Competitive Advantage in Construction

Competitive Advantage in Construction

Edited by
Steven Male
and
Robert Stocks

Department of Building Engineering and Surveying,
Heriot-Watt University

with specialist contributors

Butterworth-Heinemann Ltd
Linacre House, Jordan Hill, Oxford OX2 8DP

 PART OF REED INTERNATIONAL BOOKS

OXFORD   LONDON   BOSTON
MUNICH   NEW DELHI   SINGAPORE   SYDNEY
TOKYO   TORONTO   WELLINGTON

First published 1991

British Library Cataloguing in Publication Data
Male, Steven
   Competitive advantage in construction.
   I. Title   II. Stocks, Robert
   338.4

   ISBN 0–7506–1075–1

Library of Congress Cataloguing in Publication Data
Competitive advantage in construction / edited by Steven Male and
   Robert Stocks.
      p.   cm.
   Includes bibliographical references and index.
   ISBN 0 7506 1075 1
   1. Construction industry—Management.   2. Strategic planning.
   3. Organizational effectiveness.   4. Competition.   I.Male, Steven.
   II. Stocks, Robert.
   TH438.C636   1991
   624′.068—dc20
                                                    91–27538
                                                    CIP

Typeset by TecSet Ltd, Wallington, Surrey
Printed and bound in Great Britain

Contents

List of Contributors

Jacqueline Cannon

Jacqueline Cannon has been an economic adviser to the Building and Civil Engineering Economic Development Committee at the National Economic Development Office since the early 1970s. She has been responsible for a number of projects including the regular forecasts of national demand on the construction industry. She held a lectureship at Brunel University until 1985 and is a Research Fellow in the Department of Construction Management and Engineering, University of Reading. She is a contributor to postgraduate courses in construction management at the Universities of Bath and Reading and is a consultant specialising on the economics of the construction industry. She is co-editor of *The Management of Construction Firms: Aspects of Theory* (Macmillan, 1989) and co-author of *The Modern Construction Firm* (Macmillan, 1990) with Patricia Hillebrandt.

Roger Flanagan

Roger Flanagan is a Professor of Construction Management in the Department of Construction Management and Engineering, University of Reading. He has experience of working in the UK, USA, Canada, Mexico and the Middle East. He has co-authored books on life-cycle costing, the Japanese construction industry, the US construction industry, and Building for Joint Ventures in China.

Patricia M. Hillebrandt BSc [Econ], PhD

Patricia Hillebrandt is an economic and management consultant specialising in the construction industry. She received her education at University College, London, and the London School of Economics and Political Science. She has previously been employed as an economist to Richard Costain Ltd, the National Economic Development Office (NEDO), and as a Senior Lecturer at the Bartlett School of Architecture and Planning, University College, London. She is a Visiting Senior Research Fellow, Department of Construction Management and Engineering, University of Reading. She has been a consultant to NEDO, the Ministry of Overseas Development and DANIDA, the Danish aid organisation. Her publications include *Economic Theory and the Construction Industry* (Macmillan, 1985) and *Analysis of the British Construction Industry* (Macmillan, 1984). She is co-editor of *The Management of Construction Firms: Aspects of Theory* (Macmillan, 1989) and co-author of *The Modern Construction Firm* (Macmillan, 1990) with Jacqueline Cannon.

David Langford
David Langford is Professor of Construction Management, Department of Civil Engineering, University of Strathclyde. Prior to joining Strathclyde University, he was involved in the development of postgraduate education in construction management at Bath University and Brunel University. He has lectured to construction managers and acted as a consultant for educational and construction organisations around the world. He has co-authored *Construction Management in Practice* (Construction Press); *Construction Management, Volume 1 – Organisation Systems* and *Volume 2 – Management Systems* (Batsford); *Strategic Management in Construction* (Gower, 1991)

Peter Lansley
Peter Lansley is a Professor of Construction Management and Head of Department, Department of Construction Management and Engineering, University of Reading. He has been involved with research, consultancy and teaching for approximately twenty years, working with a large number of national and international organisations in the fields of business strategy and organisation. His work on the organisation of the construction firm, teamwork and the management of research has been published widely. He contributes regularly to executive programmes in the UK, Europe, North America and South East Asia. His AROUSAL business simulation system, winner of a Building Innovation Award, has received particular attention from industry and Government. He is a member of the Chartered Institute of Building, a Fellow of the Royal Statistical Society and a member of the International Council for Building Research and Documentation (CIB), of which he is also a Board member.

Dr Steven Male
Steven Male is a Senior Lecturer in Construction Management, Department of Building Engineering and Surveying, Heriot-Watt University. He trained as a quantity surveyor in private practice and his doctorate, obtained in 1984, focused on applying concepts of organization theory and organizational behaviour to an analysis of the quantity surveying profession. He has undertaken contract research, training and consultancy in project management, corporate strategy and value management in the construction industry. His publications include work on the quantity surveying profession, value management, and the economic management of projects. He is a co-author with David Langford of *Strategic Management in Construction* (Gower, 1991).

Charles Mathewson
Charles Mathewson is a lecturer in Construction Management, Department of Construction, Southern Illinois University at Edwardsville, USA. Prior to taking up his current occupation in construction education he was employed as a Chief Estimator for a large general contractor, Ontario Province, Canada, working on civil engineering projects,

hospitals, office blocks, educational buildings and commercial developments. He obtained his Masters degree in Construction Management from Heriot-Watt University in 1986. He is a Fellow of the Chartered Institute of Building, a corporate member of the American Institute of Constructors, and a member of the Canadian Institute of Quantity Surveyors. He was the President of the Ontario Chapter of the American Institute of Constructors in 1983 and 1984. He is a consultant to construction companies on their estimating and bidding strategy procedures.

Ronald McCaffer BSc, PhD, CEng, FICE, FCIOB, MBIM

Ronald McCaffer is currently Professor of Construction Management and Head of Department of Civil Engineering at Loughborough University, where he previously held the posts of Lecturer, Senior Lecturer and Reader. Prior to joining the University he had industrial experience with Lilley Construction Ltd, Babtie Shaw and Morton, the Nuclear Power Corporation and Taylor Woodrow Ltd. His academic work has been in the areas of construction management as applied to both building and civil engineering. He is the co-author of four text books on the subject of construction management, plant management, and estimating. His research has comprised work in the areas of contractors' estimating, planning, cost control, valuations, and the integration of major computer systems, as well as investigations in bidding strategies, tender price predictions, and data flows within contracting organisations.

Peter W. G. Morris

Peter Morris is Director, Special Projects, with Bovis Ltd. Previously he was Executive Director of the Major Projects Association (MPA), based at Templeton College, Oxford University. He continues as an Associate Fellow of Templeton College and is on the Faculty of the University of Oxford. He is Technical Director of the MPA's 'Managing Major Projects' course, run twice yearly at Templeton College. He is a Member of the Board of the International Association of Macro Engineering Societies and is on the Council of the UK Association of Project Managers. He is also on the Accreditation Committee of the US Project Management Institute.

Robert Newcombe

Robert Newcombe is Director of Executive Development, Centre for Strategic Studies in Construction, University of Reading. Prior to taking up this post he was involved in postgraduate education for construction management at the Universities of Bath and Brunel. He has extensive experience of working for constructional organisations and his research interests include business strategy in construction firms. In addition to his research, teaching and consulting interests he has co-authored *Construction Management in Practice* (Construction Press), *Construction Management, Volume 1 – Organisation Systems* and *Volume 2 – Management Systems* (Batsford).

Martin Skitmore
Martin Skitmore is Senior Lecturer in Quantity Surveying, Department of
Surveying, University of Salford. He is a Fellow of the Royal Institution of
Chartered Surveyors and a Member of the Chartered Institute of Building.
His doctoral research was on the use of models for construction contract
bidding and he is the author of *Contract Bidding in Construction: Strategic
Management and Modelling* (Longman Scientific and Technical Books,
1987).

Nigel Smith BSc, MSc, PhD, MICE, MAPM, CEng
Nigel Smith is a lecturer in the Project Management Group, Department of
Civil and Structural Engineering, University of Manchester Institute of
Science and Technology. He is responsible for Project Management
Training and Research, including funded work into BOT contracts. He is a
member of the Civil Engineers' Law and Contract Sub-Committee and a
member of the Inter-Institutional Joint Board for the Diploma in
Engineering Management.

Robert Stocks
Robert Stocks is a lecturer in Construction Management, Department of
Building Engineering and Surveying, Heriot-Watt University. He has
degrees in Business Organisation (1982) and Sociology (1989). His Masters
degree, obtained in 1984, focused on the problems of the
building/construction team as a project inter-organisational structure. He
is a Member of the British Institute of Management and the British
Sociological Association. He has undertaken research into the issues of
organisational change associated with merger activity between Building
Societies, and is currently undertaking doctoral research into the impact of
economic change on rural communities.

Monir Tayeb
Monir Tayeb is a lecturer in International Business, Department of
Business Organisation, Heriot-Watt University. She received her BA
degree (1970) in Business Studies from Tehran University, her M. Litt
degree (1979) in Organisational Behaviour from Oxford University and her
doctorate (1985) in Comparative Organisational Behaviour from Aston
University. Her research has focused on cross-national comparisons of
organisations and employee work attitudes. She has published widely in
journals on these topics and is author of *Organisation and National Culture*
(Sage, 1988).

Tony Thorpe BSc, MSc, MBCS
Tony Thorpe joined the Department of Civil Engineering at
Loughborough University in 1979 as a research assistant. He worked
extensively in developing and installing computer-aided estimating and
management systems for the construction industry. He became a lecturer
in the Construction Technology and Management Group within the

Department in 1985. His research interests include information flows in construction companies, systems analysis and design, estimating and tendering, and the use of expert systems in construction.

Anthony Walker
Anthony Walker is Professor of Surveying at the University of Hong Kong. He is a chartered surveyor and chartered builder. He has published widely in his major research areas of project management and the property and construction industries in Asia-Pacific, particularly in China. He is the author of *Project Management in Construction* (Blackwell Scientific) now in its second edition, and a co-author of *Building for Joint Ventures in China* (Levett and Bailey).

Foreword

Those already familiar with the workings of the construction industry are well aware of the challenges and changes that constantly drive the industry and make it such a complex set of dynamic and competitive processes. Although there is a constant evolution of practices and skills at all levels in the industry, nevertheless there are clear phases within which change is either accelerated or consolidated.

In short, there are cycles of growth and development, which are market led and are essentially socio-economic in nature. However, from time to time technological injections or political shifts mark significantly important areas of development. Such are the times that we are presently entering and the pace of change is increasing.

This book sets about addressing a range of issues which are of major and fundamental importance, ranging as they do from the macro to the micro scale. The changes in the world political scene, with the enormous political developments underway in what used to be the totally communist economies, marking the large-scale, and the huge investments in information technology together with robotics illustrating the small-scale influences, this book must take account of a vast array of important factors.

Added to this are the characteristics of a labour intensive industry, typically representing around 10% or more of the G.D.P. of individual countries, which is only now absorbing, applying and adapting major influences in organizational behaviour, strategic planning and man management developed for or within other business and industrial areas. Chapters in this book give these important areas their prime attention.

Quality of life has never before been so critically analysed nor heavily emphasised. Concern over the environment is, by necessity, increasing rapidly and marks another general framework for change. In the small-scale, this is emphasized by clients and occupiers demanding healthier, more satisfying buildings. The Performance Concept for buildings is being emphasized more and more at the design brief stage and the emergence of Facilities Management services for the client will increase the importance of this concept and, to some extent at least, will require monitoring as to how successfully it can be applied.

Altogether, clients are becoming much more informed, knowledgeable and sophisticated in specifying, designing, constructing and managing their building stock. They have learned hard and expensive lessons from the mistakes of the past. They want buildings of quality, to provide a lively indoor environment, to be efficient to run and to have that flexibility and adaptability built in which will provide for their changing future operational needs.

Pressures within the international construction market are bringing new responses and new challenges. The closed system response is to offer the client a package deal or a turnkey contract. The open system approach is to offer management contracting or project management. In each case geographical mobility makes the final application and realization of either system difficult. Apart from the sheer logistical problems, perhaps the associated cultural and organizationally related problems are the most obvious. Research in the recent past has shown, for example, that the most successful project managers are those who can effectively cross the cultural boundaries. We must know the values, the attitudes and the motivators of those with whom, and for whom, we work.

Knowing the individual manager, on the one hand, and the design/management team, on the other, further requires special categories of knowledge. What makes certain managers risk averse but others risk seeking? How do we make management supportive computer systems more effective? How do we improve the man/machine interface and the soft data/hard data interaction? These and other issues, such as how to make the design/construction phases better integrated, in the closed system, and how to provide a holistic I.T. system for the whole complex of process in the open system must be further researched.

Quality is a theme running through all of the foregoing. Quality of skill and professional development is a further aspect of this theme currently being comprehensively investigated in the U.K. in preparation for the workings of the European Community and to match the needs of the international market. Consequently, this book addresses current issues arising from the mapping of knowledge and skills together with pending changes in training and education which are inherent in all of the changes under discussion.

Meeting the challenges of risk, complexity and uncertainty requires particular knowledge and skills. Developing high quality change managers, capable of developing entrepreneurial, innovative and new decision-making skills is the task before us all. Those who do not manage change will have change thrust upon them, by others. This book aims to assist us to consider how to rise to the needs of challenge and opportunity while creating new areas of business and producing quality buildings within a healthier and more satisfying environment.

PROFESSOR V.B. TORRANCE
EDINBURGH

Preface

Analysing competitive advantage focuses senior managers' attention on isolating those activities where a construction company has superiority over its competitors. This book has drawn together experts, both academics and practitioners, in the field of construction management to explore, through individual chapter contributions, what competitive advantage means in the construction industry.

At the heart of any analysis of competitive advantage by managers in a construction company is the need for a broader appreciation of where this type of analysis fits into the strategic management of the firm. Strategic management, or the long-term management of the relationship between the construction company and its business environment, is an underdeveloped area of research and writing within the construction management discipline. There is a wide range of business literature dealing with the topic of strategic management, originating in the main from manufacturing industries. There is little written on how these concepts and theories can be applied or need to be modified and adapted in construction, where, to some extent, there exist a series of unique characteristics that differentiate the operations of this particular industry from other industries. Of particular relevance in this respect is the geographically dispersed nature of demand and the virtual prototype project-based requirement of the production process that can often take place under arduous political, climatic or geophysical conditions. The dearth of writing and research is even more interesting when placed within the context that construction is one of the largest industries in a nation's economy and, as Professor Torrance indicated in his Foreword to this book, can contribute on average up to 10% of a nation's gross domestic product. This book attempts, through its chapter contributions, to redress this imbalance and bring together and integrate concepts from the wider business literature with material from construction.

The editors have attempted to cover a number of important topics in the book which are of relevance to both competitive advantage and the wider issues of strategic management in the construction industry. Some chapters are heavily construction-oriented and more practical in nature; others are more theoretical and deal with a particular topic in more depth; some chapters opt for the middle ground and strike a balance between theory and practice. The chapter contributions cover areas of economics, organizational behaviour, national culture, sociology, the management of projects, and strategic management including corporate and business strategy – within both a domestic UK and an international context. The chapters draw on a wide range of material and ideas; managerial experience in the United Kingdom and international construction industries; and academic theories and concepts and empirical research to enable managers and students with an interest in strategic management to be exposed to a diversity of ideas and a number of analytical tools, techniques and procedures that can be used in practice. Extensive referencing at the end of each chapter permits the reader to delve deeper into any subject.

Finally, we would like to thank our respective families for their continued support and the editorial team at Butterworth–Heinemann, Pippa McLeish, Paddy Baker and Alison Bravington for guiding us through the production of the book.

Steven Male
Robert Stocks

Heriot Watt University,
Edinburgh

—— PART I ——
Strategic management for competitive strategy and advantage

Competitive strategy and advantage in construction

Activities taking place within the construction industry are affected by the management of two interlocking phenomena, 'companies' or 'firms' *and* projects. The important distinguishing feature between the management of these two phenomena is the fact that companies, unless they cease trading, are ongoing, relatively permanent entities that interact with their business environments. Projects, on the other hand, are temporary entities in the sense that they have a definite start and finish. Projects in construction can commence within one company, perhaps bringing together people from different departments and hierarchical levels, and can develop to an extent where people from other firms become involved. Projects in construction have the potential to span internal company environments, and also to be affected by the business environments of other participant firms, while additionally generating their own 'project environment'. Therefore, competitive advantage, the isolation and exploitation of areas of superiority over competitors, stems in construction from the strategic management of both companies and projects.

Part I is effectively split into two sub-sections, Chapters 1–4 confront those issues related more to the 'company', while Chapter 5–7 relate more to 'projects'. As suggested above, the distinction between 'company' and 'project' is, in practice, not clear cut in construction and these chapters should be read with this in mind.

Strategic management at the level of the company

A company or firm is involved in constant interaction with its business environment. Corporate strategy is concerned with the competitive position of the whole company and the management of the relationship of the total firm with its environment. Business strategy is concerned with competing in particular markets. In a construction context, corporate strategy for a contracting firm could involve issues such as the type of client, both existing and potential, that the company may be involved with; the range of projects that the firm can and could undertake and in what geographic locations; the impact of the economy on the firm; relationships with suppliers; what new companies may be entering their markets; and, finally, any new services that the firm may wish to offer. Business strategy, on the other hand, is typified in contracting by a decision to tender on a particular project. In other words, a firm's bidding strategy. Thus, competitive advantage in construction is also bound up with the effective management of the interplay between both corporate and business strategy.

   Chapters 1 and 2 set the scene for the remainder of the book. They are closely linked in that introductory ideas are developed in Chapter 1 and are elaborated in more detail in Chapter 2. The primary focus of Chapter 1 is to introduce and distinguish between industries and markets, identify how construction activities modify these relationships when compared to manufacturing, and develop a preliminary model of a construction company. Chapter 2 focuses on identifying the major concepts of strategic management, competitive strategy and advantage, and how these can be applied in construction. It also discusses production and labour strategy within a construction company and concludes with a more detailed model of a construction firm. Chapter 3 sets out the main ideas behind marketing, distinguishing between concepts that are of relevance to products or services. Stocks suggests that since construction involves the production of an object – a built facility – through the provision of a service by a contractor, strategic marketing in construction involves isolating and using those concepts and techniques that are of relevance to both products and services. In Chapter 4 Lansley focuses on innovation in construction, arguing that there is an interplay between economic cycles, markets, entrepreneurs, business leaders and innovatory behaviour within construction firms.

Bidding and project strategy

Within the firm's long term strategy, bidding for contracts is a fundamentally crucial part of its activities. It is a sub-strategy which management are required to appreciate fully. Much effort is now spent in the development of mathematical procedures and models, towards defining the most effective bidding strategy for contractor performance. Bidding models may not, however, reflect the true bidding situation, which is perhaps why contractors may not display much interest in such procedures. Standard models purport to show how to make choices in a situation of risk without accounting for both organization and environment.

   Standard bidding models presume that bidders try to maximize their expected profit. However, the contractor may be attempting to fulfil other objectives such as minimizing expected losses, minimizing profits of competitors or obtaining a contract, even at a loss, in order to maintain production.

   Different objectives require different strategies, but this diversity is not closely reflected in standard models. Morin and Blough argue [1] that before a strategy model for competitive bidding can be formulated it is necessary to investigate the competitive situation of the firm and to identify those factors which have an influencing impact on profit. Standard models fail to consider that the level of influence from these factors will vary according to the firm's competitive situation, which will be concerned with cost estimate, true cost mark-up, number of competitors, identity of competitors and class of work.

De Neufville [2] takes the view that standard models are not sensitive to the prevailing economic climate, and decisions are approached differentially in periods of expansion or recession.

Benjamin [3] points out that standard models do not take notice of differences in project size, wherein contractors are seen to bid more conservatively on larger projects which are more likely to cause substantial losses by comparison with smaller projects.

Wade and Harris [4] advocate that any competitive bidding strategies should not ignore the local market within which the firm operates.

Furthermore, construction firms individually or collectively are constrained by factors such as geographic location, class of construction, equipment parameters, government laws and regulations, building requirements and financial constraints. The effects of such constraining factors should be included in decisions regarding strategy development.

All models suggest that the analyst should develop the probability distribution for any competitor's bid by studying previous bids, although in practice certain required information is limited in its availability. The contractor may have general information on market conditions and government economic policy, for example, but will probably not have comprehensive bidding histories of competitors.

The assumption made in standard models that the value of something is a linear function of its quantity is strongly criticized. De Neufville [5] takes the view that standard models should incorporate non-linear value functions of the potential gains and losses from bids.

Competitor performance in tender bids is essential for a contractor to maintain a steady workload. A study of a contractor's competitive positioning in relation to the competitors' tender bids would reflect relative strengths and weaknesses within particular market segments. This information would assist in the formulation of bidding strategies towards improving competitive position in the market.

Competitive advantage is attained from the firm's ability to control its internal sub-systems, and exploit opportunities and lessen or avoid threats from its external environment.

Effective competitive positioning will achieve competitive advantage, hopefully leading to an increase in workload. A bidding strategy which not only responds to the environment but also attempts to shape it, is one indication of competitive advantage. Skitmore in Chapter 5 and Thorpe and McCaffer in Chapter 6 examine bidding strategy and competitive bidding. Chapter 5 reviews models of bidding strategy and provides an insight into some published work. Three separate sets of bidding data are presented as full case studies.

Chapter 6 is concerned with strategic decisions and bidding strategy at company level, while considering factors which will affect bidding success. It is also concerned with tactical decisions to tender on projects.

Finally, projects involve many participants and take place in an environment which, as the project becomes larger, can move towards increasing levels of complexity. In Chapter 7 Morris sets out a framework for understanding the range of issues that can impact a project for good or ill. This framework allows managers to take an holistic, top–down view of the factors that need to be taken into account in the strategic management of projects.

References

1. Morin, T. L. and Clough, R. H. (1977) 'OPBID – competitive bidding strategy model.' *Journal of the Construction Division, ASCE*, March, **103**, pp. 57–70.
2. De Neufville, R. (1977) 'Bidding models: effects of bidders' risk aversion'. *Journal of the Construction Division, ASCE*, March, **103**, pp. 57–70.
3. Benjamin, N. B. H. (1972) 'Competitive bidding: the probability of winning'. *Journal of the Construction Division, ASCE*, September, **98**, pp. 313–330.
4. Wade, R. L. and Harris, R. B. (1976) 'LOMARK: A bidding strategy'. *Journal of the Construction Division, ASCE*, September, pp. 197–210.
5. De Neufville (1977) *op. cit.*

— *1* —

Strategic management in construction: conceptual foundations

Steven Male

1. The international and UK domestic construction industries – a sense of scale

The construction industry is the single most important industry in any national economy, once some form of industrialization has occurred and its supporting infrastructure is in place, normally representing between 7 and 15% of a country's gross domestic product (GDP) [1]. Construction, therefore, is an important barometer of a nation's economy – both in terms of current investment in fixed capital assets and as a guide to a country's stage of economic development. Taken in its broadest sense to include the construction of all facilities – civil, building and power and process engineering – Stallworthy and Kharbanda estimate that the international construction industry is worth in the region of $US500 billion per year.

In the United Kingdom, again depending on how construction is defined, the value of the final product is approximately 9–10% of GDP; the net output – excluding materials and supplies from other industries – is approximately 6% of GDP; it employs approximately 7% of the country's labour force and contributes between 45–55% of fixed capital formation [2]. Fleming adds to this sense of scale when he indicates that the domestic construction industry of the United Kingdom is three times as large as agriculture, approximately twice as large as the largest manufacturing industry and is rivalled only in size by the broad service sectors such as distribution [3]. Construction is, therefore, a major industry in the UK economy.

Clients of construction are diverse, ranging from individuals through to large multinational companies. They also come from the private or public sector. In addition, clients are dissimilar in the degree of knowledge they possess about the workings of the construction industry. Clients of construction may also be regular or irregular procurers of facilities and approach the industry frequently, once only or on an intermittent basis.

We can conclude from the foregoing that the construction industry – both domestic and international – is large and complex.

2. The concept of the industry, market and competition in construction

The preceding section has discussed the term 'construction industry'. This section looks more closely at the idea of an 'industry' for use in strategic management and tries to answer the question of whether construction is really an industry or whether it should be viewed as a series of vertical overlapping markets.

2.1 The industry and market in construction

A major analytical problem for developing a competitive strategy in construction is to define the arena within which competition takes place. Two important facets of this are the following concepts:

(a) an industry;
(b) a market.

An *industry*, as an analytical concept, is an arbitrary boundary within which existing firms are in competition with each other to produce related or similar products, having an interdependent relationship with both supplier and buyer groupings and also facing the potential threat of new entrant firms or substitute products into the industry [4]. A substitute product is one that performs the same or a similar *function* rather than having the same form. Porter distinguishes between the concept of an industry and the decision as to where a company should compete. The latter defines the company's business and is analytically different from the former. The structure of an industry has a direct impact on, first, the nature of competition felt by firms in that industry and, second, the competitive strategies available to a company. Porter suggests that there are five major forces determining the long-term economic structure of an industry. These are set out in Figure 1.1, together with the underlying factors affecting each of the major competitive forces.

A *market* is any organization where buyers and sellers of a commodity are in close contact with each other to determine the price of that commodity [5]. Put another way, a market organizes an exchange relationship between a buyer and seller, where the buyer has a *need* which the seller can satisfy for a mutually agreed *price*.

A further useful distinction between 'industry' and 'market' is that an industry is a supply side concept whereas market is a demand side concept [6]. When considering competitive advantage in construction and the strategies that can be used to achieve this, it is important, therefore, to determine the nature and form of the competitive arena – whether industry or market – within which competition takes place. This will

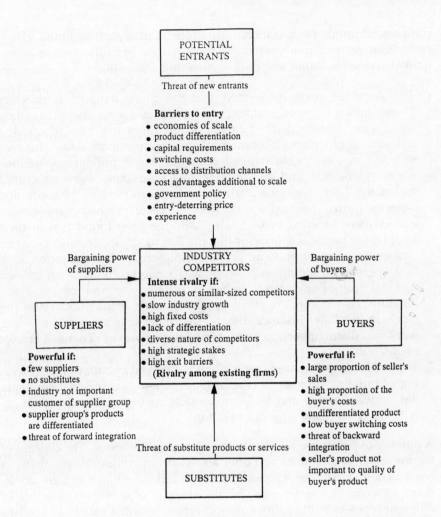

Figure 1.1 *Forces driving industry competition (Sources: Porter (1980) and Christopher, M., Majaro, S. and Macdonald, M. (1981)* Strategy: A Guide to Marketing for Senior Executives, *Wildwood House, Aldershot. Reprinted with permission.)*

determine who is or is not a key competitor of the company. However, there are divergent views on whether the concept of industry/sub-industry or market (and how that is defined within construction) is of most relevance in an analysis of construction [7].

To compound what may at times appear to be a semantic confusion, the construction industry in the United Kingdom has traditionally been viewed as being sub-divided into the civil engineering and building industries. However, by their nature, many construction contracts will involve both aspects of building and civils work. At the operational level, i.e. at the level of the company, industry/market structure impacts the company through organizational structure. Lansley *et al.* found empirically that construction companies may or may not differentiate analytically between building and civil engineering works [8]:

1. The Ashridge team discovered that for those national contractors differentiating between building and civil engineering operations, they were seen as two distinct business environments that required a different set of technical, commercial and organisational skills. This was reflected in their organisational structure where building operations were regionalised and civil engineering operations were structured nationally. There was little relationship between the two. In borderline cases the form of contract was the deciding issue on whether it was seen as a civils or building project. The Ashridge team found that in their sample, the national contractor that did not rigidly distinguish between civil engineering or building projects structured the organisation such that specialist building/civils work was undertaken by a centralised national unit. For projects below a certain size and of a general building/civils nature, regional operating units would undertake the work. In this latter instance, the difference between civils and building work was distinguished in terms of a specialist versus generalist project orientation.
2. Regional contractors were generally not involved in both civil engineering or building projects. In the instance where one regional company did undertake civil and building projects, two divisions were set up with no cross resourcing of operations.

A number of points are worth noting concerning the above. The concept of the industry, as identified by Porter above, is not without its problems in construction. First, the 'product' in construction, while normally considered in terms of a service, can be also thought of as the manufacture of different types of built facility – project types – using a variety of services to achieve this end – traditional contracting, design and build, management contracting, etc. In this latter instance projects realized as manufactured facilities are generally one-off with a tendency towards uniqueness. Second, identifying what is or is not a substitute in construction can be difficult. Langford and Male argue that readily identifiable substitutes in construction, based on a functional analysis of services, can be seen in the following four perspectives [9].

1. Design and build versus executive project management: while both are distinct types of service (product) and could define an industry boundary for competitors in their own right, both also provide the client with single point responsibility and are therefore functional substitutes.
2. Management contracting versus construction management: again, both are distinct services and yet the underlying function is that the contractor is providing management expertise to the client and design team.

3. Both 1 and 2 can also be considered as near substitutes for each other since they are alternative methods of managing the building/ construction process.
4. Other forms of substitutes in construction are new build versus refurbishment; repair and maintenance; and renovation – the substitution of new build for alterations, in one form or another, to existing buildings. A functional analysis of this substitution process would suggest that the underlying function is to provide the client with a facility that allows on-going organizational processes to proceed optimally. The solution for the client, therefore, may not be in constructing a new facility but renovating or refurbishing an existing facility.

The key issue in distinguishing what is a substitute product is to identify the functional usage(s) for the buyer (client) of a product and to investigate alternative means of satisfying that function.

Finally, the technological implications of construction services and projects cannot be ignored and neither can the impact of different forms of contract documentation.

Drawing together the various strands from different authors and the discussion above, we can deduce the following four points for construction:

1. A market is defined in terms of a buyer having a *need* for similar or closely related products which the seller can satisfy.
2. The mechanism for facilitating this exchange relationship is the price.
3. From one perspective, the notion of the market is more relevant than that of the industry or sub-industry in construction for defining the competitive arena, the demand side concept, since it is client-generated and of short-term focus. It involves the exchange relationship. For construction, however, it is contended that a broader industry categorization, where different markets are linked socially and economically, provides the context for narrower market operations, since contractors are often linked through sub-contractors and suppliers when responding to demand. Industry analysis provides the longer-term analytical orientation since a company has to work out its competitive strategy to compete in particular markets. The five competitive forces determining industry structure that have been identified by Porter set the framework and context within which markets for construction operate.
4. Since the buyer is prepared to pay a price to the seller in order to have a need satisfied, both the buyer and seller are also involved in a *value* relationship.

Depending on the size of company, there is a clear distinction between building and civils work. As company size increases, this distinction is handled through organizational structure. However, there are instances where organizational structure is adapted to take a project-based approach to this distinction.

Additionally, an overriding reason for adopting a 'market' as opposed to industry/sub-industry' view is due to the presence of procurement and tendering systems in construction that do not have a counterpart in manufacturing. Procurement and tendering strategies and the associated contractual arrangements binding the constituent parties together, to be discussed in more detail below, have a significant impact on how the market operates in construction and the method and accuracy of price determination. Furthermore, depending on the level of client knowledge of the industry, procurement and tendering strategies are invariably chosen by the design consultants in conjunction with the client. The contractor may have little if any input into this process. Therefore, the industry provides the longer-term structural context of competition whereas the market translates this longer-term perspective into a short-term exchange relationship for setting up a geographically located production process.

2.2 Market structure, price determination and competition in construction

There are two distinct types of market structure in construction with different economic forces operating in each type [10]. The market structures are as follows.

1. Contracting: this involves a company in constructing a facility to a customized design where the roles and responsibilities of the constituent parties are contractually defined. The method of price determination is the reverse of manufacturing in that the contractor determines price prior to production. Under this form of market structure the project is pre-demanded by the client.
2. Speculative projects: speculative construction, as its name implies, involves anticipating, responding to or creating demand. Typical examples in construction are speculative house building or office development. It is important to differentiate between speculative construction undertaken by a construction company as it diversifies its market base, for example through speculative house building, and that which is undertaken by a client and will eventually lead to a contracting situation.

Different skills are required for each type of market structure. In the first instance the emphasis is more on managerial and technical skills. In the second, entrepreneurial activity involves market forecasting of a different type, with market research, the assembly of financial packages and associated land banks.

To summarize, competition in construction is affected by market structure, within the context of a broader industry structure, which, operating through the five competitive forces and economic and social linkages, provides the context for market structure in construction. Under contracting, the rules of competition are set predominantly by the client and the client's advisers in the form of procurement and tendering strategies and contractual arrangements. Finally, a market in construction can be considered as either a project type or as a service. However, both are determined by a need in the market place. The following sub-section outlines the different procurement and tendering strategies and contractual arrangements that affect market operations.

2.2.1 Procurement and tendering strategies

The term *procurement strategy* is used here to describe the options available to the client for obtaining a facility, and the managerial and administrative framework that is set up to handle the process on behalf of the client. There are seven generally recognized procurement options available to the client that have varying degrees of integration between design and on-site production:

(a) traditional;
(b) management contracting;
(c) project management;
(d) design and construct;
(e) develop and construct;
(f) separate contracts;
(g) British Property Federation.

Each procurement option sets up a different set of organizational, managerial and administrative relationships between the client, the client's advisers and the contractor. Additionally, each procurement strategy also modifies the market structure faced by the contractor.

The term *tendering strategy* is used here to describe the mechanism for selecting, choosing and appointing a contractor. There are two main approaches, as follows, to contractor selection, with a series of sub-options:

1. By negotiation: where only one contractor is involved.
2. By competition: sub options are:
   (a) open competition: any number of contractors can compete;
   (b) selective competition (single stage): up to six contractors are chosen to compete, based on some form of pre-qualification process to ensure they have the competence to undertake the work;
   (c) two-stage tendering: combining selective competition in the first stage and then negotiation;
   (d) serial/continuity contracts: combining competition initially and then negotiation for a series of similar projects. This type of contract facilitates project learning but has considerable risks attached during periods of high or rampant inflation.

Table 1.1 sets out the competitive nature of each of the tendering strategies where the product of the contractor is a service. First, Scenario I is more akin to the situation where, for example, projects may be of a relatively

Table 1.1 Tendering strategies and competition

Type of selection	Stage of selection	Number of firms	Product differentiation	Type of market
Scenario I – Many firms in the market				
NEGOTIATION				
Negotiation	Pre-selection	Many	Substantial	Monopolistic competition
	Post-selection	One	n.a.	Limited monopoly
COMPETITION				
Open tendering	Tender	Many	None	Approaching perfect competition
Selective tendering	Pre-tender	Many	Substantial	Monopolistic competition
	Tender	Few	None	Partial oligopoly without product differentiation
Two-stage tendering	Pre-tender	Many	Substantial	Monopolistic competition
	Tender	Few	None	Partial oligopoly without product differentiation
	Negotiation	None	n.a.	Limited monopoly
Scenario II – Few firms in the market				
NEGOTIATION				
Negotiation	Pre-selection	Few	Substantial	Oligopoly with product differentiation
	Post-selection	One	n.a.	Limited monopoly
COMPETITION				
Open tendering	Tender	Few	None	Oligopoly without product differentiation

Type of selection	Stage of selection	Number of firms	Product differentiation	Type of market
Selective tendering	Pre-tender	Few	Substantial	Oligopoly with product differentiation
	Tender	Few	None	Oligopoly without product differentiation
Two-stage tendering	Pre-tender	Few	Substantial	Oligopoly with product differentiation
	Tender	Few	None	Oligopoly without product differentiation
	Negotiation	None	n.a.	Limited monopoly

Source: Hillebrandt 1985, p. 147. (Reprinted with permission.)

straightforward type with many companies able to undertake the work. Second, Scenario II is more akin to the situation where the project may be more complex and there are fewer companies able to undertake the work. Third, any form of pre-qualification involves assessment of a contractor's ability and competence to undertake the work. Product differentiation is based on expertise combined with a company's reputation. Fourth, once pre-qualification has taken place the assumption is that all those selected are competent to undertake the work. We would argue that the price submitted is an additional form of differentiation. The processes behind it are as complex as those highlighted previously, since, all things being equal, the price submitted reflects the ability of those involved in the tendering process within a contracting company to assess the state of the market, competition and profit level required. The tender price thus represents a quantifiable differentiation of in-house expertise (managerial, technical and commercial) between companies in the bidding strategy.

To summarize, it can be concluded from the foregoing that the nature and form of the competitive arena for the contractor in contracting is largely determined by the client's consultant advisers – architects, quantity surveyors, project managers and/or engineers. Contractor pre-selection, with final selection undertaken either through negotiation or competition, is generally undertaken by design team consultants acting as a form of distribution channel for contractors' services to the client. This has become institutionalized under the *Contracting System* [11]. The Contracting System has effectively set up *institutionalized distribution channels* for contractors' services and through their advice to clients on procurement and tendering strategies, construction consultants are acting as intermediaries in the market exchange relationship between the client and contractor. To some extent, procurement options such as 'turnkey projects' modify relationships.

2.2.2 Contractual arrangements

Contractual arrangements make up the final component locking the procurement and tendering strategies into place. The term is used here to describe the legal framework that is set up between the client, the client's advisers and the contractor. Contractual arrangements are intertwined with tendering strategy in determining price and, in the case of the former, with the method of payment to the contractor. Contractual arrangements can be broken down into the following six categories:

(a) drawings and specification;
(b) firm bill of quantities;
(c) approximate bill of quantities;
(d) schedule of rates – standard pre-priced schedules or specially priced schedules;
(e) prime cost and cost reimbursable
   cost plus percentage fee
   cost plus fixed fee
   target cost;
(f) the form of contract – standard or purpose written.

   This sub-section has reviewed the different influences on the operations of markets in construction. The following sub-section discusses the ease or difficulty with which contractors are able to enter or leave a market.

2.3 Entry and exit barriers defining construction as a project-based, vertically structured market

Entry and exit barriers to an industry or market are conceptually distinct but often related and their joint level is important in any analysis [12]. The construction industry is often quoted as having low entry and exit barriers [13], with this revolving essentially around low capital requirements and the fact that 'know-how' is the stock-in trade of the contractor and hence is easily transferable through hiring [14].

   Empirical evidence on the presence of entry and exit barriers in construction is inconclusive. Hillebrandt [15], reporting on her earlier work [16], concludes that monopoly power does not exist to any great extent in the industry since the larger contractors are not making exceptional profits when compared to industry in general. Ball [17], on the other hand, concludes from the work of Williams [18], on the profitability of different industrial sectors, that since construction has shown a consistently higher rate of return than manufacturing industry there are significant barriers to entry to the most profitable part of the construction industry. Williams' analysis was undertaken for the period 1961 to 1977. Ball, in a subsequent analysis of the period 1970–85, using different data, is unable to replicate the profitability cycles shown by Williams. Three comments are worth noting here. First, Ball has taken his data set from 1970 to 1985. Hillebrandt reported financial results from 1978 to 1980. Thus, the time spans of the two empirical analyses are quite different. Second, the trend from Williams' data for the early-1960s to late-1970s conclusively indicates higher profitability in construction. Third, during the time period from the early-1960s to mid-1980s construction companies were involved in considerable diversification away from a contracting base. Ball's data for the early-1980s indicates a consistent fall in profitability for construction compared to manufacturing, from which he concludes that some of the major construction companies experienced severe difficulties or restructuring strategies may not have been as fruitful as companies had hoped. However, we could also add a further interpretation in that, depending on the form of the restructuring, it may be that the fruits of those decisions may not pay off until the late-1980s to early-1990s. In other words, new entry barriers to profitable parts of the industry have not yet crystallized.

In order to attempt to discover if entry and exit barriers are present in construction and identify what form they might take, we will utilize sources of barriers identified by Porter [19]. These are as follows:

- *Product differentiation:* if we take the case that the product in construction is a service which embodies reputation, then product differentiation in construction occurs first via the procurement and tendering strategies adopted by the client in terms of any pre-qualification procedures and method of price determination; and second through the pressure placed on the industry to respond to clients' diverse requirements through new forms of service.

  Any form of pre-qualification differentiates one group of contracting companies from another since the group of contractors that pre-qualify are seen to have the expertise to carry out a project and, by implication those not selected do not. It must be pointed out, however, that Stokes [20] is of the view that reputation and quality have little impact on the contracting industry for obtaining work. He argues that the final arbiter of a group of pre-selected contractors is price. Situations can arise, however, where the contractor is selected through combination of price and reputation if the client's advisors are at all concerned about the lowest tender submitted for a project. Product differentiation is an important factor within international construction [21].

- *Capital requirements:* this can be broken down into two areas – fixed assets and human capital. The requirement for fixed assets in construction is lower than in other sectors of industry, especially at the lower end of company size. The requirement for human capital is high, however, especially on the more demanding projects. It has been suggested above that contractors can easily vault the human capital barrier. However, when taken in the longer term this may not be the case since the availability of human capital of the right type and quality depends on supply and the extent to which it is being replenished through training and management development. Construction has a poor training record and the stock of suitably qualified human capital is likely to diminish in the medium to long term. Thus, there is a limit to the extent to which contractors are able to continually 'poach' human capital from other companies. One final point concerns the diversification strategies of contractors. As construction companies diversify from contracting into, for example, property development, building materials manufacture or mining operations – as many UK contractors have – the extent of physical capital requirements increases due to the changing nature of investment in physical assets and technological requirements. Additionally, diversification into overseas markets also requires considerable capital investment. Diversification strategies, to be discussed in more detail in Chapter 2, are now setting up different forms of entry and exit barriers to the industry for the construction company.

- *Switching costs for buyers between suppliers:* buyers (clients) in the industry are faced with a number of options and methods for procuring contractors' services; these have been discussed earlier. We have noted that there are many different types of clients, from the individual domestic client through to large multinational companies or foreign governments, and from regular to irregular procurers. The issue of buyers switching costs in construction is complex and depends, therefore, on client type, knowledge of the industry and type of project. For the large complex project, where only a few contractors are capable of undertaking the work, switching costs can be high, especially if it is a negotiated contract [22].

- *Access to distribution channels:* distribution channels in construction can be of two types. First, those related to the distribution of manufactured goods; this would have an impact on those construction companies with, for example, building materials manufacturing subsidiaries who may channel products through the large DIY retail chains or builders' merchants. Second, as discussed earlier, clients' consultant advisers act as institutionalized distribution channels for contractors' services. In this latter instance merger and acquisition activities allow the contractor access to other client and consultant contacts and select tender lists, and hence extend contractors' access to institutionalized distribution channels.

- *Scale economies and the experience curve:* it has been argued that economies of scale are not a major issue in construction [23]. However, where they do exist they involve the following [24]: the ability to integrate the components of the production process and move sections of the workforce between projects; marketing (acting through the merchant–producer role of the contractor to increase bargaining power with clients and suppliers) and access to finance; functional specialization by trade – a sub-contracting issue for the main contractor; the degree of repetitive work that is allowed through the ability to obtain projects of a similar type – house building being a case in point. Furthermore, diversification into long-process production operations – such as certain types of materials manufacture – will allow construction companies to obtain scale economies in these activities.

To summarize, scale economies exist in contracting but they are generally of a different form than in manufacturing – they are predominantly in the areas of managerial expertise and financial management. However, to an extent, the nature of the procuring and tendering process precludes contractors developing scale economies through learning by project type. These are very much dependent on the contractor's ability to secure continuity of project types and hence retain the knowledge capability in-house and over time. Hiring-in expertise interrupts the learning cycle because new management personnel, while they may have experience of similar project types, take some time to adjust to the systems and procedures of their new company. However, scale economies through learning are possible in speculative projects of a similar type. Finally, manufacturing-type scale economies are probable within a diversified construction company.

- *Government policy:* this can be a particularly important barrier for market entry in international construction. For example, the legal requirement to use local companies is one form of entry barrier, government policy in Brazil is known to favour domestic contractors [25] and the requirement for a licence to operate in the Japanese domestic contracting market [26] can also be viewed as a barrier to entry.

To conclude, entry barriers are present for construction companies and they can be different or similar to those in manufacturing depending on the structure of the construction company and the type of market or industry being entered. This relates to the nature and form of the diversification strategy pursued by a contractor away from a contracting base, coupled with the extent of any overseas activity. What we can say is that within contracting, entry at the lower end of the company size criterion is relatively easy. However, as project size and complexity increases there are fewer companies about to undertake particular types of project – through managerial capability and access to finance. In effect, these pose barriers to entry for particular types of project and hence arrange contracting into a geographically dispersed project-based vertical market defined by project size and complexity. All things being equal, given that construction companies at the top end of the size scale have similar access to finance, the extent to which the managerial entry barrier can be vaulted by these firms and smaller companies depends on the pool of available human capital and how easy it is to continue to poach this from other companies in the long term. The alternative to poaching is considerable investment in training and management development. Furthermore, contractors, through diversification, are now involved in different types of production activity requiring different types of capital investment – both human and physical. Different types of entry and exit barriers are now present for the diversified construction company. The empirical evidence, to date, appears inconclusive as to their effects on profitability at the corporate level. As indicated earlier, issues associated with diversification strategy will be discussed in greater detail in the next chapter.

2.4 Construction as a fragmented and hierarchical industry

Since construction is often reported as being a fragmented industry, this section concentrates on defining and exploring this particular type of industrial structure for developing a competitive strategy in construction.

A fragmented industry is one in which no company has a significant market share [27]. In other words there is no market leader able to significantly influence outcomes within the industry. A fragmented industry usually comprises a large number of small- and medium-sized companies and by implication this means a small number of large companies. In addition, there is a high incidence of privately owned companies. These characteristics are common to construction. Porter adds that a fragmented industry is populated by many competitors who are in a weak bargaining position with respect to both buyer and supplier groupings, and profitability is marginal. Again, this is often seen as a characteristic of the construction industry.

Table 1.2 sets out the economic reasons which Porter identifies as being the underlying causes of fragmentation; the table then attempts to identify those present in contracting. The arguments would be different for the diversified construction company. Porter indicates that the presence of *only one* is sufficient to cause fragmentation. The table indicates clearly that many are present in contracting.

The above analysis indicates clearly that in general terms the contracting industry is fragmented for many reasons. However, if we consider construction in terms of a geographically dispersed project-based vertical market that operates world wide, from a local to international arena, as we go up the vertical market, defined by project size and complexity, there are fewer and fewer companies able to undertake particular types of project and fragmentation tends to decrease as the industry is segmented by overlapping project-based market structures. This is a relative issue. In comparison to many manufacturing industries contracting is highly fragmented. However, for particular types of project, fewer key competitors enter a market. The notion of 'contestable markets'[1] used by

---

[1] Flanagan and Norman define a contestable market as one where oligopolistic competition operates and where the danger of a potential entrant constrains companies' behaviour such that their pricing policy is affected.

Table 1.2 Economic causes of fragmentation in the construction
industry

Economic causes	Present in contracting	Comments on contracting
No scale economies or experience curve	Possible	Often argued none present. However, it has been suggested above that scale economies may be present in contracting.
Low overall entry barriers	Possible	Often argued none present. However, the analysis above suggests there is a geographically dispersed vertically structured market in contracting with entry barriers for the larger sized projects
High transport costs	Possible	Projects are geographically dispersed. Project characteristics and location are important in determining production costs. Localization of production reduces the impact of transportation costs and therefore adds to fragmentation. As project sizes and complexity increase there are fewer capable companies, higher returns are possible and transport costs can be spread across more projects. Therefore, the impact of transport costs are reduced on larger projects. Internationally, transport costs may be a crucial issue depending on the remote location of a project.
High inventory costs or erratic sales fluctuations	Possible	Sales not viewed in a traditional way in construction. Short–medium-term demand can fluctuate dramatically at times in construction for particular market sectors but when aggregated across market sectors has reduced variability. Turnover (as a proxy for sales in construction) can vary year on year. However, demand fluctuations can be reduced by the balance of project types undertaken. Inventory costs should be low in contracting due to payment system of monthly valuations.

Table 1.2 cont'd.

Economic causes	Present in contracting	Comments on contracting
DISECONOMIES OF SCALE		
Low overheads critical to success	Yes	Especially in selective tendering
Diverse product line	Yes	Each project unique. Service (as product) may not be diverse
High requirement for creativity	Not directly	Unless managerial creativity considered important
Localization	Yes	Of demand and contacts
Diverse market needs	Yes	Unique client demands
Smaller companies – greater efficiency	Yes	Industry structure favours small companies with lower overhead costs. However, larger companies gain through managerial and financial efficiency but suffer increased overhead costs
Rapid product changes	Yes if product is project. No if product is service	Each project (product) tends to uniqueness
Local regulations	Yes	Building codes/regulations
Government prohibition of concentration	Not applicable	
Newness of industry	Not applicable	
High product differentiation	Yes	Product differentiation becomes important through the pressure of client requirements and the operation of the procurement and tendering process
Presence of exit barriers	Possible	In contracting, once a project has been completed a contractor can withdraw from the market and industry, especially at the lower end of the vertical market. Generally, as project size increases, project duration increases and it becomes more difficult to disengage from a market easily, especially if subsidiaries have been set up to trade over time.

Flanagan and Norman [28] in an analysis of a tendering strategy of negotiation, appears to be a useful analytical concept of broader application in construction.

Finally, an analysis by Ball [29] indicates that construction is a hierarchical industry (designed by size of firm) where the many small companies are tending to act as sub-contractors to the large companies. Thus if we categorize the larger companies as those employing over 115 people, representing only 35% of the companies in the industry, in 1985 they accounted for nearly 40% of the total industry workload by value and undertook 51% of the value of new work, but accounted for only 19% by value of repair and maintenance work. In this latter instance, 63% of the value of R & M work was undertaken by companies employing less than 24 people. This suggests a number of issues. First, R & M work favours small companies but acts against large company operations as evidenced by the relatively small amount of work by value undertaken by the larger company categories within the industry. The trend in workload for R & M shows a continual upward trend and larger contractors can and have responded to this by setting up 'small' works divisions or subsidiaries dealing with major refurbishment projects. Fragmentation within the R & M sector is likely to continue. Second, for new build work the industry has a distinct hierarchical structure, with the larger companies capturing most of the work by value, with the other 41% of the value of work being spread in roughly equal proportions across other sizes of companies. With the decline in public sector new build projects the private sector is now the major focus of opportunities but this is the most volatile sector and it favours large company operations. Third, our previous analysis concerning vertically structured markets within construction, when overlayed with the implications of the differences between R & M and new build work, indicates that within the new build sector as we go up the vertical market significant entry barriers may well exist for companies. The height of such barriers, in the long term, is very much dependent on the quality and quantity of human managerial capital and the ease with which it can be poached from other companies or developed in-house.

To summarize, we have argued that construction comprises geographically dispersed vertical markets and is hierarchically structured in terms of company size. Fragmentation is high at the smaller end of the vertical market structure in repair and maintenance work. For new build work fragmentation decreases according to project characteristics. An analysis of entry and exit barriers to the industry has been undertaken and suggests that many are present in construction but in a subtle form.

3. An analysis of the nature of the construction company

There are a number of problems facing any analyst of the construction industry for developing ideas about strategic management in construction, either in a domestic or international sense. These problems revolve around, first, the fact that economic theory, from where a considerable proportion of the strategy literature is derived, is not easily applicable to construction [30]; and, second, the theoretical thrust of organization theory, the other strand from which much of the literature on strategic management originates, has come predominantly from an analysis of manufacturing or service companies but with little concentration on construction [31]. The primary focus of this section is to provide an analytical framework that can be used to understand the operations of a construction company as a prelude to developing ideas about strategic management for construction in Chapter 2. Sub-sections detail the theoretical perspectives from the general management field that can be used in this analysis and then applies them subsequently in a construction context.

3.1 A model of a 'company'

A company operates in a business environment. At one level, a company, thought of simply as a 'black box', transforms inputs from the business environment – money, labour, materials and equipment – into outputs that are sold to customers, either for direct consumption or as further inputs into other processes. However, a company, especially a large one, is also a complex system of decisions, processes, procedures, rules, technologies and people that are in constant interaction with each other. For analytical purposes, therefore, it is useful to think of a company as having a permeable boundary that delineates its internal workings from the external business environment. In reality the boundary of a company varies with the movement of people. Langford and Male [32] utilized the term *spheres of influence* to indicate that the boundaries of a company, especially in construction, are very moveable. For example, consider an architect: this consultant's organizational boundary can alternate between the consultant's office, the client's office(s), the contractor's site, regional or head office. The more permeable the boundary, the more the company is open to the influences of the environment. Conversely, the less permeable the boundary between it and its environment the more the company focuses on its internal workings. Events in the environment may go either unnoticed or only partially appreciated.

Taking the preceding simple analogy one stage further, over time as the company begins to grow and as its interactions with its environment increase, the set of relationships, internally and externally, become more elaborate. The result is that an internal structure develops that has both vertical and lateral components, the relative emphasis of each being dependent on the nature of the company. As the company continues to grow it is possible to discern its analytically discrete parts – the technical core or production level, the middle management or integrative level and the strategic or senior management level. Mintzberg [33] has produced a model of a large organization that is reproduced in Figure 1.2. According to Mintzberg, the primary components of an organization are as follows:

- The *strategic apex*, i.e. the strategic or senior management level: the strategic apex is concerned with the long-term survival and development of the company.
- The *middle line*, i.e. the middle management or integrative level: managers at this level will exercise formal authority and act as the linkage between the strategic apex and the operating core. Contracts managers would be an example of the middle line in construction.
- The *operating core*, i.e. the technical core or production level: managers and operators at this level are concerned with the input–transformation–output process. Site agents are involved in the contractor's operating core.
- The *technostructure:* people in the technostructure are concerned with analysing, changing and controlling the organization; they are also concerned with standardizing the operations of the organization. Those in the technostructure are not line managers but are involved in the processes associated with on-going functions of the operating core and/or strategic apex. Traditionally, the technostructure would be classified as 'staff' as opposed to 'line' managers. Examples of the technostructure for a contractor would be the accounting or training departments.
- *Support staff:* as the name implies, support staff support the on-going organization but are not normally involved directly in the main

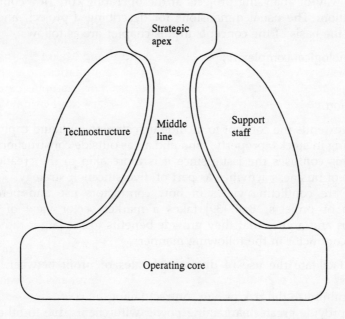

Figure 1.2   *The five basic parts of organizations (Source: Mintzberg (1979), fig. 2.1, p. 20. Reprinted with permission.)*

operational processes of the company. Mintzberg sees these as distinct from the 'staff' classification.

3.2 The operating core of the contracting company

This section discusses the nature and form of the operating core in a contracting company. It defines the concepts of project portfolios and potential capacity and then concludes with an integrated view of the operating core.

3.2.1 Project portfolios

The major feature of a project for a contractor is that any one project can form a large part of the company's annual turnover and hence an important determinant of any annual profit or loss [34]. Additionally, when taken as a totality, each project has a *life cycle* that goes through the stages of *birth*, *growth*, *decay* and *death*. The production level of a contracting company therefore comprises many projects at different stages of their respective life cycles. Furthermore, the construction project – as a resource transformation process – involves different degrees of competition at different stages of the project [35].

The concept of *project portfolios*, initially introduced by researchers at University College, London [36], and subsequently elaborated later [37], is a useful way of analysing projects at the operating core of a contracting organization. The usual dimensions for describing a project, and those forming the basis of the concepts in this chapter are as follows:

* technological complexity;
* size;
* type;
* location.

Ball [38] extends the concept to include investments of liquid capital from contracting in stocks, property, land and areas outside construction. To an extent this confuses the issue since it is more akin to the creation of a portfolio of business activities as part of diversification strategy.

There are conflicting views of how contractors use and perceive a portfolio of projects. Ball [39] takes a market sector view of project portfolios and argues that they provide benefits to the larger rather than smaller contractor in the following manner:

They facilitate the use of differential rates of profit between market sectors.
They minimize the risk of one contract failing.
They provide greater bargaining power with clients due to other work in hand.

They provide gains from acquisition of other contractors in terms of:

- access to non-construction assets;
- rapid market entry without fear of retaliation;
- additional management expertise, portfolios of contracts and contacts and membership of select tendering lists.

Lansley *et al.* [40], on the other hand, arguing from an empirical base, indicate that contracting companies do not consider demand in terms of market sectors, with the exception of housing development (which has a different economic structure), but in terms of *technologies* to execute project types. The main features that managers stated in terms of assessing projects were:

- project size;
- project complexity;
- construction method.

Implicit within this assessment are the organizational and managerial requirements of the project.

3.2.2 Potential capacity

One analytical concept that stems from the notion of project portfolios and the operating core of the contractor is that of potential capacity. For a manufacturing company, its production capacity is derived from the fact that it has a locationally fixed technical system geared to produce a certain volume of units of output. In contracting, however, the production base is transient, one-off and variable. *Potential capacity* [41] in construction refers to the capability of a company to undertake different types of work in the future and stems from its organizational structure and the accumulated knowledge of management and support functions. Potential capacity is not, therefore, idle capacity owned or financed by the company but the ability to gear up for a higher workload. In a recessionary period, operatives and the skilled workforce will be laid off first, with management and support staff retained as long as possible ready for an upturn in the economy. We can conclude that the potential capacity of contracting companies rests from site agent level upwards where a high level of sub-contracting is undertaken.

3.2.3 A synthesis of the influences on the operating core of contractors

When bringing together the various components of earlier sections we can state the following seven influences on the operating core of a contractor:

1. Aggregate and individual market sector demand is the backcloth against which the contractor operates.
2. Depending on the procurement and tendering strategies adopted by clients and their advisers and their assessment of a company's capabili-

ties, sectoral demand is translated into numerous invitations to tender for the individual company.
3. Each bid invitation is assessed in terms of executable technologies held within the company.
4. Projects in hand, the organizational structure and the accumulated knowledge of the company represent the strategies and direction the company has taken, is taking and could take in the future.
5. Project portfolios represent the total technological capability of the company across all market sectors.
6. Exploiting the profit differential of market sectors stems from a differential exploitation of the technological assessment of projects built to contract and the current and potential capacity held within the company.
7. Project portfolios, as the current and potential technological operating core of a contractor, are in a constant state of technological and competitive flux as each project goes through its life cycle of birth, growth, decay and death combined with the competitive requirements of the resource transformation process.

3.3 The construction company as an organization

Mention has been made previously of the company as a social entity. This section describes an organization as a social entity and then proceeds to highlight the major parameters of organizational structure.

3.3.1 What is 'organization'

Two definitions of organization will assist in identifying the major components. Robbins defines an organization as [42]:

> the planned coordination of the collective activities of two or more people who, functioning on a relatively continuous basis and through division of labour and hierarchy of authority, seek to achieve a common goal or set of goals (p. 5).

Hunt defines an organization as [43]:

> an identifiable social entity pursuing multiple objectives through the coordinated activities and relations among members and objects. Such a social system is open-ended and dependent on other individuals and sub-systems in the larger entity – society (p. 4).

Common threads in both definitions are *goals* or *objectives, people,* some form of *coordination* or *structure* and, finally, *continuity*. Therefore an organization is an on-going, goal-directed undertaking comprised of people whose activities are coordinated through some form of organizational structure.

3.3.2 Organizational structure

Taking common themes from a number of writers [44] organizational structure can be defined as the interrelationships between and coordination of the division of labour allotted to perform tasks or responsibilities. Organizational structure has two basic functions. First, it is concerned with reducing the variability present in human behaviour so that the organization has a common purpose. Second, organizational structure is the context within which power is exercised, decisions are made and information flows take place [45].

Coordination within the organizational structure can be achieved in five basic and not necessarily mutually exclusive ways [46]. These are as follows:

1. *Mutual adjustment* operates through informal communication. Mutual adjustment works best in simple and complex organizational situations.
2. *Direct supervision:* involves one individual having the responsibility for the work of others.
3. *Standardization of work processes:* involves specifying or programming the content of work.
4. *Standardization of outputs:* involves specifying the results of the work to be achieved. Mintzberg quotes the example of standardizing the dimensions of a product or the performance required.
5. *Standardization of skills* (and knowledge): involves specifying the training required to perform the work or task.

There are also three basic components to organizational structure, as follows [47]:

1. *Complexity:* which relates to the extent of structural differentiation. Three dimensions to complexity are usually identified. *Horizontal differentiation*, the extent of the sub-division of tasks among organizational members. These tasks can be allocated to specialists or non-specialists and hence this dimension also concerns the degree of specialization within an organization. The second dimension is *vertical differentiation* which refers to the depth or number of levels within the organizational hierarchy. The final dimension is *spatial dispersion*, which can relate to either vertical or horizontal differentiation, and refers to activities or personnel being dispersed spatially by separation of power centres or tasks.

    Contracting companies are organizationally complex. The contracting company with estimating, buying, surveying and contracts management departments is differentiated horizontally. Furthermore, the construction company with a managing director, functional directors, regional directors, contracts managers and site agents is also vertically differentiated. Finally, the existence of both geographically dispersed regional operating units (subsidiaries) and construction sites that report to the regions is an example of spatial dispersion.

2. *Formalization:* is concerned with the extent to which the norms of an organization are made explicit. Formalization is often referred to purely in terms of written rules and procedures. However, this is only one aspect of formalization since unwritten norms and standards can be as potent for controlling human behaviour as those in writing. Mintzberg views formalization and *training* (in order to standardize skills) as substitutes since they are both methods of coordination.
3. *Centralization:* refers to the extent to which power is centralized or concentrated within the organization. Centralization of power is also an indication of the extent of trust the organization is prepared to place in individuals for decision-making. A power continuum exists from centralization to decentralization. Decentralization has a vertical and horizontal component. *Vertical decentralization* refers to the formal distribution of power down the managerial line hierarchy. *Horizontal decentralization* refers to the extent to which decision-making power rests outside the managerial line hierarchy. Centralization of decision-making in construction companies will be explored further when regionalization is discussed as part of an expansion strategy.

Lansley *et al.* [48], in their study of 23 medium-sized construction companies, identified two key aspects of organizational structure. First, the degree of *control* within the company. This concerned the extent to which methods were used by the organization to ensure that individuals' roles and responsibilities complied with the aims and objectives of the company. Second, the extent of *integration*. This is concerned with the means used to relate the tasks and activities of individuals to each other. Control and integration have close affinities with the coordinating methods identified by Mintzberg and some of the components of structure identified above.

3.3.3 An organizational role model of a construction company

The basic building blocks of a company are now in place and have been described. The final stage is to bring the components together in the form of an organizational role model which can be used to complement Mintzberg's structural model identified earlier.

Each person or individual in a company has a set of expectations or views and perceptions or beliefs about how they, as individuals, behave in a social situation. In addition, an individual also holds a set of expectations, beliefs and assumptions about how other people will behave in social situations. These two sets of impressions come together within an individual to form a situational view of a company as a social organization and his or her part in it. This situational view of an individual is termed a *role* and a company, as a form of social organization, can be thought of as a role system [49].

Hunt [50] has produced a useful model for analysing organizations as role systems. The model is reproduced in Figure 1.3. Two major considera-

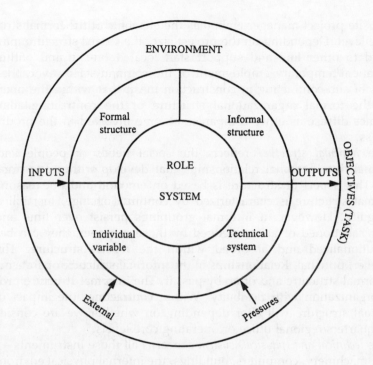

Figure 1.3 *An organization as a role system (Source: Hunt, J. W. (1972), fig. 1.2, p. 11. Reprinted with permission.)*

tions on using the model for analytical purposes in construction are that different criteria come into play at different levels in the company, namely:

1. At headquarters and regional office level: at this level there will be many similarities in the use of the model within other industries.
2. In the operating core – at project and project portfolio levels: it is at this point that the analytical use of the model in construction will differ from that in other industries.

Each component of the model will be described briefly below and the impact of the previous two influences highlighted.

The *formal structure* is concerned with the coordination and control of activities of people within the organization. It involves the distribution of individuals in a hierarchy of positions within the organization, the distribution of status, power and authority for making decisions and the rules, procedures, guidelines and records that control individuals' behaviour. The formal structure represents the past history and decisions of the organization that have become codified over time. Changing the formal structure is difficult and takes time. In contracting, at headquarters or regional office level the formal structure will be clearly delineated. At project level, the formal structure can become less clear cut. The site agent/site project manager embodies the elements of the formal structure at site level. Depending on the project size, the formal structure may also extend to other line and support staff located on-site and within the permanent/temporary employment of the company. However, the high levels of sub-contracting in construction mean that within the operating core the formal organizational structure of the contracting company becomes diffuse as other companies become involved in the production process.

The *informal structure* reflects the social needs of people and the informal, interpersonal relationships that develop within any organization. This aspect of structure is based on emotion and not reason. The informal structure is characterized by continual change, instability and ambiguity. However, if informal groupings persist over time and are either sanctioned or acknowledged by those in power they can become institutionalized and absorbed within the formal structure. This is, however, unusual. Relationships in the informal structure operate outside the formal structure and often by-pass it. The informal structure provides the organization with flexibility. Within contracting, the impact of the informal structure will alter depending on whether we are considering headquarters/regional office or operating core levels.

The *technical and (physical) system* concerns all those instruments – hand tools, machinery, computers, buildings, the internal physical environment of the workplace – that have an impact on the social system. The technical system is a major regulating influence on an organization. It is often slow to change within an organization, although individual components making up the technical system used by the organization can go through rapid changes, and computer hardware is one example that springs vividly to mind. Hunt distinguishes between the technical system and *technology*. He considers that the use of technology as a term is confusing within the research literature. Technology embodies aspects of social adaption, knowledge and skills that relate to the physical instruments used by the organization. Hunt argues that technology refers to a combination of inputs with:

(a) the machines of the technical system;
(b) the members controlling them;
(c) the knowledge of the designers of the process.

Finally, Hunt argues that a technical system can be analysed in three ways:

(a) the degree of choice allowed by instruments – technical system flexibility;
(b) the technical complexity of the instruments and the number of instruments in a process;
(c) the complexity of the technology. Since technology as defined above involves aspect of organizational structure and processes this has a total system impact and is consequently the most important factor for this reason.

For a contracting company, it has been argued that the technical system must be considered in two distinct parts. First, at headquarters/regional office the technical system will comprise, for example, word processors used by secretaries or computers used for the planning and scheduling of projects or for accounting purposes. In a design and build company with an in-house design capability the computer hardware and software used for computer aided designs will also be part of the technical system. Additionally, using Hunt's definition, the buildings and their associated internal environments will also form part of the technical system. When we consider the operating core, the technical system has two facets: (i) for the individual project; (ii) the operating core in total comprised of the 'project portfolio'. For the *individual project*, the technical system is diverse. It will comprise, in its simplest form, hand tools such as joiners' chisels, hammers or hand drills (both manual and power driven) through to heavy earth moving equipment, lorries, JCBs, dumper trucks, tower cranes and hoists. Other parts of the technical system will include scaffolding, site huts, concrete mixers and pumps. The technical system for an individual project is, therefore, highly variable. This variability can be described in terms of the following:

- The degree of mobility: typical examples of the mobile technical system in contracting would be hand tools, earth moving equipment, lorries and dumper trucks. They can operate over the total site area. Stationary examples of the technical system would be site huts and scaffolding, i.e. they are spatially fixed.
- The degree of spatial planar movement, both vertically and horizontally: different components of the technical system will operate in a horizontal plane, for example dumper trucks and lorries. Others will operate in a vertical plane, for example hoists, while others will operate both vertically and horizontally, for example a tower crane or a concrete pump.
- Temporal usage – different parts of the technical system will be required at different stages of a project: earth moving equipment is required early on in a project, concrete mixers and pumps at a latter stage and joinery tools during the finishing trades. Other parts of the technical system will be required throughout a project such as site huts and dumper trucks.
- The degree of intensity of use: there may be stages in a project when the various parts comprising the technical system will be utilized intensely compared to other parts of the project. For example, during the early stages of a project there is likely to be high usage of heavy equipment – earth moving equipment, dumper trucks, lorries, concrete batching plant, concrete pumps, JCBs. At other times, for example when the finishing trades are involved, the nature and intensity of technical system usage changes and may become more low key – a higher incidence of hand tool usage.

● Project characteristics: the nature of the project will have an important influence on the technical system. A civil engineering project will require a different mix of components comprising the technical system than that required for an office block or a project involving refurbishment. Other factors that may have a limiting effect on the choice of components making up the technical system will include, for example, the accessibility of the site, i.e. a town centre gap-site versus a greenfield site.

Using Hunt's distinction between the technical system and technology, the 'technological' capability of a contracting company is thus made up of the interactions between the technical system, the social relationships involved and the knowledge base that goes into ordering the interaction between the two. For a contractor on a particular project, this is epitomized in the 'method statement' – the way the facility is to be constructed and the 'programme' – the mix and phasing of resources to construct a project.

The total technological capability of a contractor is comprised, therefore, of the total technical system in the operating core, the impact of the dimensions identified above, operating in tandem with the aggregated project life cycles comprising the project portfolio, and the associated aggregated, managed, social interactions. This distinction between the technical system and technology is crucial and will become increasingly important in the subsequent analysis of competitive advantage for construction companies.

The *individual variable:* this refers to the impact of an individual's personality, ambitions, goals, desires and needs on an organization. The organization, as an on-going social entity that has to adapt to change, has to consider both the similarities and differences between individuals. An individual's personal objectives may run counter to a company's objectives and can generate conflict, not only within the person concerned but also in the organization. This will be explored further in Chapter 2 when dealing with strategic decision-making.

The *environment:* the external environment of a company is anything considered to be outside the boundaries of the company. The company's environment can be broken down into two parts – the general and task environments [51]. The *general environment* can be considered as anything that can potentially or indirectly affect the company. Using the variables identified by Glauck and Jauch [52] the general environment would include the economy, demographic variables, society's values and attitudes, and technological change at the societal level. Other variables would include the legal and cultural framework of a country. The *task environment* would include those variables and only those that would have a direct and immediate impact on the company's activities. The task environment is the primary source of opportunities and threats for a company and because of its proximity to the company is likely to be better understood than the general environment [53]. It has been suggested that the key aspect of the environment to the individual company is the industry (or industries) within which it competes [54]. The framework proposed by Porter for analysing industries has a close affinity to variables proposed by Dill [55] for a company's task environment.

Lansley *et al* [56] have divided the external environment faced by contractors into three broad categories. Their first category is the *common industry/national environment* embracing the economic and social background of firms, the industry's existing and potential clients, suppliers, labour and respective trade unions, trade associations, central and local government departments. This is common to all firms. The *competitive environment* is a more 'localized' business environment where the company is in competition with other firms. Key factors in this environment are the structure of demand, competitors, availability of materials, labour, sub-contractors and suppliers. As company size increases, the boundary between the competitive and industry environment will become obscure. The *operational environment* is unique to each company and is related to its position in the competitive environment and stems from the strategic choices made by the company, the business activities with which it is involved, the geographic areas it covers and the suppliers with which it deals. Using the earlier framework of general and task environments, the common industry environment is the general environment of the company, while the competitive and operational environments can be subsumed under the task environment. Markets for construction are to be found within the task environment – the competitive and operational environments using Lansley *et al.*'s terminology – and the influences of the five competitive forces of determining industry structure act primarily at this level.

An additional complication concerning the business environment facing a company is the distinction between the *actual* and *perceived environment* [57]. Managers make decisions based on their perceptions of the external environment. However, research undertaken by Downey *et al.* [58] indicate that there is little relationship empirically between the measures of the objective (or actual) environment and the perceived environment that managers use for decision-making. Robbins reports that a company will construct or invent the environment to which it responds, based on the perception of its managers. It is this perception which, in part, determines the company's structure and the assessment of uncertainty it faces.

3.4 Structural typologies and the construction company

A number of typologies exist that can be used to analyse the holistic structure of a company which are particularly pertinent to an analysis of a construction company. These underlying ideas are drawn together below [59]:

1. The *simple structure:* this structure is common in small businesses and typifies that found in the construction industry. Its major characteristics are that: direct supervision is its prime coordinating mechanism; there is a low level of formalization and organizational complexity; the important component of the company is at the strategic apex where authority is usually centralized in one person; the structure tends to be highly organic with little in the way of functional departmentalization. The main problem facing the company with a simple structure is that of growth.

   Norris [60] in his study of Nottingham-based small building companies (defined as an owner-managed company with less than 25 employees, some 95% of the companies comprising the construction industry) found that:

   - Of the total sample (*N*=112) less than 25% had any managerial experience prior to founding the company.
   - The desire for independence was given as the most important reason for company foundation, financial reward was only of secondary importance.
   - Primary business objectives were identified as financial support for themselves and their families with the provision of good service ranked second. Company growth was not considered important and growth may have been restricted in order that the owner could maintain control over the company.
   - Quality of work was the stated criterion for continued success of the company.

   In addition, Austrin [61] argues that self-employment in construction under the 'lump' system of sub-contracting results in new company formulations but does so more for tax reasons coupled with the desire to work for oneself. The net effect of new company formation under this form of work organization is not to create and revitalize the status of owner managers controlling their own capital, through the creation of a different social and economic entity, but in maintaining the economic relationship between employer and employed. In this instance the 'lump' self-employed worker remains a seller of his own labour to the contracting company. The issue of labour-only sub-contracting will be discussed in more detail in a subsequent chapter.

2. The *functional structure:* this structure evolves to handle the primary tasks of the organization. Common functional departments for a contracting company would be estimating, buying, surveying, contracts management and accounting. Companies that grow from a simple structure will usually involve development of some form of functional distribution of activities. The functional structure is, therefore, differentiated horizontally.

3. The *divisional structure:* the divisional structure creates a series of relatively autonomous smaller functionally structured units with res-

ponsibility for a defined market, product, service, geographic region, customer type or technical processes. The prime coordinating mechanism is the standardization of outputs. Each division will be responsible for its own strategic direction provided it is within corporate guidelines. The divisional structure is common in the construction industry, especially among the larger contractors, where divisional operations might be divided into, for example, construction or, more narrowly, management contracting, design and build; others include building materials or property development. Divisions may be judged on the basis of performance either as profit or cost centres. Divisionalization is a response to managing the outcome of a diversification strategy.

4. The *sector structure:* under this relatively new structural type an additional layer is interposed between divisional managers and the corporate centre. Each sector thus represents common businesses with a clearly defined industry identity. It tends to be applicable in large organizations that are adopting growth strategies where there is a danger that the span of control at the centre becomes too great. In effect, to use Robbins' term, a company structured sectorally creates 'superdivisions'. The application of sectoral structuring to construction may, for example, create a 'superdivision' called 'construction' with other, operational divisions called 'management contracting', 'design and build', 'civil engineering' and 'building'. An additional example would be the creation of geographical 'super-divisions' dealing with all aspects of construction activity in each of the subcontinents.

5. The *holding company* structure: Johnson and Scholes [62] argue that the holding company can take a number of forms, from a type that resembles a pure investment company of shareholdings in a series of unconnected businesses over which little or no control is exercised to one where a parent company manages a portfolio of virtually autonomous businesses, with different percentage stakeholdings in each. Each business unit is likely to retain its own identity and organizational structure. Hunt identifies the *subsidiary* company as a separate structural type and this is often found in construction operating under the holding company umbrella. The subsidiary company has high autonomy from the centre, the primary link being through a financial reporting and a modified management information system.

6. The *machine bureaucracy:* this structural type is characterized by very routine operating tasks, formalized rules and regulations, functional departments and centralized decision-making through the formal hierarchy. The primary coordinating mechanism is standardization of work processes. This type of structure will characterize large companies in stable environments and using highly routine technology. Line and staff are sharply delineated and there is a well-developed administrative structure. A building materials manufacturer would typically have this structure.

7. The *professional bureaucracy:* the operating core of the professional bureaucracy is the key area for this type of company. Standardization of skills is the prime coordinating mechanism. Decision-making is decentralized to specialists, i.e. professionals who have highly developed knowledge and skills with considerable work autonomy. The major difference between the machine and professional bureaucracy is that the former standardizes work flows within the organization whereas with the latter standardization occurs outside the organization through educational and professional institutions. Mintzberg highlights the *craft enterprise,* involving lengthy apprenticeship training, as an important variant of the professional bureaucracy. This is a structural type common in the construction industry. In the study undertaken by Norris of small building companies, 75% of his sample were craft-based organizations and operated primarily in the R & M sector. In addition, a divisionalized construction company with a separate design subsidiary staffed primarily by personnel who have gained their training outside the company, perhaps architects or engineers, could also be classified as a professional bureaucracy. However, the important distinguishing characteristic would be the extent to which solutions to problems are unique or standardized. In this instance, where solutions tend towards project-based uniqueness, this structure moves towards adhocracy.

8. The *adhocracy:* this is characterised by low to moderate complexity, low formalization, decentralized decision-making, high levels of horizontal differentiation, a flat hierarchy and minimal supervision. The emphasis is on flexibility for problem-solving and innovation to achieve specific objectives. Adhocracies are usually staffed by professionals with a high level of expertise. The adhocracy has as its prime coordinating mechanism mutual adjustment through interpersonal interaction. Adhocracies are team-based, primarily multidisciplinary and temporary in nature. The adhocracy would typify the project structure in construction.

   Mintzberg differentiates between the operative and administrative adhocracy depending on the nature of the skills brought to the task. The *operative adhocracy* is concerned with innovation and problem-solving directly for the client, often to contract. A key feature of the operating adhocracy is the blurring of the distinction between operational and administrative tasks, with little differentiation of the planning, design and execution of the work. Whereas the professional bureaucracy would 'pigeonhole' the solution for the client and use convergent thinking, the operating adhocracy would use divergent thinking to create an innovative solution.

   The *administrative adhocracy* is project-based but with the focus on internal performance rather than for an external client. The administrative adhocracy truncates its operating core such that the administrative component is structured as an adhocracy. This is in contrast to the operative adhocracy where the two are blurred. Mintzberg suggests truncation can take place in three ways, as follows:

(a) a need to innovate but where the operating core is to remain as a Machine Bureaucracy which can be established as a separate organization;

(b) the operating core is done away with totally and is effectively contracted out to other organizations;

(c) the operating core becomes totally automated.

9. The *matrix structure:* the matrix structure is a combination of structures operating concurrently – functional departments and products or projects, product and geographical divisions and functional and divisional structures. There are two types of matrix structure, first the temporary matrix where the structure is created as required and then disbanded. The temporary matrix is an example of the adhocracy. Temporary matrix structures are common in construction. Stocks [63] in his analysis of project structures in construction, identified the design team as an interorganizational project structure. We can term project structures in construction as a *temporary interorganizational matrix*. The permanent matrix, as its name implies, has a degree of permanency attached to it. In effect, it creates two sets of permanent managers with separate responsibilities and line reporting relationships but whose task activities overlap in some manner. The matrix structure, especially the temporary one, tends towards instability, creates ambiguities and hence conflict.

10. The *multinational company or enterprise* (MNC/MNE) structure: the most common form is the international division to manage overseas interests. Extensions of this are geographically-based divisions that evolve as part of a multinational organization, where each division operates virtually independently by country. Finally, the global product or integrated structure is an alternative to the international division. In this instance, the multinational company is split into product divisions with each managed on an international basis. The use of the matrix structure is also common in the MNE. The MNE will be discussed further in the context of international construction.

3.5 The construction company as a business and social entity

The development of the model of a company has, so far, stressed that the firm is delineated from its external environment by a permeable boundary. It has an internal structure that can be divided into analytically distinct levels that are interrelated through a role system. This sub-section attempts to draw together ideas from managerial economics with those of organizational behaviour to describe the construction company as both a business and social entity involved in various types of exchange.

Organizational economics attempts to apply economic analysis to work organization. Modern economic theories of the company have moved away from considering the small entrepreneurial company to large oligo-polistic and/or diversified companies [64]. Cannon and Hillebrandt contend that there are still inherent difficulties in applying these theories to contracting companies. One major theoretical paradigm that has been applied to construction is the analytical framework of the markets and hierarchies approach developed by Williamson [65]. In drawing together a number of writers' ideas [66] on this approach, the basic conceptual framework is as follows:

- The basic unit of analysis is the transaction or contractual exchange rather than the company or market. Transaction costs are those involved in the process of buying or selling goods and services including manpower [67].
- Key behavioural assumptions are that human beings have bounded rationality[2] and some are opportunistic. Hence it becomes difficult and costly to distinguish between those who are and those who are not opportunistic. Additionally, because of the foregoing, human beings, in making decisions in a complex situation, face an unequal distribution of information – information impactedness – and bargaining power arises due to differences in perception and understanding of the available information.
- Markets or organizational hierarchies are viable alternatives in handling transaction costs.
- The key issue for organizational design is to solve the problem of economizing simultaneously on both bounded rationality and opportunism.
- Transaction costs will be taken out of the market and internalized within the company when it is cheaper to do so. Put another way, organizations (companies) exist because they lower transaction costs. Where transactions are undertaken intermittently or on an *ad hoc* basis it is cheaper to undertake these via a series of single contracts in the external market. However, where transactions are more frequent it becomes less costly to organize the exchange within the company, i.e. internally. Thus, internalization of transaction costs within the company produces savings in information gathering, in contractual exchanges, and by substituting an employment relationship for ones undertaken totally via external contracts. Transaction costs are supplementary to the purchase directly of inputs by the company.
- Hierarchical employment relationships occur due to reasons of efficiency and the requirement for a control and monitoring function. The *vertical hierarchy* is the embodiment of the fact that ultimate control of the company rests with the owners and management representatives.

---

[2] Bounded rationality, put simply, says that individuals, when making decisions, use a decision strategy that opts for a 'good enough' fit with the circumstances they face, rather than a strategy of maximizing or optimizing. Bounded rationality will be discussed in more detail in Chapter 2.

The *horizontal hierarchy* differentiates employees in terms of grades, ranks and rewards.

● An internal labour market (ILM) – operating through some form of collective agreement (the employment contract) – differentiates labour from the external market place and allocates and prices labour internally to a company. Thus, in an ILM wages are assigned to jobs and not individuals, promotion ladders are defined and sensitive grievance structures are devised.

While intuitively appealing, a perspective that utilizes managerial economics alone possesses certain problems because, as indicated in the earlier discussions on the company as an organization, it may not reflect the realities of organizational life for a number of reasons. First, using our role model of a company, an employment contract, associated incentive systems and grievance handling procedures comprise part of the formal structure of the company – only one aspect that impinges on the functioning of an organization. Second, internalizing within the company implies some form of boundary between the internal organization and the external market place. From an organizational behaviour perspective, as Hunt [68] has indicated, individuals are involved in another form of exchange relationship within the company – one involving psychological exchanges. It is this *psychological contract* that sets and extends the permeable boundaries of the company and adds to the notion of what is internal or external to it.

A company, as a business entity, is involved in a series of exchange relationships – some are contractually defined while others are psychological. The psychological contract determines the boundary of the organization and what is inside or outside the company. Contractual exchanges – involving transaction costs – operate through the formal structure of the company. The psychological contract has more diffuse origins and stems from the interplay between the major variables comprising the role model. In essence, the psychological contract provides that sense of 'belonging' to a company and differentiates a person's feeling of being with one company and not with another. The stronger the psychological contract the greater the sense of belonging to a company. These issues will be taken up further when a preliminary model of a construction company is developed in the next section.

4. Conclusions – a preliminary model of a construction company

Construction is a major national and international industry where economic and organizational theories do not easily apply without adaption. In terms of strategic management, the construction industry is analytically complex with different types of economic market structure in evidence. A construction market – defined in terms of an exchange relationship between a buyer and seller, where the former has a need which the latter can satisfy for a mutually agreed price – is the best analytical medium in construction. The 'construction industry' comprises a series of overlapping geographically dispersed markets linked socially and economically. The five competitive forces, setting the broad context for strategic decision-making, impact each market differentially depending on whether the overlaying economic structure is contracting or for speculative purposes.

Industry and market structure impact a firm through organizational structure, and a contracting company, depending on how senior management perceive the environment and respond to it, structures the company by delineating a *strategic domain* within the broader industry environment. The strategic domain sets the parameters within which senior management chooses the company to operate. Some senior managements define a narrow domain – perhaps a regional geographic market for constructing to contract on building projects. Others may specialize by project types within this. Others may define a broader strategic domain undertaking both civil and building projects. In this latter instance senior managers' perceptions of the impact of market structures on the company can lead to alternative structural designs for handling these different commercial and technical environments. The complex market structure within construction is also affected by the institutionalized distribution channels for contractors' services – the clients' consultant advisers. The consultants, through their mediating role between client and contractor, modify the market exchange relationship, thus dictating the form of the competitive arena for the contractor. The contractor has to adjust partly to this through the merchant–producer role.

A number of entry and exit barriers have been identified in the domestic and international construction industries that structure contracting into an hierarchical industry of companies, acting as sub-contractors and/or main contractors, and a series of project-based vertical markets. In the lower layers of the vertical markets construction is highly fragmented. However, as project size and complexity increase and we move from a domestic to an international perspective, construction becomes more concentrated, with managerial expertise and access to finance becoming increasingly important. Only a relatively small number of companies are able to compete under such conditions.

The contracting company can be broken down into a series of discrete analytical parts. The main components are, first, the strategic apex, where senior managers have a primary role of linking the company to both its task and general environments. Their perception of the external environment plays a crucial role in setting the strategic direction and orientation of the company. Second, the middle line, which links the operating core with the strategic apex and where managers here have a primary role as integrators. Third, the operating core, which is in a constant state of technological and competitive flux for the contractor as projects, making up its project portfolio, go through different stages of the project life cycle.

The operating core of the contractor can be retained with permanently employed skilled, semi-skilled and unskilled operatives together with a permanently owned technical system. However, contractors face a choice, either to retain the operating core in-house or to externalize it through sub-contracting. In effect, due to demand variability, contractors have chosen to retain flexibility. The operating core, as a series of project-based production systems, has been essentially truncated at site manager level with a considerable proportion of the operative workforce and the technical system being sub-contracted out to other companies. Contractors have chosen to structure themselves at project level as an administrative adhocracy rather than an operating adhocracy. In addition, contracting companies have also responded to demand variability by moving into other markets and away from their contracting base.

Organizationally, construction companies are complex, with a number of possible corporate organizational structures depending on the degree and nature of moves into other markets. These corporate structures can move, at one extreme, from the simple structure appropriate for the small company, through a series of variations to the divisionalized structure and

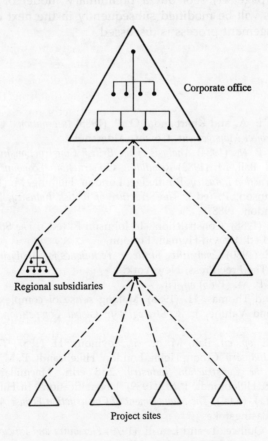

Figure 1.4 *A preliminary model of a construction company*

holding company present in the large companies. The structure of the contracting operation can also be organizationally complex with considerable horizontal and vertical differentiation linked with spatial distribution by region and project. Construction companies also operate as interlocking role systems with different types of internal exchange relationships in operation, namely, through the employment and psychological contracts. The role system within contracting is also complex, especially in the operating core as internal employment contracts are substituted for external labour contracts via sub-contracting. The internal employment contract determines the legal operation of the company through the formal structure, whereas the psychological contract energizes the company and sets the boundaries of what is within or without the company. Where sub-contracting of labour and the technical system is extensive in the operating core there will be a myriad of different employment and psychological contracts in operation for each company involved. It is the responsibility of the main contractor's site staff to weld this amorphous mass into a coherent integrated production system for achieving project objectives.

Figure 1.4 (page 41) sets out a preliminary model of a contracting company. This will be modified subsequently in the next chapter as the strategic management process is discussed.

References

1. Stallworthy, E. A. and Kharbanda, O. P. (1985) *International Construction: and the Role of Project Management*. Gower, Aldershot.
2. Hillebrandt, P. M. (1984) *Analysis of the British Construction Industry*. Macmillan, London. Ball, M. (1988) *Rebuilding Construction: Economic Change and the British Construction Industry*. Routledge, London. Fleming, M. (1988) 'Construction'. In Johnson, P. (ed.), *The Structure of British Industry*, 2nd ed. Unwin Hyman, London. 1988.
3. Fleming, M. (1988) 'Construction'. In Johnson P. (ed.), *The Structure of British Industry*, 2nd ed. Unwin Hyman, London.
4. Porter, M. E. (1980) *Competitive Strategy: Techniques for Analysing Industries and Competitors*. The Free Press, New York.
5. Hillebrandt, P. M. (1985) *op. cit.*
6. Mcgee, J. and Thomas, H. (1988) 'Making sense of complex industries'. In Hood, N. and Vahlne, J. R. *Strategies in Global Competition*. Croom Helm, London.
7. Porter, M. E. *op. cit.* Ball, M. *op. cit.* Seymour, H. (1987) *The Multinational Construction Industry*. Croom Helm, London. Hillebrandt, P. M. (1983) *Economic Theory and the Construction Industry*, 2nd edn. Macmillan, Basingstoke. Cannon, J. & Hillebrandt, P.M. (1989) 'Diversification'. In Hillebrandt, P. M. and Cannon, J. (eds.), *The Management of Construction Firms: Aspects of Theory*. Macmillan, Basingstoke.
8. Lansley, P., Quince, T. and Lea, E. (1979) *Flexibility and Efficiency in Construction Management*. Final Report. Building Industry Group, Ashridge Management College.

9. Langford, D. A. and Male, S. P. *Strategic Management in Construction*. Gower, in press.
10. Ball, M. *op. cit.*
11. Ball, M. *op. cit.*
12. Porter, M. E. *op. cit*
13. Flemming, M. *op. cit.*
14. Seymour, H. *op. cit*
15. Hillebrandt, P. M. (1985) *op. cit.*
16. Hillebrandt, P. M. (1984) *op. cit.*
17. Ball, M. *op. cit.*
18. Williams, N. (1981) 'Influences on the profitability of 22 industrial sectors', *Bank of England Discussion Paper No: 22.*
19. Porter, M. E. *op. cit.*
20. Stokes, F. H. (1977) 'Practical problems in corporate planning: II John Laing.' In Taylor, B. and Sparkes, J. R. (eds.), *Corporate Strategy and Planning*. Heinemann. Reprinted 1982.
21. Seymour, H. *op. cit.*
22. Flanagan, R. and Norman, G. (1984) 'Pricing policy'. In Hillebrandt, P. M. and Cannon, J. (eds.) *op. cit.*
23. Seymour, H. *op. cit.*
24. Ball, M. and Cullen, A. (1980) 'Merger and accumulation in the British construction industry 1960–1970.' *Birkbeck Discussion Paper No: 73.* Fleming, M. *op. cit.*
25. Verillo, J. Brazil. In Strassman, W. P. and Wells, J. (eds.), *The Global Construction Industry: Strategies for Entry, Growth & Survival*. Unwyn Hyman, London.
26. Bennett, J., Flanagan, R. and Norman, G. (1987) *Capital and Counties Report: Japanese Construction Industry*. Centre for Strategic Studies, University of Reading.
27. Porter, M. E. *op. cit.*
28. Flanagan, R. and Norman, G. *op. cit.*
29. Ball, M. *op. cit.*
30. Drewer, S. P. Scandanavia. In Strassman, P. W. and Wells, J. (eds.), *op. cit.* Hillebrandt, P. M. and Cannon, J. (1984) 'Theories of the firm.' In Hillebrandt, P. M. and Cannon, J. (eds.) *op. cit.*
31. Male, S. P. (1984) A Critical Investigation of Professionalism in Quantity Surveying. Unpublished PhD Thesis Heriot-Watt University. 1984.
32. Langford, D. and Male, S. P. *op. cit.*
33. Mintzberg, H. (1979) *The Structuring of Organisations*. Prentice-Hall Inc., Englewood Cliffs, New Jersey.
34. Anderson, S. D. and Woodhead, R. W. (1981) *Project Manpower Management: Management Processes in Cosntruction Practice*. John Wiley & Sons, New York.
35. Hillebrandt, P. M. (1985) *op. cit.*
36. Drewer, S. (1975) *The Building Process: The Mechanism of Response to Effective Demand. The Supply of Construction Services in the West Midlands*. Report by the Building Economics Research Unit. University College Environmental Research Group. University College London, June.
37. Ball, M. and Cullen, A. *op. cit.* Ball, M. *op. cit.*
38. Ball, M. *op. cit.*
39. Ball, M. *op. cit.*
40. Lansley, P., Quince, T. and Lea, E. *op. cit.*
41. Ball, M. *op. cit.*
42. Robbins, S. R. (1983) *Organisation Theory: The Structure and Design of Organisa-*

tions. Prentice-Hall, Englewood Cliffs, New Jersey.
43. Hunt J. W. (1972) *The Restless Organisation*. John Wiley and Sons, New South Wales.
44. Mintzberg, H. *op. cit.* Lansley, P., Quince, T. and Lea, E. *op. cit.*
45. Hall, R. H. (1977) *Organisations: Structure and Process*, 2nd ed. Prentice-Hall, Englewood Cliffs, New Jersey.
46. Mintzberg, H. *op. cit.*
47. Robbins, S. R. *op. cit.* Price, J. L. (1972) *Handbook of Organisational Measurement*. D.C. Heath & Co. Hall, R. H. *op. cit.*
48. Lansley, P. Quince, T. and Lea E. *op. cit.*
49. Katz, D. and Kahn R. L. (1978) *The Social Psychology of Organisations*, 2nd edn. John Wiley & Sons, New York.
50. Hunt, J. W. *op. cit.*
51. Robbins, S. P. *op. cit.*
52. Glauck, W. F. and Jauch, L. R. *Business Policy and Strategic Management*, 4th edn. McGraw-Hill, Singapore.
53. Johnson, G. and Scholes, K. (1988) *Exploring Corporate Strategy*, 2nd edn. Prentice-Hall, Hemel Hempstead.
54. Porter, M. E. *op. cit.*
55. Dill, W. R. (1958) 'Environment as an influence on managerial autonomy', *Administrative Science Quarterly*, **2**, No. 3, pp. 409–443.
56. Lansley, P., Quince, T. and Lea, E. *op. cit.*
57. Robbins, S. R. *op. cit.*
58. Downey, H. K., Hellrigel, D. and Slocum, J. W. (1975) 'Environmental uncertainty: the construct and its application'. *Administrative Science Quarterly*, December, pp. 613–619.
59. Johnson, G. and Scholes, K. *op. cit.* Mintberg, H. *op. cit.* Robbins, S. P. *op. cit.* Hunt, J. W. (1986) *Managing People at Work*, 2nd edn. McGraw-Hill, Maidenhead.
60. Norris, K. (1984) 'Small building firms: Their origins, characteristics and development needs', *CIOB Occasional Paper No. 32*.
61. Austrin, T. (1990) 'The "Lump" in the UK Construction Industry.' In Nichols, T. (ed.), *Capital and Labour: Studies in the Capitalist Labour Process*. Athlone Press.
62. Johnson, G. and Scholes, K. *op. cit.*
63. Stocks, R. K. (1984) The Building Team: An Organisation of Organisations. MSc Thesis. Heriot-Watt University.
64. Cannon, J. and Hillebrandt, P.M. *op. cit.*
65. Williamson, O. E. (1975) *Markets and Hierarchies: Analysis and Antitrust Implications*. Free Press, New York.
66. For a review of the literature see Cannon, J. and Hillebrandt, P. M. *op. cit.* Buckley, P. J. and Enderwick, P. 'Manpower management'. In Hillebrandt, P. M. and Cannon, J. (eds.) *op. cit.* Buckley, P. J. and Enderwick, P. (1988) Manpower Management in the Domestic and International Construction Industry. *University of Reading Discussion Papers in International Investment and Business Studies No: 111*. University of Reading. January. Williamson, O. E. and Ouchi, W. G. (1981) The markets and hierarchies program of research: Origins, implications, prospects. In Van de Ven A. H. and Joyce, W. F. (1981) eds., *Perspectives on Organisation Design and Behaviour*. John Wiley and Sons, New York.
67. Cannon, J. and Hillebrandt, P. M. *op. cit.*
68. Hunt, J. W. (1972) *op. cit.*

— 2 —

Strategic management and competitive advantage in construction

Steven Male

1. Introduction

The preceding chapter indicated that the construction industry – both domestically in the United Kingdom and internationally – is large, has a diversity of client types, is structured into a geographically dispersed project-based vertical market with differing degrees of fragmentation and is hierarchially structured by company size. This chapter builds on the preceding one and explores these issues in the context of strategic management and competitive advantage in construction.

2. Problems of demand forecasting for strategic management in construction

There are a number of problems associated with demand forecasting in construction. A construction project, as a process, can be broken down into a number of discrete analytical stages – inception, concept, design, construction on site, handover/occupancy – that can take many months or years before the total process is completed. For example, it can take anything between $2\frac{1}{2}$ to 17 years to undertake the stages 'inception' to 'construction on site' for a private sector funded commercial building, a public sector funded health project can take between 2 and 14 years for the same stages and public sector funded roads and harbours between 3 and 17 years [1]. The nature of construction projects and the fact that they go through these different stages, where the project can stall for any number of reasons, means that demand is felt temporally in the industry in different ways. This is explored below in a hypothetical example and set out in Figure 2.1.

The inception stage commences when the client senses a need to build a facility. As indicated above, this can take many months or years to occur within the client organization – often deep within the client organization – and will stem from a trigger either singly or in combination from the client's internal or external environment. Stage 1 – inception – illustrates the point that the client has reacted to some form of trigger in its own business environment ('business environment 1'). Additionally, at this

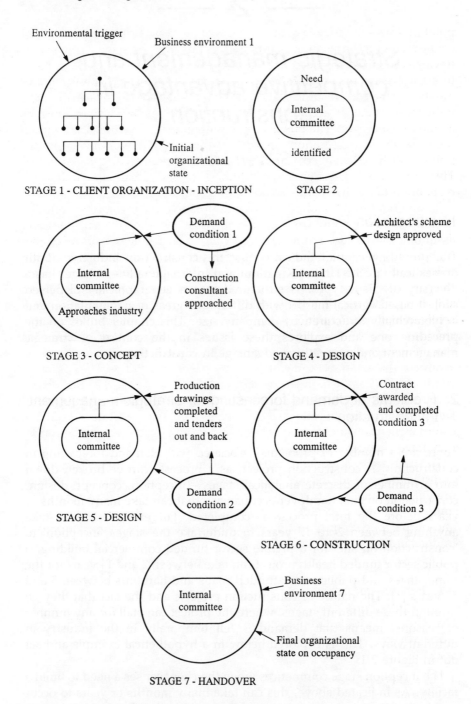

Figure 2.1 *Demand conditions throughout the building process*

point in time – the trigger point – the client has a particular organizational configuration in terms of structure and technology. At stage 2, the client, having recognized the need to build may set up an internal working party to clarify issues and requirements. At stage 3 – 'concept' these require-ments *may* have been sufficiently worked out to approach the construction industry – usually an architect, or perhaps project manager, an engineer or a quantity surveyor. The business environment faced by the client and its organizational configuration, depending on the duration of time up to this point, will have changed from that when the original trigger occurred. This can be viewed as 'demand condition 1' for the construction industry – responded to by the client's advisers, the consultants.

Assuming a traditional procurement approach, during stages 4 and 5 – design – the design and contract documents are worked up. Furthermore, assuming the facility is not cancelled due to the impact of, for example, high interest rates in 'business environments 4 & 5', invitations to tender will go out to contractors to bid on the project – 'demand condition 2' for the construction industry, responded to by contractors. At stage 5 there is still no guarantee that the project will proceed because the tenders received may be too high or the environment faced by the client may have changed dramatically. However, on the assumption that a tender is accepted, stage 6 – construction on site – is reached where the contractor is awarded the contract and commences production on site – 'demand condition 3', again responded to by the contractors. At stage 7 – handover/occupancy – the building is complete and the client takes over the facility. Depending on the duration of the process from stages 1 to 7 both the external client business environment and its organizational configuration may have changed substantially.

To summarize, a model of the construction process has been presented and then analysed in terms of a triggering event within the client organization and how this may be related to different demand conditions imposed on the construction industry. The next section reviews demand and output in construction, published forecasts and their potential use in understanding the environment faced by the construction company.

2.1 Demand and output in construction

Demand, as indicated above, is part of the environment to which senior managers must respond in construction. The nature of demand in con-struction is characterized by the following [2]:

1. The exercise of monopsonist power by clients for construction to contract in the pre-contract stages[1].

[1] However, once the contract has been signed, we would argue that power shifts to the contractor since the contracting company becomes responsible for the effective and efficient on-site production process, over which the client and its advisers have little or no direct control until the contract completion date is reached. The options to reintroduce control, from the client perspective, are not without their problems.

2. A shift to private sector demand, which is more variable in the short to medium term. This involves contractors in:
   - more land assembly than in the past for speculative purposes;
   - increased tendering activity to maintain turnover.

3. Divergent industry sectoral workloads counterbalancing each other such that individual sectoral workloads may reduce but taken as an aggregate, industry workload will not.

4. A consistent upward trend in the workload for repair and maintenance (R & M).

5. The trend line for order placing has a strong cyclical pattern similar to construction output but with a larger amplitude.

On the other hand, construction output is characterized by the following [3]:

(a) is more stable than new orders;
(b) has followed a strong trend line since World War II that conforms to the same pattern found in many other European countries;
(c) is strongly cyclical. The trend line has a period ranging from three to six years with variations from the norm of less than 10%.

Having reviewed the nature of demand and its follow-through into output, the next sub-section highlights sources of information for understanding demand in construction.

2.2 Demand forecasts and sources of information on the external environment

There are considerable problems with forecasts of demand in construction in the short to medium term, i.e. less than or greater than three years. However, in view of the limitations of these forecasts, Hillebrandt [4] argues in favour of understanding *need* – defined as the difference between the *total requirement* for built facilities and infrastructure and the *existing provision* – and the factors that contribute to it. These factors would include the following:

(a) the population of users of built facilities and any demographic changes to that population;
(b) the rate of usage of built facilities and the change in the rate of usage;
(c) standards for facilities and any changes in standards;
(d) replacement of stock due to ageing or technical factors;
(e) increases in or replacement of stock due to technological change or changes in standard.

We can conclude, therefore, that a long-term perspective in construction would require an analysis of the underlying needs going to make up demand.

2.3 Demand and strategic management in construction

The preceding sub-section has identified the fact that there can be significant problems associated with determining demand conditions in construction in the short to medium term. The point at issue here, however, is whether these forecasts are best suited for strategic decision-making – the long-term view – or operational decision-making – a short- to medium-term view. As suggested earlier, a longer-term orientation involves understanding the underlying causes of demand conditions – the determinants of market need.

Stokes [5], a corporate planning practitioner in construction, argues that any long-term forecasts for a major construction company should be based on trends in the national and international construction industries. He indicates that trends in national fixed capital formation – of which construction forms a major part – provide the context against which industry trends and possibilities should be assessed. Stokes argues in favour of long-term strategic thinking in construction with a focus away from short-term variability – the 'traditional' view of volatility in construction. This volatility would be represented more by the data in the short- and medium-term demand forecasts referred to above. Stokes' empirical data indicate that the trend line in construction since World War II is 'so stable' that forecasting in construction is possible. The key is a long-term orientation and the ability to understand and identify why changes occur in the trend line. The comparative stability of trend indicators in construction, post World War II, is also confirmed by Ball [6] who like Stokes, indicates that relatively small variations around the trend have occurred in output and order placing over the long term. Ball contends that variations, where they do occur, are not felt at the aggregate level of industry workload but sectorally. Additionally, Ball concludes, like Stokes, that the empirical evidence indicates that short-term demand variability in construction is no worse than manufacturing industry.

The picture that has emerged in this section is that a long-term, strategic orientation is possible in construction and that the indicators are present in order for strategic thinking to take place. Furthermore, many of the myths surrounding construction in terms of its uniqueness – its volatility and highly variable demand – can be refuted empirically. In the short term, construction appears no worse in terms of demand variability than that with which manufacturing companies have to contend. The consequence for managers in construction is the requirement for a long-term perspective to be adopted. Of major importance, therefore, is the ability for them to develop the skills to move away from a production orientation where the focus is on the internal working of the company and a short-term perspective, to a strategic orientation where the focus of attention is external and involves the long-term relationship between the company and its environment. This is the essence of strategic management, the subject of the next section.

3. The strategic management of a company

Strategic management is concerned with the management of the long-term relationship of the company with its external environment. As such, this will involve the company in adaptation, over time, to changes in the business environment that will have their corresponding impact on the company. This will involve managers in the management of different types of change.

3.1 *The nature of change in organizations*

Change becomes necessary when there are problems, opportunities or threats associated with the following [7]:

- the external environment;
- diversification strategies necessitating new company structures;
- technology;
- people.

The management of change is concerned, therefore, with managing the impact of any of the above on the company and hence changing the relationship between the company and its external environment.

It is important to differentiate between different types of environmental change – operational, competitive and strategic [8]. *Operational change* is familiar and can be handled by experience and the company's existing routines and procedures. Operational change does not alter the underlying relationship of the company with its environment. *Strategic change* is unfamiliar and sudden. Tichy adds that this form of change is non-incremental and discontinuous [9]. It requires managers to exercise creativity and insight. Strategic change cannot be handled by experience and existing organizational routines and procedures. This type of change involves the company in a fundamentally different relationship with its environment. *Competitive change* is a combination of both operational and strategic change. It is gradual and is likely to be more familiar. However, over the medium and longer term the environment will have shifted fundamentally. The handling of competitive change by managers involves a combination of experience, creativity and insight. It is incremental but substantial.

It is through the process of strategic management that a company adapts to the changes in its environment. Clark [10] differentiates between change that is *recurrent* – the repetition of activities over different time scales creating an 'organizational memory' that may be appropriately or inappropriately triggered by events, and *transformational* – which refers to the modification of recurrent patterns either deliberately or unintentionally. Operational change is an example of recurrent change whereas competitive and strategic change *should* involve the company in transformational change. Additionally, strategic management – the proactive management of the changing relationships between the company and its business environment – involves change that is transformational and, hopefully, deliberate.

The important point about strategic and competitive change and its management is that managers have to, first, sense the need for change and then, second, exercise choice, having worked out the appropriate way to handle the change, in order to alter the relationship between the company and its environment. However, change induces different degrees of stress in individuals. Managers, when faced by strategic change, can utilize the following five possible modes of decision-making [11]:

1. Unconflicted adherence: the triggering event goes unnoticed, no serious risk or possible opportunity is perceived and no change in the organization results.
2. Unconflicted change: managers perceive a need for change but the ensuing change is only a small variation from existing patterns – incrementalism. However, a thorough strategic analysis, had it been undertaken, of the external and internal situation facing the company may have indicated a need for substantial change.
3. Defensive avoidance: managers perceive serious risks with both new and existing courses of action and believe no solution can be found – the issues confronting the company are avoided.
4. Hypervigilance: managers have perceived the serious risks associated with current and new courses of action but feel that there is insufficient time to act.
5. Vigilance: managers have perceived the serious risks from both the current and new courses of action, believe a solution can be found and have the time to undertake the desired courses of action. Stress is controlled and acts as a motivating rather than debilitating force.

The first four types of decision-making under stress are dysfunctional. The final type – vigilance – is considered to be the best approach by Tichy for handling strategic change and he suggests the following six procedures for fostering it:

1. Managerial decisions should be thought of in terms of strategic and non-strategic types with time and resources committed to assist strategic decision-making.
2. Operational issues and crises can create 'time-traps' for managers that draw them away from important issues and can result in them operating under hypervigilance and unconflicted change modes of decision-making. Managers should be wary, therefore, of falling into time-traps.
3. A filtering system should be developed to enable the type of change problem facing the company to be addressed by the appropriate level in the hierarchy.
4. A buffering system should be developed to foster 'vigilant' decision-making and hence allow strategists time to focus their attention on strategic decisions and change.

5. Create 'advocates of strategic change' whose purpose is to draw the organization's attention to change activities.
6. Monitor time allocations to strategic and non-strategic activities.

To summarize, three different types of change have been identified that a construction company may face, namely, operational, strategic and competitive change. The management of each type of change requires a different set of managerial skills. The problem for senior managers is that strategic change is radical and can fundamentally alter the nature of the relationship between the company and its environment. Operational change is incremental. Competitive change is probably the most demanding in terms of skill requirements for managers. The company experiences a fundamental shift in its relationship with the environment. Competitive change is, therefore, both fundamental and incremental but requires both creativity, insight and experience to handle and manage it effectively. The management of change is discussed in greater detail in Chapter 10.

3.2 *Change and the strategic management process*

Strategic management and the processes associated with it are concerned with reaching decisions about answering two questions. First, *what* ought the company be doing and, second, *where* should the company be going [12]. The language of both questions is formed in a way that reflects a future orientation. The strategic management process is also about handling strategic and competitive change. Central to the strategic management process, therefore, are three key factors:

(a) a future orientation;
(b) an ability to make strategic decisions about the relationship between the company and the business environment that it faces;
(c) the management of strategic and competitive change.

Strategic management requires a different set of managerial skills than at other levels in the company – in the middle line or in the operating core. Managers at the strategic apex require conceptual and judgemental skills. They are dealing with unstructured and at times ambiguous information. Their time horizon is long-term. This is in contrast to those in the middle line who are primarily involved in an integrative function. They require organizational and political skills. Their time horizon is both long-term – to relate information of importance to the strategic apex – and short term – when they are involved in technical issues with the operating core. Those in the operating core require technical skills. Their time horizon is primarily short-term [13].

The strategic management process can be broken down into three distinct analytical stages: *strategy formulation, strategic choice* and *strategic implementation*. While analytically distinct, in reality they will overlap. The following sections discuss the important ideas within each area.

3.2.1 Strategy formulation

The primary concern of strategic analysis, as part of the strategy formulation process, is to understand the disposition of the company in relation to its business environment and hence match the capabilities of the company with the requirements of the environment through a strategy or strategies [14]. Strategy formulation is a behavioural process [15] and usually involves management within the company analysing the business environment for opportunities and threats; the internal functioning of the company for strengths and weaknesses – the SWOT analysis. Key concepts in the formulation process are – mission, objectives, strategy and policies.

3.2.1.1 Mission

A company's mission is the *fundamental reason* or underlying philosophy for its existence. The mission will usually be encompassed within some form of mission statement [16]. The mission of a company has also been described as a 'vision' of the company's future state. It is, therefore, a long-term view of the company and since it is likely to be in an idealized form may never be attained [17]. The mission will have been formed by the founder(s) or, if the founder's(s) influences are no longer felt, the major strategists within the company [18].

3.2.1.2 Objectives

Stemming from the company's mission are a series of objectives to be attained. Objectives are *ends oriented* [19] and they will be shaped by the key power holders within the company [20]. Objectives have a number of purposes, as follows [21]:

1. They facilitate the coordination and integration of decisions and decision-makers.
2. They assist in defining the relationship between the company and its business environment.
3. They can be given time horizons for attainment and hence assist the company in defining its relationship with different future business environments.
4. They set standards of performance to be met, usually in a quantifiable and hence verifiable form.
5. They can be ranked to provide sub-objectives for organizational groupings lower down the hierarchy.

Objectives are achieved through strategy.

3.2.1.3 Strategy and policies

Strategy is concerned with *the means* to achieve a given set of ends, that is, the objectives of the company. Common themes associated with the term strategy are as follows [22]:

1. The mobilization of resources to achieve long-term competitive advantage.
2. A master's plan of how a company will achieve its objectives and mission.
3. That it is top down and challenges the basis of the company in relation to the resources available to the company, in the present and future, and the opportunities and threats present in the environment.
4. A set of decision-making rules to guide organizational behaviour.
5. A strategy may be explicit or implicit.
6. A strategy is a stream of significant decisions.
7. That it falls within the realm of senior management knowledge only or is diffused throughout the company giving it an unverbalized common purpose.
8. Strategy (like organizational structure) evolves out of the minds of and interaction between individuals. Through this process strategy can be conceptualized and developed either within an individual or group.

We can therefore define strategy as:

> the implied or explicitly stated means that are developed by management, through cognitive and behavioural decision-making processes, to achieve the company's objectives and guide organizational behaviour.

There is a hierarchy of strategies [23]. *Corporate strategy* is concerned with the company as a whole. For a large diversified company it would involve issues about a balanced portfolio of businesses, diversification strategies and the overall structure of the company and the number of markets or market segments within which the company competes. *Business strategy* is focused on competitiveness in particular markets, industries or products. It is likely that for the large company an operational unit will normally be set up – termed a strategic business unit (SBU) – that will cover a particular product, market, client or geographic area. The SBU will have the authority to make its own strategic decisions but within guidelines for achieving corporate objectives. For a diversified construction company SBUs could be the management contracting, property development or materials divisions. Another example could be the regional subsidiary of a contracting company. Finally, the *operating* or *functional* strategy is concerned with maximizing productivity within particular operating functions of the company. It is also concerned with the contribution each function makes to an SBU and hence the corporate whole. The application of the idea of a hierarchy of strategies to construction will be taken up again in a later section.

A company's strategy will normally be encapsulated in a strategy statement covering the following [24]:

1. The company's *scope of activities:* key words for defining scope are *who – what – how*. Who are the company's customers, what needs of these customers are being served and how are these needs being met. Scope will involve defining the company's activities *functionally*.

2. *Use of resources:* the use of resources energizes the company in attaining its objectives. Resource allocation and the processes involved in deciding who gets what involves negotiation, the exercise of power – either covert or overt – and the acknowledgement, either explicit or implicit, of the important contributors to achieving the company's objectives.
3. *Distinctive competencies:* these are the areas where the company may believe it has a particular strength. For example, a construction company may have a commitment to training personnel at all levels, specific skills in design and build or management contracting. This issue will be explored in greater detail in the section on the SWOT analysis.
4. Areas of *synergy* within the company: put simply synergy refers to the statement 'the operation of the whole is greater than the sum of the parts' or the '2 + 2 = 5' syndrome.
5. *Competitive advantage:* this refers to those areas(s) of the company's activities that are seen to provide superiority over competitors. Ramsey notes that this differs from distinctive competencies that can also be possessed by a competitor and hence provide no apparent competitive advantage. The issue of competitive advantage will be readdressed in a later section.

Finally, policies are guides to action [25]. They are concerned with functional execution, task accomplishment and providing assistance in decision-making. Policies flow from strategy [26].

3.2.1.4 SWOT analysis
The SWOT analysis is a shorthand way of describing the techniques of analysing the strengths and weaknesses of a company and the opportunities and threats presented by the external environment. SWOT analysis will be discussed again in the chapter on marketing. The following sections introduce the main ideas.

3.2.1.4.1 Strengths and weaknesses
Porter [27] argues that there are two forms of strengths and weaknesses facing a company. The first type are *structural* and are to do with the nature of the industry structure facing the company in terms of its relative strategic positioning vis-à-vis competitors. This aspect of the strengths and weaknesses profile stems from an industry environment analysis within which the company competes. Since this aspect deals with the impact of the underlying economic structure of the industry on the company, strengths and weaknesses that are determined by industry structure are relatively stable and are difficult to overcome. These would normally form the basis of the external appraisal of the company – opportunities and threats. The second form of strengths and weaknesses are termed *implementational* by Porter. They stem from the company's ability to implement its chosen strategies, the people and managerial abilities. These are seen by Porter as transitory. It is this second set of

strengths and weaknesses – implementational – that would generally form part of the internal appraisal of the company.

The internal appraisal would normally involve identifying areas of *distinctive competence* or a *competence profile* [28]. The areas covered in the internal audit would be as follows:

- marketing and distribution;
- production;
- research and development;
- human resources;
- financial resources.

It has been suggested that the primary focus for identifying strengths and weaknesses is in the operating core, i.e. the input–transformation–output process [29]. Jauch and Glueck argue that the two fundamental questions that need to be addressed in the internal audit are:

1. *What* does the company do *well* and do these count?
2. *What* does the company do *poorly* and do these matter?

The important thing is that these questions are answered with constant reference to *competitors*.

3.2.1.4.2 Opportunities and threats

Opportunities and threats stem from the external environment and are usually dealt with as part of the *external appraisal* or *environmental diagnosis*. The five major components of the environment are as follows:

(a) the economy;
(b) demographic shifts;
(c) societal developments;
(d) technological developments;
(e) industry structure – suppliers, buyers, competitors, entrants, intensity of competition between companies.

The following section focuses on two major aspects of the external environment – competitor and strategic group analysis.

3.2.1.4.3 Competitor and strategic group analysis

The primary focus of *competitor analysis* is to profile the current and potential future strategies of competitors, to work out their possible responses to changes in strategy the company might make and anticipate their reactions to shifts in the task and general environments [30]. This would involve determining existing as well as potential competitors. The four main components of the analysis are identifying, for each competitor:

(a) their future goals at corporate and SBU level;
(b) their current strategies, both implicit and explicit and their interrelationship;
(c) the major assumptions held by the company and key managers;

(d) the key capabilities of the company – distinctive competencies, areas of competitive advantage, growth capability, capacity for the management of change and, finally, the company's staying power in the industry and its chosen strategies.

Pilot research work supervised by the editors [31] in operationalizing competitor analysis in construction indicates that a regional subsidiary of a national contractor operating in both building and civil engineering can face anything up to 55 competitors – national, regional and local – in its task environment across all market segments. To undertake a full competitor analysis as suggested above would be both difficult and time consuming. However, by concentrating on the top 10–15 key competitors – its peer group – a contracting company can obtain a very good feel for the competition it faces, and the implications that stem from this, in its task environment.

Strategic group analysis attempts to develop groupings of companies in an industry that are following the same or similar strategies [32]. Strategic groups affect the pattern of competition within an industry and where multiple groups exist, competition will not be faced equally by all companies. The two most important influences on strategic group interaction are as follows:

(a) the degree of market interdependence among strategic groups;
(b) the extent to which customer targets for strategic groups overlap.

Both influences are impacted and modified in construction through the procurement and tendering strategies suggested by clients' advisers.

Pilot research work supervised by the author [33] has indicated that the top 50 building and civil engineering contractors can be broken down into approximately six strategic groupings. However, some companies do not fall neatly into a grouping because of the diversification strategies adopted by many of these companies. The five dimensions used to identify these groupings were as follows:

(a) size (measured by turnover);
(b) corporate configuration;
(c) the extent of internalization;
(d) profitability;
(e) contribution to turnover from construction and related activities.

An in-depth case study analysis of the majority of the construction companies comprising core group 1 in Figure 2.2 indicates that strategic groupings in construction are likely to be complex. Construction is therefore a complex industry for strategic group analysis [34] and if it is to work in construction and be of practical use as an analytical tool for managers, it is best undertaken at subsidiary/divisional and bidding strategy levels. We have argued that managers' perceptions play a key part in the way they respond to the environment they face and the choices they make. Personal construct psychology [35] provides a useful approach and set of techniques that may provide the link between strategic group

STRATEGIC GROUPS

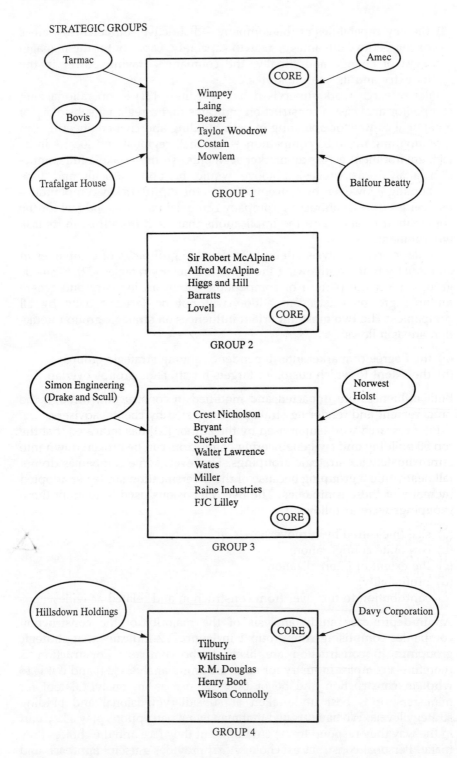

Figure 2.2   *Strategic groups in the UK construction company*

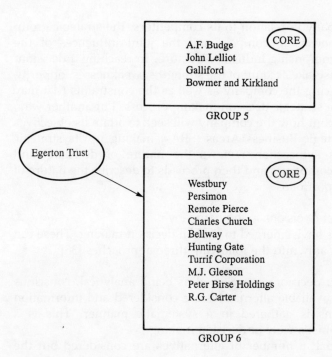

GROUP 5

GROUP 6

analysis and its impact on a company's competitive strategy at divisional and bidding strategy levels. In this instance, personal construct psychology (PCP) allows senior managers' cognitive structures and decision criteria to be made explicit in their handling of 'deep uncertainty' for strategic decision-making. Male and Aspinall [36] have explored, through the use of PCP computerized techniques, how competitor analysis can be achieved at bidding strategy level. This can be easily adapted to determine how managers perceive groupings of companies, if at all, and on what criteria.

Strategic group analysis in construction is also complicated by the fact that companies have gone through considerable diversification over the last decade and it is possible that new groupings within the industry have not as yet been consolidated. In addition, corporate diversity in construction, of itself, causes considerable problems in operationalizing strategic group analysis in the industry.

Having completed an introduction to the ideas behind the strategy formulation process, the next section explores the ideas behind strategic choice – the decision on which strategy or set of strategies the company should pursue.

3.2.2 Strategic choice among alternative strategies

Strategic choice is concerned with making long-term decisions from among a number of options that will determine the future strategic posture of the company in relation to its competitors, the strategic group within which it chooses to compete and the joint influences of the competitive forces comprising industry structure. In reaching a decision, senior managers must take account of the strengths, weaknesses, opportunities and threats facing the company as well as the constraints that may be impinging on the strategic decision-making process. Put another way, strategic choice is about how the company will seek to attain its objectives in each of the Strategic Business Areas (SBAs) making up its strategic portfolio [37]. This sub-section reviews the nature of decisions and decision-making in companies and then proceeds to describe the nature of SBAs and strategic portfolios.

3.2.2.1 The nature of decisions in the company

A number of models have emerged to explain decision-making. These can be broken down broadly into the following three approaches [38]:

1. Rational–analytic: decisions are viewed as being analytical, conscious and rational. All available alternatives are considered and information to reach decisions is gathered in a systematic manner. This is a traditional economist's view of decision-making.
2. Intuitive–emotional: a number of alternatives are considered but the decision-maker uses unconscious processes to jump through the decision-making process in reaching a conclusion.
3. Political–behavioural: this approach argues that a decision-maker is faced with competing pressures and the outcome of the decision-making process is compromise through negotiation and mutual adjustment. In reaching a decision the political ramifications of implementation are also taken into account.

In taking account of these differing approaches to viewing decision-making, other important facets that need to be considered are, first, because decision-makers and the environments they face do not allow full access to and knowledge of information and the fact that there are information processing constraints on the human mind, individuals adopt a satisficing rather than maximizing process in reaching a decision. People will decide on the first acceptable alternative – the one that is good enough – rather than review decision outcomes for all possible alternatives and then decide. Decision-makers have, therefore, *bounded rationality* [39]. Second, as we have already suggested, strategy formulation is a behavioural process involving interaction between individuals and also groups of people within the company. Therefore, objectives and strategy may be worked out over time as unanticipated events intercede in the decision-making process. Objectives and strategy can evolve through a process of incrementalism [40]. Strategic choice may not, therefore, be one neat decision but a series of discrete but overlapping decisions which when compounded have a significant effect on the company in the long term. Third, there are a number of different types of decisions in an organization that can often conflict. The four different types of decision are as follows [41]:

1. *Personal:* these are decisions made by individuals that have an impact on their personal lives, for example career moves, moving house, membership of professional institutions. Personal decisions have an impact on the organization and a person's role in that organization. They may often conflict with organizational decisions.
2. *Organizational:* these are decisions that are concerned with on-going processes within the organization such as procedures, rules, policies and budgets.
3. *Programmed decisions:* these stem from routine, repetitive and frequently occurring situations. They facilitate standard procedures.
4. *Non-programmed decisions:* these types of decisions occur when the situation is problem-oriented, novel and complex. The problem will normally be ambiguous, unstructured and lack policies or procedures to guide the decision-maker. This type of decision will require a high degree of insight and is typical of those undertaken at the strategic apex of a company.

Ansoff [42] has also distinguished between three different types of decisions in organizations. These can be classified as follows:

1. *Operating decisions:* these are concerned with the resource conversion process and preoccupy the company. Key decisions identified by Ansoff with their counterparts in construction companies are:
   • pricing (bidding);
   • establishing a market strategy (which project type/service);
   • production scheduling (site planning);
   • budgetary allocations among functions (departmental budgets, project budgets).
2. *Administrative decisions:* these are concerned partly with optimizing the use of resources of a company via its formal structure and technical system and partly with resource acquisition and development.
3. *Strategic decisions:* the focus of these decisions is on the relationship of the company to its environment. These types of decisions are externally rather than internally focused and are related to the issue of deciding what business the company is in currently and that which it should be in. Strategic decisions are generally non-programmed decisions.

To summarize, decision-making in organizations is influenced by many factors, not least that of bounded rationality. The reality is that people in organizations make decisions using different decision strategies at different times, depending on the circumstances they face. Three modes of decision-making have been presented rational–analytic, intuitive–emotional and political–behavioural. We would contend that all three have a place in organizational life. Having reviewed issues about decision-making in strategic management the following section outlines the ideas behind a strategic portfolio of SBAs.

3.2.2.2 Strategic business areas and strategic portfolios

The strategic business area (SBA) is a useful analytical concept to apply in construction. It overcomes the problems of a broad industry classification and the differing views of the importance of markets or sub-industries in construction identified in Chapter 1. Furthermore, it involves the key variables characterizing construction projects. The application of the concept of strategic business areas, as defined by Ansoff [43], when applied to, for example, contracting comprise, is as follows:

- *a future market need* (determined by the client and its advisers);
- *a technology which will serve the need* (the contractor's project technology);
- *the customers who will have the need* (the client or client type);
- *the geographic setting in which customers will have the need* (project location).

In effect, therefore, not only is a contractor involved in managing a portfolio of projects but also a portfolio of SBAs. Additionally, the use of the SBA concept also circumvents the problem of deciding whether the product in construction is a built facility (the project) or the provision of a service since both are an outcome of a need in the market place. Competitive strategy in construction – either under a market structure of contracting or for speculative purposes – evolves out of a consideration of individual SBAs. Figure 2.3 brings together themes from the preceding chapter and earlier sections of this chapter to provide an integrated view for considering a contracting company as a series of linked SBAs.

A portfolio strategy – the combination of SBAs within which a company seeks to compete – comprise the following:

1. The geographic growth vector specifying the scope and direction of the company's future business – Figure 2.4.
2. The competitive advantage the company will seek in each SBA. It achieves this through a competitive strategy – the distinctive approach the company will use in each SBA.
3. The identification and use of synergies present within the company.
4. The strategic flexibility of the strategic business portfolio. There are two components to this. First, by *external* means through diversification of geographic, market and technological scope. Second, through *internal* resource flexibility such that resources can easily be transferred among SBAs.

   The internal strategic flexibility of construction companies is also enhanced by [44]:
   - objectives that are clear and are growth- and development-oriented;
   - senior management's ability to understand the environment that they face;
   - a corporate orientation that is future directed, capable of adapting strategies and policies to environmental changes, concerned with ensuring good internal communication processes with staff, and capable historically of managing change successfully;

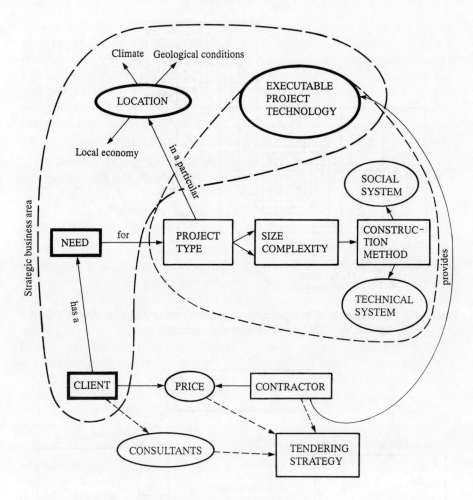

Figure 2.3 *The strategic business area in construction*

- procedures for formal strategic planning;
- a consistency of management style practised by senior managers and preferred by staff.
- a mix of people skills that reflected early work experiences, high mobility levels between companies and a wide range of project experiences

Having reviewed the strategic formulation process, the next section discussed the strategic alternatives available to senior management.

3.2.2.3 Strategic alternatives

The strategic alternatives facing a company are numerous. The problem is to group these into a framework that is meaningful for analysis. Figure 2.5 sets out an analytical framework which builds on useful ones already in existence [45] but considered to have some shortcomings. The major

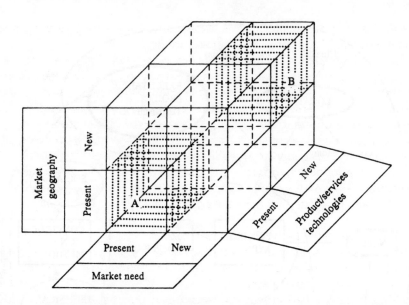

Figure 2.4   *Dimensions of the geographic growth vector (Source: Ansoff (1987), fig. 6.2, p. 110. Reprinted with permission.)*

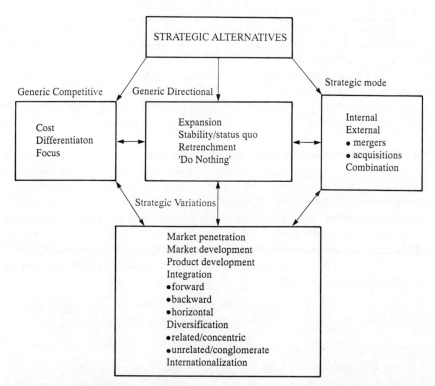

Figure 2.5   *The strategic alternatives (adapted from Johnson and Scholes (1988), Figure 6.1)*

groupings of strategy alternatives are: generic competitive, generic directional, strategic variations, and, finally, mode.

The *generic strategies* can be broken down into two categories. The first category concern making decisions to compete on *cost*, by *differentiation*, or through *focus* [46]. Each strategy requires a different set of skills, resources and organizational structure to implement. The key issue is a sustained commitment by strategists to one of these strategies only. Johnson and Scholes consider these to be the *basis* of competition [47]. This category of generic strategies is termed *generic competitive*. The second category of generic strategies involve the company in some form of movement – growth/expansion, minimal or no strategic movement, or contraction. This category of strategy is termed *generic directional*.

3.2.2.3.1 The generic competitive strategies
Cost leadership, as its name implies, requires management to focus its attention on competing on cost. This necessitates that systems and procedures are directed totally towards controlling cost.

Differentiation is concerned with creating the perception, in the industry, that something is seen by buyers as being unique. This strategy, attempting to distinguish the company from its competitors, does not ignore the issue of cost but does not make this the primary focus of attention. Differentiation crops up continually as a strategy in construction; it was discussed in Chapter 1 with respect to tendering and procurement strategies and will be discussed later in connection with international construction.

Focus is a hybrid strategy since it is effectively a combination of either of the preceding two strategies by deciding to compete more effectively than competitors on cost or through differentiation while targeting a particular buyer group, product or geographic market segment. This is a 'niche' strategy.

Each of these generic competitive strategies has its place in the construction industry. For example, tight cost control through the quantity surveying function and effective site management can follow through into an aggressive pricing policy in tendering – competing on cost. In international construction the provision of preferential financial packages combined with competing on price is an example of differentiation. Specializing in the construction of hospitals is an example of a focus strategy.

3.2.2.3.2 The generic directional strategies [48]
Expansion is a growth strategy and involves a change in business scope by developing additional markets, products, services or functions. A *stability* strategy maintains the existing business definition in terms of products or services, markets and functions, but necessitates the tracking of changes in the environment and improving performance. This strategy involves a positive decision by management to focus its attention on the internal operations of the company and can also be usefully employed if the company requires a period of adjustment following strategies involving

considerable change. Stability is also known as a consolidation strategy. A strategy of stability characterized many construction companies in the 1960s.

A *retrenchment* strategy can involve a reduction in the company's activities or functions, perhaps through an initial concentration of attention on loss-making activities or those with negative cashflows. The reduction in activities – products, markets, services or functions – can occur through choice or necessity. Retrenchment can involve divestment (or strategic shrinkage) – a planned, proactive orderly withdrawal; disinvestment – which is of a scale, magnitude and suddenness different from shrinkage; management buyouts – the company's managers, normally with the assistance of institutional investors, take over the ownership of part of the company, and, finally, liquidation – the dissolution of the company. A retrenchment strategy can often be used to turn a business around from a loss making into profit generating entity. Lansley *et al.* [49] found a number of examples of the retrenchment strategy in their sample of 23 medium-sized UK construction companies.

A *'do nothing'* strategy involves maintaining the current strategy while focusing on operational change and either ignoring or misunderstanding environmental changes that may be of major significance to the company. This typified many companies in construction during the recession of the 1970s. A do nothing strategy differs from that of stability since the latter involves proactive positive steps to implement.

3.2.2.3.3 Strategic mode
A company that opts for an *internal strategy* uses its own resources to fund expansion or undertake retrenchment by reorganization, increasing revenues, or reducing costs and assets by laying off staff or selling facilities, equipment or other assets. Internal expansion was the primary growth method of contractors in the 1960s and is often argued to be their preferred method of expansion.

A company that opts for an *external strategy* is involved in merger and acquisition activity. It has been suggested that recent trends in merger activity are primarily due to short-term financial gain and senior management job protection rather than to strategic reasons. A wide ranging analysis of mergers and acquisitions in the UK construction industry, when compared against manufacturing, highlighted the fact that the overriding reason for such activity in the former was *market diversification* [50]. A similar conclusion was reached in the in-depth five-year analysis undertaken by the author of the first core strategic group of construction companies highlighted in Figure 2.6. Market diversification also allows contracting companies to switch resources between different market sectors because the acquired company has [51]:

- a reputation in particular markets;
- management expertise;
- an existing project portfolio;

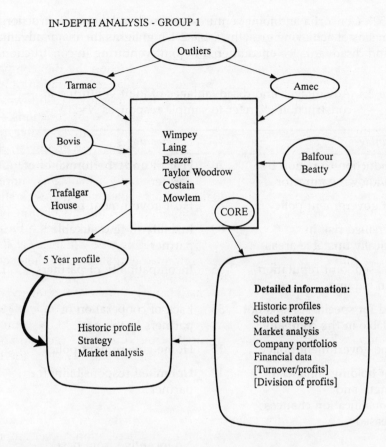

Figure 2.6 *Detailed analysis method used for strategic group 1*

- a portfolio of contacts – clients, consultants and sub-contractors;
- membership of select tender lists.

Market diversification adds to a construction company's strategic flexibility through both external and/or internal strategies.

Finally, a *combination* or *joint development* strategy involves the simultaneous pursuit of objectives strategically through both internal and external modes, where parties are linked together contractually as well as organizationally. Typical examples of a combination strategy include the following:

- Sub-contracting – commonly used in construction and considered in more depth in this chapter as part of a contractor's production strategy;
- Licensing and technology sharing;
- Franchising;
- Consortia and joint ventures. A joint venture (JV) is a single operating entity where resources are pooled to execute the total works. Different legal frameworks can exist for JVs – incorporated or unincorporated

[52]. Consortia and joint ventures are used widely in construction as a means of achieving growth. Table 2.1 highlights the major advantages and disadvantages encountered in joint venturing in construction.

Table 2.1 Advantages and disadvantages of joint venturing in construction (% refer to sample responses $N=20$)

Advantages	%	Disadvantages	%
Introduction to region by local/known contractor	70	Fear of underperformance of partner	70
Host government policy	65	Host government policy	40
Diversified risk in politically unstable areas	60	Inability to find suitable partner	35
Increased joint reputation when bidding	55	Incompatibility of partners	15
Need for specialist skills not available in the company	35	Lack of cooperation of partners in the past	10
Home government policy	15	Home government policy	5
Plant holding, financial strength and pre-qualification chances increased	10	Unlimited responsibility for partner	5
		No incentive from past experience to joint venture	5

Source: Adapted from Seymour (1987), table 6.5, p. 191. (Reprinted with permission.)

3.2.2.3.4 Strategic variations

The preceding sections have highlighted common generic strategies and the different modes that can be adopted. This section discusses other strategic variations that can occur.

The first set of strategic variations contains the expansion strategies of market penetration, market development and product development. The conceptual ideas behind each strategy will be highlighted first and subsequently discussed in the context of construction. The crux of the issues of applying these concepts to construction is the vexatious question of what is the product in construction and how it is defined. Since contractors appear to view demand in terms of technologies to build facilities (with the exception of housing development), contractors effectively sell expertise in executing different project technologies (defined here as a chosen combination of the social and technical systems unique to constructing a particular facility).

Market penetration is a minimum risk strategy, especially in growing markets, since the company is involved in penetrating existing markets only and is seeking to gain market share [53]. It involves the company in no new products, customers or technologies. A strategy of market penetration in construction involves the contractor staying with existing clients and geographic locations and obtaining more work using existing project technologies. In effect, the contractor is doing more of the same type of project for existing clients in existing locations. This strategy can be severely impacted by the procurement and tendering strategies advocated by the client consultant advisers and the fact that many of the industry's clients are one-off or intermittent buyers.

A strategy of *market development* means that the company maintains its present product line and attempts to find new markets either in the form of new segments, product uses or geographic areas. The distinctive competence of the company is with the product and not the market. Exporting is a method of market development [54]. Market development in construction would entail the contractor staying with existing project technologies and offering this expertise to new or existing clients and/or operating in new geographic areas. Again, client advisers have a major impact here on the success of this strategy. Contractors that internationalise using existing project technologies are involved in market development. Table 2.2 sets out possible market development strategies for a contractor using the same project technology.

Table 2.2 Market development strategies in construction

Clients	Geographic areas	
	New	Existing
New	X	X
Existing	X	

A strategy of *product development* is a risky strategy and involves the company in maintaining its existing markets but developing new products for those markets. In construction, product development for a contractor would require staying with existing clients and/or in existing geographic locations but developing expertise in new executable project technologies. This can take many forms. The issue is one of credibility of expertise and, again, clients' advisers have considerable influence over the success of this strategy for contractors. For example, product development for a general contractor could involve staying with the same type of project but changing the relationship between the social and technical systems involved in the project life cycle – from client inception to on-site completion. An illustration here would be moving from an involvement in general contracting to providing a service in design and build or management contracting. The technical system for on-site production may stay the same but social relationships have changed and, to some extent, the technical system may also change as the contractor moves into management involvement in the design stages. Alternatively, product development could also involve staying as a general contractor but taking on board new product types and hence executable project technologies.

A strategy of *vertical integration* involves the company in taking on board successive stages in the conversion of supply inputs – usually raw materials – into finished outputs for the final customer [55]. The strategic decision facing the company is to either *make* or *buy* in the market place [56]. This will involve the company in undertaking two or more technologically distinct production or distribution processes in-house [57]. Hence, by vertically integrating, the business definition of the company is expanded in terms of the functions performed in-house [58]. The reverse – disintegration – truncates activities or functions and contracts the business definition. Forward integration involves the company in successive stages of the distribution process. Backward integration takes a company towards suppliers. For a contractor, backward integration would involve undertaking materials manufacture or design. Forward integration would take the contractor into property development/ownership.

A strategy of *diversification* involves the company moving simultaneously from its existing products and markets or functions [59]. Diversification can involve the company in forward, backward or horizontal integration (complimentary activities). There are two types of diversification. First is *related diversification* (also termed concentric diversification), where a company enters new markets with a degree of overlap with existing activities. This can either be *market-needs-related* where a company acquires a new technology to serve existing markets or *technology-related* where a company applies its existing technology to new market needs [60]. Second, in *unrelated diversification* (also termed conglomerate diversification) a company enters new markets or activities, usually through acquisition, with no apparent overlap with existing activities. In other words, unrelated diversification is neither technology- or markets-needs-related [61]. Contractors are generally concentric diversifiers.

Finally, a strategy of *internationalization* can be viewed as a form of geographic diversification. It takes the company beyond the boundaries of its own country [62]. It will usually occur if domestic markets are slow, restricted or in a slump [63]. Seymour [64] in his survey of international contractors found that the major reasons for companies internationalizing were high overseas demand and/or low domestic demand. Protection of shareholders' interests was not seen as a major motivating force. The choice of markets to enter was determined by potential market size. British contractors have operated overseas for over 150 years but the level of international activity increased dramatically in the mid-1970s [65]. The large American contractors have considerable international interests – Parsons in 44 countries, Bechtel in 52 countries, Dravo in 41 countries and Fluor in 22 countries [66]. The internationalization of Japanese contractors into South East Asia, Australasia, the Americas and Europe may be seen as one of the major competitive threats of the 1990s for Western contractors. Japanese contractors are discussed in more detail in a later chapter and issues concerning competitive advantage in international construction will be discussed again in Chapter 12.

3.2.2.3.5 Grand strategies

'Grand strategies' [67] involve companies in using a combination of strategies at the same time or over time, for example a combination of expansion, retrenchment or stability. Many of the construction companies studied in strategic group 1 (Figure 2.6) have used grand strategies, Beazer, in its hostile takeover of the US aggregates company Koppers in 1988, adopted a grand strategy of external expansion combined with retrenchment when it sold off those parts of Koppers that it did not view as central to the business.

3.2.2.4 Choice of strategy

Johnson and Scholes [68] argue that in choosing a strategy three criteria should be used – suitability, feasibility and acceptability. *Suitability* refers to the degree of 'fit' between the SWOT analysis and the chosen strategy(s). In other words is the strategy consistent with the on-going operations of the company implied from internal and external appraisal. *Feasibility* is considering the workings of the strategy in practice, and *acceptability* is attempting to infer the consequences of the strategy when implemented within the organization.

Having decided on strategy, the next step is implementation.

3.2.3 Strategic implementation

Implementation involves the organizational structure and the setting up of control and feedback systems to ensure that the strategy 'as implemented' is consistent with the strategy 'as evolved and decided on' during the formulation and choice states of our analytical framework. The problem for the implementation process is that an organizational structure is already in place and working. The strategic management process, since it is long-term in its orientation, will involve some fundamental shifts in the structure of the organization. This invariably will draw out resistance from individuals and groups who may feel threatened by these changes [69]. The seven primary mechanisms for strategy implementation are as follows [70]:

(a) plans and policies – corporate, SBU, operational and functional;
(b) a budgetary framework for resource allocation;
(c) reward systems;
(d) political systems;
(e) control and integration systems through organizational structure – hierarchy, teams and team management, rules and procedures.
(f) training and development systems;

(g) feedback mechanisms – the comparison of actual versus expected and any associated corrective action.

Having discussed the components of the strategic management process, the next sub-section discusses an important issue in contracting, that of regionalization. This can involve important strategic decisions for a construction company as it grows (or retrenches).

3.3 Regionalization as an issue of strategic choice in construction

Regionalization, or the setting up of geographically dispersed organizational units, is a major strategic option within construction. Regionalization can involve issues associated with both expansion or retrenchment strategies.

This section draws heavily on the empirical work of Lansley and Lansley *et al.* [71] in their study of 23 regional contracting companies or regional operating units of national contractors. The four major issues to be covered in this sub-section are as follows:

(a) the processes and reasons for regionalization;
(b) the problems of regionalization;
(c) centralization versus decentralization and strategic versus operational decision-making for regional subsidiaries;
(d) regionalization as a change management process

3.3.1 The processes and reasons for regionalization

The Ashridge study identified the fact that the main impetus for regionalization came as a perceived natural consequence of growth in the company. Regionalization is a likely consequence, therefore, of an expansion strategy. However, the timing and reasons for regionalization differed among contracting companies. The four primary reasons identified for regionalization were as follows:

(a) to foster closer contacts between senior management and staff;
(b) to recruit permanent labour;
(c) to obtain raw materials;
(d) to increase market share through greater accessibility to customers.

Regionalization, therefore, is a strategic decision to create separate organizational units to bring managers in closer contact with the market place, gain better access to important production and organizational inputs and create a better working environment for staff at all levels. Regionalization can also be a process of decentralization of decision-making.

The processes used by companies to create regionalised units entailed the following:

- pilot studies to create organizational units that were essentially 'guinea pigs' in order to develop adequate control and information systems;
- using specially selected teams well versed in the company's systems and procedures. These task forces comprised groups of senior managers, junior staff and former colleagues from headquarters headed by either a prospective or current Board member;
- initial senior management thinking that regional units were to be a virtual mirror image of the centre in terms of systems and procedures.

The next sub-section reviews the major problems encountered in regionalization.

3.3.2 Problems of regionalization

The problems encountered in regionalisation were many and varied. However, the following two major themes emerge that characterize these problems:

(a) the relationship between the centre and region;
(b) pre- and post-regionalization changes.

Nine out of the 17 companies studied by the Ashridge research team that were involved in regionalization had experienced major problems between regions and the centre. These tensions were deeply rooted and had developed through a misunderstanding of the nature of the business by both the regional and head office staff. These problems generated significant levels of hostility and mistrust between regions and the centre. The four primary reasons identified by the Ashridge team were as follows:

(a) the centre applying inappropriate systems and procedures to a region;
(b) a regional unit becoming of lesser importance to the centre;
(c) a regional unit feeling isolated and ignored by the centre;
(d) the centre changing its strategic objectives and subsequently these either not been understood or fully appreciated by a regional unit.

The second set of problems are derived from the first and arose out of changes in circumstances between the pre- and post-regionalization processes. These problems can be broken down into three key areas. The first we can term the *process of succession*. Regionalization was successful in those companies where the junior staff involved in the regionalization process took over from senior colleagues who either retired or returned to head office. The second generation of senior regional managers had experience of both head office and regional procedures and therefore fostered a continued trust from the centre. Regionalization was less or unsuccessful where a new generation of regional managers was steeped in regional experience with little or no understanding of the centre. The managers had, therefore, good knowledge of local conditions but limited knowledge of conditions at the centre. This led to an inconsistency of views about the nature of the business between regions and centre.

The second post-regionalization problem can be termed *procedural inappropriateness*, i.e. the centre attempting to apply uniform systems and procedures across all regional units regardless of the size and circumstances facing the unit. The consequences for the smaller regional units was being swamped with systems and procedures more appropriate to larger units. The result was that smaller regional units were closed down due to degradation in performance. A number of the members of senior regional management subsequently set up businesses in the locality and became key competitors of the company. The final post-regionalization problem can be termed *management of the organizational life cycle*. The process of regionalization, by its very nature, sets up a series of organizational units at different stages of development. Due to the fact that short- to medium-term demand in construction is variable and geographically and sectorally diverse, over time regional units will be at different stages of the organizational life cycle – birth, growth, maturity and decline. This requires a different set of managerial skills at the centre to handle the different stages of the organizational development cycle. Empirical evidence from the Ashridge studies indicated that the centre had skills to manage regional units in the growth and mature stages but were less skilled at managing regional units in the birth and decline stages.

3.3.3 Centralization versus decentralization of decision-making

One of the primary motivations behind regionalization identified in the Ashridge studies was to bring company management closer to the market place. This, as stated earlier, involves a process of decentralization of decision-making. The degree of centralization–decentralization from the centre has two important aspects for the regionalized contracting company. The first is the impact on the strategic management process; the second is the impact on the training of senior management at regional and head office level.

If the centre retains a centralized approach to regionalization, the strategists' focus is likely to be on the similarity of issues and markets between regions rather than on their differences. Decentralization of decision-making provides regional senior managers with a great deal more decision-making autonomy and allows them to make greater use of local market knowledge. Empirical evidence from the Ashridge studies indicates that many companies failed to capitalize on regional management's market knowledge. Furthermore, those companies that decentralized decision-making avoided centre–region problems. A decision by strategists to define the contracting business from the markets served, rather than from the centre, will require greater conceptual and judgemental skills since they are managing a diverse strategic portfolio of SBUs or SBAs depending on how a construction company wishes to define its strategic domain.

The second issue, also related to the preceding one, and stemming from a decision about centralization–decentralization of regional units, is that of senior management succession and the associated management development and training. A contracting company defining its business from the centre makes all its strategic decisions at head office. Regional units will be mainly involved in administrative and operational decisions. Senior regional management will primarily be acting in the role of 'organizational managers', performing an integrative function and using political and organizational skills [72]. A decentralized regional structure, however, provides a fertile training ground for senior management with the company, both at regional and head office levels. In this instance senior regional managers will be involved in strategic as well as administrative and, to a lesser extent, operational decisions. They are in a better position, therefore, to develop the conceptual and judgemental skills required of the 'institutional manager' [73] at the strategic apex of the company. The problem for the centre, in a situation of decentralized decision-making at regional level, is managing a 'loose–tight' organizational structure [74], where there is considerable autonomy for the senior managements of regional subsidiaries but where the centre has to retain a degree of control in order to maintain an overall corporate direction.

3.3.4 Regionalization as a process of managing change

The preceding discussion has highlighted many issues associated with the strategic decision to regionalize. A critical and central theme is that this involves a construction company – as it pursues an expansion (or retrenchment) strategy – in a major process of continuing organizational change and adaptation. That is, the setting up or winding down of a series of on-going regional decision-making units, each with its own organizational life cycle, with staff and organizational structures that interconnect with decision-makers at the centre. This process of change can be facilitated by the following [75]:

- regular communication of company objectives between the centre and the region;
- managerial development and succession planning;
- staff selection and development;
- locating specialists at regional level with direct reporting relationships to the centre;
- a stress on the importance of regional success to corporate success;
- a 'bottom–up' strategic management process with complete senior regional management involvement in the corporate strategic management process and with the associated capability, within this framework, to influence thinking at the corporate strategic apex.

To summarize, regionalization is an important strategic decision for a contractor and involves a whole host of issues, not least the organizational issues associated with managing change. Regionalization issues are associated with different strategic options but each will have stemmed from some form of competitive strategy, the subject of the next sub-section.

3.4 Competitive strategy and advantage

The preceding sections have set out and discussed models of how a company or organization can be analysed, and have introduced the major components and concepts of strategic management. This sub-section focuses more specifically on issues to do with competitive strategy and advantage, drawing out some of the themes of earlier sections, expanding on them and applying them to construction. In addition, the sub-section outlines issues associated with innovation in construction – the detailed subject matter of Chapter 4 – one of the principal influences on sustained competitive advantage.

3.4.1 Competitive strategy

Competitive strategy is about positioning a company to enable it to make the best use of its abilities and hence discern it from its competitors [76]. In other words, it is the distinctive approach that will make the company stand out from its competitors. We have already highlighted the fact that construction companies can pursue different strategies at the same time or over time in our discussion on 'grand strategies'. Construction companies in each of the strategic groups identified earlier, because of their diversity at the corporate level, will have different competitive strategies.

Porter argues that there are four key elements that determine the limits of competitive strategy. These are a company's strengths and weaknesses; the personal values of the key implementers – *internal factors* – industry opportunities and threats, both economic and technical; the expectations of society – *external factors* [77]. A competitive strategy is built, therefore, on an analysis that attempts to specify the areas where a company has an advantage over its competitors.

3.4.2 Competitive advantage

Determining areas of competitive advantage requires an analysis of the *value activities* of a company when competing in a particular industry, i.e. at SBU level. Value activities are the physically and technologically distinct activities a company undertakes in building the value of its product – what *the buyer is prepared to pay* [78]. In this sense, using the differences highlighted in the preceding chapter between the technical system and technology, Porter is arguing that it is the way the company manages the relationship between people, the technical system and organizational structure and process that will determine whether its value activities provide a competitive advantage over its competitors.

Profit to a company is the difference between revenues gained from creating value for a buyer of the company's product and the costs incurred in creating that product through the value activities [79]. Using the simple 'black box' analogy from Chapter 1, the argument put forward by Porter is that value activities form a *value chain*. This chain of value activities has costs associated with it and represents the links between the *input process* from suppliers, the *transformation process* used by the company on the inputs and the *output process*, hence the creation of value to the buyer of a company's products. A company's value chain is a product of its history, strategy formulation, strategic choices and subsequent implementation, together with the cost and resourcing implications of the value activities. It represents and has both an internal company component and an external environmental component [80]. We have already argued in Chapter 1 that contractors, through their market activities with clients are involved in a value relationship. Part of any strategic analysis would be an examination of a company's value activities and an attempt to build up the value chain of key competitors. The key issue would be determining how the company can sustain a long-term competitive advantage either through *cost* or *uniqueness* and may require reconfiguring the value chain [81].

In his most recent work Porter [82] contends there are three conditions needed to sustain competitive advantage. These are as follows:

1. The *source* of competitive advantage within a *hierarchy* of sources. Examples provided by Porter of *low order* sources that can be easily copied by competitors include:
   - low labour costs or raw materials (a common basis of competition in construction);
   - economies of scale stemming from technology, equipment or methods that are also available to competitors.

   Examples of *high order* sources of advantage identified by Porter include:

   - proprietary process technology (of particular relevance in competing in engineering process and plant construction);
   - product differentiation stemming from unique products or services; brand reputation based on cumulative marketing efforts; customer relationships that are locked to the company through high switching costs (of relevance in many areas of construction and discussed in this chapter and Chapter 1).

   High order sources have a number of characteristics:

   - the requirement for more advanced skills and capabilities to achieve them; this could involve specialized and highly trained personnel, internal technical capability or close relationships with leading customers;

- a history of sustained a cumulative investment leading to the creation of both tangible and/or intangible assets in the form of reputation, customer relationships and specialized knowledge.
2. *The number of distinct sources* of advantage a company possesses.
3. *Constant improvement and upgrading* of advantage.

Using the work of Azzaro *et al.* [83] and transposing it into a value chain analysis for a contracting company in its bidding process (business strategy level), it can be stated that:

1. Empirically, the value activities in pre- and post-contract stages of a project are sharply divided.
2. In the pre-contract stage of tender production there are two major value activities that proceed in parallel – estimating and contract planning/ management. Estimators analyse a tender using labour and materials constants, seeking quotations from sub-contractors and utilizing learning curves for particular project types to produce a unit rate estimate. Their analysis does not include preliminaries. Contract planners/ management are involved in a different analytical process. They utilize a time-based, operational resource analysis involving a programme of site activities and method of working to analyse the technical system and human resource requirements of a project. Contract planners/ management are particularly involved in the assessment of preliminaries items to produce a 'preliminaries estimate'.
3. A key value activity for the contractor is the sub-contract pricing process and its relationship to the overall pricing process. The major decisions to be made that affect this are the number of sub-contract work packages and sub-contract quotations sought [84].
4. At the adjudication stage of the pre-contract process senior management, together with the estimators and contract planners/management involved in preparing the tender, will assess:
   - competitors;
   - conditions of contract;
   - the client and consultants involved;
   - the extent to which the job is required by the company, both in terms of the project itself and the level of work within the company;
   - the estimate of the time likely to execute the project versus that specified in the conditions of contract;
   - the relationship between the probability of winning the contract versus the level of mark up and expected profit.
5. In both the estimating and contracts management aspects of the pre-contract phase, experience is seen as paramount, especially in the latter instance.
6. Competitive advantage is seen to be gained in the pricing of the work preliminaries where the objective is to devise a programme of work that is shorter than those of competitors. Contractors believe that it is here that contracts are won or lost and make a profit or loss. Furthermore, they believe that unit rates in the bill of quantities are unlikely to differ

much from competitors. However, this issue will be re-addressed by Thorpe and McCaffer in a later chapter.

Bidding strategy is discussed in more detail in later chapters. The next sub-section considers innovation and its influences on gaining competitive advantage in construction.

3.4.3 Innovation in construction

Clark has identified two main types of innovation, namely, *radical shifts* and *gradual incremental innovation* [85]. Taking the case of innovation causing radical shifts, Clark contends that this type involves short, painful periods of transformation and is experienced very infrequently by most companies. The second type, incremental innovation, lasts for many years, can frequently go unnoticed and often follows radical shifts. In a construction context, Boyd and Wilson [86] in their study of technology transfer in the Canadian construction industry concluded that incremental innovation is common in construction, with radical shifts being rare. An example they quote of a revolutionary (radical shift) was the introduction of the tower crane into the United States from Europe in the early post World War II era. In our analytical framework, the tower crane would comprise part of the technical system. This example highlights the important issue of distinguishing innovation that occurs within the construction industry from that which comes from outside the industry but is utilized within both production and corporate processes.

Fleming [87] concludes that product and process innovation in construction is outside the industry's control due primarily to its service nature and the split between production and design, manufacture and construction. This issue will be taken further in Chapter 4. However, drawing together a number of different views on innovation in construction we can, preliminarily, suggest the following [88]:

1. Fleming has argued that the forms and methods of construction are largely in the hands of the designers. However, designers, especially architects, produce specifications and drawings that impact production and largely determine the spatial constraints of the production process for the contractor, but the introduction of new materials into the construction industry does not rest purely with designers. This is very much dependent on contractual arrangements. Introduction of materials by designers will only occur directly where the architect specifies nominated suppliers. Where a project is tendered for on the basis of some form of combination of specifications, drawings and bill of quantities, the wording of the bill item may allow the contractor to choose the materials or components used provided it conforms to the designer's specification. Second, innovation in materials as inputs does rest outside the contractor's control unless the company has diversified into materials manufacture, in which case product and process innova-

tion in materials manufacture can come under the umbrella of the corporate construction company.

2. Primarily, building materials innovation lies with the building materials industries but, as indicated above, the diversified construction company may well be involved in materials innovation if it has a materials producing subsidiary.

3. Innovation in construction plant rests with equipment manufacturers. Therefore, innovation in the technical system for the contractor lies outside the industry. However, the choice of plant and the manner in which it is deployed rests with the contractor. The contractor is able, therefore, to draw in plant/equipment innovation into the production process and hence gain potential advantages over competitors. The main issue here, however, is the extent to which high levels of sub-contracting of plant provide competitors with access to the same or similar types of equipment and hence nullify, in a short period of time, any sustainable advantages.

4. The primary areas for direct innovation with contractors are:
   - At site level in the 'organization' of production: where there is a high incidence of pre-fabrication off-site the contractor has to consider the timing and scheduling of these inputs together with how they might be fixed within the structure through the correct choice of craft skill. This can again lead to innovation partly in site organization and partly in craft skills. The level and type of sub-contracting has a significant impact here.
   - At the level of the company by responding to clients with new services and new forms of corporate organisational design.
   - In financial management.

   Innovation in service provision, production and corporate organization and financial management are 'knowledge-based' innovations and hence are potentially 'high-order' advantages.

5. Innovation diffusion in construction is hampered because personnel in construction appear loath to write ideas down for wider circulation to a larger audience. However, movement of personnel between companies does provide a mechanism for innovation diffusion.

6. Codes and standards are ways of achieving technology transfer in construction.

In summary, innovation for the contracting company is primarily 'knowledge-based' in that it is concerned either with alternative ways of organizing resource inputs into the production process, creating new services and hence designing new forms of corporate organizational structure, or manipulating capital flows. Technical system innovation lies primarily outside the industry and the contracting company, although skill innovation can occur at the work face. Where this latter innovation rests – within or without the company – depends on a company's strategy towards sub-contracting. Again, using our earlier analytical frameworks, contractors are principally 'technological innovators' and not 'technical system innovators' in that primarily they determine new ways for the interaction of the social and technical systems rather than improve the technical system. However, this may not always be the case. For example, Japanese construction firms, through their considerable investment in research and development, are also technical system innovators in construction since they are attempting to develop new machinery and equipment for use on site [89].

We conclude by drawing together a number of points on value activities in construction. First, competitive advantage in contracting places a heavy reliance on experience – a knowledge-based advantage and thus a high-order source of advantage. Second, the adjudication process is simultaneously an operational and strategic value activity since it brings together operational issues and strategic issues; operational in the sense that estimators and contracts management are operational staff involved in the middle line. Senior management are the company's strategists and are involved at the strategic apex. Third, the adjudication process involves aspects of both corporate and business strategy since bidding strategy is market oriented but the choice of project on which to bid seriously is also a corporate strategic decision because the relationship between the contracting company and its business environment rests on the balance of the project portfolio. Finally, the problem for senior management within a contracting company of a certain size is that involvement in the adjudication process forces them towards an operational mode of short- to medium-term thinking for business strategy, whereas corporate strategic thinking – the relationship of the total company to its environment – is long-term and holistic. It is in the small- to medium-sized company that the edges of business and corporate strategy become fuzzy and it is precisely these companies where a corporate orientation through strategic management thinking is most required for survival [90].

This sub-section has reviewed competitive strategy and competitive advantage. It has introduced the notion of the value chain and discussed value activities within a contracting company. The next section discusses production strategy.

4. Production and labour strategy in UK construction

It has been argued earlier that the on-site production process concerns the operating core of a contracting company. Construction is labour intensive and substantial use is now made of sub-contracting. The five major inputs into the production process are as follows:

1. Materials: these account for between 40 and 50% of production costs [91]. This can vary between 15% for repair and maintenance and up to 60% for contracts with a high building services element.

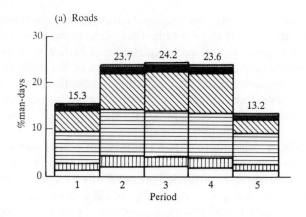

(a) Roads

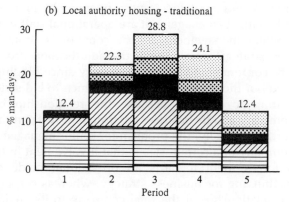

(b) Local authority housing - traditional

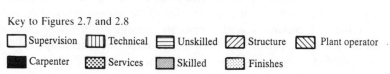

Key to Figures 2.7 and 2.8

Supervision   Technical   Unskilled   Structure   Plant operator

Carpenter   Services   Skilled   Finishes

Figure 2.7 *Site labour distributions to contract period (Source: NEDO (1978), fig. 6.4, p. 38. Reprinted with permission.)*

2. Labour: this accounts for approximately one-third of production costs [92]. Figures 2.7–2.8 indicate the relative distribution of various types of labour across different types of project.
3. Site management: traditionally, site managers on building projects have a diversity of origins, for example from a craft base, as management trainees, through technical certification such as HNC/HND/TEC/SCOTEC, through studying the Chartered Institute of Building examinations and, finally, from other building-related disciplines. Site managers in civil engineering have generally come from within the framework of the Institution of Civil Engineers [93].

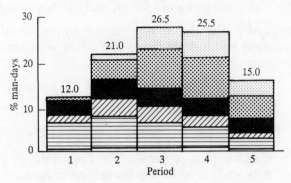

(c) Hospitals: treatment units - traditional construction

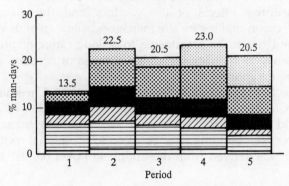

(d) Hospitals: alterations and extensions

Figure 2.8 *Site labour distributions to contract period (Source: NEDO (1978), fig. 6.4, p. 39. Reprinted with permission.)*

4. Plant and equipment, which can be owned, leased or hired: all things being equal, civil engineering projects are normally more equipment oriented than building projects.
5. Money/finance for working capital: requirements for working capital can usually be kept to a minimum due to the monthly valuation process and the various opportunities available to manipulate finance through credit arrangements with materials and equipment suppliers and payment procedures with sub-contractors. The judicious management of capital flows by contractors can result in a positive cashflow.

This sub-section, by exploring different issues associated with the production process, attempts to highlight factors that need to be taken into account by senior managers of construction firms when they decide on a strategy of:

- internalizing technology, that is, owning within the company the relationship between the technical and social systems;

• externalizing a major part of technology to the market place through, for example, sub-contracting out labour and machinery/equipment.

We have suggested earlier that internalization within or externalization outside the company will include issues associated with both contractual and psychological exchanges.

4.1 The on-site production process

The on-site production process, unlike the opportunities presented in manufacturing, is characterized by few routine procedures. Site managers make many *ad hoc* decisions, often without reference to senior managers, due to the diversity of inputs, the one-off nature of the product from site to site, the disruptive effects of the weather and the diversity of the workforce. Decision-making by site managers uses a great deal of personal knowledge and has to be responsive to a wide range of problem situations. Site managers manage through a process of constant intervention rather than by exception [94].

This sub-section draws heavily on the work of Cheetham [95] and NEDO [96]. Cheetham based his work on a combination of observation, structured and unstructured interviews with company management and operatives on seven building sites between four national contractors. The NEDO report was derived from the findings of over 60 case studies.

4.1.1 Site practices

Site practices found through observation and interviews by Cheetham, Marsh *et al.* [97] and NEDO suggest clearly that statements of company personnel policy and the realization of that policy in practice may differ considerably. For example:

1. Managements of contracting companies state that they would welcome permanent employment of operatives in the industry. Much of the inability to offer permanent employment is stated by managements to be a result of workload variability and the nature of the industry.
2. Of the companies studied by Cheetham, managements reported there were clearly defined, well-used procedures that worked well in practice for transferring men between sites. However, in reality, head–regional office recruitment, transfer or dismissal was mainly concerned with site-based clerical staff, foremen and some charge hands. The centre was rarely involved in any activity involving tradesmen or labourers.
3. Recruitment by companies at site level appears to be a passive activity. This was confirmed in the studies conducted by Cheetham and Marsh

et al. The primary method of recruitment to site is through informal approaches and casual applications. Cheetham indicates that only when this method failed was there any attempt to invoke activity from the centre through advertising or transfers from other sites. Furthermore, his case studies indicate that recruitment interviews, as a method of pro-active employee selection, were rarely undertaken with this in mind. The majority of those that applied for jobs were taken on and unsatisfactory recruits were discouraged from continuing employment by either reducing bonus payments or giving the operative the most unpleasant work. Site agents rarely conducted operative recruitment interviews. In all but one case this was delegated to trades foremen or, occasionally, charge hands. These informal recruitment procedures at site level often led to misunderstandings about bonus payments which subsequently resulted in voluntary cessation of employment.

4. In the case studies conducted by Cheetham many left jobs on site in anticipation of redundancy and very few operatives were declared formally redundant. However, some were dismissed for misconduct or poor quality of workmanship. Slow working rarely led to dismissal. Some firms were prepared to pay a premium to basic wage rates for certain key workers, termed 'leading hands', to keep them on during project start up and completion.

5. Bonus is one of management's major motivating forces at site level. Procedures for bonus payments were found to be a common cause of problems and were highlighted as such in both Cheetham's and the NEDO study. This will be discussed in more detail in a later section. However, Cheetham discovered significant differences between and within companies for calculating bonus payments. Management appeared to accept the fact that high levels of labour mobility are a consequence of employees seeking improved bonus payments and overtime.

6. Little use is made of formal planning techniques or modern technology to increase the ease of communication with and between sites. Cheetham indicates that all sites he visited displayed bar charts that were prepared prior to the commencement of the project. However, these only provided an indication of the general sequence of work, were not kept up to date and, with the exception of one site agent, agents were not prepared to accept the responsibility for the programme. None of the programmes indicated any resourcing assumptions. In the instance where the programme was used, the site agent had prepared it himself and used it to control sub-contractors as opposed to controlling the operations of the firm's employees. The NEDO study indicates that few sites had computers and where installed they were underutilized in terms of resource planning and control. In addition, modern communication equipment such as fax machines, cordless or radio telephones were rarely seen.

4.2 Sub-contracting as a production strategy

The increasing technical complexity of projects, changes in employment legislation over the last 20 years, increasing pressures on employers to reduce fixed costs [98] and the inherent short-term variability of geographically dispersed construction workloads, necessitating organizational flexibility, have now resulted in much of the on-site production process being sub-contracted out to other firms. NEDO [99] report up to 90% of the production process as being sub-contracted out, while the London Research Centre [100] indicate that of their pilot sample of ten contractors in the London area, five firms sub-contracted 67–100% of all work to indirect employees, three firms sub-contracted out 34–66% of all work to indirect employees and the remaining two firms sub-contracted out up to 33% of all work in this way. A number of different types of sub-contractor operate in construction. These can be broken down into four distinct groups as follows [101]:

(a) design, manufacture, supply and fix;
(b) design, supply and fix;
(c) supply and fix;
(d) fix only.

The five most frequently used sub-contractors highlighted in the NEDO case studies were as follows:

(a) heating, ventilating and electrical contractors;
(b) structural steel and concrete contractors;
(c) window and curtain walling contractors;
(d) lift contractors;
(e) roof, ceiling and floor contractors.

Thus the operating core of the contracting company is now characterized by a myriad network of sub-contractors of various types, employed with different contractual obligations, rights and liabilities, where, in addition, certain categories of sub-contractors often sub-let the fixing and installation of products to self-employed specialists. The implication of this level and form of sub-contracting in an industry is a wide loss of control over training and the skills of the workforce. With such high levels of sub-contracting the main contractor's primary role has now become one of [102]:

• organizing, coordinating and procuring inputs into the production process;
• providing core services of management expertise, experience, backup and resources from an established organization and an ability to carry contractual risks and obligations for large and complex projects.

Notwithstanding this, the long-term applications of sub-letting out the production process combined with the issue of short-term workload variability creates a strategic paradox for the contractor. The requirement for organizational flexibility means that the main contractor has to ensure a minimum of capital lockup in fixed and human assets. In essence this necessitates, as we have indicated earlier, sub-contracting out much of the production process to others. However, there are long-term trade-offs associated with this. First, the avoidance of investment in machinery by contractors means that management within a contracting company is denying itself the opportunity to substitute machines for labour and hence reduce costs through mechanization [103], as has happened in the industrialization of manufacturing. This maintains construction as a highly labour intensive industry. Second, with the increasing use of sub-contracting, the main contractor could be in danger of losing the role of the foreman, a key technical and managerial knowledge-based asset. The result would be a loss of information about and control over tasks executed on site [104]. Taking a cross-cultural view this is why Italian contractors are reported as preferring not to operate a sub-contract strategy, except for specialized work, on overseas projects. Their philosophy is one where construction knowledge of site tasks and procedures is an asset and can be lost if a 'service orientation' is adopted with detailed production knowledge sub-contracted out to other firms [105].

Sub-contractors are also increasingly involved in design and there is now a move in the industry away from nominated specialist sub-contractors to named sub-contractors. In the case of the former, the contractor is obliged to accept the employment of the sub-contractor nominated by the architect (unless under exceptional reasons). The 'named list', generally produced by the architect, allows the contractor to choose among a number of sub-contractors deemed suitable by the client's advisors. While the contractor is not bound by this, empirical data indicate that most contractors choose sub-contractors from the architect's approved list [106]. The upshot is that the client is now expecting the contractor to take responsibility for all sub-contract work and the increased burden that this now places on site management is a requirement for a combination of both high levels of technical *and* managerial competence. (In addition, understanding the organizational and contractual relationships between main contractor and sub-contractor is now of major importance.)

4.2.1 Organizational and contractual issues associated with sub-contracting

Sub-contracting, as a production strategy for a main contractor, allows fluctuations of workload and uncertainty to be handled relatively flexibly. Sub-contracting also provides access to specialist knowledge that could be expensive to retain in-house. It is also argued to be a low-cost method of organizing the work [107] since parts of the production process are sub-let for a known price [108]. Empirical evidence indicates that some contractors treat sub-contractors as suppliers and handle their procurement through the buying department. Other firms treat sub-contractors as specialized inputs, requiring specific negotiations that are handled by site managers or other contracts staff [109]. In effect, sub-contracting, while handled organizationally in different ways by contractors, is seen as an effective mechanism for production cost control by sub-letting work packages at a known price, generally through competition. The extent to which these cost savings are realized is dependent on the manner in which sub-contracts are handled on site.

The NEDO study [110] indicated a number of organizational and contractual problems associated with sub-contracting. First, increasing precision is required in defining the content and duties to be included in the sub-contract work packages. This is often left implicit with sub-contract manning levels, supervision and site programmes remaining unspecified. Second, ambiguities often surrounded responsibilities for providing plant, tools, power, assistance with setting out and attendance. The writer knows of instances where, for example, main contractors can easily abdicate responsibility for all but the barest provision of such items by writing into sub-contract documents that these become the responsibility of each sub-contractor. Boundary management in these instances is not the domain of the main contractor but, via contract conditions, becomes the responsibility of each sub-contractor and should but may not be taken account of in their pricing. NEDO conclude that main contract conditions are no longer an adequate method for regulating the obligations and rights of the main contractor in a situation where much of the work is sub-let to other firms engaged through different contractual terms.

A case study analysis by Waterfall of the labour only sub-contracting (LOSC) strategy by a national contractor indicates that the argument for cost savings anticipated by adopting this form of labour strategy is not clear cut and may not be maintained in reality for the following five reasons [111]:

1. Savings accrued through staff reductions in the wages department due to lower levels of direct employment may be offset by the increased need for quantity surveying staff for on-site measurement and agreement of sub-contract payments. However, this may also be balanced by a lower requirement for bonus surveyors with increasing levels of LOSC.
2. Savings will occur as the costs of employment legislation are forced on to the LOSC, as is the case with a sub-contract strategy in general.
3. Some sub-contracted trades appear more profitable than others. For example, brickwork and groundworks are normally profitable for the main contractor provided supervision is good. Joinery work, on the other hand, may be less profitable and exceed bill rates due to the larger number of labour items to be measured and the individual nature of the work.
4. LOSC daywork costs can be expensive for the main contractor due to variations in sub-contractor work programmes or patterns due to material shortages or main contractor disruptions.
5. Design changes and consequent LOSC claims for additional payments:

if these are, however, of major significance they will eventually be claimed back from the client through the final account.

Sub-contracting as a labour strategy is discussed in more detail in the following section.

4.2.2 Sub-contract labour strategy

Labour, like materials and equipment inputs, can also be viewed as a key supplier into the on-site production process in construction. Porter [112] argues that the three key issues in any assessment of the strategic implications of procuring labour are as follows:

1. The scarcity of different types of labour: this has two significant impacts – first, the ability of a company to expand, and second, the degree of constancy of labour supply. The more scarce a particular type of labour the greater its bargaining power. Both of these effects were felt in the London area in the mid to late 1980s during the boom [113]. Recruitment difficulties were experienced by contractors for good quality skilled labour in plastering, bricklaying, carpentry/joinery. Contractors had long-term recruitment problems with bricklaying and carpentry, with unfilled vacancies for over 12 months. Contractors did not believe that access to capital would place limits on company growth but that difficulties in the recruitment of sufficient skilled labour would. Interviewees suggested that any industry expansion over 5–10% would cause difficulties for those firms experiencing major problems filling vacancies [114].
2. The degree of labour organization: tightly organized labour, through unions or trade associations, has greater bargaining power. The labour force in construction has become highly fragmented and there has been a consistent decline in union membership in construction since 1948 [115]. NEDO found only 40% union membership among the operatives they interviewed [116]. More recently, following the increase in LOSC, certain types of skilled labour-only are starting to organize, for example the formation of the Federation of Brickwork Contractors. This issue will be discussed in more detail in the chapter dealing with industrial relations.

Porter suggests that the key influences on a firm that stem from considering labour as a supplier are, depending on the above two issues, that it can threaten to, first, raise prices and hence squeeze industry profitability if the firm is unable to recover these increased costs in its own prices and, second, reduce quality. In construction, the ability of con-tractors to raise prices is dependent on the tendering strategy adopted by the client and the economic climate prevailing at the time. However, the continued fragmentation of the production process in construction favours the main contractor. During a boom period, when labour is likely to be short, especially certain types of skilled labour, labour costs will be bid up. However, it is highly likely that there will be a relatively small number of main contractors capable of undertaking particular types of project. Furthermore, there may be such a high supply of work for contractors to bid on, as happened in the mid- to late-1980s in the South East of England, that there are insufficient numbers of main contractors available anyway. Higher labour costs can be passed on to the client (buyer) through higher tender prices. In a recession, where there are many firms chasing less work, the main contractor is in a relative position of power with respect to sub-contractors but in a position of weakness with respect to the client (buyer). Clients are in a position to obtain a more favourable price from contractors, who, in turn can bid sub-contract prices down *provided* sub-contractors remain relatively unorganized.

4.2.3 Labour mobility in construction

Labour mobility into, out of and within the construction industry is a key issue in the production process and has future resource implications for skills development in the industry. The study undertaken by Marsh *et al.* [117] indicates the following:

- Approximately 50% of the labour force entered the industry for positive reasons – open air work, to obtain a trade or follow a family tradition. One-third of skilled entrants entered the industry reluctantly because it was the only work available, and the majority of unskilled workers put this as their primary reason.
- In terms of obtaining employment, 38% of the sample believed they had a free choice of employment. 56% believed they had to take whatever job is going.
- Most skilled men have worked in the industry for most of their working life while only 50% of the unskilled have remained in the industry. Approximately one-third of unskilled men have worked outside the industry. Quite large numbers of older men, especially the unskilled, are invalided out of the industry.
- The reasons given for changing jobs in the industry are redundancy, better pay and job satisfaction.
- The single most important factor that is strongly associated with mobility is age. The highest level of mobility is in the age group 20–35 years old. When controlling for age, however, sharp differences occur between occupational categories. Electricians and plumbers have the most job security, with bricklayers and scaffolders being least secure. Labourers are more mobile than skilled men and young labourers are highly mobile.

Cheetham's [118] findings suggest that within construction, high levels of labour turnover and stability can coexist easily. The relative importance of each is very much dependent on whether the employee works for a main contractor or sub-contractor. Greater continuity of employment is provided by sub-contractors; they are likely to transfer three times as many peratives between sites as main contractors, with the latter recruiting twice as many men for a particular site as the former. Cheetham also discovered a higher incidence of voluntary cessation of employment with main contractor employees. On closer examination, however, as in the Marsh *et al.* study, there were marked differences in turnover of occupational groupings of main contractor employees. We can divide these mobility groupings into three. First, four times as many *general labourers* left voluntarily as were transferred between sites. This compliments the Marsh *et al.* study. Second, unlike the Marsh *et al.* study, *labouring specialists* – scaffolders, reinforcement fixers and drainlayers – were more likely to be retained and transferred than those with certain *crafts skills*, our third category. In this craft grouping fall the bricklayers and carpenters and joiners.

4.2.4 Production strategy and the degree of skill transferability

The degree of skill transferability between companies depends on the level of standardization of tasks. At the operative level most skills and abilities are readily transferable. The reverse will be true at senior levels of the hierarchy. Here the organizational setting or context becomes more important. Therefore, the extent to which individuals are able to move easily between firms is dependent on the degree to which standardized skills have been developed and the degree to which different companies vary the responsibilities attached to the same task/function for which a particular skill is required. The key aspects associated with the ease of transferability are the interplay between skills, the techniques required for tasks performance and the context within which these are exercised [119]. Using our earlier distinction between programmed and non-programmed decisions, a further feature of the degree of transferability of skills between organizations is, therefore, the extent to which skill requirements within the organizational structure are programmed – for which performance yardsticks can be determined or unprogrammed – where task execution requires the exercise of judgement, initiative and discretion [120]. Unprogrammed activities by their nature, have less scope for control to be exercised over the person executing the task. Common examples of programmed activities in construction are as follows [121]:

- bricklaying;
- plastering;
- glazing;
- painting.

Examples of unprogrammed activities in construction are as follows [122]:
- joinery;
- trade and general foreman;
- contracts management;
- design

4.3 Relationships between site management and sub-contractors

The focus of much of the discrepancy between company policy and actual site practice surrounds the behaviour of site management. Empirical studies indicated the following to characterize site managements' behaviour [123].

1. Site agents organize work by experience and adopt a short-term time horizon of between one and two weeks for anticipating problems.
2. An informal network of contacts operates between site agents within the same company via regular telephone contact. Transfers of staff are arranged between site agents, and head office may be told as a *fait accompli*. Site agents use this system to retain good labour and also to encourage unwanted labour to leave.
3. Many site agents consider it pointless to undertake any form of labour forecasting for each trade for the following reasons:
   • problems associated with sub-contractor coordination;
   • availability of plant and equipment;
   • disruption due to materials deliveries;
   • revisions to the design;
   • frequent updating of progress due to variations from labour output due to differing degrees of competency and effort.
4. Site agents often alter the manner in which bonus payments are calculated. This leads to bonus payments being the focal point for grievances by operatives. Operatives find bonus systems difficult to understand, indicate they do not appear to be related to output and suggest they are often exaggerated in terms of earning prospects when seeking recruitment. The NEDO study [124] also found that sub-contract payment procedures caused friction between site management and sub-contractors. For example, the indiscriminate withholding of payments as a contra charge, as contract retention and also slow payments, especially for additional work carried out by the sub-contractor.
5. Site agents are often unaware of the level of labour changes taking place on site since they keep few if any records of such changes.

Other issues that affect site management/sub contractor relationships are as follows [125]:

1. The general level of management competence of the main contractor. Two issues here are:
   • sub-contractors' perceptions that the main contractor is not in control of the process on site;
   • the main contractor being unable to commit himself to a firm programme and provide the sub-contractor with adequate notice.
2. The ability of the sub-contractor to deliver work on time and to the quality required. Common deficiencies of sub-contractors include:

- inadequate resourcing;
- poor or erratic attendance;
- a reluctance to complete work to the required detail;
- producing properly dimensioned information on time;
- clashes over the use of space where sub-contractors are working in close proximity to each other; this is a particularly common problem in the coordination of services.

3. In certain instances operative and site management views are the mirror image of each other. Where a 'them and us' situation pervades, site management may perceive operatives as concerned only with pay and this may also be reflected in the attitudes of workers. However, on sites where management broaden motivational influences, pay may not become such a prominent issue [126].

The foregoing discussion indicates clearly that a production strategy of sub-contracting places on site staff increasing coordination and organizational problems between the various sub-contractors. Waterfall [127] indicates that LOSC will often attempt to determine from main contractors, in advance, which site agent will be in charge of a project, and price their tender submission accordingly, clearly indicating that sub-contractors place a pricing premium on the abilities – either good or bad – of site management. This necessitates that site management become increasingly adept at boundary management skills. It is argued that this is assisted by the sub-letting of work packages and off-site fabrication rather than by trades [128]. Furthermore, it is also argued that the increasing commitment to quality assurance programmes and the subsequent control over site processes will favour direct employment rather than sub-contracting [129]. The major problem in the long term is, however, that the industry at all levels has become used to operating with a short-term perspective and the subsequent reversal of the internalization of the production process – disintegration. The result is fragmentation of a company's control over the total production process, of the labour force, of training and of intimate production knowledge. The following sub-section attempts to place the UK experience in the context of German and French construction industry experience to allow a comparative assessment of the production process to be produced in the final section of this chapter.

4.4 A comparative assessment of production strategy

A number of issues were raised at a recent policy conference entitled 'Construction Training in the 1990s' [130]. The analyses presented at the conference allowed a comparison to be made between UK, German and French production practices. The conference occurred prior to German reunification. In Germany a highly trained workforce in construction is seen as the key to long-term success. This is to be achieved through a reform of the apprenticeship system, backed by both employers and the construction union, creating a common core of training across fourteen trades. It allows the following:

- a flexible workforce to be created;
- workers to adapt to future unknown techniques and materials;
- increased possibilities of worker re-deployment.

The German experience of attempting to rationalise work processes in the construction industry has resulted in the view that [131]:

- Fabrication does not constitute a significant proportion of building operations.
- Technological substitution of labour (Taylorism) has failed in construction.
- Product quality and quantity in construction will not be determined by technology as in manufacturing but by the level of qualification of and through employment of labour.
- Organizational innovation is the key in construction by lowering fixed costs through 'just-in-time'-type techniques, intensifying work processes and increasing work pace by utilizing the flexible potential of the workforce.

In essence, this future strategy for the workforce requires a high level of training [132] and the cooperation of employers and unions to produce a training programme that will allow different crafts to take over the site from each other without delay, friction and extensive managerial coordination. This is one of the contributing reasons why German skilled construction workers share 12 months basic training that is identical across fourteen craft occupations [133].

In France the main focus of attention is on changing the status of construction training by creating a high-status route through the educational system – the 'Bac Pro' or vocational baccalaureat – that stresses the integration of both vocational and theoretical skills. Through this process it is hoped that the move between technical planning and execution and management will be made easier. Bobroff [134] indicates that some French construction companies are now questioning the traditional criteria of qualification – the capacity to perform and master a single task – by putting forward a different perspective of thinking in terms of *competencies* – taking charge of a whole process or function. The crux of this view is that operative flexibility is stressed and new skills and knowledge are acquired outside of their specialisms. The operative would acquire abilities in planning and site production, adapting to new situations, boundary management and organizational skills, safety and quality. The next section draws the themes in this chapter together in order that an insight may be obtained into competitive strategy and advantage in construction.

5. Conclusions

This section draws together the themes running throughout this and the preceding chapter to produce an analytical model of a construction company. In this instance the model encompasses that fact that construction companies have diversified away from a contracting base to form corporate organizational structures where the divisional structure is common and the contracting/construction division forms one part of a wider organizational configuration. Within the construction division it is probable that there will be a regionalized 'subsidiary' structure. Much of our earlier discussion has focused on the operation of strategic management within the context of contracting only and elaborated on, where necessary, to encompass this wider corporate configuration.

Demand in construction is spatially dispersed, creating a 'process-based' requirement for a project-oriented production system. Demand, to which contractors have to respond, is highly variable in the short term but this volatility is no worse than that experienced by the manufacturing industry. In the long term the trend indicators for construction demand and output are relatively stable. This suggests that the call for the 'uniqueness' of construction compared to manufacturing industries has its limitations. What it does mean is that those unique characteristics have to be identified and research and theoretical insights developed to address them.

Strategic thinking is concerned with the long term and the indicators are present for this type of conceptual and judgemental decision-making to occur within construction. However, what this does require is a mental focus that is oriented away from a short- and medium-term, technically-based production orientation – where the impact of demand variability can be high – towards the long term and a strategic corporate orientation concerned with managing the relationship of the construction company with its environment. However, it does not mean that production is ignored as part of the strategic management process. A strategic orientation in construction necessitates understanding the underlying derivatives of the *need* for facilities.

A strategic orientation, since it involves managing the company–environment relationship in the long term, also involves managing change. Two major types of change have been identified. First, recurrent change which is associated with an operationally based internal production orientation. Recurrent change creates an organizational memory that can respond either appropriately or inappropriately to external events. The second type of change that has been identified is termed 'transformational change'. Within this second type of change, two sub-sets have also been identified, termed 'competitive change', which is incremental but fundamental in nature, and strategic change, which is radical, discontinuous and also fundamental. Transformational change involves the company in a different relationship with its environment and will require considerable adaptation of the organizational memory if the firm is to survive in the long term. The construction company that is able to respond to transformational change and adapt its organizational memory for long-term survival can be termed a *learning organization*. Underlying the management of these different types of change is the requirement for varying types of managerial skills at different levels in the hierarchy. The management of transformational change – both competitive and strategic – requires a future orientation, and the ability to be able to live with high levels of ambiguity and handle and integrate unstructured information that can often be conflicting. This places a heavy reliance on conceptual and judgemental skills that are able to blend experience with creativity and insight.

Three distinct processes associated with strategic management have been identified which, while analytically distinct, will in reality overlap. Key concepts in the formulation stage are the company's mission, its objectives and how these are achieved through strategies and policies. A hierarchy of strategies was identified: corporate strategy – affecting the whole company, be it a divisionalized construction firm or one that concentrates totally on contracting; business strategy – concerned with competing in particular markets, bidding strategy is an example in contracting; finally, the operational or functional strategy – concerned with the operating core. Important techniques highlighted for assisting in the formulation process are the SWOT analysis and competitor and strategic group analysis. The second stage of strategic management is the strategic choice process, involving making decisions about which strategies to adopt. An analytical approach was suggested that viewed a construction company as a portfolio of strategic business areas reflecting different market needs, customers, geographic locations and project technologies. A number of strategy alternatives were identified: the generic strategies – competitive and directional; strategic variations; and strategic mode. The processes and issues associated with regionalization, as part of an expansion or retrenchment strategy, were identified. Key issues in regionalization are as follows:

- centre–region relationships;
- changes that stem from the pre- and post-regionalization process;
- centralized versus decentralized decision-making; the dilemma here is the choice between top–down decision-making, where decisions are taken at the centre and bottom–up decision-making, where decisions are market led. It was suggested that regionalization with decentralized decision-making may require skills at the centre in managing a 'loose-tight' organizational structure;
- succession planning and management development;
- the process of managing change over the organizational life cycle.

Strategic choice involves senior managers in making decisions about the competitive strategy that the company must adopt to utilize its capabilities to the fullest and position itself advantageously with respect to its competitors. The major construction companies in the United Kingdom have used 'grand strategies' in their strategic development, that is, the use simultaneously or over time of the generic directional strategies of expansion, retrenchment or stability. Competitive strategies will be based on isolating, in the formulation stage, the areas where the company has distinctive competencies that provide superiority over its competitors; in other words isolating areas of competitive advantage. It has been suggested by some authors that distinctive competencies are found in the operating core of a company. If this is the case and since we have identified people as one of the key resources in construction, then areas of distinctive competence for a contractor would be located at site management level – a team specific advantage [135]. However, we would also argue that because of the nature of contracting, requiring a construction company bidding for the opportunity to set up a continual series of prototypical project-based production systems, team specific advantages will also be operating, for example during the adjudication process as part of bidding strategy, where key personnel from the middle line and strategic apex come together to produce the final project tender price.

Isolating competitive advantages in construction is difficult since we are dealing with a high incidence of knowledge-based advantages that reside in project teams. Competitive advantage requires the analysis of value activities and how these are configured into a value chain. The value chain has both internal and external components and is a product of a company's history, the impact of the strategic formulation, choice and implementation stages and the cost and resourcing implications of these. Value chain analysis should be undertaken both for one's own company and for those of key competitors. In addition, the isolation of competitive advantage requires the determination of the number of distinctive sources of advantage that a company has, among a hierarchy of sources. An analytical model was put forward for highlighting the value activities making up the bidding process for a contractor. This revealed that contractors compete on both low- and high-order factors. Low-order factors, primarily inputs of materials, capital, equipment and labour may be easily obtainable by competitors. In the case of equipment and labour, depending on the choices made by the company, they may remain in-house or be sub-contracted out. Where both are sub-contracted in sizeable proportions low-order advantages become very transient and can be easily eroded by competitors. High-order advantages for a contractor, as identified by the model and highlighted above, are knowledge-based and invariably team-based, leading to the development of team specific advantages. These require constant upgrading and improvement, through training and management development, in order to provide sustainable advantages. High-order advantages that are knowledge-based and team specific follow through into the development of reputation and expertise in the execution of particular project technologies. The dilemma for the individual construction company is that, to an extent, these high-order advantages can be easily 'poached' in the short term by other contractors.

However, if the company's competitors do not actively pursue training and development programmes for the continual upgrading of managerial skills, then 'poaching' cannot, in the long term, lead to sustained advantages for these competitors.

The final stage of the strategic management process is that of implementation. This involves adapting and modifying the existing organizational structure and the allocation of resources. The organizational structure can be difficult to change. Resistance to change is a natural phenomenon and is typical of any social system. The crucial distinction is the difference between resistance that dissipates over time as people see the benefits of change and begin to accept it versus that which becomes dysfunctional and pathological. Implementation will involve the use of power, either overt or covert. Successful implementation will encompass determining the key coalitions with the company and acknowledging those that are seen as important in achieving corporate objectives.

The concluding stage of the analysis of competitive advantage in construction, within a domestic context, concerns production. The analysis undertaken here of production on site indicates clearly that the competency of site management is a key issue. Site management has a significant impact on production efficiency, especially where sub-contractors are concerned, and they price site management accordingly. Site management manage by constant intervention rather than by exception, making many *ad hoc* decisions, often without reference to more senior managers. Site management is thus in a powerful position to adapt and modify the company's policies at production level and this is, in certain instances (primarily the modification of bonus and overtime payments), a cause of considerable labour discontent. This chapter has also highlighted that site management are not trained with the right skills for the emergent role of the main contractor. The role of the main contractor, with the substantial increase in the use of sub-contracting, has moved towards one of managing organizational and contractual risk and the coordination and control of interorganizational boundaries on site. Due to this change in main contractor role, site management are now increasingly required to combine high levels of both technical and managerial competence. The evidence suggests that they are insufficiently trained in the latter.

With the increasing use of sub-contracting the production process has become fragmented in terms of managerial control, intimate and detailed production knowledge and methods of labour employment. It has been shown that the workforce in construction experiences high levels of mobility, especially among the unskilled. However, sub-contractors appear to have a more stable workforce than main contractors. There is a general acceptance of mobility and redundancy by both management and the workforce and they see it as endemic to the structure and operations of the industry. In essence, both parties to the production process are attempting to maximize the benefits each can gain from industry structure – employers by lowering costs and labour through higher earnings.

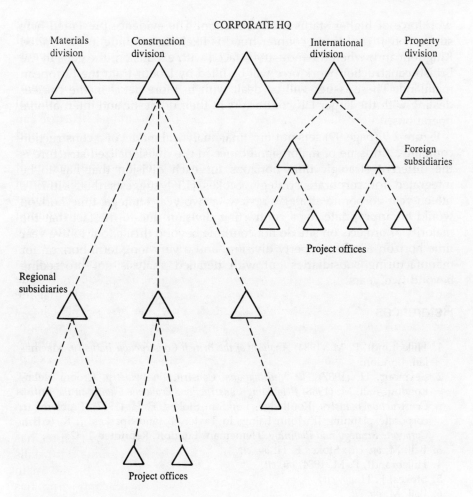

Figure 2.9 *A model of a construction company*

However, the upshot of this has been a sustained erosion of training opportunities, the utilization of methods of employment that are divisive and an industry that is in danger of becoming de-skilled in the medium to long term in comparison to our European partners. In addition, the continued emphasis on self-employment in the industry has had repercussions for the structure of the main contractor's organization. In those craft skills that have been designated as programmed, where performance yardsticks are easy to establish and measure, the main contractor can potentially obtain the maximum benefit from self-employed labour operating on a piecework system. However, for those craft skills designated as unprogrammed, joinery being a prime example, the main contractor is unlikely to reap the benefits of self-employed sub-contract labour due to the requirement for increased levels of measurement by quantity surveyors. Finally, as alluded to earlier, our European partners are gearing up to develop a better trained, multiskilled and adaptable workforce of higher status in construction. The evidence presented here suggests that the strong counter trend is likely to continue in the United Kingdom and, when the industry is faced with expansion, the gaps in the British construction workforce will be filled by labour from the European mainland. These issues will be dealt with in more detail in the chapter dealing with the larger UK contractors in their domestic and international operations.

Figure 2.9 (page 99) sets out our final analytical model of a construction company. An issue of major significance in the divisionalized structure is the different strategic time horizons for each division that has to be integrated for corporate strategy. Stokes [136] suggests that within a fifteen-year corporate strategic review, a two-year strategic time horizon would be appropriate for a contracting division due to the fact that the majority of projects on site do not continue beyond this, a four to five year time horizon for the property division, and a very long term horizon for manufacturing subsidiaries but with detailed analysis not proceeding beyond two years.

References

1. Hillebrandt, P. M. (1984) *Analysis of the British Construction Industry*. Macmillan, London.
2. Seymour, H. (1987) *The Multinational Construction Industry*. Croom Helm, London. Ball, M. (1988) *Rebuilding Construction: Economic Change in the British Construction Industry*. Routledge, London. Stokes, F. H. (1977) 'Problems in corporate planning II': John Laing. In Taylor, B. and Sparkes, J. R. (eds.), *Corporate Strategy and Planning*. Heineman, London. Reprinted 1982.
3. Ball, M. *op. cit.*; Stokes F. H. *op. cit.*
4. Hillebrandt, P. M. 1984. *op. cit.*
5. Stokes, F. H. *op. cit.*
6. Ball, M. *op. cit.*
7. Tichy, N. M. (1983) *Managing Strategic Change: Technical, Political and Cultural Dynamics*. John Wiley & Sons, New York.
8. Lansley, P., Quince, T. and Lea, E. (1979) *Flexibility and Efficiency in Construction Management*. Final Report. Building Industry Group, Ashridge Management College.
9. Tichy, N. M. *op. cit.*
10. Clark, P. (1989) 'Social technology and structure'. In Hillebrandt, P. M. and Cannon, J. (eds.). *The Management of Construction Firms: Aspects of Theory*. Macmillan, London.
11. Tichy, N. M. *op. cit.*
12. Howe, S. (1986) *Corporate Strategy*. Macmillan, London.
13. Kast, F. E. and Rosenzweig, J. E. (1981) 'The modern view: a systems approach'. In *Systems Behaviour*. Open Systems Group (eds.), 3rd edn. Harper and Row, London.
14. Johnson, G. and Scholes, K. *Exploring Corporate Strategy*, 2nd edn. Prentice-Hall, Hemel Hempstead.
15. Hunt, J. W. (1986) *Managing People at Work*, 2nd edn. McGraw-Hill, Maidenhead.

16. Glueck, W. F. and Jauch, L. R. (1984) *Business Policy and Strategic Management*, 4th edn. McGraw-Hill, Singapore.
17. Ramsey, W. (1984) 'Business objectives and strategy'. In Hillebrandt, P. M. and Cannon, J. (eds.), *op. cit.*
18. Glueck, W. F. and Jauch, L. R. *op. cit.*
19. Glueck, W. F. and Jauch, L. R. *op. cit.*
20. Johnson, G. and Scholes, K. *op. cit.*
21. Glueck, W. F. and Jauch, L. R. *op. cit.* Howe, W. *op. cit.* Ansoff, I. (1987) *Corporate Strategy*, 2nd edn. Penguin, London.
22. Christopher, M., Majaro, S. and McDonald, M. (1989) *Strategy: A Guide to Marketing for Senior Executives*. Wildwood House, Aldershot. Wheelen, T. L. and Hunger J. D. (1987) *Strategic Management*, 2nd edn. Addison-Wesley. Ansoff, I. *op. cit.* Hunt, J. W. *op. cit.* Mintzberg, H. and Waters, J. A. (1984) 'Researching the formation of strategies: The history of Canadian Lady 1939–1976'. In Lamb, R. B. (ed.), *Competitive Strategic Management*. Prentice-Hall, Englewood Cliffs, New Jersey.
23. Wheelen, T. L. and Hunger, J. D. *op. cit.* Bowman, C. and Asch, D. (1987) *Strategic Management*. Macmillan, London.
24. Ramsey, W. *op. cit.*
25. Hunt, J. W. *op. cit.* Glueck, W. F. and Jauch, L. R. *op. cit.*
26. Wheelen, T. L. and Hunger, J. D. *op. cit.*
27. Porter, M. E. (1980) *Competitive Strategy. Techniques for Analysing Competitors and Industries*. The Free Press, New York.
28. Ansoff, I. *op. cit.* Jauch, L. R. and Glueck, W. F. (1988) *Business Policy and Strategic Management*, 5th ed. McGraw-Hill, Singapore.
29. Jauch, L. R. and Glueck, W. F. *op. cit.*
30. Porter, M. E. *op. cit.*
31. Spiteri, J. (1989) Competition and Strategy for a Construction Firm. MSc Thesis, Heriot-Watt University. Duncan, J. 1989 Competition in the Scottish Construction Market. MSc Thesis. Heriot Watt University.
32. Porter, M. E. *op. cit.*
33. Rice, J. (1989) Strategic Group Analysis Within the UK Construction Industry. MSc Thesis. Heriot Watt University. Aluvaala, A. (1990) Strategic Group Analysis Within the UK Construction Industry. MSc Thesis. Heriot-Watt University. Moodley, K. (1990) Strategic Group Analysis in the Construction Industry. MSc Thesis. Heriot-Watt University.
34. McGee, J. and Thomas, T. (1988) 'Making sense of complex industries'. In Hood N. and Vahlne, J. R. (eds.), *Strategies in Global Competition*. Croom Helm, London.
35. Kelly, G. A. (1955) *The Psychology of Personal Constructs*. W. W. Norton, New York.
36. Male, S. P. and Aspinall, P. A. (1986) 'A computerised, interactive, interrogative, analytical decision technique for strategic management in construction companies', *Proceedings of the 10th CIB Congress 'Advanced Building Technology'*, Vol III, pp. 1019–106, Washington DC.
37. Ansoff, I. *op. cit.*
38. Glueck, W. F. and Jauch, L. R. *op. cit.*
39. Simon, H. A. (1976) *Administrative Behaviour*, 3rd edn. The Free Press, New York.
40. Bedeian, A. G. (1984) *Organisations: Theory and Analysis*, 2nd edn. Holt–Saunders.

41. Feldman, D. C. and Arnold, H. J. (1983) *Managing Individuals and Group Behaviour in Organisations*. McGraw-Hill.
42. Ansoff, I. *op. cit.*
43. Ansoff, I. *op. cit.*
44. Lansley, P., Quince, T. and Lea, E. *op. cit.*
45. Johnson, G. and Scholes, K. *op. cit.* Jauch, L. R. and Glueck, W. F. *op. cit.*
46. Porter, M. E. *op. cit.*
47. Johnson, G. and Scholes, K. *op. cit.*
48. Jauch, L. R. and Glueck, W. F. *op. cit.* Johnson, G. and Scholes, J. *op. cit.*
49. Lansley, P., Quince, T. and Lea, E. *op. cit.*
50. Ball, M. and Cullen, A. (1980) 'Merger and accumulation in the British construction industry 1960–1970'. *Birkbeck Discussion Paper No: 73.* 1980. Ball, M. *op. cit.*
51. Ball, M. *op. cit.*
52. Ashley, N. (1988) 'Relationships with partners'. In 'Overseas projects: Crucial problems', *Proceedings of the Conferences on Crucial Problems Encountered in the Execution of Overseas Projects*, pps. 35–43, Institution of Civil Engineers, 27 April, 1988. Thomas Telford. London.
53. Howe, S. *op. cit.* Johnson, G. and Scholes, K. *op. cit.*
54. Johnson, G. and Scholes, K. *op. cit.*
55. Howe, S. *op. cit.*
56. Jauch, L. R. and Glueck, W. F. *op. cit.*
57. Howe, S. *op. cit.*
58. Jauch, L. F. and Glueck, W. F. *op. cit.*
59. Jauch, L. R. and Glueck, W. F. *op. cit.* Johnson, G. and Scholes, K. *op. cit.*
60. Ansoff, I. *op. cit.*
61. Ansoff, I. *op. cit.*
62. Ansoff, I. *op. cit.*
63. Jauch, L. R. and Glueck, W. F. *op. cit.*
64. Seymour, H. *op. cit.*
65. Ball, M. *op. cit.*
66. Strassman, P. W. (1989) 'The United States'. In Strassman, P. W. and Wells, J. (eds.), *The Global Construction Industry: Strategies for Entry, Growth and Survival*. Unwin Hyman, London.
67. Jauch, L. R. and Glueck, W. F. *op. cit.*
68. Johnson, G. and Scholes, K. *op. cit.*
69. Ansoff, I. *op. cit.*
70. Johnson, G. and Scholes, K. *op. cit.*
71. Lansley, P. (1981) 'Corporate dislocation: a threat for the 1980s', *Journal of General Management*, Summer, 1981, pps. 28–38. Lansley, P., Quince T. and Lea E. *op. cit.*
72. Male, S. and Stocks, R. 'Managers and the organisation'. In Hillebrandt, P. M. and Cannon, J. (eds.) *op. cit.*
73. Male, S. and Stocks, *op. cit.*
74. Peters, T. J. and Waterman, R. H. (1982) *In Search of Excellence: Lessons from America's Best Run Companies*. Harper & Row, New York.
75. Lansley, P. *op. cit.*
76. Porter, M. E. 1980 *op. cit.*
77. Porter, M. E. 1980 *op. cit.*
78. Porter, M. E. 1985 *Competitive Advantage. Creating and Sustaining Superior Performance*. The Free Press, New York.

79. Porter, M. E. *op. cit.*
80. Johnson, G. and Scholes, K. *op. cit.*
81. Ramsey, W. *op. cit.*
82. Porter, M. E. (1990) *The Competitive Advantage of Nations*. Macmillan, London.
83. Azzaro, D. Hubbard, J. and Robertson, D. (1987) 'Contractors' Estimating Procedures: An Overview'. *Occasional Paper*. Royal Institution of Chartered Surveyors.
84. Flanagan, R. and Norman, G. (1989), 'Pricing policy'. In Hillebrandt, P. M. and Cannon, J. (eds.) *op. cit.*
85. Clark, P. *op. cit.*
86. Boyd, A. D. and Wilson, A. H. (1975) *Technology Transfer in Construction*. Background Report No: 32. Science Council of Canada, January.
87. Fleming, M. (1988) 'Construction'. In Johnson P. (ed.), *The Structure of British Industry*. 2nd edn. Unwin Hyman, London.
88. Ball, M. *op. cit.* Boyd, A. D. and Wilson, A. H. *op. cit.* Fleming, M. *op. cit.* Lansley, P. R. (1987) 'Corporate strategy and survival in the UK construction industry', *Construction Management and Economics*, 5, pp. 141–55.
89. Bennett, J., Flanagan, R. and Norman, G. (1987) *Capital and Counties Report: Japanese Construction Industry*. Centre for Strategic Studies. University of Reading.
90. Lansley, P., Quince, T. and Lea, E. *op. cit.* Langford, D. and Male, S. P. *Strategic Management in Construction*. Gower, 1991.
91. National Economic Development Office (1978) *How Flexible is Construction*. HMSO, London. Hillebrandt, P.M. (1985) *Economic Theory and the Construction Industry*. 2nd edn. Macmillan, Basingstoke.
92. Hillebrandt, P.M. 1985 *op. cit.*
93. Hillebrandt, P. M. 1984, *op. cit.*
94. Enderwick, P. (1989) 'Multinational contracting'. In Enderwick, P. (ed.), *The Multinational Service Firm*. Routledge, London.
95. Cheetham, D. W. (1982) 'Labour management practices', *Construction Papers*, 1, No 3, pp. 37–53.
96. National Economic Development Office. (1988) *Faster Building for Commerce*. Millbank, London.
97. Marsh, A., Heady, P., and Matheson, J. (1981) *Labour Mobility in the Construction Industry*. HMSO, London.
98. Gray, C. and Flanagan, R. (1989) *The Changing Role of Specialist and Trade Contractors*. Chartered Institute of Building, Epsom.
99. NEDO (1988) *op. cit.*
100. London Research Centre (1987) *Skills Shortages in the London Building Industry*. Report by the Economic Activities Group.
101. Gray, C. and Flanagan, R. *op. cit.*
102. NEDO (1988) *op. cit.*
103. Ball, M. *op. cit.*
104. Ball, M. *op. cit.*
105. Norsa, A. (1988) Italy. In Strassman, W. P. and Wells, J. *The Global Construction Industry: Strategies for Entry, Growth and Survival*. Unwin Hyman, London.
106. NEDO 1988 *op. cit.*
107. Buckley, P. J. and Enderwick, P. 'Manpower management'. In Hillebrandt, P. M. and Cannon, J. (eds.) *op. cit.*
108. Ball, M. *op. cit.*
109. Lansley, P., Quince, T. and Lea, E. *op. cit.*

110. NEDO (1988) *op. cit.*
111. Waterfall, M. H. P. (1989) The Profitability of Labour Only Sub Contracting. MSc Thesis. Heriot Watt University.
112. Porter, M. E. *op. cit.*
113. London Research Centre *op. cit.*
114. London Research Centre *op. cit.*
115. Farnham, D. and Pimlott, J. (1986) *Understanding Industrial Relations*. Holt, Rinehart and Winston, London.
116. NEDO 1988 *op. cit.*
117. Marsh A., Heady P. and Matheson J. *op. cit.*
118. Cheetham, D. W. *op. cit.*
119. Lansley, P., Quince, T. and Lea, E. *op. cit.*
120. Lansley, P., Sadler, P. J. and Webb, T. D. (1975) 'Managing for success in the building industry', *Building Technology and Management*, July, pp. 21–23.
121. Lansley, P., Sadler, P. J. and Webb, T. R. *op. cit.*
122. Lansley, P. Sadler, P. J. and Webb, T. J. *op. cit.*
123. Cheetham, D. W. *op. cit.*
124. NEDO 1988 *op. cit.*
125. NEDO 1988 *op. cit.*
126. NEDO 1988 *op. cit.*
127. Waterfall, M. H. P. *op. cit.*
128. Lansley, P. R. (1987) *op. cit.*
129. Lansley, P. R. (1987) *op. cit.*
130. Construction Industry Studies Group (eds.) (1989) 'Construction training in the 1990s and beyond: a policy conference', University of Warwick, 13–15 December.
131. Syben, G. (1989) 'Rationalisation and new technology in the West German construction industry'. In Construction Industry Studies Group (eds.), *op. cit.*, pp. 12–13.
132. Syben, G. *op. cit.*
133. Streeck, (1989) W. 'Developments in initial and further training in the West German construction industry', In Construction Industry Studies Group (eds.), pp. 14–16.
134. Bobbroff, J. (1989) 'Training in construction trades: Difficulties and developments in the face of new demands', In Construction Industry Studies Group (eds.), *op. cit.*, pp. 7–11.
135. Enderwick, P. *op. cit.*
136. Stokes, F. H. *op. cit.*

—— 3 ——

Strategic marketing management

Robert Stocks

1. Overview

The enigma of marketing is that it can be both simple and complex at the same time, a state of mind and a dynamic business function [1]. It may, or may not, be adopted by firms to any great extent. It is a function which is patently necessary to bring together the producer and the consumer, the buyer and the seller.

Examples of the many definitions of marketing, including The Institute of Marketing [2], Perreault *et al.* [3], Slater [4], indicate that marketing is a management function concerned with identifying, analysing and antici- pating the needs of the customer with a view to supplying these specific needs, at a profit, to the identified target market and within the bounds of a company's capabilities; in short, trying to establish what the market wants and what it is prepared to pay for it.

The marketing concept takes a somewhat wider approach in that it is a way of thinking – a management philosophy about an organization's entire activities. This philosophy affects all efforts of the organization, not just the marketing activities [5]. This concept of marketing and an orientation towards its functions and processes remains concerned with the basic tenet of satisfying customers' objectives while achieving organi- zational goals.

These marketing functions and processes highlight an important dyna- mic business activity which is closely related to the corporate strategic processes. It is within an overall strategy that marketing assumes the two dimensions of philosophy and function, with marketing as a business philosophy stemming from the recognition that the firm depends on the customer for its survival and growth. Perreault *et al.* [6] identify the three elements of this philosophy as, customer orientation, total company effort, and profit objective.

A business organization exists only because of its customers and, in order to survive, the needs of these clients will be identified and satisfied, while providing a profit for the firm: 'The real power of marketing philosophy is the firm's perception that its prosperity is built up by meeting customers' needs profitably.' [7] It is also crucial that customers are created by the firm and the marketing philosophy plays an important role in this activity.

Marketing is an organizational function which is part of the overall system. The integration of all organizational activities is essential. A total company effort is required for success, and in any event marketing affects everyone within the organization. The management function, as a dimension of the marketing profile, is concerned with evaluating and analysing markets and providing, for example, the resultant information in terms of quality, price and service allied to the needs of the customer. Use is made of market research, forecasting and advertising in the performance of this function.

Marketing management includes all the decisions involved in setting up and executing marketing plans, in order that the firm implements the concept of marketing in conjunction with its environment. It is essentially involved in the planning of marketing activities and the direction and control of these plans. Baker [8] shows the distinction between the market plan and the strategic marketing plan. The latter is seen to involve four sets of related decisions: defining the business; determining the role of the business; formulating functional strategies and budgeting. It is therefore clear that the strategic marketing plan is concerned with long-term issues as part of an organization's overall corporate strategy. It is likewise identified with the SWOT analysis which is integral to the formulation of long-term strategy.

The process of marketing planning is outlined in Figure 3.1 where the sequence produces a model similar to that applied to corporate strategy formulation. When any business is posed with the question of what business it is in today, and where it will be five to ten years from now, a self-analysis is vital. Furthermore, the attitude portrayed by a company

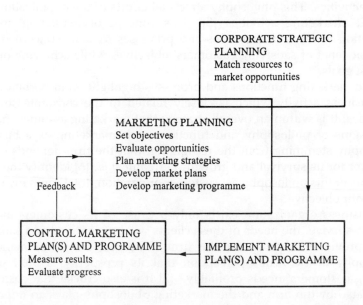

Figure 3.1 *The marketing process (Source: E. J. McCarthy, U.D. Perreault and D. Richard (1984), Basic Marketing, Irwin Inc. Reprinted with permission.)*

and its management will show a reactive or proactive approach to the future of its industry. If the proactive approach is considered the more positive attitude to future events, an examination of internal strengths and weaknesses, and of external opportunities and threats, is an inherent part of the planning process.

An internal appraisal or audit of strengths and weaknesses indicates that marketing efficiency is no less important than, for example, technical efficiency. Having the most technically efficient plant in the world is of no use if there is no accessible worthwhile market for one's product or service. From the marketing philosophy viewpoint, the question, therefore, is of how sufficiently management are marketing orientated. If any business firm can be viewed as operating within a customer-solving process more than anything else, then marketing of course plays a vital role. Neither technical leadership nor superior quality control are, of themselves, enough. Management has to organize the business to be competitively effective in terms of being in the right markets, with the appropriate products and services to sell and deliver at the time the customer wants them, at a price which the market can absorb and at a profit which makes it worth while to the supplier. Basically, therefore, marketing is all about having a satisfied customer who has a good feeling about doing business with the firm.

There is a paramount requirement for making the marketing concept work, and the chief executive and his top management colleagues must be fully committed to the concept and involved in its implementation.

Quality control and high standards of after-sales service allied to market research, i.e. customer feedback, are also of importance.

Any internal analysis of the company would also require that there are effective internal lines of communication to explain and sell the marketing concept at every level within the organization. Everyone must be convinced that he or she can make a vital contribution to servicing the customer. As the essence of good marketing is team effort, the marketing function should be part of an integrated, functional whole.

Every firm has to ask itself where its strengths and weaknesses lie, and has to try and develop some kind of unique advantage or special competence which will provide it with a competitive edge – and which effective and efficient marketing policies will subsequently exploit.

2. Market choice and segmentation

Most companies recognize that they normally cannot service all the customers in some broad market: 'The customers are too numerous, widely scattered and varied in their buying requirements.' [9] A firm will therefore identify a segment within which to compete rather than the mass market. This target marketing enables the firm to identify marketing opportunities more effectively. There are three steps of target marketing in which the company divides a market into distinct groups of buyers,

evaluates the attractiveness of segments and positions the firm competitively in the target market.

> An industry is a wide group of manufacturers producing a wide range
> of products. A market segment is a much more distinct group of
> customers who have similar requirements that may be served by
> alternative products and technologies. [10]

David [11] defines market segmentation as 'the subdividing of a market
into distinct subsets of customers according to their needs and the way
they buy and use a product or service'. This sub-sectioning of the
marketplace is seen as an important variable in strategy implementation
for the following three reasons [12]:

1. Many company strategies, including market development, product
   development, market penetration and diversification, require increased
   sales through new markets and products. To be effective in these
   implementations new or improved segmentation approaches are
   required.
2. A firm which has limited resources and specialization is able to
   implement segmentation policies because mass production, distribution and advertising are not required. The smaller firm is often in an
   advantageous position of competition against the large company by its
   maximization of per-unit and per-segment sales.
3. The market-mix variables of the four Ps: product, place, promotion and
   price, depend on how the market segmentation is a central issue for the
   firm's strategy implementation.

Marketing managers will attempt to fulfil the individual needs and tastes
of customers while attempting to win long-term customers: 'Choice of
market is a choice of the customer and of the competitive, technical,
political and social environments in which one elects to compete.' [13]
Many industrial companies tend to think of a market as one large market
place which buys and uses similar products. This could describe a sales
'segmentation' which involves a concentration of effort in a non-global
view of markets. Companies with a total market approach direct one type
of product at the total market in an endeavour to create an awareness for
the customer that their product is a better choice than that of competitors.
The single marketing mix in this situation compares with a marketing mix
or mixes as required in the segmentation approach for these prospective
customers within the selected segments.

   A number of circumstances must be present for market segmentation to
be effective [14]. The segments of the market must be identifiable and able
to be divided up, with information available regarding the attributes of
buyers for measurement. Segments should be set against one another in
respect of sales, costs and profits estimates. At least one of the segments
should then be able to vindicate its marketing mix (product, place,
promotion, price) selection by showing sufficient profit potential. It then

follows that the firm's marketing mix can be applied to such a segment; and its accessibility therefore enables effective commitment by the firm. However, the segment must be sufficiently profitable to justify marketing costs. To further qualify as an agreeable choice the segment should be able to be defended against concentrated market competitors, and the uniqueness carried by the segment should be assumed to be long lasting. Finally, compared to major competitors, the firm should have a relative advantage in the types of skills required to serve the particular segment which is chosen. The four major and common bases for segmenting a market lie under the broad headings of geographic, demographic, psychographic and behaviourial [15, 16]. Pride and Ferrell [17], in labelling these four sets of major variables geographic, socio-economic, psychographic and product-related, point out that these segmentation variables are for consumer markets.

A consumer market 'consists of purchasers and/or individuals in their households who intend to consume or benefit from the purchased products and who do not buy products for the main purpose of making a profit' [18].

Industrial markets, on the other hand, consist of individuals, groups or organizations who purchase products in order to produce other products. A lamp producer buying electrical wire for the production of lamps is one example. Other types of market would include the producer markets which include buyers of new materials, and industries such as agriculture and construction where raw materials are used in their operations. Segmenting for customer markets is usually much easier and simpler than for industrial markets. The major reason is that industrial products can have multiple applications and can appeal to diverse customer groups. For industrial firms, there is a need for segmentation when, on evaluation of a market segment, the following four points apply as criteria to be considered before deciding which segments to serve [19]:

(a) the market growth potential;
(b) the level of market domination by large and powerful competitors;
(c) the entry barriers and the prospect of being able to attain and maintain a certain 'critical mass' to be an efficient producer;
(d) the value added by the manufacturer. If the value added is high, it gives the manufacturer leverage in pricing and remaining competitive.

If the producer does not offer something new or better to the customer, proceeding to target the segment will result in inefficient allocation of resources which could have been better used in a different segment.

Segmentation is not difficult and does not call for exceptional skills in marketing, but it does require detailed market and customer knowledge [20].

The benefits of segmenting rather than treating all segments as one homogeneous marketplace, should not be neutralized by a lack of monitoring for change in competitive position and environmental changes which may shift market boundaries.

3. Customers

Conventional wisdom would affirm that customers are involved in making decisions on a rational basis. This is to say that they have goals or wants which they attempt to satisfy, within the means available to them and at a certain cost. Following rational principles, they choose on the basis of these goals or wants. The marketing implications point to the perception that by identifying what people say, do or are, market research can identify customers' wants and beliefs.

However, it cannot be assumed that customer goals are given, or even that consumers know what they want. Marketing managers therefore need to consider this irrationality which leaves potential customers open to persuasion, in the knowledge that they in fact have multiple and conflicting wants [21]. It is also questionable as to whether or not customers are always informed about products, or about what they are being offered.

Five stages of consumer buying behaviour can be outlined in the buying decision process; problem recognition; information search; evaluation of alternatives; purchase; and post-purchase evaluation [22]. This process may be employed by individuals who are engaged in extensive decision-making, although all five stages are not always included. For example, not all decision processes result in a purchase.

Pride and Ferrell outline the following three possible areas of influence on the decision process which are interrelated in their effects:

1. Demographic or socioeconomic factors are individual characteristics such as age, sex, race, income, family and occupation.
2. Situational factors are those circumstances or conditions which exist when a purchase decision is made.
3. Psychological influences help to determine behaviour and consumers may be affected by elements such as perception, motives, learning, attitudes and personality.

'All companies should examine their customer base to establish just who the key customers are and what their loss would mean to the firm.' [23] The whole market should likewise be appraised for potential customers, or small customers who could be promoted to key positions. From this examination, the firm can trace three types or groups of customers: existing key customers, existing non-key customers and non-customers. Key-customer marketing is essentially similar to any other type of marketing, except that it is more frequent and intense and entails a different level of contact. There is seen to be a need for a change of attitude towards key customers and potential key customers, and towards the market itself [24]. In this respect, importance is placed on working relationships, negotiating skills, internal coordination, back-up services, follow-up and better information-gathering intelligence systems.

Markets and buying behaviour of consumers have to be understood in order for marketing managers to develop effective marketing plans. The various influences on the decision process must also be appreciated by marketers.

4. The marketing plan

Planning is a management function at all levels, for all companies, and corporate planning involves all functional areas of the organization.

Although typical documentation would include an organization chart and corporate plan, the information required for a marketing plan should not be confused with a corporate plan. Also, the strategic marketing plan is concerned with all aspects of the firm's strategy in the marketplace. A marketing plan, on the other hand, deals primarily with implementing the market strategy as it relates to target markets and the marketing mix [25].

Market planning 'is a systematic process that involves the assessment of marketing opportunities and resources, the determination of marketing objectives, the development of a marketing strategy and the development of a plan for implementation and control' [26]. Marketing managers need to begin with the firm's current situation and assess the future opportunities and constraints which the organization faces.

The marketing audit is the intelligence system which collects the information required to determine if the company's marketing strategy is working. This methodological inventory informs the firm as to how effective is its marketing function in helping to achieve objectives and recommends future marketing activities to improve the company's marketing performance. The marketing audit is, therefore, the systematic examination of a company's marketing position.

In examining the company's marketing position, the marketing audit is seen as an input to the overall corporate strategy and the basis for the detailed marketing plan [27].

The scope and components of the marketing audit are applied to the environment, strategy, organization, systems, productivity and function. Figure 3.2 displays the position of the marketing audit within the marketing plan relative to the strategic marketing plan and the firm's overall corporate strategy.

With regard to the environment, and from a marketing viewpoint, corporate image and reputation, customers and competitors are important external variables requiring appraisal. A discipline and mechanism is provided by the SWOT analysis to ask pertinent questions about the nature of the firm's business, the present circumstances in which it finds itself and the expectations for the future. However, it is only a tool to enable the firm to ask the correct questions.

If, as it is said, more companies fail because of poor marketing than for any other reason, the SWOT analysis, which is vital to an organization, thereafter places great importance on marketing philosophy, management and strategy, and a significant part of marketing planning.

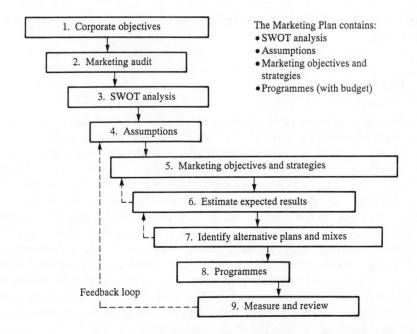

Figure 3.2   *The marketing planning process (Sources: M. J. Baker (1985)*
Marketing Strategy and Management, *Macmillan, p. 47. Reprinted with
permission.)*

5. Market research

Management requires a marketing information system in order to monitor
the marketing environment. The marketing audit, with this requirement,
will focus on the basic functions of marketing and in doing so highlight
the relevant sources of data which management require.

Market research is the systematic collection, recording and analysing of
data concerning problems relating to the marketing of goods and services.
There are five basic steps in the process, as follows:

1. Exploratory research is carried out in order to define the problem and
   objectives of the research.
2. The research plan is developed and secondary data from within and
   external to the firm is examined.
3. Data is collected and information generated.
4. Information and data is analysed.
5. The findings are presented and recommendations made.

One of the most important functions of market research is that it enables
the firm to concentrate its resources on those parts of the market which are
most likely to help it achieve its objectives. The up-to-date information

gained from an effective marketing research exercise assists in reducing the risk and uncertainty associated with marketing decisions.

Marketing research for construction firms may gather information to identify profit opportunities, ascertain the demand for particular types of building or obtain data on categories of customers within the market. Market research will allow firms to identify suitable target segments of the market.

The use of marketing research in construction may appear to be extensive, at least potentially. However, Moore [28] sees little scope for it, in certain contexts. While the consumer goods industries can use market research to estimate demand closely, establish correct pricing, alter design to customers' needs and make the product more competitive, the contractor, other than those in house building, can do none of these things. Rather, the contractor has to contract according to the design of the consultants and price their requirements. If a strength of the business firm lies in its marketing prowess, the ability to identify new and profitable market segments through effective market research is an important element.

6. Marketing of services

One definition of a service views it as 'any activity or benefit that one party can offer to another that is essentially intangible and does not result in the ownership of anything. Its production may or may not be tied to a physical product.' [29] Furthermore, unlike a product which is produced and then consumed, a service is consumed as it is being produced [30].

There is a basic question as to whether or not there is sufficient difference between the marketing of goods and the marketing of services to warrant separate attention. However, the differences between goods and services themselves are highlighted when the following features of services are outlined.

- *Intangibility:* one cannot physically touch a service and it can also be difficult for the mind to grasp. Services therefore can also be mentally intangible.
- *Heterogeneity:* services cannot be standardized in the same manner as goods because services are performed and there is always a human element involved. A service is always subject to some variation in performance.
- *Perishability:* services cannot be produced before they are required and then stored to meet demand.
- *Inseparability of production and consumption:* a service is generally consumed while it is being performed and usually consumers are actively involved in the performance of the service they are using.

Rushton and Carron [31] take the view that neither goods nor services are marketed. What is marketed is a bundle of benefits with both tangible and intangible features. Kotler [32] offers a range of four categories wherein the service component varies in amount from a pure service to a pure tangible good, and the service element is either in the majority or just playing an accompanying part in the product.

A product can become both mentally and physically intangible and thus marketing becomes necessary, with a need to clarify the service for customers. Both goods and services possess tangible and intangible benefits; accordingly marketing will assist customers' evaluation of products.

The traditional controllable decision areas in marketing incorporate the four Ps of the marketing mix, product, price, promotion and place (distribution), together with planning and control. When applied to the marketing of services, these variables are seen to require a different blend in order to produce the response which the firm wants in the market [33]:

1. *Product:* services marketing requires discernible substitutes for evaluation of the intangible whenever possible. Product features and benefits are difficult to recognize in respect of the intangibility of services. Most services are supplied by people and this human element may require more 'man management, people skill and probably greater liaison with personnel and industrial relations, than with a tangible product'.
2. *Price:* customers may often perceive a stronger association between price and quality for services than for goods.

   As skill and expertise need to have values placed upon them, it is difficult to cost a service constituent. In some cases one will not know what is involved with the service until it is completed.
3. *Promotion:* a service commodity cannot be displayed because it has no physical presence. This means that it depends largely on promotional activity and material to provide an image. Promoting the service organization is one way of helping to make the intangible tangible, although it involves something different than creating an image for a tangible product. Services cannot be held in stock, in tandem with high and low demand periods, as can goods. Services therefore require promotion which spreads demand as well as creating it.
4. *Place:* having no goods to store or distribute, services producers will not typically have a physical distribution system. A vital ingredient in the overall marketing mix of most, if not all, services is the site at which the service is performed. Facilities location decisions are therefore marketing rather than operating decisions.
5. *Planning and control:* service products cannot be controlled in the same way as tangible products either in terms of what is provided to the customer or in terms of what is 'received' by the customer. Individuals function differently from day to day, with their output unable to be controlled in the same way as can machines. There is also less control over the service as it is acquired by the client. The customer will assist in determining the quality of service received from his input of information.

Marketing an intangible is vital in winning construction orders within an environment which seems to exemplify the views that services are overwhelmingly people-based and that if people are alright, the majority of other components will be correct also.

However, it would seem that the construction industry is not entirely a service industry. Apart from speculative house building, which can be likened to the proverbial 'can of beans' on the vendor's shelf, the industry is a mixture of service and product. In effect an expectation is, in many instances, marketed. The customer is given to expect a certain product, based usually on either price, time or quality, in combination or total of all three. The marketer will promote this expectation which he or she has promoted and offered for sale. The services of an architect in the form of drawings, specifications and reports is evidence that the client's expectation will be fulfilled at some later, specified, date when the product is handed over. The contractor in his or her promotional guise will, in terms of place, present an image from premises, plant and offices.

Cowell [34] states that within a service business there will not normally be found the following functions: procurement, production, warehousing, engineering, security, distribution, quality control, and research and development. While this may be a further indication that the construction industry is not entirely services orientated, the example of marketing for professional firms within the industry highlights the position of the services input. For example, the quantity surveying (QS) firm typifies the specialized marketing requirements of an organization which provides professional services to the construction industry.

In common with the marketing of products, the QS firm, with its objective of finding its niche within the total market, will employ the following six methods to aim at its chosen market segment [35]:

1. Establishing the target market will initially require the internal management audit which demonstrates the company's requisite skills. The firm will decide on a segmentation or specialization policy aimed at, for example geographical areas or a concentration on highly specialized sectors of the market.
2. The particular problems associated with quantity surveying marketing arise from the nature of the services provided by the firm, and these must be understood. There is the general 'problem' associated with the marketing of services, intangibility. Also, the question arises as to how the services offered by one firm can be tested against a competitor. The client is buying a building rather than the quantity surveying firm's services, and although the methods of producing that building may be similar, each contract is unique. Given the above, image building within the chosen market segment is imperative.
3. A client profile based on information from previous contracts would outline groups of regular, occasional, lost and potential clients, and failed offers, this analysis of clients within the chosen segment being based on frequency of awarded contracts.

4. A client is initially and irresistibly concerned with obtaining 'efficient procurement of construction' and not quantity surveying services as such. The firm thus has to convince the client of how valuable the quantity surveying service is to him or her and, in particular, how the firm is superior to its competitors.
5. Promoting the company creates an awareness in prospective clients while attempting to persuade them to use the firm's services. It may also correct false impressions about the service or the company. The methods utilized are those widely used by marketers of products in general, and include: personal selling; sales promotion through direct mail and brochures; publicity from exhibitions; and advertising either generally or selectively. Image building is of course a prime objective of promotion in a professional service organization.
6. Feedback and control is essential for all marketing, generally through the marketing audit, with the typical restatement and refinement which control systems provide.

It is clear that there are differences between the marketing of goods and services, but also similarities which necessitate the use of certain marketing tools for companies in all industries.

7. The marketing of marketing

The position of marketing within a company is largely determined by the firm's orientation towards, say, production, sales or marketing. There are five distinct functions involved in the operations of a business. One of them is likely to be dominant and may thus cause the firm to be orientated towards that function. Each of the following is a stereotype which, however, contains a sufficient element of truth to indicate that a predisposition to any one, will importantly affect the firm's reaction to its environment.

7.1 Technology orientation

An emphasis upon research and development or technology is to be found in many companies and comprises the following five key features:

1. Emphasis is on research and engineering *per se*, with little recognition of economic considerations.
2. Market criteria to guide research and development are inadequate or non-existent.
3. The product is considered to be the responsibility of the technical organization, with little product planning influence from marketing.
4. There is a tendency to overengineer products to satisfy internal inclinations, or even whims, beyond what the customer needs or is willing to pay for.

5. Basic development, product and facility decisions are often made between engineering and manufacturing management, without marketing participation.

7.2 Production orientation

This is the classic orientation in economies where demand exceeds supply:

1. The factory floor is considered to be the business.
2. The focus and emphasis are on making products.
3. Little attention is given to marketing research and product planning.
4. There is a tendency to base price on cost and cost alone, with value and competitive considerations largely ignored.
5. Cost reduction efforts may sacrifice product quality, product performance and customer service.
6. The role of the sales organization is to sell whatever the factory chooses to make.
7. If customers aren't happy, the salesmen are told to go out and find new ones.

7.3 Sales orientation

This is often confused with a marketing orientation because it places heavy emphasis on customer considerations; however, it has fundamental differences. Its major features include the following:

1. The focus is on volume, not on profit.
2. The prevailing point of view is that the customer should be given whatever he wants, regardless of the cost to the business.
3. There tends to be a weak linkage between true customer needs and wants and the planning of products to be offered.
4. Pricing, credit, and service policies tend to be loose.
5. Production scheduling is overinfluenced by subjective estimates from the field force.
6. Market guidance of engineering and manufacturing is commonly inadequate.

7.4 Financial orientation

This orientation frequently prevails without being clearly recognized. Its dominance may be indirect, through the influence of the accounting, auditing, and treasury personnel on general management decisions. During the 1980s this orientation was much more pervasive than it used to be and has been severely criticized by authors such as Hayes and

Abernathy, who believe that this orientation has been responsible for much of the loss in economic vigour in many western industrialized economies in the post-World War II period. The five key features of the orientation are as follows:

1. The emphasis tends to be on short-range profit at the expense of growth and longer-range profit.
2. Budgeting and forecasting frequently preempt business planning.
3. Efficiency may outrank effectiveness as a management criterion.
4. Pricing, cost, credit, service and other policies may be based on false economy influences and lack of marketplace realism.
5. The business focus is not on the customer and market but on internal considerations and numbers.

7.5 Marketing orientation

The five basic features of this orientation are as follows:

1. The focus is on the marketplace – customers, competitors, and distribution.
2. A commercial intelligence system monitors the market.
3. It requires recognition that change is inevitable, but manageable in the business arena.
4. The business is committed to strategic business and marketing planning, and to creative product planning.
5. The emphasis is on profit not just volume, with growth and profit kept in balance.

These business functions should be coordinated to achieve the overall objectives. However, in practice, interdepartmental relations and rivalries damage this necessary integration of functional activities. Some departments, often manufacturing, finance and research and development do not wish to see the expansion of marketing because it jeopardizes their power in the organization.

Marketers argue [36] for a customer orientation in which all functions cooperate in order to satisfy customers' needs and wants. To fulfil the role of providing customer satisfaction, the company requires that the marketing function assumes the important integration role of harmonizing the customer with other organizational functions such as production, finance and personnel. In order to carry out this role, marketing needs to be able to control and influence these other departments, thus explaining the resistance resulting from within the organization.

General management pursues different goals, including attainment of profit, consumer satisfaction, prestige, etc., each of which may conflict with one another [37]. As functional groups develop their own interests and strategies, the marketing department has to be sufficiently powerful to impose its influence on other departments. The marketing function thus has to deal simultaneously with its internal and external markets, and the success of the latter is highly dependent on that of the former.

Generally speaking, the marketing function is created after the other functions and has to establish its own variability or legitimacy. This is made even more difficult if, as is often the case, marketing managers are not given an advanced role in the organization's hierarchy.

An internal marketing strategy tries to create enthusiasm, in services firms particularly, wherein a large number of employees are in direct personal contact with customers. The internal marketing of marketing is seen to be necessary given the weak position of the marketing function within service firms, and the lack of hierarchial power for the marketing manager. The basic condition is that the marketing function carries sufficient weight inside the firm to create an effective general customer orientation. This internal power is therefore directed at the external and internal markets to attempt to influence them simultaneously.

The marketing manager, generally, should work through persuasion rather than authority in order to convince all departments to work together to satisfy customer needs and expectations. However, given the internal interactions and pressures on the marketing function, in order to sustain the company's position in the market the marketing department may require to utilize means other than persuasion to market internally. Manipulation, authority and coercion are means which may need to be used because of the frequent division which exists between marketing and other functions.

8. The marketing unit

Marketing orientation is not simply a particular framework for an organization chart. It is the organizational structure adopted by the marketing department but also, vitally, the use of that orientation as a management philosophy.

Marketing departments, as units, can be organized by functions, products, geographical regions or types of customers [38] [39].

8.1 Functional organization

The most common form of marketing organization comprises functional marketing specialists reporting to a marketing executive manager who coordinates their activities. Such specialist functions would include, sales, advertising and promotions, distribution, product development, market research and customer relations.

This structure is seen to work effectively for the smaller firm with a centralized marketing operation, but coordination of managers in larger decentralized organizations becomes problematical, especially where products and types of customers are diverse.

8.2 Product organization

Where the organization produces and markets varied products, the functional approach may be inappropriate and if there are large numbers of different products the functional form may be unable to cope.

A product manager supervises several product group managers, who in turn supervise product managers in charge of specific products. There is an inbuilt flexibility from this form of marketing organization. Marketing mixes can be developed for each product and each product manager can react more quickly to changes in his specific product marketplace. Disadvantages include the duplication of marketing activities by different product groups and the situation where product managers become experts in their product but rarely become experts in any functions.

8.2 Organizing geographically

The large company which markets its products nationally, and perhaps internationally, may organize its marketing activities along geographical lines. All regional marketing managers report to their regional marketing manager, and managers of marketing functions for each region report to their regional marketing manager. This organizational form is especially appropriate where the company has customers whose characteristics and requirements vary a great deal between regions.

8.3 Customer-type organization

This organizational form is effective where the firm has different and differing groups of customers, in respect of their needs and problems. For example, a manufacturer may sell products to retailers, wholesalers and institutions. The marketing activities and decisions for these customers will vary, perhaps appreciably.

The marketing manager for each customer group reports to the top-level marketing executive while directing most marketing activities for his group. Usually, there will be a marketing manager for each of the various marketing functions, and he will supervise the activities of marketing products to a specific customer group.

'Proper implementation of a marketing plan depends on the co-ordination of marketing activities, the motivation of personnel who perform those activities and the effectiveness of communication within the marketing unit.' [40] Marketing managers require to work closely with other functional managers within the organization to ensure the harmonization of marketing with these other functions. Integration of marketing activities with those of relevant external organizations is also a necessary coordinating function, for example with wholesalers, retailers, advertisers, etc.

In order to motivate marketing personnel towards high levels of performance, marketing managers are obliged to identify the goals of employees and provide rewards with some means of goal at attainment. Marketing managers can neither coordinate nor motivate without good communication. Marketing managers are required to communicate with the organization's top-level management and personnel at the operations level also. Marketing personnel need to communicate with production staff. An information system within the marketing unit, and between it and other departments, would be patently beneficial.

The modern marketing department has followed a long process of evolution from the simple sales department, and yet a company with a modern marketing department is not necessarily a modern marketing company. It is only by integration of all other functional departments into a combined approach and philosophy which directs its efforts towards the customer that it will become so.

9. Small firms

As a very large number of construction contracting companies in the United Kingdom are considered to be small businesses, marketing issues need to be applied to these companies also. In the main, the necessity to plan the firm's future progress or expansion in its development, within the business strategy frame, applies to all sizes of business organization. Random development rather than directional planning, can be harmful to every size of company.

Every firm needs customers or clients. If an opportunity is required to sell a good or service, some level of marketing is essential in order to explicate the 'article'.

Small firms have obvious different characteristics from large companies, including scale and scope of operations, ownership and management style and their state of independence [41]. The lack of financial resources is an inhibiting factor for small firms, which is problematical, not least in their undercapitalization.

Style of management is highlighted by the situation where specialists will not be employed. This will therefore mean that, as no marketing manager exists, the owner of the small firm becomes his own 'expert' in this field, as in other areas of the business for these, typically family-owned, concerns. Three broad types of constraint on marketing may therefore be highlighted, namely, limited resources, lack of specialist expertise and a limited impact on the marketplace, factors which in themselves 'define' the small firm. Once a decision has been made for a firm (any firm) to accept the philosophy of marketing, the methods used to instigate its techniques will vary according to a number of components, including the size of the firm, although the basic problems to be solved and decisions to be taken are unlikely to be very different across all sizes of organizations. It will not require many meetings, discussions or consultation procedures with the directors, or sizeable numbers of staff, who operate within medium-sized or large firms. The marketing function within small companies will be covered, as an additional responsibility, by a top manager who will probably be a director.

However, every general contracting company regardless of size, will require the basic functions of estimating, tendering, production, accounts, surveying and purchasing, although in small firms there may not be separate managers for each function. The marketing function will therefore 'take its chance' as an additional duty here also, although in any event a considerable volume of transactions arise from personal contacts with satisfied and prospective clients.

10. Competitiveness

A company needs to be noticed, distinguishable or even conspicuous. Until the firm is known to a potential client, nothing happens except by chance and the object of marketing is to reduce that likelihood by providing the potential customer with information to allow him to make a choice. However, there are those managers who wait for things to happen, those who hope that nothing happens, those who have no idea of what is happening and those who make things happen. It is within the market-place that firms will assume differing positions of competitiveness, given their size, differentiation, amount of available resources and their object-ives. Kotler [42] and Baker [43] highlight the diverse competitive positions which firms will occupy:

1. *Dominant:* this firm controls the behaviour of other competitors and has a wide choice of strategic options. It would be a very rare situation that would be monopolistic or strongly protected technological leadership.
2. *Strong:* this firm can take independent action without harming its long-term position which it can preserve irrespective of competitors' actions. Strong competitors can usually, therefore, pursue their chosen strategies with relative ease.
3. *Favourable:* this firm has a strength which is exploitable in particular strategies, and has an above-average opportunity to improve its posi-tion. In fragmented industries with no distinct competitor, these favourably positioned firms tend to be leaders.
4. *Tenable:* this firm performs satisfactorily at a level which warrants carrying on in business. It exists at the sufferance of the dominant company and has a below-average chance of improving its position. Profitability can be maintained through specialization.
5. *Weak:* this firm's unsatisfactory performance, albeit with improvement potential, means it must either change or exist. It may either be too small to compete effectively or big and inefficient.
6. *Non-viable:* this firm has unsatisfactory performance and no opportun-ity for improvement.

It follows, that within a target market firms will adopt competitive positions which are, first of all, decided by their location within the industry. A firm may be a market leader, a challenger to a leader, or if unwilling or unable to challenge that leader, will be a follower. Small companies or small divisions of large firms may specialize in parts of a market where they are not in competition with larger firms.

The firm will specialize along market, customer, product or marketing-mix lines in occupying a market niche. Marketing strategies are highly dependent on which one of the following four competitive positions the firm occupies: leader; challenger; follower; or nicher. A market leader will either wish to expand the total market, protect his market share or expand that share. The challenger will forcefully attempt to expand its market share from other firms in the industry, including the leader. A market follower will not create a disturbance lest it loses more than it gains. Its strategy will aim at using its expertise to participate in the growth of the market. The nicher is a small firm which operates in these specialized parts of the market to which larger firms are unlikely to be attracted.

The firm's competitive position is established by a combination of its market share and other factors resulting from past strengths and weaknesses, and competitive economics.

A firm's competitive differential advantage must be identified and signalled to the market segments within which it operates. Those strengths may lie in areas of competence which provide a competitive edge, such as a particular skill, resource, facility, expertise or combination of them. Potential clients must be made aware of these strengths and a continuous monitoring, reviewing and developing of the firm's competence must be carried out, as in time it is likely that they will be copied by other firms.

Kotler [44] uses Ansoff's framework to examine intensive growth strategies – those strategies of integration and diversification in pursuit of growth towards closing the strategic planning gap that is the difference between the desired and expected sales of the firm. However in reviewing the performance of its existing business, the firm considers three major intensive growth strategies.

Market penetration is the strategy employed by the firms in seeking increased sales for its present products in its present markets through more aggressive promotion and distribution. Market development is where the company pursues increased sales by taking its present products into new markets. Where the firm attempts to increase its sales by developing improved products for its present markets, this is seen as a product development strategy. The marketing role therefore assumes great importance for those firms wishing to improve performance without entering the fields of acquisitions and diversification.

Within an industry are firms which, if a company were monitoring, would be perceived as competitors. 'A company's competitors include these seeking to satisfy the same customers and customer needs and making similar offers to them.' [45] The company needs to know the strategies of competitors in order to determine which firms are its closest rivals, and act accordingly. It also needs to be aware of competitors' objectives so as to anticipate their future movements. Knowing competitors' strengths and weaknesses enables the company to improve its own strategy, enabling it to benefit from competitor weakness and take avoiding action where competition is strong. The reaction pattern of competitors should also be known to the company as this helps it to time and choose its moves. Some firms react quickly to moves by an adversary. Others react only to certain situations, some only to incursions on their own ground and others have no predictable reaction pattern: 'Market signals are indirect means of communicating in the marketplace, and most if not all of a competitor's behaviour can carry information that can aid in competitor analysis and strategy formulation.' [46]

The firm must thus carry out an objective assessment of competitors and what they can offer in their particular skills, how they promote themselves and the quality of all areas of staffing. The firm's own performance is then compared against these standards and competitor weaknesses exploited. Any weakness shown in the firm's own performance standards must be improved until they become strengths which they have to be marketed as such to clients and potential clients.

11. Discussion

Marketing is seen as trying to establish what the market needs and wants, and what it is prepared to pay. Selling ensures that the firm gets the opportunity to meet that need. For construction companies, it is not sufficient to ask a price for a job; the firm must set out its previous experience, particular expertise, current workload, and convey enthusiasm and credibility to the prospective client.

It has in the past been noted that marketing was not widely accepted by building industry contractors, except those engaged in speculative house building [47]. The industry has been slow to accept the marketing concept and until the late 1970s at least, failed to grasp the functions of marketing. Construction companies, on the whole, were unable to perceive how marketing would fit into the management process and how it could assist in working towards achieving the company's objectives. Numerous reasons are put forward for this unwillingness to accept the marketing function: the construction industry is claimed to be unique, there are differences between buildings and consumer durables, the nature and terms of investment are different, building construction involves artificial addition and alteration to the environment [48].

Further reasons suggested for the industry's disinclination to accept the marketing concept include the following [49]:

1. Confusion in the industry as to the meaning of marketing and where it begins and ends in terms of the firm.

2. Contractors failing to appreciate that the adoption of marketing would lead to increased profitability or reduced risk.
3. A belief by contractors that if the services and end products are good enough they are sufficient to sell the firm to future clients. Contractors tend to be product, not consumer, oriented.
4. A belief by contractors that the industry is a service industry and therefore cannot create demand. This belief is further entrenched by the fact that the building is commissioned by the client and its subsequent design is under the control of the architect.
5. The erratic nature of public sector spending in the industry which makes future planning and forecasting difficult or impossible.
6. The argument that the structure of the industry has hindered the penetration of marketing ideas since it is effectively an agglomeration of service firms who, while loosely connected, are only used infrequently by clients.
7. There are few established procedures relating to marketing in the industry.
8. The construction industry is basically conservative.
9. Contracting companies are prone to bankruptcy.

A number of these reasons have been disputed. In terms of the distinction between a service, and product orientation, it is argued that both are important in construction marketing. Companies therefore have the advantages associated with both service and product-related marketing techniques. It has been argued that the widespread use of both selective and negotiated tendering, and the subsequent requirement for pre-qualification evaluation by the client or architect, has provided contractors with a greater opportunity to market themselves and increase their prospects of being included on tender lists. Moore has also suggested that erratic public expenditure by government within the construction industry is an inadequate area to be put forward as a reason for a lack of forward planning and adoption of marketing techniques. Changes in public sector demand can affect other industries also, and those industries are capable and willing to implement forward planning procedures.

Bell [49] has indicated that the marketing function is being accepted by contractors in the construction industry and, for example, that function may be diffused among a number of the firm's senior personnel. The essence of a number of short studies [50] reinforces Bell's views. Segmentation, customer and competitor evaluation, market research, promotion and image building, and a general link to overall strategic management are of significant importance to larger firms. For larger companies, all departments are expected to agree with marketing policy and support it.

Smaller companies' views of the marketing function, in these studies, take on an understandably different course. Bell's study was restricted to contracting companies with more than 500 employees, although the majority of firms in the construction industry are within the small- to medium-size range. These smaller firms are in many cases seen to employ marketing activities and to perceive product diversification as essential for long-term survival. Marketing is essential for this expansion and other factors of importance are public relations, extending market share and development and training staff in order to keep abreast with innovation and produce the necessary dynamism within the firm.

There is, however, a remaining apathy towards advertising as a method of promoting smaller firms. In general, small firms formulate a plan which incorporates some level of marketing. Larger companies ranging from medium to large diversified companies require, and today often have, a marketing strategy. The marketing process commences after the corporate plan has been produced and subsequently feeds back into the strategic management process.

Business organizations in all industries have to make themselves visible to potential clients. They must let themselves be known and distinguished by association with their particular competencies and must continually develop these particular strengths. Even if these can be copied by competitors in the long-run, it is marketing which converts potential clients into new customers and retains existing clients.

However a commitment by all to the marketing philosophy is essential, and making things happen rather than waiting for them to happen is fundamental in bringing together the manufacturer and user, the vendor and purchaser of goods and services.

References

1. Baker, M. J. (1985) *Marketing Strategy and Management*. Macmillan, p. 15.
2. McDonald, M. and Gattorna, J. (1985) *'Marketing', Essential Guides for Managers*, 4 BIM, Gee and Co.
3. Perreault, W. D. and McCarthy, E. J. (1954) *Basic Marketing*, Richard D. Irwin Inc.
4. Slater, A. G. (1981) International Marketing: *The Role of Physical Distribution Management*. Institute of Marketing.
5. Pride, W. M. and Ferrell, O. C. (1985) *Marketing: Basic Concepts and Decisions*, 4th edn. Houghton Mifflin Company, p. 13.
6. Perreault, W. D. and McCarthy, E. J. *op. cit.*
7. Perreault, W. D. and McCarthy, E. J. *op. cit.*
8. Baker, M. J., *op. cit.*, p. 45.
9. Kotler, P. (1988) *Marketing Management: Analysis, Planning, Implementation and Control*, 6th edn. Prentice-Hall International, p. 279.
10. Hlavacek, J. D. and Reddy, N. M., (1986) 'Identifying and qualifying industrial market segments', *European Journal of Marketing*, 20.2.
11. David, F. R. (1986) *Fundamentals of Strategic Management*. Merrill, p. 262.
12. David, F. R. *op. cit.*
13. Hlavacek, J. D. and Reddy, N. M. *op. cit.* p. 8.
14. David, F. R. *op. cit.*
15. Baker, M. J. *op. cit.* p. 150.

16. Kotler, R. *op. cit.*, p. 286.
17. Pride, W. M. and Ferrell, O. C. *op. cit.*, p. 46.
18. Pride, W. M. and Ferrell, O. C. *op. cit.*, p. 35.
19. Hlavacek, J. D. and Reddy, N. M. *op. cit.*, p. 18.
20. Wilson, A. (1985) 'Target your market priorities to maximise marketing effort.' *Contract Journal*, 14 March.
21. Dickinson, R., Herbst, A. and O'Shaughnessy, J. (1986) 'Marketing concept and customer orientation', *European Journal of Marketing*, **20.10.**
22. Pride, W. M. and Ferrell, O. C. *op. cit.*, p. 74.
23. Wilson, A. 'Key customers provide focus for organised marketing effort.' *Contract Journal*, 8 August, p. 14.
24. Wilson, A. *op. cit.*, p. 15.
25. Pride, W. M. and Ferrell, O. C. *op. cit.,,* p. 547.
26. Pride, W. M. and Ferrell, O. C. *op. cit.*, p. 559.
27. Baker, M. J. *op. cit..* p. 186.
28. Moore, A. B. (1984) *Marketing Management in Construction. A Guide for Contractors.* Butterworth, Surrey, p. 12.
29. Cowell, D. (1988) *The Marketing of Services.* Heinemann, p. 23.
30. Cowell, D. *op. cit.*, p. 93.
31. Rushton, A. M. and Carson, D. J. (1985) 'The marketing of services: Managing the intangibles'. *European Journal of Marketing*, **19.3,** p. 26.
32. Kotler, R. *op. cit.*, p. 477.
33. Rushton, A. M. and Carson, D. J., *op. cit.*
34. Cowell, D. *op. cit.*, p. 2.
35. Greenhalgh, B. (1987) 'Marketing and the Q.S.' *Chartered Quantity Surveyor*, July, p. 24.
36. Kotler, R. *op. cit..*, p. 24.
37. Flipo, J. P. (1986) 'Service firms: Interdependence of external and internal marketing strategies'. European Journal of Marketing, **20.8.**
38. Pride, W. M. and Ferrell, O. C. *op. cit.*
39. Kotler, R. *op. cit.*
40. Pride, W. M. and Ferrell, O. C. *op. cit.*, p. 590.
41. Carson, D. J. (1985) 'The evolution of marketing in small firms'. *European Journal of Marketing*, **19.5,** p. 7.
42. Kotler, R. *op. cit.*, p. 318.
43. Baker, M. J. *op. cit.*, p. 49.
44. Kotler, R. *op. cit.*, p. 47.
45. Kotler, R. *op. cit.*, p. 254.
46. Porter, M. E. (1980) *Competitive Strategy: Techniques for Analyzing Industries and Competitors.* The Free Press, p. 45.
47. Moore, A. B. *op. cit.*
48. Moore, A. B. *op. cit.*
49. Bell, R. (1981) 'Marketing and the larger construction firm.' Occasional Paper No. 22. Chartered Institute of Building.
50. Heriot-Watt University, Dept of Building Engineering and Surveying. Various unpublished papers. R. K. Stocks.

—— 4 ——

Organizational innovation and development

Peter R. Lansley

Summary

This chapter reviews the implications of a conventional Schumpertian perspective of innovation for construction organizations. It highlights the differences between technological and organizational innovation, between process and product innovation and the contribution of these different types to competitiveness. Particular issues addressed are the existence of long waves in the economy as a reflection of different levels of innovative activity, the influence of markets on the level of innovation, and the importance of entrepreneurs and business leaders. Evidence from the construction industry is discussed with special reference to research work on the commercial success of contracting organizations.

1. Introduction

The ability of the construction industry to achieve even modest levels of innovation has been a feature of the debate on the effectiveness of the industry since at least the 1920s. The debate reflects both the realities of the industry, which in many of its activities is slow to change, and some fundamental misunderstandings about the nature of the industry and of where innovation might be found within it.

The debate has taken different orientations: macro-economic, political and contextual factors, the development of the industry, inter- and intra-industry relationships, change and innovation within firms and the role of the individual and groups in developing new products and processes. This has produced a range of perspectives that is both rich and confusing. In construction, innovation occurs largely at the level of individual work processes on specific projects, rather than at some total system level. Innovation is seen to take place when practices are so new that traditional design and construction operations which follow a set pattern are replaced by new approaches requiring deliberate and informed management and control. Also, the project-based context of construction provides opportunities for innovation and risks and rewards which are quite different from those of non-project-based industries.

The aim of this chapter is to provide a brief review of one common view of innovation and to consider the experience of the construction industry in the light of this perspective.

Although much of this review relates to innovation in general terms, it is useful to distinguish organizational innovation from technological innovation.

A straightforward example of technological innovation is that of a machine, which in its development utilizes new knowledge or techniques to provide an article or service at a lower cost or with higher quality. However, organizational innovation can take forms which do not require technological advances, for example the establishment of new kinds of business organization, e.g. the change from unitary to multidimensional forms of organization among large corporations in the 1930s. In construction, examples of organizational innovation are new forms of contract (e.g. design and build), the opening up of new markets and major government initiatives in controlling demand and managing R & D (e.g. the establishment of the Building Research Station and the National Building Agency). Naturally, the dividing line between technology and organization is vague, but the latter can be usefully considered in terms of management as a social technology, working with attitudes, values and behaviours.

It is also customary to distinguish between product innovation and process innovation. Product innovations are advances in technology which result in superior products. In some cases these may have a low dependence on hardware, the innovation being the better utilization of resources. An example of an organizational product innovation would be the development and application of project network systems such as CPA and PERT.

Process innovations result in substantial increases in efficiency, but without a significant advance in technology. An example of low-hardware-dependence organizational process innovation might be found in the application of enhanced quality control methods, and improved staff appraisal systems.

2. Long waves

The processes of invention, innovation and utilization were not studied systematically until the end of the nineteenth century, when a significant contribution to the theory of innovation and the role of the entrepreneur was offered by Schumpeter [1].

Schumpeter's basic premise was that significant economic changes were triggered by major inventions and the innovator and entrepreneur were key figures in creating employment and wealth. He referred to such changes as the alpha-innovation stage in which rapid growth occurred as the result of the invention, drawing heavily on labour and material resources. These innovations set new standards, for example in the design of products and in industrial processes, by drawing on advancing but existing technologies and thereby creating new composite technologies or end products. Although this alpha stage growth eventually slowed down there were many spin-off developments which sustained the impact of the initial innovation. This was the beta-innovation stage. Eventually, however, competitive forces led to an oversupply of the benefits of the innovation, thereby neutralizing its impact and, as a result, growth.

Schumpeter's theory drew heavily on, and provided an explanation for, the long-term cycles in economic activity which had been identified by the Russian economist Kondratiev and even earlier by others. Schumpeter suggested that the first 'Kondratiev Cycle' represented the Industrial Revolution with an upswing commencing in 1790 and peaking in 1826. This arose from the invention of steam power. The second cycle (1845–76) arose from improvements in communications – railways and steamships, and the third cycle (1895–1929) from the generation of cheap electricity and motors which could use electricity and from the invention of the automobile. A fourth cycle appears to have commenced around 1950, peaking in the late-1960s and to have been triggered by advances in computers, aircraft design and synthetic polymers.

While Schumpeter's work identified the role of the entrepreneur in creating wealth and in founding business empires, he clearly distinguished the entrepreneur's role as a managerial decision-maker from that of inventor; his later thinking was modified by changes in the organization of the business enterprise which took place in the mid-twentieth century. The role of the individual entrepreneur was supplemented by corporations which provided new managerial and technological roles and which together contributed to invention and innovation in different ways.

Although in recent years Schumpeter's work has been criticized, especially the implication that investment in scientific effort leads to innovative success (a closely held belief of research funding agencies in the immediate post World War II period), it did provide a starting point for many studies of long wave cycles and of the stimulus of technological innovation to change.

3. Long waves and construction

Evidence of long waves in construction activity is well established and has been studied in the United Kingdom by Lewis [2], who considered the building economy since the early-1700s and in the United States by Abramovitz [3] who considered long waves in construction from the end of the American Civil War. Both identified the historical period of these waves to be between 15 and 25 years, rather than the 50 years of the Kondratiev cycle. The waves were associated with economic shocks arising from wars, famines, population changes, the supply of finance and credit, and inflation. They were characterized by very large or protracted upswings lasting between 5 and 15 years, followed by extended periods of stagnation or decline.

While Abramovitz was able to link aggregate construction activity for the United States with overall industrial activity, the findings of Lewis in the United Kingdom were much more complex, due to leads and lags between different types of construction activity and overall economic activity. Lewis highlighted the importance of social and managerial innovations in the form of industrialization and urbanization, new forms of financing (e.g. joint stock acts and the emergence of building societies) which led to a move away from individuals to institutions being the suppliers of finance and to the eventual emergence of the property developer as financier and speculator. These innovations, which took place largely in the external business environment of the industry, can be viewed as serving principally to have shaped the market in which the industry operated, rather than coming from the industry itself.

4. Diffusion

Rogers [4] has suggested that the market for innovation can be considered in terms of the willingness of potential users to experiment with new ideas. A small proportion are keen to test new ideas. These, representing the leading edge of industry, are termed 'innovators'. A rather larger proportion, the early adopters, follow after monitoring the experience of the innovators. The vast majority of potential users fall into the categories of early and late majorities, leading to the laggards, those who resolutely resist change.

Work in construction by Fredriksson and Larsson [5] supports the general validity of the diffusion model with regard to innovation on site, with the 'normal' curve applying for straightforward innovations where clear advantages can be seen and where substitution of a new method for an existing method can take place. Where advantages are not clear and require more complex judgements (e.g. on the economics of form work systems), or the development of new skills and knowledge (e.g. flowing concrete), the pattern of diffusion can be very irregular. Indeed, in practice the pattern can diverge quite markedly. Innovations can 'run out of steam', be modified by the market and in turn their markets can change.

5. Markets

The work of Schumpeter emphasized the role of the innovator and entrepreneur, and particularly the role of new technology. But while growth was seen to be both stimulated and caused by technological innovation (i.e. technology push), the pull of the market for new products and processes was also shown to play a significant role in generating innovations (i.e. market pull). A construction example of market pull is given by Lea [6] who cites some of the very earliest building research as focusing on insulation for steam pipes and cold stores, where the economic incentive was strong. However, while Utterback [7] found that between 60 and 80% of important innovations occurred in response to market pull, a detailed review by Parker [8] suggested a more complex picture. Necessity is the mother of invention, and at times there are great men of genius, but much new knowledge comes from a cumulative synthesis of what has come before and of insight leading to the resolution of existing 'discontinuities', of technology building on technology.

Further, Hayes and Abernathy [9] suggest that the observed weightings towards the large proportion of innovations derived from market pull could be partly due to a dependence of business on market pull strategies and a reluctance to engage in more speculative strategies: a result of a short-term focus on return on investment and cost reduction and of the analytical dependence of managers rather than insight from hands-on experience.

6. Technology push or market pull?

Generally, researchers in the field of innovation have suggested that the process is unpredictable and chaotic and that innovations often occur unexpectedly as a 'by-product' of innovation programmes with some other aim, or purely by chance. The relative importance of technology push and market pull varies in relation to such factors as pure chance, changes in market structure and industrial structure, demographics, new knowledge, changes in confidence, gestation periods, supply of finance and commercial opportunities. Stoneman [10] suggests that there is strong support for the view that new technologies which are expected to generate high profits diffuse faster than those with low profit expectations; technologies which are complicated and require large capital investment diffuse slower than cheap simple technologies; and that factors such as liquidity, market structure and supply difficulties influence the speed of diffusion.

7. Competition in construction

At a general level there are clear market pull factors in construction arising from the adoption of new and innovative designs and the increasing complexity of projects. Often the challenge of these projects is organizational rather than technical, with the £800 million Broadgate Project in the City of London providing many examples. A further market pull factor comes from the dynamics of competitive behaviour. Especially when markets are depressed, companies seek a competitive edge through cost reduction exercises and through providing new services to clients. While new technologies may be developed, in recent years competitive advantage has been sought through organizational innovation, such as new organization forms to satisfy new systems of procurement, increased emphasis on marketing and the development of ancillary services, especially those which contribute to a 'total service'. Clearly, if a company's market becomes threatened by other companies which have adopted a particular organizational innovation, that company is likely to adopt a similar innovation. Other examples of market pull are easy to find, especially from clients who are demanding more contractual options, new types of building and imposing new performance criteria on designers, consultants and contractors. Legislation concerning safety, the environment and pollution provide other examples of market pull factors. Building regulations are also a powerful influence.

8. High tech and technology push

Technology push can also be identified in the construction industry, for example in the building of The Crystal Palace and the Eiffel Tower and, a century later, the Renault Centre, the Lloyds Building and the Pompidou Centre. Obvious current examples relate to building services engineering (e.g. the intelligent building), robotics, CAD and other computer-based innovations. In some instances technology push has been introduced from other industries. A recent example of both technical innovation and organizational innovation is the use of pre-fabricated high-quality stainless steel toilet modules in the Lloyds building in London which were designed and constructed by a firm with its roots in aerospace, nuclear and process plant engineering, and who have little previous experience of building construction. Often, technology has come from overseas, in better designed products and more professional services, e.g. cladding, curtain walling, services engineering. Indeed, between 1979 and 1984 imports of construction materials and components rose by nearly 50% despite a depressed market – NEDO [11]. Among many basic building materials much of this growth was in products with a technological or design edge.

9. Resources

Clearly, supply and demand are a spur to innovation. For example, high building costs can stimulate a search for a new building design and high wages can lead to the development of labour saving methods. There is the need to reduce project-financing costs of capital locked up in work-in-progress, especially important for speculative work, and to avoid the problems arising from scarcity of labour and materials. This has led to indigenous materials being replaced by standard materials (e.g. bricks for stone), substitutions to take place (e.g. board for plaster) and increases in site pre-fabrication (e.g. timber, steel, services, ready mixed concrete). It has also led to the use of easier technologies which have often been developed outside the construction industry.

The state of the labour market has had a particular impact on the development of new building methods in some countries. Shortages of labour, especially skilled craftsmen, in post World War II France and Germany, and in Scandinavia, where climatic conditions have provided an added incentive, have been most important. On the other hand, in those countries which have had a surplus of labour and where labour has been relatively cheap, Italy and Spain, and to some extent the United Kingdom, the development of new materials and methods has proceeded more slowly.

10. Product and process innovation and long waves

A final insight into considering technology push and market pull, given by considering one of the overriding implications of the long wave theory, is that there are periods when innovation may be easier and more appropriate than others. For example, during periods of economic decline the need for rationalization through process innovation may be more pressing than in periods of recovery. Van Duijn [12] has shown that the product innovations which led to the emergence of new industries occur during that part of the wave where the economy is most favourable and when innovation is most required, the recovery phase. On the other hand, new product innovation in existing industries tends to occur at an earlier stage, during the depression phase, as a response to demand saturation, a better understanding of product life cycles and of the need to change technologies. Process innovations in existing industries are seen as responses to the need to meet demand increases during periods of prosperity and to accommodate cost increases during periods of recession and depression. Innovations in basic industrial sectors appear as a response to increasing demand from other sectors occurring largely during the prosperity phase (Table 4.1).

For construction, this suggests that innovative activities as a whole might be at their greatest during periods of depression and recovery, but during periods of prosperity and recession such activities would be largely focused on cost saving and productivity enhancement via process innovation.

This is entirely consistent with the results from empirical studies carried out by Ashridge Management College (Sadler *et al.* [13], Lee *et al.* [14], Lansley *et al.* [15]) which has shown that during the prosperous 1960s the commercial development of firms was through a focus on efficiency (i.e. process innovation) within the boundaries set by a quite limited range of

Table 4.1 The propensity to innovate during different phases of the
long wave

Type of innovation	Depression	Recovery	Prosperity	Recession
Product innovation (new industries)	+	++++	++	+
Product innovation (existing industries)	+++	+++	+	+
Process innovation (existing industries)	+++	+	++	++
Process innovation (basic industries)	+	++	+++	++

Source: van Duijn [12].

markets. In the 1970s period of depression, business development which
was linked with the adoption of highly flexible approaches to identifying
and exploiting new markets, to resource utilization and to the organization of work (i.e. product combined with process innovation), was much
more important. The 1980s' period of recovery has witnessed the substantial introduction of new technologies and approaches to organization, but
such an innovation surge appeared complete by the time the period of
prosperity had been reached in the late-1980s.

Further evidence of the fall off in innovative activity is given by
Uzomaka [16] who, drawing on his experience of UK industrial research
organizations, argues that when competition is low (i.e. periods of
prosperity) firms do not apply research, even though it could increase
their efficiency or financial performance. However, when it gives them a
competitive edge (e.g. in periods of depression) they become more
interested in research, although the picture is very complex. To a large
extent, technological innovation can be seen to be determined by the level
of innovativeness of the design professions, and the plant and equipment
sector, together with changing client needs. Each of these ingredients has
its own complex innovation cycle, which, when combined, leads to
uncertain forces for technological innovation while emphasizing the need
for high levels of organizational flexibility, for example in the contracting
firm.

Dosi [17] summarizes the technology and markets debate in the following way. New technologies (product innovations) emerge through an
interaction between complex economic forces (e.g. search for new profit
opportunities and new markets and pressure for cost saving), together
with powerful institutional factors (e.g. interests and structures of existing
firms, the effect of government agencies), while technical change (process
innovation) along established technological paths is much more endog-

enous to normal economic mechanisms. Periods of depression seem much more likely to generate a questioning and breaking of those paths.

11. Leaders

Schumpeter's work emphasized that the qualities of inventors and entrepreneurs are quite different. The qualities of the entrepreneur and the business leader have been defined as those of identifying opportunities, obtaining capital and taking the risks necessary to turn inventions into innovations. This stems from a belief, expressed by March and Simon [18], that policy-makers are more able to take a broader view than both those more closely involved with invention and those who are responsible for operational issues.

Research within organizations has suggested that organizational position and role influence innovative behaviour. For example, innovation adoption is strongly influenced by those with power, communication linkages, and with the ability to impose sanctions. Other work has suggested a link between innovativeness and length of service. It seems that long service enables the development of knowledge of how to handle political systems, and it provides legitimacy in its own right. Also, successful firms have long-serving executives due to the compatibility between organizational and personal values. In turn this provides organizations with continuity and latitude for managers to change the firm in response to changing environments.

Other factors include educational background, cosmopolitanism, perceived levels of personal risk by potential top management innovators, personality factors and organizational climate. Also, industrial environments (e.g. experience, education, productivity, growth) can strongly affect the types of managers found in senior management positions, and hence the potential innovativeness of firms.

Indeed, contextual factors such as the age of an industry do appear to be conditioning factors, such that the technical features of its processes may be more or less susceptible to improvement. For example, Salter [19] notes that industries which are more scientifically based possess greater capacity to benefit from technical change. From these findings, the expectation is that the production aspects of construction would be relatively slow in innovatory activities, while design activities would be more innovative.

12. Leaders in construction

Some of the most useful models for understanding personal styles of leadership are based on the twin concepts of employee or people centredness and task centredness (e.g. Blake and Mouton [20], and which accommodate a contingency view of leadership. For example, the selection of an appropriate style has to be judged against the type of work being carried out, the degree of clarity of the task and the associated uncertainties.

Although the relationship between leadership characteristics and innovative activity is complex, and in many cases it is difficult to disentangle the influence of contextual variables, the Ashridge studies mentioned earlier provide strong evidence that the commercial performance of construction firms and organizational innovation are related to styles of leadership. From these it appears that a people-oriented style is appropriate for uncertain and changing conditions, whereas strong task orientation may be more appropriate where tasks are well defined. Further, process innovation in the 1960s was shown by these studies to be facilitated by task-oriented styles, and product innovation in the 1970s by people and corporate-oriented styles. This latter factor, which represents and accords with currently popular notions of 'vision', was shown to have a significant impact on the climate for innovation and change.

13. Conclusion

The chapter has raised three important and recurrent themes in theories and research on innovation. First, there is the importance of the individual or institutional entrepreneur. Second, there is the apparent existence of long waves which reflect the impact of innovative activities on the economy and which carry with them implications for the type of innovation most likely to succeed during any particular phase of the cycle. Finally, there is the issue of technology push versus market pull.

Evidence concerning the construction industry is not extensive, but that which does exist suggests that the industry is largely reactive, shaped by opportunities and threats in its environment, and with innovative ideas from outside rather than from within. Market pull would appear to be a more dominant influence than technology push. The influence of the market, the supply of credit and the general economic climate seems more important in influencing the development of the industry than does research.

However, such a situation should not be taken at face value to imply that the industry is necessarily backward. It could be argued that the strength of the industry lies in its ability to develop competence in using many different types of materials and different technologies in order to adapt to changing conditions and demands. Instead of development work leading to 'hardware' innovations in products or processes, Fredriksson and Larsson [5] consider that the successful firm develops competence and flexibility in problem-solving and as an adopter of new technology developed by others.

For the practising manager, the implication of this broad view of innovation is that there are clear factors which influence the level of innovativeness over which the manager and his organization have some control. To a large extent these factors represent potential constraints to innovation, making it important for the manager to identify areas for innovation which are likely to have a greater probability of success, and of understanding how these probabilities are influenced by timing. There are periods when certain types of innovation can be achieved quite naturally, and others when they go very much against the affairs of the industry.

References

1. Schumpeter, J. A. (1939) *Business Cycles*, McGraw-Hill.
2. Lewis, J. P. (1965) *Building Cycles and Britain's Growth*. Macmillan.
3. Abramovitz, M. (1964) *Evidences of Long Swings in Aggregate Construction Since the Civil War*. National Bureau of Economic Research.
4. Rogers, E. M. (1962) *Diffusion of Innovation*. The Free Press of Glencoe.
5. Fredriksson, G. and Larson, B. (1984) 'Adoption of new technology in the contracting firm', in Handa, V. (ed.) *Organising and Managing Construction. Proceedings of International Symposium on Organisation and Management of Construction*, University of Waterloo.
6. Lea, F. M. (1971) *Science and Building*. HMSO.
7. Utterbuck, J. (1974) 'Innovation in industry and the diffusion of technology.' *Science*, February.
8. Parker, J. E. S. (1974) *The Economics of Innovation*. Longman.
9. Hayes, R. H. and Abernathy, W. J. (1980) 'Managing our way to economic decline.' *Harvard Business Review*, July–August.
10. Stoneman, P. I. (1985) 'Technological diffusion: The viewpoint of economic theory'. *Warwick Economic Research Paper No 270*, University of Warwick.
11. NEDO (1985) *Strategies for Construction R and D*, NEDO.
12. van Duijn, J. J. (1984) 'Fluctuations in innovations over time,' in Freeman, C. (ed.), *Long Waves in the World Economy*. Frances Pinter.
13. Sadler, P., Webb, T. and Lansley, P. (1974) *Management Style and Organisation Structure in the Smaller Enterprise*, Ashridge Management Research Unit.
14. Lea, F. E., Lansley, P. and Spencer, P. (1974) *Efficiency and Growth in the Building Industry*. Ashridge Management Research Unit.
15. Lansley, P. R., Quince, T. and Lea, F. E. (1979) *The Flexibility and Efficiency of Construction Management*. Ashridge Management Research Unit.
16. Uzomaka, O. (1977) 'The management of research (discussion)', in Alsop, K. (ed.), *Construction Research International Vol 2: Discussion*. Construction Press.
17. Dosi, G. (1984) 'Technological paradigms and technological trajectories. The determinants of technical change and the transformation of the economy.' in Freeman, C. (ed.) *Long Waves in the World Economy*, Frances Pinter.
18. March, J. G. and Simon, H. A. (1958) *Organisation*, John Wiley and Sons.
19. Salter, W. (1966) *Productivity and Technical Change*. CUP
20. Blake, R. R. and Mouton, J. S. (1964) *The Managerial Grid*. Gulf Publishing.

—— 5 ——

An introduction to bidding strategy

Martin Skitmore

Modern bidding strategy effectively started with Lawrence Friedman's brilliant 'A competitive-bidding strategy' [1], presented at a New York meeting of the American Society of Operations Research on 4 June 1955 and published in the Society's journal the following year. Friedman's work, which resulted in the first ever doctoral thesis in operations research, is perhaps the most influential of any in the construction management field and is still quoted frequently today. It is remarkable on several counts. First, the bidding problem is carefully defined. Second, the problem is formulated in terms of a statistical model with an explicit objective function. Third, a means is proposed for solving the problem in terms of an 'optimum' bid. Fourth, the formulation and solution of the problem is general enough to incorporate differing amounts of information concerning both the identity and number of competitors. Fifth, an extension is proposed for situations involving multiple simultaneous bids.

There have been many other efforts (over 1000 papers/theses, etc.) since Friedman, but none has proposed any fundamentally different alternative approaches. Whether the lack of basic alternatives is good, in concentrating efforts on sound incremental refinements, or bad, in restricting imaginative competing approaches, remains to be seen. Meanwhile, Friedman's original framework may still be used to examine progress in the subject.

1. Problem definition

Friedman's first step was to reduce the problem to a convenient size for mathematical treatment. This is covered by three statements, or assumptions, concerning 1. the bidding situation, 2. the bidders, and 3. the objectives.

1. A bidding situation is typified by the case where 'a government agency invites a . . . number of companies . . . to bid for contracts' and 'each company interested in obtaining a contract must submit a closed bid and the company submitting the lowest bid gets the contract' [2]. As it happens, the method proposed by Friedman is not dependent on the type of agency involved. The important point is that a contract is placed in a market for such contracts.

The concept of a contract market enables us to define the method of contract acquisition in terms of the rules of the market. UK construction contract markets, for instance, are known to have a variety of potential rules, mostly in the hands of the contract seller (client), such as the sets of rules for selective, negotiated, two-stage tendering, package deals, etc. A popular name for a set of rules is a procurement system, the selection of which is an interesting problem in itself. Friedman's procurement system contains two rules: (a) bidders enter closed bids; and (b) the lowest bidder acquires the contract. This implies for (a) that one unqualified bid only per bidder is allowed and no other bidders may know its value, and for (b) that no post-bid bargaining or shopping will take place. Thus Friedman's system, in excluding several of the alternative options, represents a special case in procurement system formulations generally, an important point in practical applications.

A few alternative formulations have been considered by others in the field. Overt open bidding, for example, has long been the subject of game theory, even pre-Friedman, albeit at a rather modest and extremely simplified level. Covert open bidding or collusion has been examined but rather superficially [3], its effects generally being ignored. Qualified bids in the form of non-price features, sometimes encountered in construction bidding in terms of alternative construction periods or designs, have also been considered [4].

A surprisingly neglected area is the lowest bidder assumption contained in Friedman's second rule, as a good proportion of UK construction contracts, for instance, are not acquired directly by the lowest bidder but by the second or third lowest, negotiation, retendering or even completely abandoning the tender. The existence of various normative approaches, including Cauwelaert and Heynig's [5] 'Belgian Solution' involving the identification and rejection of unrealistic or suicidally low bids, suggests this to be an important issue in several countries.

2. '. . . the number of competititors who will actually submit bids on each contract may be unknown'. Friedman actually considers two possible events: (a) the number and identity of all the bidders for a contract are known; (b) neither the number of bidders nor their identity is known. Some other work after Friedman has extended these possible events to cases where (c) the identity of some, but not all, bidders are known; and (d) there is sufficient historical bidding data concerning some, but not all, bidders. The approaches used for (c) and (d) are essentially the same as Friedman's approach to (b), involving the aggregation of unknown or insufficiently documented bidders into one 'average' bidder. The unaggregated bidders, usually termed 'key' competitors, are treated individually in a similar manner to Friedman's approach to (a).

It is clear now that there are a variety of possible events concerning the identity and number of bidders involved in the auction. We may know the identity of bidders with differing degrees of certainty for each bidder and each auction. Similarly, we may know the number of bidders involved with differing degrees of certainty for each auction. In other words, the issue centres on the uncertainties involved. The methods by which these uncertainties are handled depends on the way in which they are modelled.

3. Friedman [6] considers the existence of several possible objectives, or combination of objectives, that a bidder may wish to achieve, including:

(a) maximize total expected profit;
(b) gain at least a certain percentage of investment;
(c) minimize expected losses;
(d) minimize profits of competitors;
(e) keep production going.

As Friedman points out, each of these and other objectives, together with their combinations, produce different solutions. More obscure objectives, such as keeping the workforce happy, obtaining special experience for the managers, improving status in the community, etc., involve formulations not as yet addressed by anyone in the field. Similarly, dynamic aspects of construction contracting, involving forecasts of future events such as the state of the various contract markets, competitors, bidding opportunities, and the outcome of bidding activities as reflected in cash flow forecasts, etc., have also received little treatment, although Atkins [7] is a notable exception.

In view of this, Friedman's choice of (a) – to maximize expected profit alone – has to be regarded as rather simplistic. Later efforts to incorporate non-monetary goals by means of utility maximization (Willenbrock [8], for instance) have offered some improvement towards realism. Utility theory, however, is not without its critics, more recent studies [9] and [10] tending to reject single unit measures such as profit or utility in favour of multiple objectives.

Applications of multiple objectives, multiattribute, or multiple criteria decision-making (MCDM) to bidding problems, however, have been very limited even in simplified form, and extensions to dynamic and uncertain situations have still to be tackled.

2. Problem formulation

In its most general form the bidding problem consists of choosing a set of actions in a bidding situation that will bring about a desired set of results, i.e.:

$$R_{max} = A \qquad (1)$$

The idea is that there are several alternative sets of actions A1, A2, A3, etc., associated with which there are several corresponding sets of results R1, R2, R3, etc., one of which, the 'best' set of results, is particularly preferred by the decision-maker.

From this formulation it is clear that the selection of this 'best' set of results will automatically lead to the corresponding best set of actions. A brief glance at the antirationalist economics literature suggests that the 'best' set of results is very much dependent on the priorities of the individual decision-maker and his perception of the situation. This suggests that problems of this kind should be split into two components – the mechanisms governing the choice among possible results, and the relationships between actions and results. The first component is primarily concerned with human behaviour, a specialized field of study not dealt with here. The second component is primarily concerned with information, the provision of which is essentially the task undertaken by management information systems (MIS) or, to be more precise in bidding situations, decision support systems (DSS).

The role of the DSS is to provide objective information concerning specific decisions, leaving the more intuitive, experiential aspects to the decision-maker. In terms of the bidding decision this involves the provision of some useful information concerning the relationships between the **A** action sets and the **R** result sets. As with all disaggregating approaches, however, some residual problems occur in the interface between components. In this case the major difficulty is that, in order to completely specify the DSS for bidding, some prior knowledge is needed of the type of action and result sets that may interest the decision-maker. Fortunately, the informational requirements of bidders is reasonably well documented.

2.1 Action sets

The standard texts on construction contract bidding provide a very concise set of alternative actions for bidders. These have been adopted by Fellows and Langford [11] in their important formal formulation of the static multiattribute approach. When taken together with Simmonds' non-price features, and Eastham's [12] 'rough' cost estimates, the range of direct action alternatives is as follows:

(a) return tender documents;
(b) enter a 'cover' price;
(c) calculate a 'rough' cost estimate and add a mark up;
(d) calculate a detailed cost estimate and add a mark up;
(e) add 'non-price features';
(f) no bid.

As the tender period is usually at least three weeks, the 'no bid' option may be exercised at any time, though the intention is that some prior analysis of options (b)–(e) is made, rather than the pre-emptive option (a).

Several indirect actions are also available. These include actions more often associated with organization structure and marketing such as those involving reorganization of resources in the advent of an unaccustomed type of building, construction method, etc., or a project contract that would provide some publicity for the company. Although of relevance to the bidding decision, such considerations essentially concern the nature of the interface with organizational and marketing functions of the company.

Perhaps the most important indirect action concerns the resourcing of the bidding operation itself. The most obvious of these concerns the costs involved. Clearly, the direct action alternatives (a)–(e) listed above have an increasing impact on estimating and adjudicating resources, returning the tender documents being the cheapest and entering a detailed cost-estimate-based bid with non-price features being the most expensive option in these terms.

Further, and seldom mentioned, potential indirect actions relating to resources for bidding are the measures that bidders sometimes take to gain an advantage over competitors. These include the legal acquisition and analysis of data relating to competitors, their previous bidding patterns, current workload and intentions.

Finally, some mention should be made of potential rule breaking actions that may be made by participants in the bidding process. These include the possibility of collusive or cartel agreements (strictly forbidden by the US antitrust laws for instance), bribery and corruption of clients or their representatives, etc. Although it would be naïve to ignore such possibilities in considering the whole range of bidding actions, their very nature tends to prohibit any serious empirical attempts to examine their potential. Also it is currently considered unseemly to give any serious thought to the subject at this level in case it is regarded as encouraging such unfair practices.

2.2 Results sets

Designing a DSS to accommodate the full range of all possible sets of results that may interest bidders is a daunting task. The most commonly reported quantities of interest – profits, losses, turnover, workload – clearly relate to monetary outcomes. Non-monetary outcomes of interest include the personal development of the people involved, career prospects, position in society, etc., which can be loosely called human aspirations. This leaves a residual collection of non-monetary, non-aspirational outcomes such as the acquisition of property in the form of buildings, plant, etc. The little empirical work that has been done in this area (Niss [13], Mannerings [14]) indicates, unsurprisingly, that monetary, personal and property outcomes are usually prioritized in just that order.

Analysis of the measures of these various types of outcomes suggests that a few basic quantities would suffice to enable their calculation. A record of the state of finances at several points in time, for instance, would allow the necessary measures of profit, losses, turnover, etc., to be calculated. Similarly, records of the state of human development and aspirations and property should, at least in theory, provide the equivalent derivational basis.

One of the most important yet in many ways most neglected aspects of result sets concerns the dynamics associated with bidding problems. The notion that result sets may be best modelled as state variables naturally leads to the consideration of bidding situations as a part of a continuum of such situations. As the execution of bidding contracts is a relatively long-term rather than an instant affair, the outcome of today's actions is dependent to some extent on the outcomes of previous and even future actions. The knowledge that a particularly desirable contract will become available soon can affect the desirability of one currently under considera-tion. Also it is possible that the action taken on the current contract, for example returning the tender documents, may have some influence on the availability of future contracts. Thus there exists an archetypal dynamic situation – the past, present and future all interacting in a continual state of change.

Finally, there is the matter of uncertainty to consider, a ubiquitous feature of bidding problems. In every conceivable aspect, the results of bidding actions are to some degree indeterminate.

Bidding uncertainties comprise four components: (a) uncertainties caused by the variability in outcome states that occur generally irrespect-ive of any bidding actions, e.g. the variability of monetary states due to macro-factors such as national and international economic, legal, social, and technological developments, and micro-factors such as management and productivity; (b) uncertainties caused by inaccuracy in estimating outcome states due to imprecision in the estimating methods used, inability of the estimating personnel, inadequacy in information acquisi-tion, and insufficient acquisition and use of feedback from previous estimating activities; (c) uncertainties caused by differences between the bidding models and the real or perceived bidding situation; and (d) uncertainties concerning the acquisition of contracts.

These four distinct types of uncertainty are illustrated in a situation where a person is contemplating entering a clay pigeon shooting competi-tion. He practises the game incessantly in his back yard using an air rifle to pop off some old tin cans on a wall. To his surprise and embarrassment on entering a preliminary qualifying competition he misses the clays on every occasion. He calls a meeting with the tournament director and a local expert shooter to sort out his problems. 'You did not fire off the clays consistently' he accuses the director. 'Rubbish' cries the director 'You are just a hopeless shot.' I am a very good shot' retorts our innocent. At this point the expert intervenes 'You might be a good shooter, but not a good clay pigeon shooter.' The analogy is, of course, that: the moving target represents a type (a) variability, the accuracy of the straightline tin-can shooting is a type (b) variability, the difference between tin-can and clay pigeon shooting is a type (c) variability and all three types of variability contribute to the overall failure. The type (4) uncertainty in this case turns out to be whether he can even make the competition proper. It is instructive to note that if our competitor was to seriously seek optimal improvements, he would be best advised to analyse the relative influence of each of the variability components and concentrate his further efforts accordingly.

In the bidding situation such an analysis is also necessary, but by no means easy, as the components and their interactions are usually extremely complicated. How each of the four types of uncertainty are incorporated into bidding strategies can be seen from the various models employed.

3. Bidding models

Before attempting to propose a solution to the bidding 'problem', it is first necessary to formulate, or model, the situation in a way which will enable a possible solution to be found. In undertaking this task, two factors need to be borne in mind: (a) the relevant characteristics of the situation that constitute the 'real world' decision-making environment; and (b) the existence of some technique, or collection of techniques, that can be adopted or adapted to generate a solution. The complicated nature of the 'real world' situation described above and the relatively simple nature of extant techniques suggest that these two factors are not particularly compatible. Consequently, the usual approach at this stage is to propose a simple model of one part of the situation to suit a known solution technique. Although this is clearly short sighted – the development of solution techniques being faster than changes in the characteristics of the 'real world' situation – it is nevertheless acceptable provided the overall problem situation is continually kept under surveillance. Ideally, a research programme should exist aimed at coordinating activities on the various parts of the problem. The worst that could happen is that every researcher works on one same small part of the problem, forgetting the overall picture – exactly the situation that has occurred in bidding strategy research.

Until now, with very few exceptions, only the monetary aspects of results sets and the mark-up level in the actions sets have been introduced into bidding models. Even this grossly simplified version of the bidding situation has been sufficient to tax researchers to the limits of their abilities and patience.

Various proposals have been made concerning the identity of the competitors in Friedman's model. These are said to vary with the type and size of contract, client and location (Benjamin [15]) and 'classes of work' (Morin and Clough [16]). Very few models have been reported, however, to provide the necessary identification of bidders for a future contract. Shaffer and Micheau [17] briefly mention a predictive technique called the multidistributional model (MD), which predicts 'with a high level of confidence' the identity of competitors on a specific project, but unfortunately details are not provided. Skitmore [18] has suggested a linear model based on contract value.

There is also some evidence of a relationship between market conditions and the number of bidders (De Neufville *et al.* [19], Skitmore [20]), but no model has as yet been proposed.

4. Parameter estimation and reliability

Although it is normally useful to consider model identification and parameter estimation as separate tasks in the analysis, it is clear that some degree of duplication often exists in practice. The contract may not be acquired or contracts that are acquired may have an underestimated expenditure. Parameter estimation moves down a level to estimating the probability of acquiring a contract and the probability of underestimating expenditure should the contract be acquired.

Parameter estimates may be obtained in several ways. These are usually classified as either 'objective' (derived from carefully and explicitly recorded data) or 'subjective' (not so derived). The distinction between these methods of deriving estimates is of vital importance in bidding problems, mainly due to the rather extreme data demands of some models, particularly Friedman's. Consider the following example:

(a) A meteorological office collects a vast amount of historic 'objective' climatic data for the purposes of long range weather forecasting.
(b) Fred Farmer has a subjective 'feel' for future weather conditions, which he claims to be based on the (unspecified) state of the frog spawn in his duck pond.

How can we judge whether (a) or (b) is the best method? The answer is clearly an empirical matter – we compare the (a) and (b) forecasts with the actual outcome over a period of time to see which is the most reliable. Similarly for bidding model parameter estimates, the true judge of 'bestness' must be based on the reliability of the estimates rather than their source.

The above considerations raise the broader issue of reliability of models generally. We may have a good model which reflects many of the salient features of the problem but with unreliable parameter estimates. Conversely, we may have an oversimplified model but with very reliable parameter estimates. It is the combination of the two – reliability of model identification and parameter estimation – that determines the appropriateness of the model in practical applications. For bidding models, separation of these two reliability components is not an easy task, as the 'true' outcomes are seldom (if ever) observable. Even the assessment of the reliability of parameter estimates is sometimes difficult, as this assessment is itself an estimate – leading to considerations of the reliability of the reliability etc.

What is difficult to understand is the marked lack of attempts to assess the reliability of bidding model parameter estimates. Friedman's work, for instance, once again set the trend in not only omitting to indicate reliability but failing to specify the values of any parameters at all for the proposed models. In fact, only relatively recent work with the multivariate approach seems to have addressed the parameter problem in a systematic manner. This places us in a difficult position when having to choose between the three approaches described in the last section. With no objective criteria available, the best that can be attempted at this time is a discursive analysis of information utilisation of the three approaches.

First, let us examine the Hanssmann and Rivett [21] 'lowest bidder' approach. This model has several desirable characteristics – in considering only the lowest bid entered for contracts, irrespective of the bidder's identity, only one set of distribution parameters (μ and σ) needs to be estimated, and neither the identity of the lowest bidder nor the number of bidders is needed. This makes data collection and analysis a relatively simple matter. On the other hand, it may be that the identity of the bidder is important in that some bidders may be more efficient, more competitive or make more mistakes in bidding than others. Furthermore, and there is a growing amount of empirical evidence in support of this (cf Skitmore) [22], greater numbers of bids entered for contracts tend to produce diminishing lowest bid values.

Friedman's approach, in considering all bidders, overcomes the disadvantages of the Hanssmann and Rivett approach, but at a cost of producing data demands of alarming proportions. Friedman recommends that a bidder records his own cost estimate/competitor bid ratios for each auction in which he has participated. From these data the bidder is supposed to construct a frequency distribution and thence an appropriate probability distribution (with the associated parameter estimates) *for each competing bidder*. With the quantity of data that a construction contractor can collect in this way, it is considered by many (cf Hackemar [23], for instance) that the resulting parameter estimates will be extremely unreliable. Friedman in fact anticipated this by introducing what he calls 'the average bidder' concept, which involves pooling the data of competing bidders for whom data is insufficient to provide reliable parameter estimates, or where the identity of bidders is simply unknown. By doing this, the advantages of the identified bidder approach are of course lost. Varying numbers of bidders are, however, accommodated in this approach, the probability of entering the lowest bid diminishing with increasing numbers of competitors, as expected.

The multivariate approach aims to retain the identified bidders' approach while increasing the amount of useable data. By this method all bids entered by identified bidders are considered by our bidder *irrespective of whether our bidder was involved*. Friedman's assumption, that individual competing bidders behave in the same (statistical) way when bidding against 'our' bidder, is extended to assume that individual bidders will behave in the same way irrespective of whom they bid against. Friedman's other assumptions, that individual bidders behave in the same way irrespective of time, contract characteristics or number of competing bidders, are retained, although the model could be extended to accommodate these (but with corresponding data demands). The effect of this change in assumption is to increase the amount of data available, and thus the reliability of parameter estimates, quite dramatically.

In view of these considerations it would seem likely that the multivariate approach may offer the most reliable results in terms of parameter estimates, and ultimately perhaps the bidding problem (certainly as defined by Friedman) solution. It is this observation, together with the progress that has been made to date in developing the multivariate approach, both in terms of parameter estimation, reliability and model validation, that provides the motivation for the next section, which examines the multivariate approach in more detail.

5. The multivariate approach

The central issue in all bidding problem specifications concerns the probability that the bidder enters the lowest bid. The multivariate approach prescribes this probability in terms of a set of candidate statistical equations derived from a general equation. This, in turn is derived from the general proposition that in all sealed bid auctions,

> A sealed bid can be adequately modelled as being a random value drawn from a probability distribution unique to the bidder at the time of bidding.

First, the following comments are particularly relevant concerning this general proposition:

1. *Sealed bid:* the bid is a value entered supposedly simultaneously with bids from other competitors for certain rights, e.g. to obtain or deliver services in return for the value of the bid.
2. *Adequately modelled:* as there can be no certainty in attributing causal rules to phenomena, the best hope is to devise a model exhibiting similar behavioural characteristics to the phenomena under investigation. The adequacy of the model depends on the circumstances. One method of measuring the degree of adequacy might be to examine the cost consequences of differences between the behaviour of the model and that of the 'real world'.
3. *Random value:* a random value is regarded here in the strict statistical sense, sometimes termed the 'noise' in the system.
4. *Probability distribution:* associated with random values is the statistical concept of the probability of a value occurring. Many theoretical

probability distributions have been studied and, in some cases, their properties well defined.

5. *Unique to the bidder:* each bidder has his own unique probability distribution, different from other bidders.

6. *The time of bidding:* changes in bidding behaviour take place over time. Following Friedman [24], we take the assumptions contained in comments 1–3 as 'given' for construction contract bidding without further discussion. In so far as comments 4–6 are concerned, it is practically impossible to obtain objective empirical estimates of the required parameters. It is therefore clear that some generalized version of the equation is necessary if suitably reliable objective parameter estimates are to be obtained.

This is done by empirical analysis in three stages: (a) model propositions; (b) parameter estimation; and (c) model selection and validation.

Once this analysis is completed, it is possible to go on to consider the several types of strategies available. These are presented below in the form of a case study.

6. A case study

Fortunately, bidding strategies can be illustrated quite well graphically. For this purpose we will examine a set of 'live' bidding data consisting of the values of all bids entered for a series of construction contracts, together with the identity of the associated bidders. To preserve confidentiality, all the bidders were assigned a code at random, the bidder providing the data having code 304. From the data, the mean and variance of each bidder is estimated. Figure 5.1 shows the probability curves for bidders 304 and 55. These are slightly skewed due to the nature of the probability distributions (a type of lognormal) used to model the data. The third curve shown

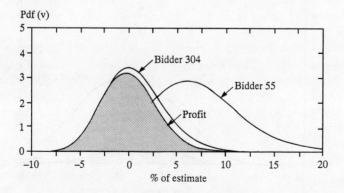

Figure 5.1 *Distribution of bids and profits (0% mark-up)*

in Figure 5.1 is the profit probability distribution for bidder 304 should he bid against bidder 55 with a zero mark-up and the area under this curve is the probability that bidder 304 underbids bidder 55, 0.769 in this example.

Figures 5.2–5.4 show the situation for mark-up values of 5, 10 and 20% with the probability of underbidding bidder 55 being 0.593, 0.264 and 0.024 respectively. From this it can be seen that the profit probability curve becomes progressively flatter with its mean value diminishing relative to the mark-up value – the winner's curse.

The object of a bidding strategy is to choose a mark-up value which will bring about some preferred state of the profit probability curve. One obvious choice is to have a profit probability curve that has no possibility

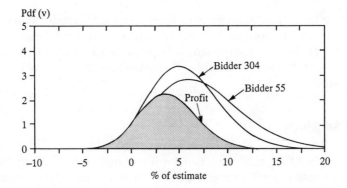

Figure 5.2 *Distribution of bids and profits (5% mark-up)*

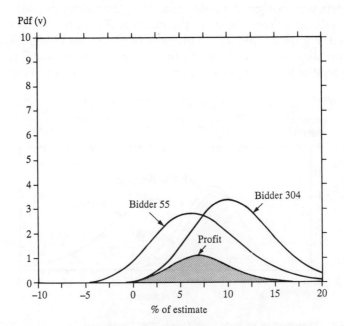

Figure 5.3 *Distribution of bids and profits (10% mark-up)*

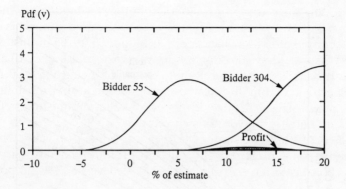

Figure 5.4 *Distribution of bids and profits (20% mark-up)*

of negative values, i.e. the 'no loss' option. The infinite tails of the normal curve, however, from which this model is derived, makes it theoretically impossible to completely avoid the possibility of making a loss. The usual way to handle this is to define some small probability as being the greatest that can be tolerated, for example 5% (one in twenty contracts makes a loss) is a popular criteria. In terms of Figures 5.1–5.4 this means finding a mark-up value which will produce a profit probability curve with a left-hand tail that is very close to zero on the horizontal axis. Using the 5% criterion, this implies that 5% of the area under the profit probability curve is to the left of the zero point.

It is also of interest to note that if, instead of 5%, 50% is used as the criterion, i.e. there is an equal chance of making a profit or loss, the mark-up value necessary to produce this situation is the 'break even' mark-up.

One way to calculate 'no loss' and 'break even' mark-up values is to calculate the percentage points of the profit probability curve over a series of mark up values. Figure 5.5 shows the position of the 5,10, 20 . . ., 80, 90, 95 percentile points over mark-up values ranging from minus 10 to plus 20%. By drawing a horizontal line through the zero profit point we can find the desired mark-up values at the intersection with 5 and 50 percentiles for 'no loss' and 'break even' strategies respectively. These turn out to be 6.795 and 0.475% respectively in this example.

A criticism of the 'no loss'-type strategies is that they are essentially defensive and overly conservative in their philosophy. In ignoring likely profit levels associated with alternative mark-up values, the bidder is neglecting an opportunity to make profit gains. Friedman's approach, to maximize expected profit, certainly overcomes this criticism.

Figure 5.6 shows the expected profit curve over a series of mark-up values. The mark-up value which produces the maximum expected profit in this example is 6.46%.

Finally, there are strategies that take into account both the probability of profits and losses. A simple way to do this is to multiply the profit

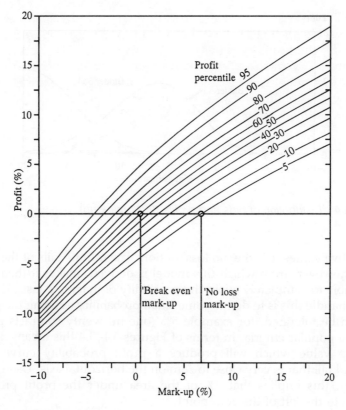

Figure 5.5 *Profit percentiles*

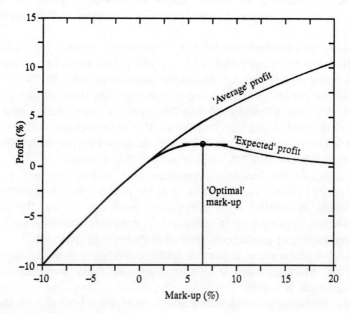

Figure 5.6 *Expected profit*

probability percentiles for a given mark-up by the probability of entering the lowest bid for that mark-up. This means combining Figure 5.6 with the area under the profit probability curve in Figure 5.1. The result is shown in Figure 5.7. Now by finding the maximum value of the curve at any desired percentile, we can obtain the required risk-related maximum. In this case the 'high-risk' strategy (on the 95 percentile) is 12.42%, and 'low-risk' strategy (on the 5 percentile) is 3.97%.

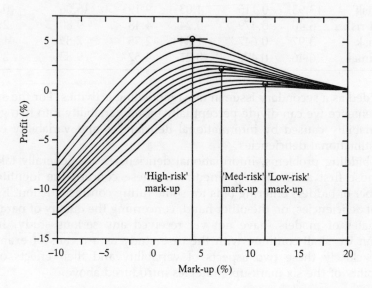

Figure 5.7 *Expected profitiles*

Table 5.1 summarizes the correct mark-up values, together with the associated probability of underbidding bidder 55, likely profit at the 5, 50 and 95 percentiles, and the expected profit for each of the six bidding strategies considered above. The similarity of the medium risk and maximum expected profit strategies is due to the closely symmetrical nature of the profit probability functions – the medium risk and maximum expected profit mark-up values being equivalent to median and mean strategies respectively.

7. Reliability

The distinction was made earlier between variability in the 'real world' and variability in perceptions of the 'real world'. Up to this point we have attempted to encapsulate the variability in the first of these classes by means of statistical models, statements of the assumptions implied by the models, and tests on the validity of some of these assumptions. The second class of variability is generally less well understood and tends to be

Table 5.1 Six strategic mark-up values for bidder 304 ($\alpha=0.0$, $\sigma^2=0.014$) against bidder 55 ($\alpha=0.213$, $\sigma^2=0.020$)

Type	Mark-up (%)	Prob. winning	Profit (%) 5% prob.	50% prob.	95% prob.	Expected
'No loss'	6.80	0.453	0.00	4.75	10.09	2.03
'Breakeven'	0.47	0.855	−4.34	0.00	4.90	−0.04
'Lo-risk'	13.93	0.115	4.03	9.19	15.06	0.92
'Med-risk'	6.40	0.479	−0.24	4.48	9.80	2.04
'Hi-risk'	3.97	0.647	−1.84	2.75	7.89	1.72
'Optimal'	6.46	0.476	−0.21	4.52	9.83	2.04

regarded as a secondary issue in most modelling activities. For the sake of convenience we can divide perceptually based variability into two groups – variability caused by informational deficiencies and variability caused by estimational deficiencies.

In bidding problems, informational deficiencies are generally taken to be those first addressed by Friedman. These concern the identity and number of bidders entering bids for some future contract auction. Estimational deficiencies, on the other hand, concerning the quality of parameter estimates of models, have not yet received any serious study. In this section we shall continue with the case study as a means of examining more closely these two aspects of variability and their effects on the reliability of the six mark-up strategies introduced above.

7.1 Informational deficiencies

7.1.1 Identity of some bidders not known

In the above analysis we were able to make the assumption that one bidder, bidder 55, was the only competitor in the auction. If we assume that we only know the number of competitors but not their identity, then it is possible to adjust the models by reference to the data base (that we may have other external partial knowledge of a competitor's probability of participation is not considered here).

One approach is to model all competitors as equal – the 'average' competitor. This approach, however, relies on the validity of the 'homogeneity assumption', which is inappropriate for the data under study. We estimate the probability that a specified bidder will participate in an auction by a linear regression involving the contract value. The results using this technique for a contract valued at £1m are given in Table 5.2.

7.1.2 Number of bidders not known

Where the number of bidders is not known, we estimate the number by another linear regression involving the (log) contract value. This has the

Table 5.2 Six strategic mark-up values for bidder 304 against exactly five unknown competitors for contract size £1 million

Type	Mark-up (%)	Prob. winning	Profit (%)			
			5% prob.	50% prob.	95% prob.	Expected
'No loss'	14.39	0.006	0.00	3.87	7.68	0.02
'Breakeven'	3.34	0.265	−4.23	0.00	4.16	−0.03
'Lo-risk'	22.39	0.000	1.96	5.68	9.41	0.00
'Med-risk'	6.28	0.119	−2.35	1.28	5.30	0.14
'Hi-risk'	1.57	0.389	−5.18	−0.90	3.36	−0.40
'Optimal'	6.51	0.111	−2.76	1.37	5.38	0.14

Competitors' IDs estimated to be bidder 55 ($\alpha=0.213$, $\sigma^2=0.02$), 221 $\alpha=0.233$, $\sigma^2=0.030$), 134 ($\alpha=0.170$, $\sigma^2=0.013$), 152 ($\alpha=0.079$, $\sigma^2=0.027$), and 170 ($\alpha=0.246$, $\sigma^2=0.008$)

advantage that both the number and identity of bidders may be estimated from the contract value, and thence the six strategic mark-up values as before. Figure 5.8 gives the results for a series of contract values.

7.1.3 Contract value not known

We use a loglognormal probability distribution to model the frequency of contract values. Thus, where even the contract value is not known, a prediction may still be obtained by taking the mean value of this distribution. In our example this is £1 105 108 which is then used to estimate the number and identity of bidders and thence the six strategic mark-up values as before (Figure 5.8).

7.2 Estimational deficiencies

Several parameters had to be estimated in the above study, e.g. the bidders' means and variances, and number of competitors. The estimates of these parameters can be thought of as variables themselves, each with a mean and variance of their own. Up to this point, we have concentrated on the mean or 'best' estimate of these parameters. There is an error associated with this 'best' estimate, usually termed the standard error, which reduces as more data is introduced into the analysis so that with a very large sample of data the standard error becomes quite close to zero.

In order to ascertain the impact of the size of data set on the estimates of the parameters, the easiest procedure is to conduct a simulation study. This is done stochastically by repeated random sampling of values from some hypothesized probability distribution of the parameter estimates. Fortunately we can often call upon the central limit theorem for this purpose which enables most of the parameter estimates to be treated as normally distributed.

By generating independent random values for each of these parameters in each informationally deficient situation, a measure of estimational

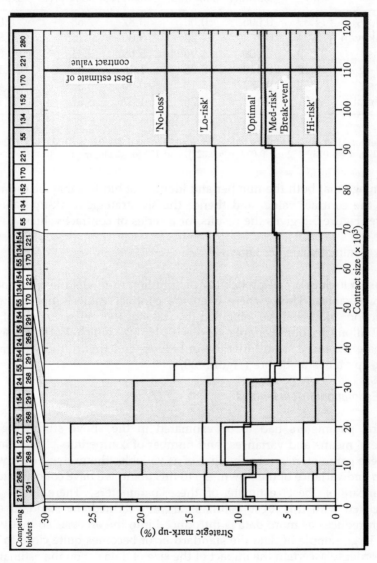

Figure 5.8 *Six strategic mark-up values – by contract size*

reliability is obtained. Figures 5.9 and 5.10 illustrate the effects of randomizing parameter estimates of bidder means and variances on the probability of bidder 304 underbidding bidder 55 alone. The effects in terms of the mark-up strategies is shown in Figure 5.11 and Table 5.3, the 'no loss' mark-up being between 4.46 and 9.50% and the 'optimal' mark-up being between 4.56 and 7.82%.

Figure 5.12 shows the effects on the optimal mark-up of randomizing all parameter estimates for a fixed number of competing bidders (100 trials for each number of competing bidders). This figure clearly shows the decreasing reliability of the optimal bid recommendation for contracts with increasing numbers of competitors. Assuming a minimum reliability

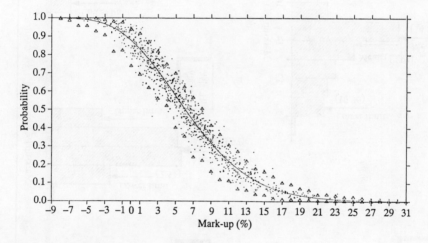

Figure 5.9   *Reliability of probability curve*

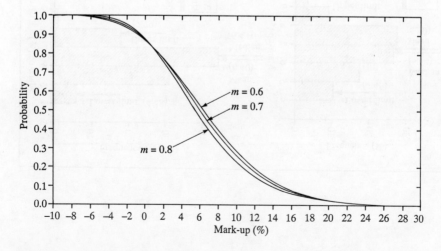

Figure 5.10   *Reliability of probability curve*

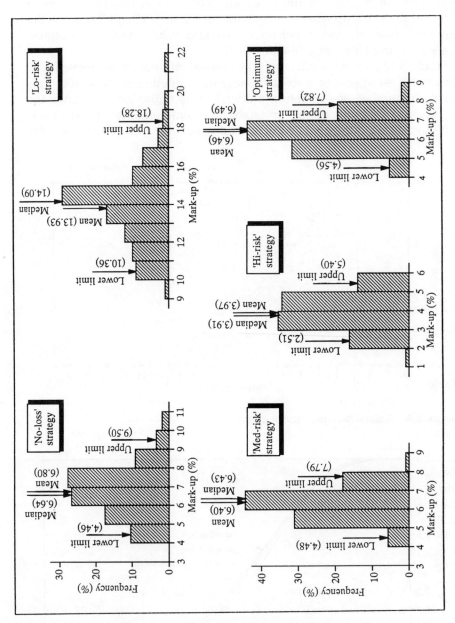

Figure 5.11 *Mark-up strategies*

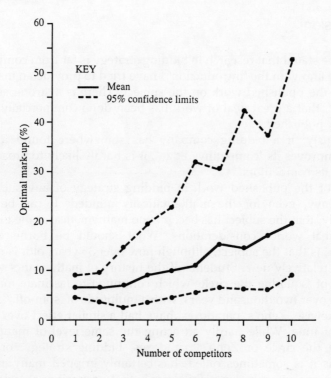

Figure 5.12 *Optimal bidding – results of reliability trials*

Table 5.3 Reliability analysis for six strategic mark-up values for bidder 304 against bidder 55.

Type	Mark-up $(2\frac{1}{2}\%)$	(%) confidence intervals (50%)	$(97\frac{1}{2}\%)$
'No loss'	4.46	6.64	9.50
'Breakeven'	0.12	0.42	0.97
'Lo-risk'	10.36	14.09	18.28
'Med-risk'	4.48	6.43	7.79
'Hi-risk'	2.51	3.91	5.40
'Optimal'	4.56	6.49	7.82

of, say, ±1% to be acceptable, then clearly a great deal more data is required before a reliable optimal mark-up can be ascertained, even in the presence of only a few competitors.

Conclusion

It must be stated that research in bidding strategy is far from complete – as far as we know. In the 'Introduction' I have tried to provide an insight into some of the published work on the subject. There is a strong suspicion, however, that a great deal of work has been done commercially that has not been published.

Obviously, if a bidding company has somewhere found a method which improves its 'competitive edge', it is hardly likely to broadcast the news to its competitors.

Most of the published work in bidding strategy of any substance is quite heavy, even for the mathematically minded. It can be argued, justifiably, that the subject has become too mathematical at the expense of many 'real world' considerations. What should be borne in mind, however, is that the subject, although now over 35 years old, is nevertheless still relatively new. Students of the history of mathematics will recall the lure of 'squaring the circle' which continued to fascinate mathematicians for over two thousand years, with a multitude of 'spin-offs' along the way. Likewise, Zeno's 'paradoxes' have had a similar effect over a similar period of time. While hardly attracting the same level of manpower as squaring the circle or Zeno's paradoxes, bidding strategy, or bidding theory as it is sometimes called, has certainly gripped many academics and industrialists alike since Friedman's first propositions. Indeed, over 60 PhD theses alone have been produced on the subject, although very few specialist books have been published – another indication of the newness of the work.

The major barrier to direct progress in the field at the moment would seem to be the proliferation of approaches, albeit Friedman-based, that have been proposed, making even a literature review a major undertaking. What seems to be needed is a reconciliation of approaches into a more general model upon which further work may be based. Unfortunately, most approaches are prescriptive, even normative, in nature, with relatively few considering empirical evidence in their formulation. This suggests the need for a restatement of the 'problem' in such a way as to enable suitable methods of testing and validation to be developed.

In considering such a 'restatement', two basic sets of factors appear to be relevant. The first of these concerns what may be termed macro-factors covering such matters as the objectives of the bidder, the state of the market, bidding opportunities and the 'knock on' effects of bidding decisions on future events. An examination of the structure and role of these and other macro-factors can be found in Skitmore [25] to which the reader interested in the broader aspects of the subject may wish to refer.

The second set of factors, micro-factors, has also been dealt with to some extent in this chapter. These centre on the probability of entering the lowest bid and are essentially concerned with the efficacy of statistical models of the variables associated with this probability. A first attempt at a statement of this problem is the proposition given in my examination of the multivariate approach, in which I try to identify the basic assumptions involved. My own attempts over the last eight years to check out these assumptions have been restricted to identifying a suitable probability distribution for bids while maintaining generality as far as possible. The main conclusion so far is that a three-parameter lognormal is reasonable for all bidders, but with different scale and location parameters. Current techniques should enable us to examine some of the other assumptions, particularly those of randomness and independence of bids, in a similar manner. The scope for yet further work involving the introduction of further influencing variables affecting bidding behaviour and their changes over time is, however, problematic, data limitations being the major factor.

For readers wishing to pursue the subject further I should offer some final words. Those interested in the subject as a field of academic study will find a sufficient opportunity for original work. The objectives of bidders, the frequency and characteristics of contract opportunities and the effect of bidding decisions on future objectives and opportunities at the macro-level are all poorly researched areas. At the micro-level, the analysis of large sparse matrices and small sample statistics is of particular relevance in bidding and, coincidently, an emerging topic in mathematical statistics at the same time. Those looking for an immediate solution to their commercial bidding problems are, however, not so fortunate. Bidding strategy still has a considerable distance to travel before it can offer any neat tidy packages for the busy industrialist. Like squaring the circle, the problem, though simple in appearance, is rather less so when faced with the rigours of scientific analysis. The best advice is to wait patiently for developments, and hope that this is not another two-thousand-year problem!

References

1. Friedman, L. A. (1956) 'Competitive bidding strategy'. *Operations Research*, **1** (4), pp. 104–112.
2. Friedman, L. A. *op. cit.*, p. 105.
3. Sheldon, I. M. (1982) 'Competitive bidding and objectives of the firm, with reference to the U.K. process plant contracting industry'. Occasional Paper 8210. Dept of Management Science, The University of Manchester Institute of Science and Technology.
4. Simmonds, K. (1968) 'Competitive bidding – deciding the best conditions for non-price features'. *Operational Research Quarterly* **19**(1), pp. 5–14.
5. Cauwelaert, F. V. and Heynig, E. (1978) 'Correction of bidding errors – the Belgian solution'. *Journal of the Construction Division: Proceedings of the American Society of Civil Engineers*, **105** (CO1), pp. 13–23.
6. Friedman, L. A. *op. cit.*, p. 105.
7. Atkins, K. J. (1975) Bidding, Finance and Cash Flow in the Construction Industry. PhD Thesis, University of Bradford.

8. Willenbrock, J. H. (1979) A Competitive Study of Expected Monetary Value and Expected Utility Value Bidding Strategy Models. PhD Thesis, Pennsylvania State University.
9. Fellows, R. F. and Langford, D. A. (1980) 'Decision theory and tendering'. *Building Technology and Management*, October, pp. 36–9.
10. Ibbs, C. W. and Crandall, K. C. (1982) 'Construction risk – multiattribute approach.' *Journal of the Construction Division: Proceedings of the American Society of Civil Engineers*, **108** (CO2), pp. 187–200.
11. Fellows, R. F. and Langford, D. A. *op. cit.*
12. Eastham, R. (1988) Unpublished Postal Survey of Bidding Practices of 50 UK Construction Companies.
13. Niss, J. (1965) Custom Production, Theory and Practice, with Special Emphasis on the Goals and Pricing Procedures of the Contract Construction Industry. PhD (EC) Thesis, University of Illinois.
14. Mannerings, R. (1970) A Study of Factors Affecting Success in Tendering for Building Works. MSc. Thesis, UMIST.
15. Benjamin, N. B. H. (1969) Competitive Bidding for Building Construction Contracts. PhD Dissertation, Stanford University.
16. Morin, T. L. and Clough, R. H. (1969) 'OPBID: Competitive bidding strategy model'. *Journal of the Construction Division: Proceedings of the American Society of Civil Engineers*, **95** (CO1), pp. 85–106.
17. Shaffer, L. R. and Micheau, T. W. (1971) 'Bidding with competitive strategy models'. *Journal of the Construction Division: Proceedings of the American Society of Civil Engineers*, **97** (CO1), pp. 113–26.
18. Skitmore, R. M. (1982) 'A bidding model', in *Building Cost Techniques: New Directions*, Brandon, P. S. (ed.). Spon.
19. De Neufville, R. D., Hani, E. N. and Lesage, Y. (1977) 'Bidding model: effects of bidders risk aversion'. *Journal of the Construction Division: Proceedings of the American Society of Civil Engineers*, **103** (CO1), pp. 57–70.
20. Skitmore, R. M. (1982) 'A bidding model', in *Building Cost Techniques: New Directions*, Brandon, P. S. (ed.). Spon.
21. Hanssmann, F. and Rivett, B. H. P. (1959) 'Competitive bidding'. *Operational Research Quarterly*, **10** (1), pp. 49–55.
22. Skitmore, R. M. (1986) A Model of the Construction Project Selection and Bidding Decision. PhD Thesis, University of Salford, 1986.
23. Hackemar, G. C. (1970) 'Profit and competition: estimating and bidding strategy'. *Building Technology and Management*, December, pp. 6–7.
24. Friedman, L. (1956) 'A competitive bidding strategy'. *Operations Research*, **1** (4), pp. 104–112.
25. Skitmore, R. M. (1989) *Contract Bidding in Construction: Strategic Management and Models*. Longman Scientific and Technical.

───── 6 ─────

Competitive bidding and tendering policies

Tony Thorpe and Ronald McCaffer

Summary

The background to market conditions; the importance of estimating in the strategic and tactical decisions of acquiring new work; the bidding process including all decisions in the estimating and tender adjudication process; the factors affecting bidding success; estimating accuracy; data support; and monitoring competitors' performance. The chapter highlights the decisions and judgements required in competitive bidding and emphasizes the inherent variability in the process which makes planning and control a difficult and dynamic process.

1. The competitive environment

Two main influences on the manner in which contracts are awarded to UK construction contractors still predominate. The first is the traditional practice of the construction industry which separates design from construction, and the second is the practice of public sector clients. The traditional strength of the independent consulting engineers and architects in the United Kingdom has fostered and sustained the separation of design from construction and the forms of contract that are derived to suit the completion, or near completion, of design before inviting contractors to bid for the contracts. Although the predominance of these forms of contract is weakening with the growth of design/construct, management contracting and contracts which allow the contractor to undertake detailed design, the traditional form is still the major source of work for contractors.

The public sector clients, namely local and central government, with a need for public accountability, have developed many of the practices for competitive tendering and the private clients have tended to follow suit. Thus, most construction contracts are awarded after several contractors have prepared estimates and submitted tenders.

The construction industry is, however, changing. The vagaries of the tendering process have long been known and the contractor's response has been to develop a design/construct capability and to participate more in development whereby the contractor acts as client as well as designer and constructor. These newer forms of business practice are more prevalent in building projects rather than civil engineering, but even this may change as contractors prepare to participate in power-generation projects for a privatized electricity industry and in privately funded road development. The best example is, of course, the Trans-Manche Link which was financed by a share issue by a company formed from a consortium of construction contractors.

In all these forms of business practice the contractors face severe competition with all its attendant risks. Thus many of the strategic decisions taken by contractors are influenced as much by reducing risk as by seizing opportunities. Contractors are in a risky business, as is evidenced by the bankruptcies and liquidations statistics. Thus, in strategic decisions, contractors are seeking business opportunities with reduced competition and reduced risk. The fundamental laws of economics make such opportunities hard to find.

Strategic decisions by contractors, include directing their marketing efforts at finding opportunities which are believed to be advantageous to the company. The type of work, client, size of contract, type of contract, and geographical location are all issues for consideration by the contractors in seeking to fill their order books. Companies have needed a flexible approach to strategic decisions in the volatile construction market where demand has moved significantly from the peak of 1973 to the trough of 1981, growth thereafter, and decline in the early 1990s.

Since 1980 there have been major shifts in the structure of construction markets. This is illustrated in Figure 6.1, which shows how output has been distributed between three markets, housing and non-housing, the public and private sectors, new work and repairs and maintenance. Throughout the period (except when mortgage rates were unusually high), housing work has maintained or increased its share. This increase has

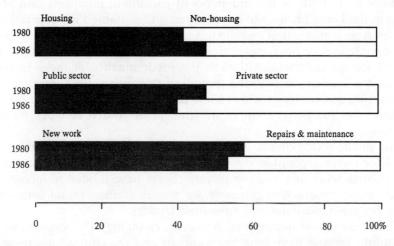

Figure 6.1   *Division of construction output – 1980–1986 (Source: HMSO [1].)*

evolved from the private sector and is one cause of the sharp decline in the public sector share of output as Figure 6.1 shows. This trend is continuing, reflecting controls on central and local government spending and the privatization of previously state-owned companies.

The trend for repairs and maintenance to displace new work is a phenomenon of recent years, resulting from expenditure constraints and a poor business climate early in the decade. However, this trend ceased in 1985, reflecting the improved economic climate. The breakdown of the volume of work for the various construction sectors in 1988 is shown in Figure 6.2.

The effect of these market changes has brought about changes to the structure of the construction industry, and in the 10 years to 1987, the growth of sub-contracting in the United Kingdom has been exceptional. This is shown in Table 6.1 by the increase in the number of small firms (1–24 employees). This change, brought about by an industry unable to sustain employment for its own workforce, has found a partial solution in sub-contracting sections of work formerly undertaken by themselves. This use of sub-contracting has also altered the distribution of risks within the contract.

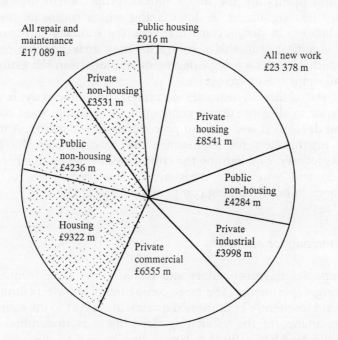

Figure 6.2 *Breakdown of the total £40 600 million of construction during 1988 Repair and maintenance shaded. (Source: HMSO [1].)*

Table 6.1 Details of size of firm and output

	Value of work done (£m)	Number of firms	Value of work done (£m)	Number of firms	Value of work done (£m)	Number of firms
1–24	1535.6	107 558	2401.9	165 163	3075.3	170 463
25–114	996.7	5 063	1213.8	4 023	1529.4	3 876
115–299	580.8	663	641.3	555	851.3	507
300–599	471.4	208	416.9	144	576.7	143
600–1199	429.4	92	407.4	74	592.2	71
Over 1200	711.9	48	771.3	40	918.8	35

Source: HMSO [1].

2. The importance of estimating

At the heart of all strategic and tactical decisions within a company are the company's assessments of its ability to construct building or civil engineering works at an estimated cost. In competitive tendering, the tender is based on the estimated cost, which may represent as much as 90% of the tender. The additions and allowances added for risks, overheads and profits are the much smaller proportion of the tender and therefore less significant in determining which contractor shall be the lowest bidder. In design/construct work the estimate can assume even greater significance in that a contractor may guarantee his price to the client, and this needs a high degree of confidence in the estimated cost that underpins the offered price.

Thus the ability to estimate accurately and efficiently is of critical importance to all construction companies. As a result, most have organized and developed well-defined procedures for estimating. A description of the organization for estimating, the process, and the estimating methods follows, highlighting the critical areas where judgements have to be made and where the decisions in the process are of particular importance in implementing company policies [2] [3].

2.1 Organizing for estimating

All companies have estimators and medium and large companies have estimating departments. The large companies also have planning departments and frequently both these departments report to the same director. The importance of the estimating department is underlined in that it virtually always has a director in charge.

Depending on the 'style' of the company, the director in charge of estimating would have responsibility for other functions. A company that saw 'estimating' as part of a technical service, and technical decisions and competence as the major determinants of the company's actions, would also have such functions as 'temporary works design', 'engineering design' and 'work study', reporting to the same director. This style would be found in major engineering companies. Other 'styles' would be represented by companies that saw 'estimating' as part of the marketing function and there are examples where the director in charge of estimating is also responsible for marketing. Such companies hold the view that heightening the awareness of market-place trends and demands, in an essentially technical function, maintains a forward looking attitude in the estimating department which is in the front line of the battle for new work.

3. The tendering (bidding) process

The process undertaken to produce a competitive bid for a project is illustrated in Figure 6.3. The process consists of the following stages:

(a) decision to tender;
(b) programming the estimate;
(c) preliminary project study;
(d) project study including production of method statement;
(e) preparing the direct cost estimate
    (i) collecting or calculating cost information;
    (ii) calculating direct costs;
    (iii) calculating on-costs;
(f) calculation of site overheads;
(g) preparing reports for tender adjudication.

In all companies of any size this process has been developed and refined until it is efficient in terms of number of estimates produced per estimator, consistent and reliable. Efficiency is required in both depressed and buoyant markets. In depressed markets the success rate declines, and more tenders, and hence estimates, need to be produced to maintain the company's turnover. In buoyant markets the increased bidding opportunities need evaluating to ensure that the company makes the best use of its opportunities.

Consistency or reliability is required, otherwise senior managers using the estimate as a base for commercial decisions on 'risk', 'overheads' and 'profit' are severely hampered if wide fluctuations in calculated costs are produced.

In the larger companies, consistency used to be achieved by producing company manuals detailing how calculations were to be undertaken, the factors to be considered and the output or productivity figures to be used. Nowadays these manuals have been replaced by computer systems which achieve the same effect by producing a framework of control within which the senior estimators can supervise the work of others.

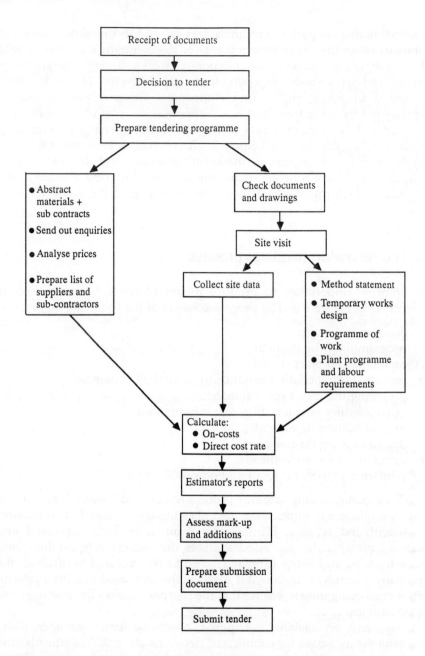

Figure 6.3 *Preparation of tender (Source: Harris and McCaffer [2].)*

3.1 Decision to tender

All companies have a corporate plan, some more detailed than others. This corporate plan will detail the company's turnover targets broken down into its various divisions or sectors of work. Against this corporate plan senior managers will take the decision to bid for a specific contract, the factors considered will include the following:

(a) the potential contribution of the contract to the company's turnover in a particular sector, the overhead recovery and profit;
(b) the likely demands of the contract on the company's financial resources;
(c) the company's resources available;
(d) the type of work;
(e) the location;
(f) the client;
(g) the contract details.

Companies will avoid contracts that are too large for their size, outwith their experience range, likely to stretch their available resources including cash, well outside their normal geographical area of operation, or contracts that have unusually onerous conditions of contract.

In taking the decision to tender, the company's senior managers are making judgements that balance market opportunities and risk. The actual decision to tender may be taken at three stages within the tendering process.

The first is during the pre-selection stage, if this is used. Pre-selection allows contractors to examine brief details of the project in order to allow them to indicate their willingness to proceed to produce a complete tender. This process is used on large projects where producing a tender will involve considerable time and cost to the contractor.

Pre-selection information provided to support the decision to tender includes the following:

- the names of the promoter and engineer or architect;
- the names of any consulting engineers with supervisory duties;
- the location of the site;
- a general description of the work involved;
- the approximate cost range of the project;
- details of any nominated sub-contractors for major items;
- the form of contract to be used;
- the procedure to be adopted in examining and correcting priced bills;
- whether the contract is to be under seal or under hand;
- the anticipated date for possession of the site;
- the period for completion of the works;
- the approximate date for the dispatch of tender documents;
- the duration of the tender period;
- the period for which the tender is to remain open;
- anticipated value of liquidated damages;
- details of any bond requirements;
- any particular conditions relating to the contract;

Part of the contractor's consideration, particularly with respect to a private client, will be to determine the financial strength of the client. The history of the industry is littered with tales of private clients failing to pay and offering contractors numerous alternatives such as shares in hotels, squash clubs and even part ownership of a racehorse! Recurring doubts as to financial security of clients has encouraged contractors to develop skills in financial engineering. This benefits clients for whom contractors can often make financial arrangements on terms more favourable than their clients are able to secure, and at the same time it ensures payment for the contractor. This type of action can be seen as both providing an attractive service to a client, thereby increasing a company's competitive advantage, and reducing risk. If the contractor indicates his or her willingness to submit a tender at the pre-selection stage and he/she is invited to do so by the client's representatives, he/she will normally proceed through the stages outlined above.

However, he/she has two further opportunities to withdraw from the tendering process, that is, after a careful examination of the full contract documentation and after the estimate has been prepared and the tender is ready to submit.

3.2 Programming the estimate

Having taken the decision to tender for the project and having received the full contract documentation, the estimator's first task is to establish a schedule of estimating activities against key dates so that the process can be effectively monitored and controlled. This is vital as the submission date and time are precisely defined and the time available to produce the tender is limited. This action of internal management is to ensure that no in-company errors put the estimating and tendering procedure at risk, and to ensure that each stage in the process is given adequate and due consideration. By these actions the company minimizes risks of leaving decisions too late and being forced to substitute 'guesstimates' for 'estimates'.

3.3 Preliminary project study

The purpose of the preliminary project study is to aggregate the material, plant and potential sub-contractor items within the project, so that enquiries for quotations can be made as early in the process as possible. The preliminary project study ascertains the following:

- the principal quantities of the work;
- an approximate estimate;
- the items to be sub-contracted;
- the materials and plant for which quotes are required;
- the key delivery dates;
- whether design alternatives should be considered.

The four main cost headings of any estimate are 'labour', 'plant', 'materials' and 'sub-contractors'. Quotations are required for materials and sub-contractors. Typically materials account for between 30 and 60% of a project's value; sub-contractors can typically account for between 20 and 40%.

If in an estimate the materials account for 50% of the project cost, and the materials element was entered inaccurately because quotations could not be obtained in time, then the consequences are not difficult to calculate. Chadwick [4] analysed national expenditure on materials and indicated the high increases in company profits that could be delivered from modest savings in material costs.

With respect to materials, the main difference between companies bidding for the same work is their skill in buying, not their efficiency in constructing. It is therefore critical to get enquiries out early to ensure that the vast majority are returned in time for inclusion in the estimate, or, even better, in time for some negotiation to take place with a view to obtaining the best 'price'. This early issue of enquiries is both for competitive reasons and the reduction of risk.

3.4 Project study

The project study starts with the receipt of the contract documents and concludes with the submission of the tender. It includes the preliminary study previously described and the main study which results in the method statement and pre-tender programme. Because of the inter-relation of both planning and estimating at this stage, both functions are involved. The study includes the following:

(a) a study of the contract documentation;
(b) a site visit;
(c) the preparation of a method statement determining how the project will be constructed.

3.4.1 Contract documents

Although the preliminary study will have identified any aspects of the project which require clarification by the engineer or architect and the approximate principal quantities involved, the appraisal now undertaken refines this initial information for detailed analysis. It also requires a detailed listing of any unusual conditions contained in the contract.

3.4.2 Site visit

A site visit is normally arranged through the engineer or architect. In building contracts such visits are not always arranged, in which case the contractor will make his own arrangements for a visit. The purpose of the site visit is to prepare a report containing the following:

- a description of the site;
- the position of existing services;
- a description of ground conditions;
- available access and restrictions;
- any potential security problems;
- topographical details;
- details of any temporary work or demolition to adjoining buildings;
- facilities for the disposal of spoil;
- an assessment of the availability of labour;
- any other 'intelligence' that can be acquired with regard to the contract or competitors.

This report is used in the production of the method statement and is also essential in that the major forms of contract require the contractor to take account of circumstances that could be foreseen by an experienced contractor.

3.4.3 Preparation of method statement

In the larger companies the method statement is usually prepared jointly by the estimator and planner. This statement specifies the methods and procedures to be adopted in executing the work and defines the initial estimates of activity durations, sequence and interactions in the pre-tender construction programme.

The preparation of the method statement involves liaison and consultation with site staff, plant managers and temporary works designers. It is at this stage that design alternatives to the works may be considered. This process produces a description of the proposed construction method based on the pre-tender programme and the global quantities of labour, plant and temporary materials required. These may be reworked several times before the tender is finally submitted.

3.5 *Preparing the direct cost estimate*

The estimator's main task is to determine the most likely cost to the contractor in undertaking the work described in the contract documents. The preparation of the direct cost estimate comprises the following:

(a) collecting or calculating cost information;
(b) calculating the direct cost;
(c) calculating the site overheads;

The mark-up, which includes allowances for head office overheads, profit and risk, is considered separately by senior managers and added to the estimated direct cost to give the tender sum. The assessment of mark-up is described later.

3.5.1 Collection of cost information

The cost information required by the estimator comprises details of labour, plant, materials and sub-contractors.

3.5.1.1 Labour

The cost of the company's own labour is usually calculated either per hour, per shift or per week. The cost to the company of employing their own labour is greater than that paid directly to the employee. The elements in the calculation include the following:

- basic rate;
- overtime payments;
- plus rates for additional duties;
- bonus;
- tool money;
- travel monies;
- holiday stamps and death benefit;
- sick pay;
- national insurance;
- CITB levy;
- employers' and public liability insurance;
- allowances for severance pay;
- allowances for supervision.

The basic data for the calculation is contained in the working rule agreements [5]. However, estimators have to make a number of assumptions that cannot always be supported by calculations. These include the bonus, whether guaranteed or based on productivity, which may be the most significant element and may not be precisely determined until on-site negotiations have taken place. Other assumptions include the hours lost due to inclement weather and time off due to sickness. Abdel-Razek and McCaffer [6] attempted to quantify the risk inaccuracy by creating a sensitivity model to study the effect of estimators' assumptions in these calculations.

3.5.1.2 Plant

Plant may be obtained for a contract either internally or externally. Quotations for the plant required are therefore obtained from external hirers or from the company's own plant department.

It is rare for UK contractors in the domestic market to calculate the all-in plant rate from first principles, this calculation usually being undertaken by the plant hire company. Such calculations are undertaken for overseas contracts. Details on calculating plant rates are contained in Harris and McCaffer [7]. An explanation of the sensitivity of variables contained in the calculations to the overall plant rate are given by Abdel-Razek and McCaffer [8].

3.5.1.3 Materials

Materials form a significant percentage of most projects typically ranging from 30 to 60%, and up-to-date quotes are usually obtained for the majority of material items. The material enquiries include information on the required quantities, the delivery dates, the specification and any terms and conditions on which the quotation is being sought.

The materials quotation received would only normally include delivery to site and the estimator would add allowances for unloading, storage, handling and wastage. These allowances, if inaccurately judged, could lead to significant underestimating of material costs. Abdel-Razek and McCaffer [9] describe the sources of variability in material costs.

One aspect that estimators take care to check is that the supplier has quoted for materials specified and not an available alternative.

3.5.1.4 Sub-contractors

The estimator will in the preliminary study have identified items of the work to be sub-contracted. The decision to sub-contract depends upon the specialization of the work involved. In undertaking large projects or projects of a unique nature, the company may decide to sub-contract work normally undertaken by themselves, in order to access additional resources and spread the financial risk.

Each sub-contractor quotation has to be adjusted for attendance and other allowances. Each sub-contract quotation will vary by the amount by which the sub-contract expects to be serviced by way of access scaffolding, cranage, air compressors, etc. The estimator must therefore allow for this in the final sub-contract rate included in the estimate.

The choice of sub-contractor is important and most companies maintain a list of approved sub-contractors for various trades. Abdel-Razek and McCaffer [10] highlight the growth of sub-contracting and the differing risks between sub-contracted work and contractors undertaking their own work.

3.5.2 Calculating direct cost rates

A direct cost rate is the cost to the contractor of undertaking the work described. The cost will include the costs of all labour, plant, material and sub-contractors employed in constructing the section of work concerned. The real 'art' of estimating is in selecting the detailed resources of labour, plant, materials and sub-contractors. An estimator's skill lies in being able to define the configuration of labour, plant and materials required to undertake specific items of work. Having selected the resources the amount of these resources required to undertake the work needs to be estimated, in hours for labour and plant and quantities for materials. Having determined the resources and usage (time or quantity), the remaining task is combining this information with the collected or calculated costs to produce a direct cost rate as illustrated in Figure 6.4.

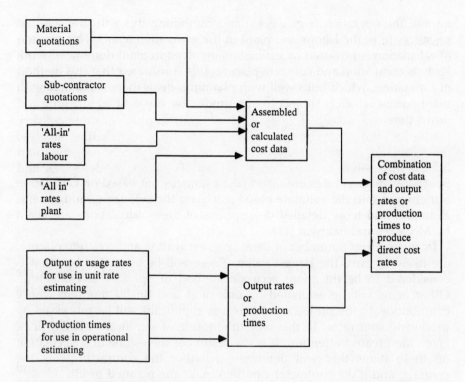

Figure 6.4 *The selection of production rates and cost data and their combination to produce cost rates*

The main calculation techniques adopted by the estimator include the following:

(a) unit rate estimating;
(b) operational estimating;
(c) spot rates.

3.5.2.1 Unit rate estimating

Unit rate estimating is the selection of the resources (labour, plant and materials) required and the selection of output or usage rates for these resources.

Thus for each resource the calculation is the output or usage rate combined with unit cost. An output rate is work quantity per hour (e.g. labour for steelfixing tonnes/hour), and a usage rate is time or resource quantity to do a fixed quantity or work (e.g. hours of labour to fix/tonne of steel). This method of calculating gives rates that can be entered against bill item rates and therefore is commonly used.

3.5.2.2 Operational estimating

Operational estimating is based on calculating the total quantity of work involved in an operation (e.g. excavation), estimating the total elapsed time of the operation (e.g. weeks) and combining this with the selected resources (e.g. the labour and plant in the excavation team). This method of calculation is favoured by estimators involved in plant dominated work such as excavation and concrete placing. It is considered that this method of estimating, which links well with planning, deals more accurately with plant output which is subject to non-productive travel time, idle time and down time.

3.5.2.3 Spot rates

Spot rates or gash rates are direct cost estimates not based on calculation but entered into the estimate based solely on the estimator's judgement. Examples and more detailed descriptions of these calculations are given by McCaffer and Baldwin [11].

In any contract a number of items, e.g. excavation and concrete placing, are likely to carry the largest value. These will be estimated by what is considered to be the more accurate method of operational estimating. Other items will be estimated by unit rates and finally the item whose contribution to the project's value is less significant will be processed by producing spot rates. In this way the more cost significant items will be given the greatest attention. It is the results of the estimator's calculation on these items that will determine whether the contractor wins the contract, and if the contractor can then make the planned profit.

3.5.3 Calculation of site overheads or on-costs

The estimator also calculates the site overheads (or on-costs) for the project. These include allowances for the following:

- site management and supervision;
- plant;
- transport;
- scaffolding;
- miscellaneous labour;
- accommodation;
- temporary works and services;
- general items;
- commissioning and handover;
- sundry requirements.

These items are usually contained in a checklist prepared by the company. This gives guidelines on the appropriate allowances to be made in each category with the estimator determining the total costs.

The calculated site-overheads are often allocated to the 'preliminary' section of the bill, but may be allocated to the bill item rates according to the contract programme or cash flow requirements.

3.6 Preparing reports for tender adjudication

The estimator prepares a set of reports on the estimate to present at the tender adjudication meeting. These reports allow senior management to decide on the appropriate level of mark-up to apply. These reports contain the following:

- a brief description of the project;
- a description of the method of construction;
- a list of problem areas or risks associated with the projects not adequately covered by the contract documents;
- any non-standard contract details;
- an assessment of the state of the design process;
- any assumptions made in preparing the estimate;
- an assessment of the profitability of the works;
- any pertinent information concerning market and industrial conditions;
- a review of any past project undertaken for the same client.

In addition to the above, the estimator will prepare detailed cost reports itemizing the quantities and costs of labour, materials, plant, sub-contractors, nominated sub-contractors and suppliers, provisional sums, dayworks, contingencies, attendance on domestic and nominated sub-contractors and amounts included for material and sub-contractor discounts. The estimator may also calculate a projected cash flow for the project based on a range of 'likely' mark-ups. The purpose of these reports is to convey the details of the contract and the assumptions made in the estimate to senior management.

4. The adjudication process

The transformation of the total calculated direct cost of a project into a tender is accomplished at the tender adjudication meeting. This meeting, attended by representatives of the senior management of the company and the estimating team responsible for producing the tender, considers the commercial implications and decide on additions and allowances. These include the following:

- adjustments to the direct cost estimate;
- additions for head office overheads;
- additions for profit;
- assessment of, and additions for, risk;
- allowance for inflation;
- adjustments for rate-loading or bid-unbalancing;;
- assessment of the project cash flow.

4.1 Adjustments to the direct cost estimate

At the meeting the estimators will present the proposed construction programme for the project. This will include the basic assumptions and decisions implicit in the estimate, with regard to the following:

- labour, plant and material requirements;
- plant and labour output rates;
- wastage assumptions;
- site overhead requirements.

The senior management will satisfy itself as to the adequacy of the estimate by interrogating the estimator.

Decisions made by the panel will include any adjustments required in the resource levels of the project and output or wastage levels.

4.2 Additions for head office overheads

Each project undertaken must contribute to the cost of maintaining the head office and general overheads of the company. If the anticipated (or planned) turnover of the company is known, the required monthly contribution to service the annual head office overhead can be calculated. According to the size (i.e. monetary value) of a particular project in relation to total turnover, and its planned duration, the required contribution can be determined. Competitive pressures keep overhead expenditure low. However, the most difficult circumstances a company has to cope with, are a falling market and a falling turnover. As turnover falls the attendant fall in head office overheads will lag and by keeping the same overhead recovery element in tenders, the company will underrecover. If the company increased its overhead-recovery element in its tenders it would reduce its success rate and consequently worsen the overhead recovery. If it reduced the overhead-recovery element to increase its competitiveness, it may drive up turnover sufficiently to compensate, but it would be likely to exacerbate its *underrecovery*. In such circumstances good management hope to foresee the difficulties and make provision to shed overheads, which are usually staff, early rather than late.

4.3 Additions for profit

In assessing the percentage profit margin to be added to the direct cost of the project the following factors are considered:

- the volume of on-going work;
- the anticipated level of new orders;
- the prevailing market conditions;
- the risk inherent in the work;

- the 'attractiveness' of the project;
- likely competitor actions.

Out of any profit made by the company after servicing loans the following are the main heads of disbursement:

(a) dividends to shareholders;
(b) corporation tax;
(c) retained profits for re-investment.

The critical financial ratios that determine the company's well-being are:

$$\frac{\text{Profit}}{\text{Turnover}} \quad \text{and} \quad \frac{\text{Turnover}}{\text{Capital}}$$

During most of the 1970s and 1980s the profit/turnover ratio experienced by the UK construction companies was very low, typically around 3%. The turnover/capital ratio, however, was relatively high, in the order of 8 to 16, with 10 being a typical figure. This high turnover/capital ratio reflected the ability to run a construction company on a low capital base. Little capital is required because companies can hire plant, rent offices and receive monthly interim payments from clients.

The combination of the two ratios gives the return on capital viz:

$$\frac{\text{Profit}}{\text{Turnover}} \times \frac{\text{Turnover}}{\text{Capital}} = \frac{\text{Profit}}{\text{Capital}}$$

Thus a profit/turnover ratio of 3% and a turnover/capital ratio of 10 gives a return on capital of 30% and perhaps viability. Before servicing debts contractors would be looking for a return on capital of 30–50%. Thus the following simplified example would hold.

Capital employed (equity + loans)	= £100 000
Planned turnover ratio	= 10
Planned retained profits	= 25%
Corporation tax	= 35%
Planned returns on capital	= 50%
(pre-tax and debt servicing)	
∴ planned turnover	= £1 000 000
∴ planned profit	= £50 000
retained profits	= £12 500
corporation tax	= £17 500
return to equity investors	= £10 000
∴ profit margin	£50 000 on £1 000 000 = 5%

this 5% being larger than the achieved margins of most companies during the last 15 years.

The major adjustments to these figures arise from turnover increasing or decreasing with respect to capital employed, decisions regarding the amount of profit to be retained and the return to the equity investors.

Thus if the market forces suggested a smaller margin, to be healthy the company would need to increase its turnover with respect to its capital employed or reduce its retained profits, thereby allowing the company to shrink or decrease the returns to the equity shareholders.

In a buoyant market, with high levels of both on-going work and anticipated orders, the profit margin would be raised and a much happier scenario would emerge.

4.4 Additions for risk

The risk associated with the project must be identified and commercially quantified. This will involve the estimator in identifying potential construction problems with alternatives, areas of the project where insufficient information is available and item quantities in the bill which appear unrealistic.

The senior management must assess these factors and quantify them in terms of a percentage lump sum addition or subtraction.

Complex mathematical models have been developed for the assessment of risk but these are rarely used in practice. Simulation techniques which are more acceptable to practising company managers are little used because of the time constraints.

4.5 Allowance for inflation

Depending upon the client and the prevailing level of inflation, the contract may contain price adjustment clauses using NEDO indices and the appropriate formula. In times of high inflation contractors will take particular care to satisfy themselves that they are not overexposed due to inflation.

4.6 Assessment of project cash flow

A project cash flow will normally have been produced during the estimating process. This is examined to determine whether it fits into the overall company cash flow requirements. Adjustments may be undertaken to improve the project's cash flow and minimize the contractor's capital locked up in the contract and thereby minimize the contractor's risk. This may be achieved by some form of rate loading.

4.7 Adjustments for rate loading or bid unbalancing

Rate loading is the process of adjusting rates throughout the bill while keeping the total constant. The purpose of rate loading is to minimize capital lock-up and optimize cash flow without compromising the competitiveness of the tender. Rate loading may be undertaken to obtain greater early income by increasing the rates of the initial site activities (this is known as front-end loading). It may be undertaken to increase profit by increasing the rates on items of which the quantities are believed to have been underestimated and decreasing the rates on items similarly believed to be overestimated.

Manually redistributing rates around the bill is a time-consuming and laborious process. However, the advent of computer-aided systems has greatly enhanced the contractor's ability to manipulate rates and fine tune the tender to his own requirements.

4.8 Writing up the bill

Having considered the various factors and quantified them, the estimator must finally adjust the bill of quantities, if it is a bill of quantities type contract, by the amounts decided in the adjudication meeting. This may be achieved by increasing all bill item rates by a single percentage, including a lump sum addition as an adjustment item, or by a combination of both.

Usually the time available between the tender adjudication meeting and the submission of the tender is limited. Estimators therefore often include a notional percentage mark-up to the bill items at the estimate stage and include lump sum adjustments to implement the adjudication panel's decisions.

The introduction of computer systems has enabled these final adjustments to be made faster and more comprehensively than was previously possible.

5. Factors that affect bidding success

In competitive bidding, where all competing contractors are judged equally suitable, the project is awarded to the contractor submitting the lowest bid or tender. Bidding success is defined as submitting a tender figure which is competitive enough to win the contract, yet realistic enough to cover the contract costs, service an appropriate proportion of the company overheads and provide the required level of profit.

Thus the factors that affect bidding success include the following:

- the accuracy of the estimate;
- the level and variability of the mark-up;
- the market conditions;
- the level of competition;
- the company efficiency and size.

5.1 The accuracy of the estimate

In producing an estimate, the estimator is required to make many assessments of both a quantitative and qualitative nature. These assessments may be based on recorded data, experience, the prevailing market conditions and a multitude of other factors. Different estimators will obviously weigh these factors differently and hence produce a range of estimates for a particular project.

Abdel-Razek [12] suggested that the overall level of inaccuracy of a cost estimate is the result of combining the effects of seven individual elements, as shown in Figure 6.5. These are as follows:

(a) the all-in labour rate;
(b) the all-in plant rate;
(c) material costs;
(d) sub-contractor costs;
(e) labour productivity rate;
(f) plant productivity rate;
(g) site overheads.

The importance of the general level of estimating accuracy and the individual company's own accuracy has been modelled and the results are reported in Harris and McCaffer [13]. It is clear that if all companies have a high standard of accuracy then the skills in choosing a construction

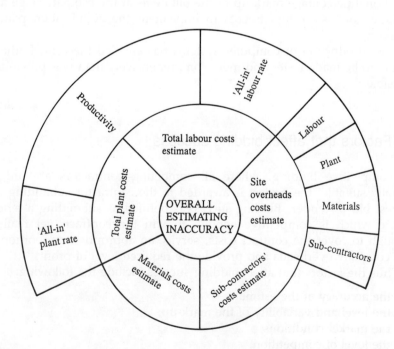

Figure 6.5   *The constituent elements of the overall estimating inaccuracy*

method, buying materials and selecting sub-contractors will play their full part in determining the most efficient, and hence most economic, contractor. If estimating accuracy is low then the incidence of the unrealistic bid winning against carefully constructed bids will be higher. Unrealistic bids are likely to lead to loss-making contracts and so not only deprive the 'winning contractor' of a profit but also deprive all the more sensible contractors of a potential profit as well. This is unhealthy for the industry and frustrating for company managers. The improvement of general estimating accuracy has taken two forms in recent years. One is the improvement of the process of estimating largely through the disciplines imposed by computer systems. The second is by more widespread and improved education and training of practising estimators across the range of companies. The main contributors in this latter improvement have been professional institutions such as the Chartered Institute of Building and the larger companies who realized that if all companies were staffed by competent estimators, general estimating accuracies would rise to the benefit of all.

5.2 The level and variability of the mark-up

The tender figure is a combination of the direct cost estimate and the mark-up. The mark-up, as previously described, is the amount added to the estimate to allow for company overheads, risk and profit. One cause of mark-up variability is the process of assessing and allowing for these elements which varies from company to company. The factors on which these assessments are based are described in the section on the adjudication process.

Another cause of mark-up variability is due to the fact that the mark-up is based on the estimated cost of the project. Thus any variation or inaccuracy in the estimated costs is reflected in the level of mark-up applied. Consequently, companies frequently assess their mark-up in absolute rather than percentage terms. Studies of variability in mark-ups [14] suggest that mark-up differences between companies are small, mark-ups are fairly tightly bunched and that as a means of distinguishing companies' tenders the mark-up element is not the most significant. A review [15] of literature on accuracy and variability of contractors tenders revealed variability in bids, as measured by the coefficient of variation (standard deviation/mean × 100) ranging from 5 to 8%. It is clear that most of this variability is derived from the direct cost estimate and not the mark-up. This once again reinforces the importance of the estimator's calculations in determining the competitiveness of companies' bids.

Mark-ups do vary with market conditions and buoyant markets do lead to higher mark-ups. However, when markets are buoyant, they are buoyant for all competitors and contractors' bids tend to drift upwards together.

5.3 Market conditions

Since 1968 the movements of tender prices and input prices have been monitored by tender price and building cost indices [16]. The differences between these two indices can be attributed to market conditions.

Market conditions is an all-embracing subjective term which on a macro-(industry) level includes such factors as the following:

- the total construction order for all work;
- the total orders for each market sector;
- projected future orders;
- current and projected governmental policy and legislation;
- construction (input) price levels;
- cost of capital.

On a micro-(company) level it will also include an assessment of:

- local, national and international opportunities;
- competitor activity;
- volume of on-going work;
- order books.

There is no generally accepted way of quantifying the effect of market conditions on tender price levels. Studies by South [17] and McCaffer, McCaffrey and Thorpe [18], demonstrated that changes in tender prices in response to market conditions could be modelled using regression techniques.

The tender price indices measure the general movement of tender prices. Contractors' tender prices comprise direct costs plus contractors' mark-up. Contractors' direct costs are an aggregate of all labour, plant, materials and sub-contractors' costs. All the material costs contain the suppliers' mark-ups, all the plant costs contain the hire companies' mark-ups, all the sub-contractors' costs contain the sub-contractors' mark-ups. Consequently, what the tender price index is measuring is not only the underlying movement in costs, but also the aggregate movement in all the suppliers', plant hire companies', and sub-contractors' mark-ups as well as that of the main contractor. Therefore, measuring the difference between the cost indices and the tender price indices indicates the movement in contractors' prices to the client and reflects the aggregate movement in all these mark-ups, not simply that of the main contractor. As markets rise, all the suppliers will tend to increase their mark-ups. This is particularly true when an industry is recovering from a severe slump.

Statistical analysis [19] of the data indicates that the gap between tender prices and costs rises after a rise in demand, and falls after a fall in demand. The lag between movements in tender prices following changes in demand is largely due to the time taken for the new orders to filter through into company output. The evidence is that the companies respond to their own forecasts of their own output (i.e. turnover) rather than movements in demand.

5.4 The level of competition

The level of competition as a determining factor of the success of a contractor's bid, is obviously a critical factor. As the demand fell during the 1970s the level of competition consequently rose and margins on contracts fell. This was no more than responses to market forces. The number of potential bidders in the market place remained high. Earlier, comment was made on the high turnover/capital ratio resulting from the relatively low capital requirements of a construction company. One consequence of low capital requirements is that more companies can be created to service the construction market and so competition is maintained at a high level.

Advice notes [20] on tendering practices recommend levels of bidders per contract. However, in depressed markets the pressures from contractors frequently see these recommended norms usurped. It is well recorded in research and companies' data that contracts won against a large number of bidders are unlikely to be profitable. The mechanism at work here is the interplay between estimating accuracy and number of bidders. This has given rise to a phenomenon known as the 'margin lost in competition' [21].

Assuming that a contract has a 'likely cost', the range of estimates produced by each company will be 'likely cost' $\pm$ A%, where A% represents the accuracy of the estimators' prediction of likely cost. Thus

Cost estimate range = likely cost $\pm$ A%

To calculate the tender, contractors add a mark-up to their cost estimate, i.e.

Tender = cost estimate + applied mark-up.

The estimator who produces the lowest estimate, say likely cost minus A%, gives his company the best chance of winning the contract. It is probable that most winning tenders will have cost estimates which are low in the range 'likely cost' $\pm$ A%.

The difference between the mean of the winning bids and the mean of all the bids, is the average margin lost in competition. Thus the winning tender based on a cost estimate, which is probably less than the likely cost, usually results in the mark-up achieved on the contract being less than the mark-up included in the tender. Over a large number of contracts, the average difference between mark-up included in tenders and achieved mark-up is the average difference between the likely cost and the estimated costs. This average difference has been called the break-even mark-up.

If a contractor did not wish to make a profit but wanted merely to break even and attempted to do so by adding a zero profit mark-up to his tenders, he would, because of estimating inaccuracies, make a net loss over a number of contracts. In order to break even in the long term he would have to apply a profit mark-up greater than zero to compensate for differences between the likely cost and estimated costs of his winning tenders. The mark-up needed to break even depends on the general level of estimating accuracy and the number of competitors.

Figure 6.6 gives an illustration of the theoretical magnitude of the margin lost in competition based on calculations and several simplifying asumptions. A more detailed description is given by Abdel-Razek [22] and Harris and McCaffer [23]. Understanding this mechanism, most contractors' attempt to improve their estimating accuracy and avoid competition with excessive numbers of bidders. Regrettably, an individual contractor with a well-developed estimating database and good estimating procedures producing very accurate estimates may well lose to the less accurate companies. In this respect, the need has long been recognized that it is in the industry's interests to generally improve the quality of estimating via education and training.

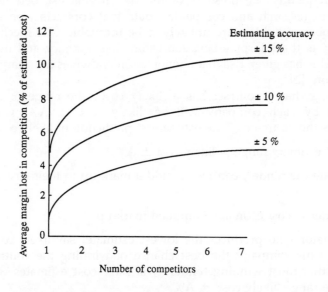

Figure 6.6 *Average margin lost in competition*

5.8 Company efficiency

Due to the nature and previous history of construction companies, each will have a unique level of competence in different types of work and corporate efficiency. The different levels of competence result in companies specializing, or preferring, certain market sectors or types of work. The detailed knowledge gained from previous works puts them at an advantage when tendering for similar projects. In addition, required items of specialized plant may be available in-house.

The organizational structure and management style of companies also influence their efficiency. Companies which have developed streamlined head-office procedures, implemented systematic and orderly site monitoring and control techniques, can operate on reduced overheads thus reducing the overhead recovery apportioned to each project.

6. Strategies for improving estimating and increasing competitive advantage

Competitive tendering based on contract documents prepared by the client's advisers is still the most common method of gaining work in the construction industry. Despite the growth of negotiated contracts and construction management packages, the requirements of public accountability and the acceptance that competitive bidding is fair while producing the lowest commercial price for the work, competitive tendering sustains its position of importance.

Clearly, for a company to continue in business and to generate an appropriate return on the capital employed, it must submit tenders that are lower than those of its competitors yet high enough to cover the construction costs, service overheads and provide profit. Given the random nature of the bidding process this is a difficult task. The actions companies take to ensure that their estimates are sound and to monitor the competition are as follows:

(a) improve data support to estimators;
(b) monitor the performance of competitors;
(c) check the sensitivity of success rate changes in mark-ups.

6.1 Improved data support

As described earlier, the estimating process relies on the estimator's assessments and assumptions of numerous factors. The knowledge and judgement of the estimator is therefore critical for estimating accuracy. Any method which supports the estimator's decision-making is thus beneficial to the bidding success of the company.

Traditionally this has been achieved through the creation and use of estimators' manuals. These contain details of construction methods, resource inputs to each construction operation, and typical output rates. The manuals also describe how all-in labour and plant rates are calculated, company standard details of bonus payments, allowances for inclement weather and allowances for supervision. These manuals have largely been made redundant with the arrival of micro-computers and the availability of computer-aided estimating systems. These systems provide well-structured data libraries to support the estimator. They also perform the tedious calculations involved quickly and accurately. It is their information storage and retrieval facilities which have greatly improved decision-support to the estimator.

The typical supporting files of a computer-aided estimating system are shown in Figure 6.7. These are as follows:

- cost files;
- performance data files;
- operational group build-ups;
- bill details.

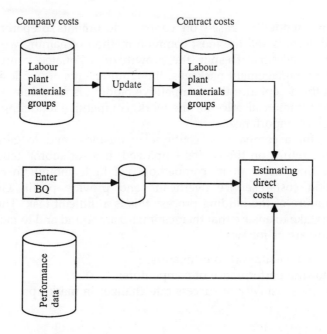

Figure 6.7 *Typical components of the supporting files of a computer aided estimating system*

The purpose of these supporting files is to provide the estimator with the data required for the direct cost calculations. These files reflect the structure of the estimating process which was previously divided into 'cost collections' and 'rate calculations'. Such files and the file management system are similarly divided with 'costs' held on one separate sub-system, subject to its own data management and the files containing the performance data. The following is a brief description of the content of these files.

6.1.1 Cost files

The company data cost files contain the all-in costs for different categories of labour, different items of plant and materials prices. Within these cost files, data relevant to either individual resources or to gangs may be stored. The contract specific cost files are the company cost files transferred by the estimator for use in a specific contract. The estimator can either accept the company data, amend it to suit his own requirements for a particular contract or, as is the case with most materials, mark it as awaiting quotes. If the awaiting-quotes-facility is used then any resultant calculation of direct cost rates by the estimator will be held separately until the buyer or estimator supplies the quotation to the system.

6.1.2 Performance data files

Performance data files contain build-ups on a unit rate basis with resources and usage rates for commonly recurring items of work. These build-ups are recorded against a set of codes that enable the estimator to identify the build-up required. In the more sophisticated systems, usually developed within large companies for their own use, the codes have also been specially devised by the companies to suit their own estimating and to link to their cost control systems. This ability to link data into other systems has emerged as a major benefit from computerized estimating.

The data contained in these build-ups which prescribe the configuration of labour, plant and materials, together with their associated outputs required to execute a particular item of work, are usually derived from the companies' own estimating data. Some proprietary systems supply data as part of the computer systems, i.e. an electronic version of the price and estimating data books. For the major companies the data are from their own estimating manuals or their work study exercises.

6.1.3 Bill details

The remaining file is to allow data describing a specific contract to be entered. The most common form in the United Kingdom remains entering details from the bills of quantities. The bill details entered by the estimating clerk or estimator's support staff, include bill number, section number, page number, bill reference and, if appropriate, a reference code which links the item with the data in the performance data file. This code would have been pencilled against the bill items by the estimator. These data are then available on recall for use by the estimator without having to re-enter them.

6.1.4 Data management

The management of the data supporting the estimator is usually the responsibility of a named individual who is normally an estimator reporting directly to the chief estimator.

The 'company' cost files will be maintained with the latest costs for labour, plant and commonly used materials. Systems provide estimators with the facility to edit (i.e. alter) such cost data, but the 'system' will record the change and it will be known to senior managers. Thus the cost management system ensures that the 'cost data' is consistent from estimator to estimator and between contracts. This provides an improved reliability in the data used and an improved understanding within the company of the factors included and excluded in the cost data. It also ensures that where estimators consider changes are necessary, the information relating to the change is not 'lost', 'overlooked' or 'forgotten'. Thus the existence of these cost-data management systems greatly improves the reliability of the cost data used.

Similarly, data contained in the performance data file are managed by a nominated person. This gives the chief estimator the managerial control to create and manage a file of performance data. In this there are descriptions of the configuration of labour or plant and their respective outputs required to undertake certain items of work. In the larger systems there are many thousands of these item build-ups. The fact that the creation of these build-ups has taken place outside the pressures of producing estimates, does potentially result in more carefully considered item build-ups. Again, the estimator's 'right' to alter such data remains, but in an accountable way. More carefully assembled performance data linked to its monitored use therefore offers greater reliability and consistency.

These benefits of improved reliability, consistency and accuracy are all derived from the improved housekeeping of the data by the disciplines imposed by the use of computer systems.

6.2 *Monitoring the performance of competitors*

All companies monitor, to some degree, the bidding performance of their competitors. This involves collecting the bids of all competitors for each contract for which the contractor has tendered, recording what companies are holding the major contracts and picking up any items of gossip it can.

6.3 *Other bids*

In many competitive bidding competitions the submitted bids are notionally confidential. However, the data relating to the bid submitted by each contractor can usually be accessed by any contractor who tries hard enough. Contractors can then find themselves able to compare their submitted bid or underlying estimate with the bid of others. Given the degree of variability in each contractor's estimate the data so collected are not particularly useful other than in providing a general guide to current trends. The comparison which contractors undertake is that between their estimate or bid and the winning or mean bid.

6.4 *Contractor's estimate v. winning bid*

If the contractor's estimate is compared to the winning bid, then some measure of the reduction in the applied mark-up required before the contractor could come close to the winning bid would be given. Due to the variability in the estimates these data on a single contract are useless. Calculating over a number of contracts it may indicate a trend. However, this trend cannot be acted upon without other supporting information.

6.5 Contractor's estimate v. mean bid

In the jargon of statisticians the 'winning bid' is an unstable statistic. If the five or six bids submitted for one contract are regarded as belonging to the same distribution of 'possible bids', then to compare the company's estimate to the lowest is to use a very variable item of data for comparison. This can be corrected by comparing the company's bid with the mean of all bids submitted, given that the calculated mean is a more stable statistic. Thus monitoring the company's estimate against the mean of bids will more accurately indicate how the company's estimating is moving with the trend. However, it is the lowest bid that wins, so a second statistic, the average difference between mean and lowest, needs to be calculated. This needs to be calculated for each number of bidders, i.e. three, four, five and six, as the difference between mean and lowest will vary with the number of bidders, (see Harris and McCaffer [24] for a more detailed description).

6.6 Difference between the winning bid and the next lowest

In competition, the statistic calculated is the gap between the winning contractor's bid and the second lowest. Colloquially this is known as the 'money left on the table'. It is another measure of the movement of the contractor's bid relative to the competition, and is as relevant as the statistics calculated in Sections 6.1 and 6.2 above.

It is frequently said that when a contract is 'won', a check is immediately made to determine where the error was. A large gap between the winning bid and the next lowest would indicate that indeed there was a great error. This is just one more argument for improving the quality, reliability, consistency and accuracy of the estimate.

6.7 Sensitivity of success rate to changes in mark-up

Having collected data relating to most of the bidding competitions entered, contractors have the opportunity of exploring what would have happened if some other bidding policies had been followed.

There is obviously a relationship between mark-up and success rate, and increases in the mark-up will reduce success rate. Sometimes the advice given is to increase the applied mark-up and compensate for the reduced success rate by bidding for more contracts. This advice may have a firm theoretical basis but can only be applied if extra contracts are available and should only be applied if the sensitivity of success rate to changes in mark-up is known. If the applied mark-ups in the contracts for which contractors have data are adjusted, and the new number of winning bids calculated, then the effects of alternative policies can be explored. For example, if all mark-ups on all large contracts were reduced by 1% how many more would have been won? If all mark-ups on all small contracts were increased by 2%, would any more have been lost?

Experimenting with bidding data in this way provides a better insight into the contractor's bidding behaviour relative to the competitors.

7. Conclusion

The construction market has seen the total demand on the industry slump in the 1970s, grow since 1981, and decline again in the early 1990s. It has also seen significant changes in the mix of demand between the various sectors. The industry has survived remarkably well the demand fluctuations which it has experienced, demonstrating a great robustness. The initial response of the industry to demand fluctuations was a 'price response'. As markets fell the price charged for construction work decreased. This was achieved by squeezing the margin not only of the main contractor but also all the materials suppliers, plant hire companies and sub-contractors. However, the fluctuations in demand were so severe that this response alone was not adequate, and the industry had to demonstrate even greater flexibility.

The industry has shown itself to be flexible in shedding and recruiting labour and has responded to a lack of continuity in work and tighter and more competitive markets, by a significant shift to sub-contracting.

The industry has also demonstrated a flexibility in the services it is prepared to offer to clients, and imaginative forms of contract have emerged.

Individual companies have demonstrated abilities to move into new geographical regions, to seek work abroad and to survive by takeovers and mergers. In the search for a workload, companies have also changed market sectors, developed repair and maintenance units or house building capabilities. The most common change forced on companies has been to seek private clients to replace the decline in work from the public sector client.

The decisions of company managers regarding target-market sectors have had to be taken against this ever-changing background. The market-place is just one more factor that adds uncertainty into an inherently uncertain industry. This uncertainty arises from the general economy, the marketplace, the bidding process, site conditions, productivity, the weather and many other factors. This has meant that the industry has had to develop managers capable of managing in these turbulent conditions. These are managers with a flexible attitude well able to plan, monitor, replan and adjust to the ever-changing situation. Not for them the comfort of long-term plans that hold good over a considerable period.

Thus decisions on market sector, public or private client, new work, engineering or building, repair and maintenance and decisions on geographical region are always kept under constant review, subject to the judgement of the individual managers and their interpretation of current trends. If the government announces a new spending programme on roads then these managers will seize on that for guidance, although frequently the information required for them to take such decisions is not so readily available.

One decision that is reviewed bid by bid is the price. The key to this is the reliability of the company's estimate of the cost of the work. Thus the decision in estimating and tendering becomes a key instrument in the company's response to market changes.

Governing all these decisions, both strategic and tactical, is the balance between opportunity and risk.

References

1. Government Statistical Service, Department of the Environment, *Quarterly Bulletin of Housing and Construction Statistics*, HMSO.
2. Harris, F. and McCaffer, R., (1989). *Modern Construction Management*, 3rd edn, BSP.
3. McCaffer, R. and Baldwin, A. N. (1984) *Estimating and Tendering for Civil Engineering Works*, BSP.
4. Chadwick, L. (1982) 'Materials management, profitability and the construction industry', *Building Technology and Management*, CIOB.
5. Civil Engineering Construction Conciliation Board for Great Britain (1988) *Constitution and Working Rule Agreement*, Federation of Civil Engineering Contractors.
6. Abdel-Razek, R. H. and McCaffer, R. (1986) 'The range of inaccuracy in the estimated all-in-labour rate', *International Journal of Construction Management and Technology*, **1**, No. 1.
7. Harris, F. and McCaffer, R., *op. cit.*
8. Abdel-Razek, R. H. and McCaffer, R. (1987) 'Evaluating variability in the estimated all-in plant rate'. *International Journal of Construction Management and Technology*, **2**, No. 2.
9. Abdel-Razek, R. H. and McCaffer, R. (1986) 'Evaluating the variability in estimates of material costs'. *International Journal of Construction Management and Technology*, **1**, No. 2.
10. Abdel-Razek, R. H. and McCaffer, R. (1987) 'A change in the UK construction industry structure: implications for estimating', *Construction Management and Economics*, **5**, No. 3.
11. McCaffer, R. and Baldwin, A. N. *op. cit.*.
12. Abdel-Razek, R. H. (1987) *Computerised Analyses of Estimating Inaccuracy and Tender Variability: Causes, Evaluation and Consequences*. PhD Thesis, Loughborough University of Technology.
13. Harris, F. and McCaffer, R. *op. cit.*
14. Grinyer, P. H. and Whittaker, J. D. (1973) 'Managerial judgement in the competitive bidding model'. *Operational Research Quarterly*, **24**, No. 2.

15. Ogunlana, O. and Thorpe, A. (1987) 'Design phase cost estimating: the state of the art'. *International Journal of Construction Technology and Management*, 2, No. 4.
16. Tysoe, B. (1981) *Construction Cost and Price Indices: Description and Use*. E & F. N. Spon.
17. South, L. E. (1979) *Construction Companies and Demand Fluctuations*, MSc Thesis, Loughborough University of Technology.
18. McCaffer, R., McCaffrey, M. J. and Thorpe, A. (1973) 'The disparity between construction cost and tender price movements'. *Construction Papers*, 2, No. 2.
19. McCaffer, R., McCaffrey, M. J. and Thorpe, A. *op. cit.*
20. The Institution of Civil Engineers, The Association of Consulting Engineers and the Federation of Civil Engineering Contractors (1983) *Guidance on the Preparation, Submission and Consideration of Tenders for Civil Engineering Contracts.*
21. Harris, F. and McCaffer, R. *op. cit.*
22. Abdel-Razek, R. H. *op. cit.*
23. Harris and McCaffer 1989.
24. Harris, F. and McCaffer, R. *op. cit.*

——— 7 ———

The strategic management of projects

Peter W. G. Morris

1. Introduction

The subject of this chapter is the outlining of an overall strategy for
managing projects successfully. This is a vast topic. It is hardly been
attempted anywhere before, not even in that literature which singularly
addresses the management of projects. Attempting it in a book which
deals primarily with the construction industry is in a sense even more
ambitious. Nevertheless, recent research conducted through the Major
Projects Association at Templeton College gives me sufficient confidence
to believe that we can now outline comprehensively, and briefly, the
elements needed to ensure that projects are initiated and accomplished
successfully.

Modern project management, as I shall show shortly, is a relatively
young discipline – perhaps 20–30 years old. It is a discipline which is
predominantly practitioner-led: only very recently has there been any
academic support to the research and teaching of the subject. Much of the
practitioners' enthusiasm has been associated with the development, from
the 1960s onwards, of computer systems to plan and control project
activities and costs. Unfortunately, this has led to the discipline of project
management being centred on these systems, supplemented as well by an
interest in the organizational practices required to make projects successful. Vitally important though both these are, they are by no means
sufficient to ensure project success.

Successful projects require the following:

- the effective strategic and technical definition of what the project is
  about, as well as the management of that definition as it unfolds;
- the active management of the interplay between the project's definition and the political and financial environments in which it finds
  itself;
- the careful defining of the timing of the project, both in its total
  duration and in its phasing;
- the creation of the right organizational attitudes among all the parties
  involved in the project's success;
- the active development and implementation of the project as it
  evolves.

The process of managing this bigger framework I have called 'The management of projects' to distinguish it from project management, which has come to retain a more limited interest in tools and techniques.

What is now needed to understand the management of projects is an holistic, top-down approach to looking at projects and managing them rather than merely a middle-management, tools and techniques orientation. Those engaged in projects, whether in the building industry, petrochemicals, or any of the countless other areas in which projects are to be found, need to be thinking of their projects in this broader framework so that they can understand the 'whole' that their enterprise involves, and the part that their efforts are playing in that totality.

This chapter attempts to provide such an holistic view of the management of projects.

2. Projects and the strategy for managing them

Projects have been around for years. Man's earliest records illustrate a profound desire to engage in major building projects. Many were performed exceptionally well. Indeed, the Pyramids of Giza stand among the greatest and most successful projects of all time. Why then is there this interest in the art and science of managing projects today, if we could do them so well thousands of years ago?

During the last 100 years the environment in which projects have been accomplished has changed totally. Whole new technologies have arisen; technically and organizationally, projects have become much more complex; the intellectual apparatus with which people think about their work has changed radically – 100 years ago there were virtually no theories of management; views of social responsibility and of science and engineering were vastly different from what they are today; and latterly, the needs of financing have become particularly wound up with the way a project will be defined and carried out. So it is not that previously we were unable to manage projects so much as that now the context in which we address projects is new and requires a new language.

Modern project management, as I have shown in detail elsewhere [1], grew initially out of the interests of the US Air Force and Exxon in the late 1920s and 1930s in creating a project coordinator function. (This function was defined precisely by Gulick in a paper in 1937 [2].) There was some use of modern project management terminology in World War II, particularly by the US Corp of Engineers, but the real development of modern concepts and practices and terminologies came with the US missile programme in the mid-1950s, particularly Atlas and Polaris [3].

Atlas saw the emergence of systems engineering and systems and program management. Polaris elevated the program as a form of organization to an extremely high level within the military hierarchy. Admiral Raborn, the program manager for Polaris, managed the program as a full blooded project in the round, very much along the grounds to be outlined in this chapter. Great attention was given to political, community and funding matters; enormous effort was given to the technical and engineering issues; huge emphasis was put on team building and motivation; and of course, Polaris is famous for the development of the first really well-known project management system, PERT. (Raborn was created head of Polaris in 1955; when the first Polaris missile was launched in 1960, press coverage of PERT proved almost as great as the coverage of the launch itself.)

The 1960s were to see a dramatic championing of project management through NASA's Apollo program. Huge TV audiences watched as Neil Armstrong and Buzz Aldrin stepped on to the moon. As they did so none could fail to be impressed by the enormous engineering management achievement of NASA in accomplishing this task just eight years after President Kennedy set the goal 'before this decade is out of landing a man on the moon and returning him safely to earth'. The myth of project management, with all the arcane language which NASA so delighted in using, was promoted and broadcast liberally.

By the late 1960s to mid-1970s the subject of project management was attracting enormous attention. Management systems were being developed in their profusion largely, though not exclusively, in the US defence–aerospace field. (Many indeed still continue as core project management systems and practices: methods such as the Critical Path Method (CPM), Precedence, GERT, VERT, resource scheduling, C/SCSC, earned value, work breakdown structures, and configuration management.) Yet despite the development of these systems and techniques, in the real world most projects were still not performing well.

Even in defence/aerospace the record belied the seeming simplicity of the project management message. Several studies during the 1960s, particularly by the Rand Corporation [4], showed that the cost, schedule and technical performance of projects was anything but satisfactory with cost and schedule overruns of up to 400% being experienced. Indeed, by the late 1960s the Pentagon was considering the problem to be little short of a crisis. The new Assistant Secretary of Defense, David Packard, implemented a range of new and fruitful practices,[1] most particularly greater emphasis on front-end definition and an insistence on avoiding production before thorough prototype testing. (That is, the avoidance of 'concurrency' – concurrency being the process of simultaneously developing, testing and producing a product. Several studies have shown that concurrency is nearly always associated with cost or schedule overruns [5].)

---

[1] One of the least successful was that of the total package procurement (TPP) under which the Pentagon attempted to transfer all responsibility for the program as a 'total package' onto the contractor. This might have worked had the Pentagon not made frequent changes and had there not been such large cost inflation. Unfortunately these two factors led to the virtual bankruptcy of TPP contractors, particularly McDonnell Douglas, and in 1972 the process was abandoned.

The consequences of inadequate project definition and poor technology development were meanwhile being experienced in a number of other industries. Britain, for example, suffered severely on several projects, most notably Concorde and the TSR 2. The development of the UK AGR nuclear power reactors similarly exhibited an almost wanton disregard for technical risk while simultaneously shifting responsibility massively, and unfairly, onto the contractors. The AGR programme was a disaster and the contractors essentially went bankrupt [6].

Meanwhile as this new management paradigm was taken and used – in completely new contexts by people who were neither at the level, nor had the responsibilities, of the original pioneers of project management – projects in the 'civil domain' began to suffer dramatically from their impact on the social environment. Politicians, local communities, financiers and other 'external' groups began to restrain the ability of managers to accomplish projects successfully. California's BART, London's third airport, several major road schemes, Concorde, the Trans-Alaskan pipeline, the US Supersonic Transport and several other projects were all stopped, or at any rate delayed, as a consequence of community and environmentalist opposition. Nowhere was this tension more fought over than in the nuclear power industry where political push and technological bloody-mindedness caused the merit of the environmentalists' arguments to be ignored for far too long [7].

As Sayles and Chandler perceptively wrote in 1971 of the management lessons of Apollo:

> compared to some of the socio-technical programs [on the horizon], NASA had a simple life. NASA was a closed loop – it set its own schedule, designed its own hardware and used the gear it designed. The populous did not feel threatened by the program; on the whole the popular mood was supportive. As one moves into the socio-technical area, this luxury disappears. Housing and environmental protection for example will have to deal with political complexities never dreamed of. Management and organizational skills will be many times more critical in these inherently unwieldy public-private systems. [8]

They were nearer to the truth than they realised. It was the unwillingness of Nixon, facing an overheated economy and the drain of Vietnam, to fund massive space programs that led to the downsizing of the space shuttle program which led to the technical disaster that the shuttle program essentially became [9]. By the early 1970s the ability to manage political forces was clearly an essential element in the successful management of projects.

This combination of economic, organizational and political forces was to be a characteristic of the project world throughout the 1970s and 1980s. Yet most of the professional project management practitioners acted as though they did not matter. By the early 1970s project management had become taken up by groups of largely middle managers fascinated by intraproject organizational issues and by the systems and jargon of the US aerospace community. This inward-looking attitude was further reinforced by the emergence at this time of a new form of management structure – the matrix – which was at this period being launched in hundreds of major organizations. As a result, thousands of professionals were suddenly propelled into operating, for the first time, in a project environment. Simultaneously, professional societies were formed in America and Europe which encouraged practitioners to share their knowledge and disseminate their systems and intraorganizational perspectives of project management.

The net result was that project management was launched in the early 1970s as a discipline immediately out-of-date with reality. But so mesmerizing was the jargon hardly anyone noticed. This situation continued almost without change for the next 20 years.

By the end of the 1980s this marvellous discipline, which by now was attracting the attention of thousands around the globe, and in which an absolute industry of publication was burgeoning, had achieved almost everywhere little short of a trail of disasters. The defence industries on both sides of the Atlantic were riddled with massive tales of overruns and botched projects. NASA, with its space shuttle program, was deteriorating. The oil and gas industries were experiencing huge cost overruns in the North Sea, particularly in the early and mid-1970s, due to technical uncertainties and economic overheating. The power, civil engineering and building industries were suffering from poorly conceived projects and substantial cost overruns, particularly in the nuclear power and third world sectors (where 'loan pushing' caused by the recycling of some $500 bn of petrodollars had been responsible for hundreds of badly set-up projects). Telecommunications and information system projects similarly had a terrible record of overruns and poor performance.

The 1980s were, however, to see some improvement in both our understanding and the practice of managing projects. As the price of oil fell and as experience was gained, North Sea oil projects improved dramatically. Defence projects, at least in the United Kingdom, began to improve with the new practices introduced under Sir Peter Levene; at the same time the increasing tendency towards consortia and joint ventures in defence – and indeed other sectors – brought significant improvements in project performance. Although the onset of the third world debt crisis from August 1982 led to the highly regrettable cessation of commercial lending to developing countries, the emergence of privatization schemes and build–own–operate (–transfer) projects led to an increased and beneficial focus on defining the project as a whole: of viewing its operating performance capabilities jointly with its construction and financing efficiency. Further, and ironically, just as third world commercial lending was drying up and aid lending began to be severely cut back, a series of writings on aid by Cassen, Moris, Paul and others in the early-1980s was making as clear as anybody could probably ever wish, the lessons for successful development projects [10]. The growth in use of the environmental impact procedure was a further development which was to prove extremely beneficial during the decade. By requiring a full definition of the project in its early stages and coupling this with extensive consultation with local and national groups, the dangers of poorly defined and ill-communicated projects were substantially diminished.

There were of course still many problems. The US defence industry in particular continues to be an Aladdin's cave of problem projects. NASA continues to find enormous problems with its principal project, the space station 'Freedom'. The Channel Tunnel has not exactly proved itself a model of how to manage a project, nor, sadly, a very good advertisement for the build–own–operate (–transfer) method. The power industry continues to be substantially troubled by the after-shocks of the nuclear program (Chernobyl, Shoreham, the UK programme, etc.). Nevertheless, by and large the track record of projects has improved substantially during this last decade.[2]

Amazingly, however, the writings on project management were largely – at least until the late-1980s – oblivious to all this change and rage in the firmament about it, and the implications that this must have on the discipline of managing projects. Where it was reflected was more in the work of newly formed major project associations and macro-engineering societies around the world [11].

In this chapter, I wish to synthesize insights that have been made through my research at Templeton College, the home of the UK Major Projects Association, in building a general model for the management of projects, incorporating both the traditional intraproject insights and our knowledge on these external and strategic issues.

So, what, then, can one say about the strategic management of projects?

3. The strategic management of projects

The way one sets up a project determines largely how successful it will be. The crucial point about the model I am about to present is that *all* the items in the model must be considered from the outset if the project's chances of success are to be optimized, not just, as is often supposed, those of, say, project definition, financing and planning approvals. The project must be seen as a whole and it must further be managed so as it is implemented.

The model is shown in Figure 7.1. Its logic is essentially that described at the outset of this chapter:

1. First, the project will be in great danger of encountering serious problems if its *objectives, technical base* and general *strategic planning* are

---

[2] Details of the developments noted here for the 1970s and 1980s are copiously documented in 'The first 50 years of project management lessons in the management of projects'.

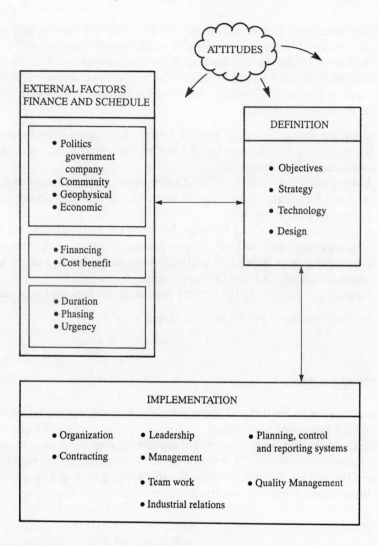

Figure 7.1 *The management of projects*

inadequately considered or poorly developed, or if its *design* is not firmly managed in line with its strategic plans.

2. The project's *definition* both affects and is affected by changes in *external factors* (such as politics, community views, and economic and geophysical conditions), availability of *financing* and *project duration*, and that therefore this interaction must be managed actively and well. (Many of these interactions operate, of course, through the forecast performances of the product(s) that the project will deliver once completed.)

3. Both the project's definition, its interaction with these external, financial and other matters, and its implementation, will be much harder to

manage and quite possibly damagingly prejudiced if the *attitudes* of the parties essential to its success are not positive and supportive.

4. Pre-eminent issues in the *realization* of the project as it is defined, developed, built and tested – the crucial 'project management' stage of developing the project within its defined schedule, cost and technical scope definition – include:

- deciding the appropriate project–matrix–functional orientation and balancing the involvement of the owner, as operator, and the project implementation specialists;
- having contracts which reflect the owners' aims, are motivational, and appropriately reflect the risks involved and the ability of the parties to bear these risks;
- establishing checks and balances between the enthusiasm and drive of the project staff and the proper conservatism of its sponsors;
- developing team attitudes, with great emphasis being put on active communication and productive conflict;
- having the right tools for project planning, control and reporting.

Let us examine these points in brief detail.

3.1 Project definition

The project should be defined comprehensively from its earliest days in terms of its purpose, ownership, technology, cost, schedule, duration, financing, marketing and sales, organization, energy and raw materials supply, transportation, etc. If it is not defined properly 'in the round' like this from the outset, key issues essential to its viability could be missed or given inadequate attention resulting in a poor or even disastrous project later.

3.1.1 Objectives

The extent to which the project's objectives are not clear, are complex, do not mesh with longer-term strategies, are not communicated clearly or are not agreed, will compromise the chances of project success. The Apollo program, for example, was technically extremely difficult; its chances of success were helped immeasurably by the clarity of its objective however.

Comparison with NASA's space station – currently the largest civil project in the world – is interesting. Superficially clear (in President Regan's words 'to develop a permanently manned space station and to do it within a decade'), the objective is in fact far from being very clear. What, for example, does 'develop' really mean – just design and construct? Surely not. Also, these difficulties reflect fundamental uncertainties over the station's real long-term strategy. Earth observation? A way-station to inter-planetary travel? Celestial observation? Micro-gravity and other experimental purposes? A combination of these? The space station illustrates that project, or programme, objectives must match with viable long-term strategies.

3.1.2 Strategies

Strategies for the attainment of the project objectives should similarly be developed in as comprehensive a manner as possible from the outset. This means that at the pre-feasibility and feasibility stages, for example, industrial relations, contracting, communications, organization and systems issues should all be considered, even if not elaborated upon, as well as the technical, financial, schedule and planning issues.

Some of the most valuable work on the need for comprehensive planning has come from R & D and new product development, and indeed for development aid projects.

Hirshman's 1967 'Development projects observed' [12] was one of the first writings explicitly to pull the 'project success' question into project management. The 1980s insights of Cassen and Moris encapsulate most of what anyone of good sense would expect regarding what it takes to produce successful development projects [13].

Cooper's, Manfield's, and others' writings on new product development, similarly relate product implementation performance to environmental and market success [14].

3.1.3 Technology and design

The development of the design criteria and the technical elements of the project should be handled with the utmost care. The design standards selected will affect both the difficulty of construction and the operating characteristics of the plant. Maintainability and reliability should be critical factors in determining the project's operating characteristics. The technical risk in particular should be assessed. The rate of technology change in all relevant systems and subsystems should be examined. Many studies have shown that technical problems have a huge impact on the likelihood of project overrun [15]: thorough risk analysis is therefore essential.

No design is ever complete; technology is always progressing. A central challenge in the effective management of projects is the conflict between meeting the schedule against the desire to achieve improvement in the technical base. The orderly progressing of the project's sequence of review stages, the level of detail becoming progressively tighter with strict control of technical interfaces and of proposed changes (through configuration management), is now a core element of modern project management.[3]

Projects as widely different as weapons systems, process plants and information systems now generally employ project development methodologies which emphasize careful, discrete upgradings of technology, thorough review of cost, schedule and performance implications and rigorous control of subsequent proposed changes. (Civil engineering and building, however, because of the split between design and construction still common in most countries, alone of today's major project-based industries, still tend not to have design management practices as a central part of the evolving total project management process.)

A major issue in project specification is how great a 'technological reach' should be aimed for without incurring undue risks of cost overruns, schedule slippages or inadequate technical performance. Up until about the 1980s this was perhaps the most difficult issue to get right on projects. During the 1980s, however, practice has become better (though there have still been some spectacular disasters) partly because our basic technologies are not progressing into new domains at quite the rate they were before, but partly also because of the greater caution, care over risk assessment, use of prototypes, etc., which are now more common in project practice. It is barely conceivable that we should embark on a brand new nuclear power reactor (AGR) or aerospace project (Concorde) today with the bravura that we did 20–25 years ago.

Therefore, in setting up projects care should be taken to appraise technological risk, prove new technologies and validate the project design, before 'freezing' the design and moving into implementation.

3.2 External factors, finance and timing

Many external factors affect a project's chances of success. Several may be identified but the project's political context, its relationship with the local community, the general economic environment and its location and the geophysical conditions in which it is set are particularly important.

3.2.1 Political, environmental and economic factors

Project personnel have had notable difficulty in recent years in recognizing and dealing with the project's impact on the physical and community

---

[3] Configuration management is the project management term for ensuring that the project's shape and technical features evolve in a consistent and orderly manner. Changes must be carefully vetted and implemented in a controlled way so that everyone on the project knows and agrees them. Technically, configuration management is change control coupled with documentation management. A standard term in aerospace, telecoms and information systems management, it is still, curiously, relatively unknown in construction.

'environment' and, in consequence, in managing the political processes which regulate the conditions under which projects are executed.

Most projects raise political issues of some sort and hence require political support: moral, regulatory, and sometimes even financial. National transportation projects, R & D programs and many energy projects, for example, operate only under the dictate of the politician. The civil nuclear power business has been heavily pushed politically. Third world development projects are especially prone to political influence. Even where the public sector is supposedly liberated to the private, as in build–own–operate projects, political guidance, guarantees, and encouragement, are needed.

Do non-major projects also need to be conscious of the political dimension? Absolutely: even small projects live under regulatory and economic conditions that are directly influenced by politicians. Intraorganizationally, the project manager must also secure 'political' support for his project.

The important lesson, therefore, is that these political issues must be considered at the outset of the project. The people and procedures which are to work on the project must be attuned to the political issues and be ready to manage them. To be successful, project managers must manage *upwards* and *outwards*, as well as downwards and inwards. The project manager should court the politicians, gaining allies by providing them with the information they need to champion his or her programme. Adversaries should be coopted, not ignored. (The environmental impact assessment process is showing how substantive dialogue can help reduce potential opposition, as will be described shortly.)

Although, as has been noted, 'environmentalism' has been prejudicing project implementation since at the least the 1960s, most project personnel ignored it as a serious force, at least until 1987–88 when Mrs Thatcher, the World Bank and others suddenly made it 'establishment'. Now, at last, most project staff realize that they must find a way of involving the community positively in the development of their project. Ignoring the community, leaving everything to planning hearings, is often to leave it too late. A 'consents strategy' must be devised and implemented [16]. Dialogue must begin early in the project's development.

Getting the support of the local community is, in a different sense, particularly important in those projects where it is, so to speak, the user, as, for example, in development projects and information technology. The local community may also be the potential consumer or purchaser for the project. Carrying out a market survey to see how variable are the project economics, is an essential part of the project's management.

Changes in economic circumstances affect both the cost of the project's inputs and the economic viability of its outputs. The big difference today, compared with 20 years ago, is that then we assumed conditions would not vary too much in the future; now, after the economic dislocation of the 1970s and 1980s, we are much more cautious in appraising and managing our projects. Externalities and longer-term social factors are now recognized as important variables which can dramatically affect the attractiveness of a project. In the area of cost-benefit discounting and other appraisal techniques, practice has moved forward considerably over the last few years. Indeed, the basic project appraisal techniques of the 1960s have now largely been replaced with a broader set of economic and financial tools arrayed, in the community context, under the Environment Impact Analysis (EIA) procedure.

Initially resisted by many in the project community, the great value of the EIA process is that it allows consultation and dialogue between developers, the community, regulators and others, and forces time to be spent at the 'front end' in examining options and ensuring that the project appears viable. Through these twin benefits the likelihood of community opposition and of unforeseen external shocks arising is diminished.

Further, in forcing project developers to spend time planning at the front end, the EIA process is emphasizing precisely the project stage which has traditionally been rushed, despite the obvious dangers. Time spent in the project's early stages is time well spent – and furthermore it is cost-effective time well spent – yet all too frequently this stage is rushed.

3.2.2 Finance

During the 1980s there was a decisive shift from public sector funding to the private sector. There is a belief that projects built under private sector funding inevitably demonstrate better financial discipline. Where projects are built and financed by a well-managed private sector company this is doubtless true, but private financing alone does not necessarily lead to better projects, as the record of third world lending in the 1970s shows (weak project appraisals, loan pushing, cost and schedule overruns, white elephants, etc). What is required is funding realism. The best way to achieve this is by having all parties accept some risk, and making them face up to this squarely by undertaking a thorough risk assessment. Full risk analysis of the type carried out for limited-recourse project financing, for example, invariably leads to better set up projects and should therefore be built into the project specification process. The use of this form of funding in methods such as build–own–operate has had the healthy consequence of making all parties concentrate on the continuing economic health of the project by tying their actions more tightly to that goal.

The raising of the finance required for the Channel Tunnel from the capital markets in 1986–87 is a classic illustration of how all the elements shown in Figure 7.1 interact, in this case around the question of finance.

Raising the £6b finance called for certain technical work be done, planning approvals obtained, contracts signed, political uncertainties removed, etc. Since the project was raising most of its funding externally, there was a significant amount of 'bootstrapping' required: the tasks could only be accomplished if some money was already raised, and so on. Actions had to be taken by a certain time or the money would run out.

Further, a key parameter of the project's viability was the likelihood of its slippage during construction. A slippage of three to six months meant not just increased financing charges but the lost revenue of a summer season of tourist traffic. The Channel Tunnel thus demonstrates also the significance of managing a project's schedule and of how its timing interrelates with its other dimensions.

3.2.3 Duration

Determining the overall timing of the enterprise is crucial to calculating its risks and the dynamics of its implementation and management. How much time one has available for each of the basic stages of the project, together with the amount and difficulty of the work to be accomplished in those phases, heavily influences the nature of the task to be managed.

In specifying the project, therefore, the project manager will spend considerable effort ensuring that the right proportions of time are spent within the overall duration. Milestone scheduling of the project at the earliest stage is crucial. It is particularly important that none of the development stages of the project be rushed or glossed over, a fault which has caused many project catastrophes in the past. A degree of urgency should be built into the project, but too much may create instability.

Avoid specifying implementation to begin before technology development and testing is complete. This is the 'concurrency' situation. Concurrency is sometimes employed quite deliberately – to get a project completed under exceptionally urgent conditions – but it often brings major problems in redesign and reworking.

Concurrency is now increasingly synonymous with Fast Track: that is building before design is complete. If faced with this, be under no illusion as to the risk. Analyse the risk rigorously, work-breakdown element by work-breakdown element, milestone phase by milestone phase. 'Fast Build' is now used to distinguish a different form of design and construction overlap – that where the concept, or scheme design, is completed, but then the work packages are priced, scheduled and built sequentially within the overall design parameters, with strict change (configuration) control being exercised throughout. With this 'Fast Build' situation the design is secure and the risks are much less.

There are, in short, several lessons on how to deal with the challenge of managing urgent projects. First, do not miss out any of the stages of the project. Second, use known technology and/or design replication as far as possible, avoiding unnecessary innovation. Third, test technology before committing to production (prototyping); avoid concurrency unless prepared to take the risk of failing and of having to pay for the cost of rework. Fourth, avoid making technical or design changes once implementation has begun; choose design parameters broad enough to permit development and detailing without subsequent change ('Fast Build'); exert strict change control/configuration management. Fifth, order long lead items early. Sixth, prefabricate and/or build in an as predictable an environment as possible, and set the organizational factors to support optimum productivity. Seventh, put in additional management effort to ensure the proper integration, at the right time, of the things that must be done to make the project a success – teamwork, scheduling conscious decision-making, etc.

Each of the three areas of external factors, finance, and duration is affected by, and affects, the viability of project definition. They must all be managed by the project executive. They must then be implemented through the project's life cycle.

3.3 Attitudes

Implementation can only be achieved effectively if the proper attitudes exist on the project. Unless there is a major commitment towards making the project a success, unless the motivation of everyone working on the project is high, and unless attitudes are supportive and positive, the chances of success are substantially diminished.

It is particularly important that there is commitment and support at the top. Without it the project is probably doomed. But while commitment is important it must be commitment to viable ends. Great leaders can become great dictators. It is important that if sane and sensible projects are to be initiated they are not insulated from criticism. Thus, criticize the project at its specification stage, and ensure that it continues to receive objective and frank reviews as it develops.

3.4 Implementation

Project management, I have suggested, has in the past been concerned primarily with the process of implementation. This is a pity since it implies that developing the definition of the project is somehow not something which is the concern of the project's management. As the foregoing shows, this is absurd. To avoid this confusion I have suggested that a better term for the discipline might be 'the management of projects'.

The key conceptual point is therefore not only that the specification process must be actively managed, but that the specification process must consider all those factors which might prejudice its success – not just technical matters, economics and finance but ecological, political and community factors and implementation issues also.

3.4.1 Organisation

The two key organization issues in projects are, to decide the relevant project–matrix–functional orientation and the extent of owner involvement. Both of these must be considered from the earliest stages of project specification.

On the former, it should be noted that a full project orientation is expensive in resourcing terms. Also, many projects start and finish with a functional orientation but 'swing' to a matrix during implementation. Implementing a matrix takes time, and effort must be put into developing the appropriate organizational climate. Organization behaviour assistance should therefore be considered when designing and building a matrix organization. (Indeed, this is also true for other forms of project organization.)

Crucial issues regarding the extent of owner involvement centre around the extent to which the owner does not have the resources, skills, outlook or experience, but does have legal or moral responsibility for assuring the implementation is of a satisfactory standard.

The first constraint is the most common. In building and civil engineering, for example, because of the nature of the demand, the owner rarely if ever has sufficient resources in-house to accomplish the project. Outside resources – principally designers, contractors and suppliers – have to be contracted in. The owner, quite properly, focuses more on running his business.

However, some degree of owner involvement is generally necessary, for if no project management expertise is maintained in-house, then active, directive decision-making of the kind which is generally necessary will not be available. On the other hand, if operators who are not really in the implementation business get too involved, then there is a danger that the owner's staff may tinker with, and refine, design and construction decisions at the expense of effective project implementation.

The solution to this dilemma is not an easy one to determine. There is in fact no standard answer and what is correct will be so for each given mix of project characteristics, organizations and personalities.

The key point is ultimately for owner-operators to concentrate on pre-determined milestone review points – the key markers in the project's development at which one wants the project to have reached a certain stage satisfactorily – to schedule these properly and to review the project comprehensively as it passes across each of them. Milestone scheduling by owners is in fact now much more accepted as appropriate rather than the more detailed scheduling of the past.

3.4.2 Contract strategy

The degree of owner involvement is clearly related to the contractual strategy being developed. It is now generally recognized that the type of contract – essentially either cost reimburseable or incentive (including fixed price) – should relate to the degree of risk the contractor is expected, and able, to bear. If the project scope is not yet clear it is probably better not to use an incentive or fixed-price type of contract and the contract can be converted to this form later. Contracts should be motivational with top management support and positive attitudes should be encouraged.

The parties should put as much effort as possible, as early as possible, into a contract to identify their joint objectives. It is better to spend longer working out how to make the contract a success than how to 'do down' the other party. While competitive bidding is healthy and therefore to be encouraged, adequate time and information must be provided in order to make the bid as effective as possible. Time should also be spent ensuring that the bases upon which the bid is to be evaluated are the best, as price alone is often inadequate.

3.4.3 People issues

Projects generally demand extraordinary effort from those working on them (often for a comparatively modest financial reward with the ultimate prospect of working oneself out of a job). Frequently, significant institutional resistance must be overcome in order for the many factors to be even approaching a satisfactory situation! This therefore puts enormous demands on the personal qualities of all those working on the project, from senior management through the professional team(s) to the workforce.

The different roles of manager, leader, champion and sponsor should be distinguished (Figure 7.2). Each is needed throughout the project but the initial stages particularly require the latter three.

Project manager:	A manager is someone who gets others to do what he or she is not able to do himself. He or she is a manager of resources.
Leader:	A leader is someone who gets people to follow him or her.
Project champion:	A champion promotes something. The project champion has an extremely important role early in the project particularly in ensuring the project receives the attention and resources it will need to survive.
Project sponsor:	The sponsor is the provider of resources. The sponsor must ensure the project will make operational sense once it is completed.

Figure 7.2   *Different project manager roles*

One should guard against unchecked champions and leaders, and the hype and overoptimism which too often surrounds projects in their early stages. The 'sponsor' must be responsible for providing the objective check on the feasibility of the project.

One should recognize the importance of team working, of handling the inevitable conflicts which arise positively, and of good communications. Consideration should be given to formal start-up sessions at the beginning of a team's work (mixing planning with team building). The composition of the team should be looked at from a social angle as well as technical one, as people play social roles on teams, and these will be required to vary as the project evolves.

All projects involve conflict: cost schedule and technical performance are in conflict; contracts potentially include conflict. Conflict can in fact be used positively as a source of creativity. On the best projects, conflict is managed in this way but on some projects it is ignored or brushed over – at best a creative tension is lost, at worst it becomes destructive.

Every effort should be made to plan for good industrial productivity. The last 20 years are rich in lessons, ranging in the United Kingdom for example from NAECI and the Thames Barrier to BP's Acetyles 5.

3.4.4 Planning and control

Plans should be prepared by those technically responsible for their work and integrated by an organizationally distinct planning and control group. Planning initially should be at a broad 'systems' level with detail only being provided where essential, and in general on a 'rolling wave' basis. Similarly for cost, estimates should be prepared by work-breakdown element[5], detail being provided as appropriate[4]. Cost should be related to finance and assembled into forecast out-turn cost, related both to the forecast actual construction price and to the actual product sales price.

Implementation of systems and procedures should be planned carefully so that all those working on the project understand them properly. Start-up meetings should develop the systems procedures in outline and begin substantive planning while simultaneously 'building' the project team.

A final word of caution. It is vital that attention be given to managing the plant computer systems. There have recently been some spectacular cases of plant hardware being complete but the plant being unable to start up because the computer systems themselves had not been managed effectively as projects.

---

[4] The work–breakdown structure is a tool developed in the early 1960s: a 'product-oriented family tree of hardware, software, services and other work tasks which organizes, defines and graphically displays the product to be produced, as well as the work to be accomplished to achieve a specified product' [17]. Though little known in the construction industries, the work–breakdown structure provides a logical, coherent complete statement of what the project comprises; it also allows a coding system to be developed which enables cost, schedule, technical and other data to be identified and cross-related. It is fundamental to project control .

4. Conclusions

The message of this chapter is, in short, that a model of the strategic management of projects does exist. The framework sketched in Figure 7.1 indicates the main items that should be considered; the lessons outlined in the second half of this chapter, and detailed elsewhere, furnish the 'meat' that goes on to that framework. All the items identified in Figure 7.1 should be considered from the earliest stages of the project and should be kept in review as the project develops, receiving particular scrutiny at the major life cycle change points.

The model presented in Figure 7.1 is of course a high-level one (it is bound to be since its essence is its comprehensiveness). Note, therefore, that as one gets into any particular 'sub-systems' the level of detail will increase. The two sub-systems where models have more commonly been developed in detail are financing and implementation.

Ideally, at a higher level both these sub-systems should converge around a 'what does it take to make this project as a whole a success?' kind of model, and indeed this is what is beginning to happen now in 'best practice'. BOT/project-finance and contractor-led project and programme management are two examples of such best practice convergence.

Construction is in fact witnessing a long overdue synthesis of overall project management practice. Increasingly, one will see the best contractors, financiers and others working together to secure the best management of projects.

References

1. Morris, P. W. G. 'The Management of Projects – Lessons From The First 50 Years Of Modern Project Management', forthcoming.
2. Gulick, L. (1937) 'Notes on the theory of organization', in Urwick, L. (ed.) *Papers on the Science of Administration*, Institute of Public Administration, Colombia University Press, New York, pp. 1–46.
3. Beard, E. (1976) *Developing the ICBM*, Colombia University Press, New York. McDougall, W. A. (1985) *The Heavens and the Earth: a Political History of the Space Age*, Basic Books, New York. Putnam, W. D. (1982) *The Evolution of Air Force System Acquisition Management*, Rand Corporation, R–868–PW, Santa Monica, California, August. Sapolsky, H. (1972) *The Polaris System Development:Bureaucratic and Programmatic Success in Government*, Harvard University Press, Cambridge, Massachusetts.
4. Harman, A. J. assisted by Henrichsen, A. (1970) *A Methodology for Cost Factor Comparison and Prediction*. Rand Corporation, R–6269–ARPA, Santa Monica, California, August. Large, J. P. (1974) *Bias in Initial Cost Estimates:How Low Estimates can Increase the Cost of Acquiring Weapon Systems*, Rand Corporation, R–1467–PA & E, Santa Monica, California, July. Marschak, T., Glennan, T. K. and Summers, R. (1967) *Strategy for R & D: Studies in the Microeconomics of Development*, Springer-Verlag, New York, 1967. Marshall, A. W. and Meckling, W. H. (1959) *Predictability of the Costs, Time and Success of Development*, Rand

Corporation, p. 1821, Santa Monica California, December. Peck, M. J. and Scherer, F.M. (1962) *The Weapons Acquisition Process: and Economic Analysis*, Harvard University Press, Cambridge, Massachusetts. Perry, R. L., Smith, G. K., Harman, A. J. and Henrichsen, S. (1971) *System Acquisition Strategies*, Rand Corporation, R–733–PR/ARPA, Santa Monica, California, June. Perry, R. L., DiSalvo, D., Hall, G. R., Harman, A. L., Levenson, G. S., Smith, G. K. and Stucker, J. P. (1969) *System Acquisition Experience*, Rand Corporation RM–6072–PR, Santa Monica, California, November.

5. Cochran, E. G., Patz, A. L. and Rowe, A. J. (1978) 'Concurrency and disruption in new product innovation', *California Management Review*, Fall. General Accounting Office, 'DoD's Defense Acquisition Program:A Status Report', NS 1AD–86–148. Government Printing Office, July 1986. Harvey, T. E. (1980) 'Concurrency today in acquisition management', *Defense Systems Management Review*, 3(1), Winter, pp. 14–18.
   Morris, P. W. G. and Hough, G. H. (1988) *The Anatomy of Major Projects*. John Wiley and Sons, Chichester.

6. ibid; Thomas, S. D. (1988) *The Realities of Nuclear Power: International, Economic and Regulatory Experience*. Cambridge University Press 1988. Cambridge Energy Series. Williams, R. (1986) *Nuclear Power Decisions. British Policies 1953–78*, Croom Helm, London.

7. ibid; Bupp, I. C. and Deriean, J-C. (1978) *Light Water: How the Nuclear Dream Dissolved*, Basic Books, New York. Hall, P. (1980) *Great Planning Disasters*, Weidenfeld & Nicholson, London. Horwich, M. (1982) *Clipped Wings: the American SST*, MIT Press, Cambridge, Massachusetts, Morne, J. G. and Woodhouse, E. J. (1989) *The Demise of Nuclear Energy?: Lessons for Democratic Control of Technology*, Yale University Press.

8. Sayles, L. R. and Chandler, M. K. (1971) *Managing Large Systems. Organizations for the Future*, Harper & Row, New York

9. Trento, J. J. (1987) *Prescription for Disaster*, Crown Publishers, New York. McConnell, M. (1987) *Challenger*, Simon Schuster, New York.

10. Cassen, R. and Associates (1986) *Does Aid Work?*, Clarendon Press, Oxford. Moris, J. (1981) *Managing Induced Rural-Development*, International Development Institute, Bloomington, Indiana. Paul S. (1979) *Managing Development Programs: the Lessons of Success*, Westview Press, Boulder, Colorado.

11. Details can be obtained from the International Association of Macro Engineering Societies, Templeton College, Oxford, OX1 5NY, United Kingdom; see also Davidson, R. P., and Huot, J.-C. (1989), 'Management trends for major projects', *Project Appraisal*, 4(3) September, pp. 133–142.

12. Hirschman, A. O. (1967) *Development Projects Observed*, The Brookings Institution, Washington DC.

13. *op. cit.*, p. 10.

14. Baker, N. R., Green, S. G. and Bean, A. S. (1986) 'Why R&D projects succeed or fail', *Research Management*, November–December, pp. 29–34. Balachandra, R. and Raelin, J. A. (1980) 'When to kill that R&D project', *Research Management*, July–August, pp. 30–33. Cooper, R. G. (1982) 'New product success in industrial firms', *Industrial Marketing Management*, 11, pp. 215–223. Gerstenfeld, A. (1976) 'A study of successful projects, unsuccessful projects and projects in progress in West Germany', *IEEE Transactions on Engineering Management*, EM-23(3), August, pp. 116–23. Mansfield, E. and Wagner, S. (1975) 'Organizational and strategic factors associated with probabilities of success and industrial R & D, *Journal of Business*, 48(2), April 1975. Whipp, R. and Clark, P. (1986) *Innovation and the Auto Industry*, Francis Pinter, London.

15. *Op. cit.* [4] see also Morris, P. W. G. and Hough, G. H. (1988) *The Anatomy of Major Projects* John Wiley & Sons, Chichester.
16. Stringer, J. (1988) 'Planning and inquiry process', *MPA Technical Paper No. 6*, Templeton College, September.
17. Department of Energy, Washington DC (1977) 'Mini-PMS Guide', *Performance Measurement Systems Guidelines, Attachment 1*, pp. A1–4. Reported in Lavold, G. D. (1988) 'Developing and Using the Work Breakdown Structure' in the *Project Management Handbook* (2nd ed.), New York, Van Nostrand Reinhold, pp. 302–3.

— PART II —

Organization and the construction company

Construction companies are both business and social entities that are arranged in some form of hierarchical organizational structure. In order to survive in the long term they have to change and adapt to the business environment. This should involve a regenerative process as people leave, join or progress through the firm. A construction firm can also be viewed as a legal framework that sets up a contractually defined employment relationship between those that manage and those that are managed. In addition, a construction company, especially if it operates in an international environment, will often comprise of employees from different national and cultural backgrounds. The four chapters comprising this part of the book focus on different aspects of the operations of a construction company as a collection of people charged with meeting strategic objectives.

In Chapter 8 Langford and Newcombe argue that the most important resource of a construction company are its workers, and they have to be developed as part of the regenerative process mentioned above to continue their effective contribution towards the attainment of company objectives. Langford and Newcombe put forward a number of tools and techniques that can assist construction firms in pursuing a policy of management development. In Chapter 9 Tayeb addresses the effects of culture on organizations. Culture is the shared meaning, values and beliefs that are held by a community or society and influence, or have the potential to influence, behaviour. The chapter focuses attention on the issues that need to be considered by managers when operating in a multicultural environment. The ideas in this chapter are of particular relevance to those managers working in the international divisions of construction companies.

Chapter 10 addresses the fact that a construction firm is constantly undergoing change. Earlier chapters have identified that a construction company experiences different types of change, incremental, sudden, planned and unplanned. This has to be managed effectively and has behavioural implications for those either managing or experiencing change. Stocks provides an in-depth insight into the issues that need to be considered in change management, and demonstrates by way of a case study from another industry the impact that 'planned' change can have on organizations. Closely allied to the issue of management of change is that of industrial relations. From one perspective, much of the industrial relations climate in the United Kingdom over the last decade has been the re-establishment, through different forms of legislation, of the right of management to manage. The construction industry has a chequered history of industrial relations. There have been periods of intense industrial conflict, and at other times quiescence. Much of the industrial relations climate within construction is worked out at site level, although there are times when it has taken on national dimensions, usually involving the relationship between methods of payment and the employment of direct versus sub-contract labour. In Chapter 11 Stocks and Male adopt an organizational and sociological analysis of industrial relations in construction, focusing on management of the operative workforce.

— 8 —

Management development in construction

David Langford and Robert Newcombe

1. Introduction

Management development is the process by which construction organizations' managerial resources are nurtured to meet these organizations' present and future needs. This process involves the interaction of the needs of the organization, and the needs of the individual manager in terms of development and advancement.

Systematic management development in the construction industry is a relatively recent phenomena which is not helped by the heterogeneous and fragmented nature of the construction industry. Frequently, a construction manager's working life is characterized by variety, brevity and fragmentation. The job primarily involves organizing people to integrate their activities within a project setting. This has meant, as Fryer [1] has pointed out, that coordination and social skills are essential elements of a construction manager's job. In this context management development in construction has to concern itself with the reality of the manager's job if it is to be effective. This approach has often spawned a conclusion that only experience develops construction managers. While this view may have had some validity in a more stable organizational context, the turbulent environment of the construction industry of the 1980s and the forecast changes for the 1990s has meant that a more structured approach is necessary. This chapter introduces some concepts of management development, and reviews several models which the construction organization can use to develop its most precious resource – its people.

2. What is management development?

Management development is often confused with the education and training function within organizations, and yet there are important differences. The Manpower Services Commission [2] defines education, training and development as follows:

> Education is any activity which is aimed at developing knowledge, skills, moral values and understanding of all aspects of life . . . the purpose of education is to provide conditions essential for people to

develop an understanding of . . . the society in which they live and enable them to make contributions to it.

This definition suggests that education has a soft focus, with its objectives being non-specific. In contrast, training is 'a planned process to modify attitude, knowledge or skill behaviour . . . to achieve effective performance in an activity or range of activities. Its purpose is to develop the abilities of the individual and to satisfy the current and future manpower needs of the organization.' Training has a harder focus and is concerned with more immediate needs. Development is, by contrast, continuous and life long and is wider in scope than education or training: 'It is a personal as well as an organizational process with "growth" or realization of a person's ability, through conscious or unconscious learning.' In the context of construction management, education is instruction in basic subjects, disciplines, techniques and principles relevant to the practice of construction management. Construction management training is instruction concerned with developing skills required to practise specific managerial duties (i.e. prepare a contract programme), while development seeks to integrate personal needs with those of the organization for which a manager works. Ashton and Easterby-Smith [3] identify four perspectives of management development. These are as follows:

1. Management development can be seen as an organizational function, an integral part of the organization's structure, with characteristics similar to those exhibited by other functions such as personnel, finance and marketing.
2. Management development can be seen as a style or philosophy of management adopted by the organization. Here management development is seen as a reflection of the way things are done in the organization. The relationship and behaviour of managers in all aspects of work are constrained and guided by the organizational culture.
3. Management development can be seen as bringing about changes in the managers' behaviour in order to achieve set organizational objectives. A good example is when management development is used to develop a sense of belonging and identity with the organization.
4. Management development can be seen as the progressive development of an individual manager's abilities at all stages of his or her career.

The above perspectives can be categorized into what Ashton and Easterby-Smith [4] call structural and process perspectives, 1. and 2. are structural, while 3. and 4. are process perspectives.

The definition of management development has to recognize and differentiate between the two groups of perspectives. Failure to do so leads to both ineffectiveness in the implementation of management, development and disillusion among the intended recipients.

Among the various definitions of management development Ashton *et al.* [5] view it as: 'A conscious and systematic decision-action process to control the development of managerial resources in the organization . . . for the achievement of organizational goals and strategies.'

Morris [6] defines management development as: 'The systematic improvement of managerial effectiveness within the organization, assessed by its contribution to organizational effectiveness. The British Institute of Management [7] sees management development as: 'The process of finding, keeping and developing managers to meet the current and future needs of the organization . . . and ensuring that the right people are developed in the right way.'

The important features which emerge from these definitions are as follows:

1. Management development relates to the overall organizational strategy, that is, it should mirror and be congruent with the organization's present and future policies and strategy [8].
2. The success of management development is measured by the extent to which the organizational goals are achieved [9].
3. Management development tries to harmonize the development of a manager, so far as is possible, both in career and personal terms within the organization context [10].
4. Management development is not limited to the formal activities of education and training, but includes conscious and unconscious learning, informal – accidental learning processes, and integrated – opportunistic learning processes [11].

3. Who should be developed?

Who should be developed is a difficult question and for an answer one needs to know the individual and his or her skills and the needs of the employer. Consequently it is not easy to be prescriptive. The numbers of administrative, professional, technical and clerical staff employed in the construction industry may be used as one indicator of the growth in the demand for people who may benefit from some form of management development. While it is recognized that this is a crude measure, it is probably one of the best-documented indicators.

One of the paradoxes of the construction environment during the late 1980s, and for the foreseeable future, was the growth in the number of administrative, professional, technical and clerical (APTC) staff, and an almost universal shortage of such staff. Housing and construction statistics [12] records the extent of APTC staff employed in the industry. It is noticeable, that while the absolute numbers of such staff has declined in response to the recession of 1978–83, the proportion of such staff in the workforce has increased. Table 8.1 charts the growth in percentage of this grade of staff.

It is evident that there was a greater managerial intensity in the construction industry in the late 1980s in that more managerial and technical staff were required to service the declining operative population.

Table 8.1 Growth of APTC staff

	APTC	Operatives	APTC as a percentage of operatives
1980	235	760	31%
1981	236	659	34%
1982	214	587	36%
1983	214	600	36%
1984	214	585	37%
1985	213	586	36%
1986	212	530	40%
1987	220	541	41%
1988	236	566	42%

Source: *Housing and Construction Statistics*, HMSO, 1989.

Certainly, the increased use of sub-contractors in the site-work end of the business created demands for more co-ordination. Greater technical sophistication within buildings and different procurement methods con- tributed to the growth of the proportion of managerial staff. The shortage of managerial staff can be seen if the number of APTC staff are indexed and compared against the changes in workload since 1980 (Table 8.2). As can be seen the pressure on staff has intensified with the building boom of the mid-1980s. This phenomena has led firms to consider how their managers should be developed and encouraged to participate in the development process. Development programmes can be used to attract and retain managers in the construction industry, although this approach is not altruistic, as many firms are now strongly committed to developing their managers in order to secure improved managerial performance.

Table 8.2 Shortage of managerial staff

	Index of APTC staff	Index of workload
1980	100	100
1981	99	90.5
1982	91	91.8
1983	91	95.7
1984	91	99
1985	90	100.1
1986	90	102.8
1987	93	111
1988	99	129

Source: *Housing and Construction Statistics*, HMSO, 1989.

The availability of CITB grants has encouraged this process and in 1987–88 the CITB gave over £6m to aid management supervisory and technical training [13]. Selection for such schemes will often depend upon a manpower audit. This audit will help organizations to identify management potential, and Figure 8.1 illustrates the issues which need to be reviewed in order to indicate who should be proposed for management development.

```
                         What recruitment needs
                         to take place and how are
                         these recruits to be
                         developed as high flyers?

What are the organization's                    Level and function in
current and future needs?        Who?          the organization?

                         What management staff
                         are available within
                         the company?
```

Figure 8.1   *Management development*

Williams [14], in a review of management training for civil engineers, found that, generally, management development was largely inadequate, and employers, whether local authorities, consultants or contractors, were critical of the amount and direction of management development. Consultants and contractors were particularly keen to have junior staff developed in fields of leadership, communication, problem-solving and decision-making. There was, according to Williams, an understanding that construction organizations could do much to rectify the inadequacies that they had perceived. This conundrum – a recognition of a development need and the failure to provide for this need – is puzzling. In theory, to be effective, management development needs to commence in undergraduate degree programmes and be a continuous process throughout a career. In practice, Williams found that employers were only providing development opportunities for selected senior staff. Despite this view, management development is seen as a direction for the future, and Williams has provides a basis for its provision. He found that the construction industry saw the relative importance of various processes to their organizations in accordance with the following:

(a) communication skills;
(b) leadership;
(c) problem-solving and decision-making;
(d) organizational functions and objectives;
(e) self-development;
(f) groups and motivation;

(g) design technology;
(h) personnel;
(i) new materials;
(j) civil engineering law;
(k) computing;
(l) politics and general legislation.

Organizations saw the main reasons for implementing development programmes as preparing their staff for future responsibilities and to satisfy organizational needs.

4. Why management development?

There are two types of benefits which can be identified, those which benefit the organization and those which are of benefit to the manager.

4.1 Benefits to the organization

The following four benefits accrue to the organization as a *result* of management development:

1. Presumably if the training is effective the people involved will be more efficient at their jobs.
2. The firm's audit of its strength and weaknesses will reveal areas where there are skill shortages impeding the efficiency of current operations. These gaps can be filled by a short-term management development programme.
3. Forecasting of the future direction of the company will also highlight the need for training tomorrow's managers. Again, gaps can be identified and filled by long-term development programmes.
4. Following the above points, a management development programme can be used as a 'test-bed' for aspiring people, in order to distinguish the 'high-flyers' from the rest.

In addition to benefits to the organization which stem from training, there are benefits which come from the *process* of development. The present difficulties of recruiting and retaining staff in the current highly competitive construction market may be eased if staff, receiving company support, are committed to a long-term management development programme.

4.2 Benefits to the manager

1. A programme of self development can be very motivating to ambitious people.

2. In order to remain a practising professional, mandatory, continuing professional development can be incorporated into the development programme.
3. Managers need to be kept up to date in a rapidly changing organizational world.
4. External courses provide opportunities for managers to broaden their perceptions of their jobs through exposure to people from other organizations.

5. When should management development take place?

The ideal answer is *continuously*. The idea of training a person once-and-for-all at the beginning of their career is now thankfully dead.

If the concept of continuous development is accepted, then a management development plan tailored to each manager's needs will be prepared. This will map out the stages and levels of a manager's career and synchronize a development programme to fit the manager's needs at particular points in time.

6. What is the practice of management development?

It has been noted that the style and content of management development will take different forms in different firms within the industry. The management development needs of consultants are likely to be different from those of contractors. Even within one firm, discipline or profession, such differentiation will require different approaches to management development. Ashton *et al.* [15] have proposed a pattern of management development which may be useful in classifying the organization's attitude to the management development function.

Ashton *et al.* suggest that there is a continuum in the development process, as shown in Figure 8.2. Phase I is characterized by a very low level of commitment by top management to the development function, and the level of possible activities in this function is relatively small. In this phase, development is not part of the culture of the firm and is restricted to selected personnel attending external courses.

Phase II suggests a higher level of commitment to management development which is accompanied by a level of visible activity. Training courses are likely to be available within the firm and, in order to send people on external courses, training budgets are expanded. Typically, firms in this phase have developed formal appraisal schemes and are undertaking audits of managerial talent within the firm. Also, there may be conflict concerning the orientation of the development activity. Top management may see development objectives merely in terms of satisfying the goals and mission of the organization, for example extending the technical skills of

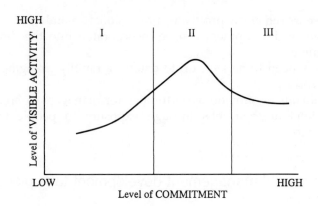

Figure 8.2   *Patterns for management development (Source: Ashton* et al. *(1975).
Reproduced with permission.)*

staff so that the firm may enter a new area of the construction market. On
the other hand, existing site-managers may see the development opportunity in terms of developing individual needs either as a manager or as a
person.

In Phase III the level of visible activity declines and training events are
not so prominent in the firm. In this phase it is assumed that management
development has become an integral part of the organization, with
managers at all levels being committed to management development.

From this generalized model there need to be some positive activities
which make up the management development function in construction
firms. The components of management development in practice are as
follows:

(a) appraisal;
(b) career development;
(c) development activities.

6.1 Appraisal

Barratt *et al.* [16] have argued that the foundation for a management
development scheme is the appraisal process. It will be recalled that
appraisal is a systematic process where staff are evaluated in respect of
their work, comparing it with pre-determined targets. Following this
comparison a realistic plan is agreed for the next period. Appraisal is not
assessment, for assessment suggests a review of what has happened in the
past; appraisal uses the past performance as a vehicle to look forward more
effectively. Assessment is a one-way process whereas appraisal is a
two-way, negotiated part of the development process. The appraisal
component of a management development system can be modelled as
shown in Figure 8.3.

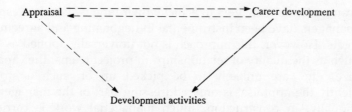

Figure 8.3 *Interaction of management development activities (Source: Ashton and Easterby-Smith (1979). Reproduced with permission.)*

The appraisal process has many purposes, of which the following are some:

(a) Human resource considerations for the firm;
   - to identify the manager's strengths and weaknesses;
   - to set targets for personal performance;
   - to explore the necessary changes in duties, i.e. more work, different work, etc.;
   - to eliminate obstacles to work, over which the employee has little or no control.

(b) Training:
   - to identify training needs.
   - to agree on personal development needs.

(c) Promotion:
   - to assess the person's promotion prospects.

(d) Organization development:
   - to assist in the planning of company operations by taking stock of the jobs currently done and the people doing these jobs.

(e) Personal and career development:
   - to inform staff what is expected of them.

6.1.1 Appraisal methods

There are several approaches to undertaking appraisals, some of which are described below.

6.1.1.1 Results orientated
This approach uses a management-by-objectives approach and considers how a job is done rather than the individual doing it. This approach typically establishes targets to be achieved, and at the end of the appraisal period the achievements of the individual are compared against the target, with differences between target and performance as the focus of the appraisal discussion. This approach has the benefit of measuring performance in an objective way, and the very act of establishing quantifiable

targets can motivate managers to achieve their targets, which is especially true if managers have been instrumental in negotiating and agreeing their own targets. However, this approach is not universally applied as 'softer' issues such as the quality of relationships in project teams, the capacity to empathize, etc., are unlikely to be picked up on such a structure; consequently the appraisal is only addressing part of the manager's job.

Additionally, in construction, much managerial work is carried out within management or project teams and individual targets have less relevance to the construction environment.

6.1.1.2 Narrative methods

The narrative method of appraisal simply allows the appraiser to write a narrative about the person being appraised. This may be a totally free correspondence or it may be confined to certain aspects of the job or manager's performance or behaviour. This review is then used as the basis for the appraisal interview. The method offers flexibility but requires the exercise of fine judgement by the appraiser. However, comparisons are difficult to make and no uniform standards can be applied.

6.1.1.3 Rating scales

Rating scales can be of two kinds:

(a) semantic scales;
(b) fixed rating scales.

Semantic scales are used to appraise set components of a job. For example:

	Outstanding	Very effective	Effective	Below average effectiveness	Unsatisfactory
Leadership ability					
Technical ability and know-how, etc.					

This approach creates a universal yardstick for all employees in one grade or type of job, and such types of appraisal are relatively easy to complete. However, the disadvantage of this method is that it appraises a person's abilities in the context of the current job, and opportunities need to be created to explore causes or limits of particular performance levels. Appraisers also need to be alert to bias with halo effects (the practice of letting one good or bad characteristic override all others) distorting the overall picture. Finally, uniformity can be a problem, with different appraisers offering different interpretations of the semantics provided in the appraisal document.

In fixed rating scales, a list of statements is prepared (usually by the personnel department) and the appraisers are invited to mark the statement which best describes the behaviour of the manager. For example the appraiser may have to choose between the following:

Best description

Set 1
- does not anticipate potential delays on site;
- grasps project information quickly;
- good communication skills;
- rarely wastes time.

Set 2
- provides leadership to project teams;
- wastes time;
- cool and calculated in a crisis;
- works hard.

Clearly, the combination of the descriptions needs to be carefully chosen to elicit a profile of performance and behaviour, but this system does have the advantages of rater bias being reduced as there are no right or wrong answers. The personnel department can then undertake the appraisal interview with date provided by a large number of separate appraisers.

While the construction industry is a difficult setting for full appraisal schemes, there is recent evidence which suggests that the practice of providing management staff with appraisals is gaining ground. Aboobucker [17] reviewed appraisal behaviour in 30 construction companies, 15 of them contractors and 15 consultants. He found that 20 firms had adopted formal appraisal schemes, but there was a greater propensity for contractors to use the procedure (90% of the contractors had schemes while only 45% of the consultants used it). Size was the key determinant in the use of appraisal schemes; the larger the firm the more formal was the appraisal. Construction organizations used appraisal for a mixture of organizational and personal development reasons. Assessment for promotion was prominent in the reasons given for using appraisal, but evaluating training needs and discussions concerning individual career plans were also heavily cited. Narrative and rating scales were the primary techniques used in making appraisals in construction.

As a part of the research, personnel managers were interviewed to obtain the views of the advantages and disadvantages of appraisal schemes. Among the advantages perceived was the identification of training needs, but more subtle advantages such as increased managerial involvement with work and improvements in communication between manager and subordinate, were cited. Two of the disadvantages which personnel managers reported, were uneven standards of appraisers in the conduct of interviews and the quality of feedback given. This point was often reinforced by a lack of standardization of procedures across the organization. Finally, a lack of commitment to appraisal from line managers was noted.

7. Career development

The issue of career development is closely linked with the appraisal process. To the construction organization, career development may be concerned with manpower planning. Careers can be developed so that the firm has sufficient site managers, senior surveyors, etc., to meet expected needs arising from growth or shift in workloads. The individual manager will have a narrower perspective and will be concerned with making progress within the firm in terms of gaining interesting work, increased responsibility and seniority. These factors are associated with improved incomes, which may be another important drive in career development. Activities in career development interact with appraisal schemes, to be synthesized into management development activities. Ashton and Easterby-Smith [18] have represented this interplay in the model in Figure 8.3, which shows that activities within the management development function are determined both by the information available from assessment of managers in the appraisal, and the career development decisions of the manager and the organization.

8. Management development activities

The development process can be classified into the following three generic types:

(a) formal management development;
(b) informal management development;
(c) integrated management development.

8.1 The formal process

Mumford [19] sees formal management development taking place when there are changes in the job and job context, and this is coupled with a programme of development activities such as training courses.

The catalyst for such programmes is often a change in job associated with promotion, job rotation, secondment, or allocation of special duties such as committees or task forces. The activities which can help the individual manager cope with this change are 'coaching', i.e. direct discussions, and guided work to help colleagues do a better job. This may be supported by 'counselling', which involves the giving of advice about a particular aspect of the job. Usually a mentor is appointed to act as a father figure to a young aspiring manager, and oversees the overall development of the younger person's skills and job attitudes. Finally, 'mentoring' is a fashionable way of providing for development. This is the process of developing attitudes and behaviour associated with the whole career and the whole job. It is a general dispersal of a philosophy of management, rather than 'coaching' for better performance in one aspect of the job. These in-house activities need to be supported by training. Such training initiatives can either be internal company courses or external courses. In-company courses tend to be directed to specific company objectives and Ascher [20] noted that in-company courses sought to integrate technical and managerial knowledge, which was modelled on the practice of managers at work. Behavioural topics such as team building, leadership and the management of change were also represented in the contents of in-company courses. The content of such courses is dependent on the relevant level within the organization, and, for example, contrast with junior managers, the top management of construction firms tend to rely on external courses. The reasons for this relate to issues of status and breadth of vision. Top managers can resist attending courses which are taught or organized by employees lower than themselves in the organizational hierarchy. Moreover, in-company courses do not provide a peer group for senior management, who need a wider view of the firm which can be provided by external courses, added to which is the creation of networking opportunities from external courses in providing a forum for managers to meet those in similar positions in other organizations. Koudra [21] also claims that senior managers are more receptive to external rather than in-company courses because they are more likely to respect outside experts than in-company specialists.

8.2 The informal process

Informal development can be said to take place when 'the learning process is essentially subsidiary to the activity of carrying out the job' (Mumford [22]). Such peripheral development is seldom planned in advance, and frequently the organizational intention is for a manager's task performance to be enhanced. An example of informal development would be if the site quantity surveyor were charged with running a project because the firm had no other site manager to assign to the project. This change in job content would enable the surveyor to experience on-the-job management development. However, this experience is likely to be unstructured and the development gains made subsequent to the surveyor having managed the project for some time.

8.3 The integrated process

This approach synthesizes the informal, incidental, process with the formal, structured, process. In the integrated model, twin objectives are stated; there is concern for learning which develops the individual, and for the task which satisfies the needs of the firm. Because the process is planned and has objectives, the results can be evaluated, but probably the most powerful advantage is that the superior and the subordinate negotiate the content and structure of the development process. This is best done by a combination of appropriate courses interspersed with in-company projects and assignments.

9. How is management development organized and costed?

During the 1980s many large construction organizations initiated programmes of investment in management development. Most of the management development activities come under the aegis of training departments. In one sense, construction organizations are not typical of firms who have a strong commitment to management development. Mangham and Silver [23] found that size was an important variable in the propensity of a firm to undertake management development, with large organizations undertaking more training and development activities. A further variable was the technology of the industry, with high technology firms (i.e. the R & D budget was greater than 1% of sales) more likely to undertake management development. Also, owner-managed and single-company firms (no subsidiaries and not part of a group of companies) were less likely to develop their managerial staff. Notwithstanding these findings, the activity is reasonably well understood in the construction industry. In a survey of 38 of the top 100 construction companies, 17 had formal management development policies and the same number explicitly recognized the importance of management development for the efficiency and profitability of a company.

The importance of management development in many ways relates to its position within the firm. There are several choices of reporting structure for management development units. The most frequent arrangement is for the management development function to be part of the personnel department. Where an organization has a separate training department, management development is often embraced by training. In rare instances the management development staff report directly to the chief executive.

Some construction organizations will tend to see expenditure on management development as an unnecessary cost to be avoided. Those construction firms which do develop their managers see it as an investment. Kenney and Reid [24] see investment in management development in the same way as other forms of investments – it should only be undertaken when a cost and benefit appraisal has been carried out. They suggest the following two questions which may be used to test the efficacy of management development:

1. What benefits can an organization obtain from investing in management development?
2. What costs are involved in the proposed development programme?

The six benefits which may accrue from the management development function may be listed as follows:

1. Development of managers helps them to learn their jobs quickly and effectively, thus minimizing 'learning costs'.
2. The present and future work requirements are likely to be met and maintained if there is management development in the organization.
3. Management development is an agent for growth in an organization, helping both to stimulate and control expansion. Where growth has already started, management development should be of urgent priority if growth is to be sustained [25].
4. The general morale of employees is improved by management development activities. The organization's ability to accept and implement changes, to become proactive and take advantage of new opportunities, is enhanced by management development.
5. Labour turnover among new managers, if caused by efficient learning and inadequate development, can be reduced by staff induction and training activities. Managers can learn their jobs rapidly and are more likely to achieve high levels of job satisfaction, thus remaining with the organization longer.
6. Retention of staff is an advantage to an organization only so long as their skills and knowledge contribute to its operations. With management development new skills and knowledge replace obsolescent ones.

This is not to say that there are no difficulties in valuing the benefits of development. Pepper [26] records that the development process is fraught with uncertainty about whether development of talent actually takes place and over what period. Further, if performance is improved can it be directly attributed to the development process? – the 'Hawthorne effect' may be at work. In short, quantifying the benefits is difficult as some may be intangible (yet vital) and others may be more pertinent to the individual than to the organization.

The costs are more easily quantified but there are different ways of looking at development expenditure. One view is to integrate opportunity costs into the costings. If a development activity is costed at £1000 but during this development the firm loses an opportunity to win a contract which would have rendered £10 000 profit, then the opportunity cost of the development is £11 000. A further approach is to minimise these learning costs. They may be defined as payments made by organizations to staff who are less effective and efficient. These costs, for example, could include the costs of wasted materials or wrong decisions while learners are acquiring competence, and the reduced output of colleagues who have to partake in the training and induction costs as a result of learners leaving because of the job demands. Thus development costs reduce learning costs and the objective is to minimize the cost of development. However, this approach is conceptual rather than practical as the learning costs are difficult to quantify.

A third approach is to catalogue the principal costs as follows:

(a) establishment costs;
(b) marginal expenditure costs;
(c) interference costs.

Establishment costs are those which pay the salaries and operating costs (rental or office space, etc.) of the management development group.

Marginal expenditure costs are those which add to the costs of providing a development function, such as course fees, consultants' fees, expenses for individuals attending development events, etc.

The greatest costs incurred are likely to be the interference costs. These occur when the manager is missing from the place of work and, for example, productivity may drop on site if a key number of the management team is missing.

10. How does the construction industry undertake management development?

Ascher [27], in her research, found that some construction organizations place heavy emphasis on management development activities. Some have offered internal courses which are accepted as a qualification towards professional examinations. This preference for internal courses was also reported by Fryer [28]. The direction of such courses is interesting and Ascher regards construction as an industry where technical qualifications are important and, consequently, sponsorship for technical qualifications is widely accepted. As an activity towards management development, Fryer found job rotation used as a vehicle to widen managers' skills, supported by 'coaching' from senior managers. Despite these encouraging trends the budgetary allocation for management development is small. The Industrial Society (1985) found that construction organizations spend less than ½% of their annual turnover on development activities. Mphake [29], in a review of management development in the construction industry, estimates that approximately £300 per manager per year is a typical figure for the provision of management development in the construction industry. This figure seems small given the evidence concerning the methods used to develop managers. In-company and external courses are the methods most used and in the survey 22 of the 38 responding firms had experience of in-company or external courses. Also popular was the 'coaching' method. Surprisingly, in the light of Fryer's findings above, Mphake found that project attachments, job rotation and self-directed learning were not widely used. Interestingly, the content of the courses attended was heavily biased towards management techniques and Figure 8.4 illustrates where development activity took place.

	Courses for junior managers %	*Courses for middle managers* %	*Courses for senior managers* %
Functional management e.g. finance, marketing, personnel, safety and training	33	35	33
Management techniques e.g. team building, IR, communications, delegation, motivating, leadership	58	51	42
General management business policy, strategy, decision making	9	14	25
TOTAL	100	100	100

Figure 8.4   *Course content (Source: Mphake (1980).)*

It is noticeable that Mphake's survey reveals that the focus towards management development in construction is the provision of appropriate courses. However, as has been seen earlier this is not the whole of management development and the skills and personal qualities of a manager have to be developed alongside the knowledge required by a construction manager. The survey shows that developing skills of empathy and understanding is not well provided for.

11. Conclusions

There is little doubt that in successful companies, management development is not just a set of training courses but a way of life and an integral part of the organization's outline. It is reflected in the attitudes of all managers at all organizational levels. The company is seen by people as a place for learning and growing and not just as an employer.

This chapter argues that this approach to management development does not arise by accident. Management development has to be deliberately designed into the strategy and fabric of the organization.

References

1. Fryer, B. G. (1979) 'Management development in the construction industry'. *Building Technology and Management* (11 May) pp. 16–18.
2. Manpower Services Commission (1981) *Glossary of Training Terms*. London, HMSO.
3. Ashton, D., Easterby-Smith, M. and Irvine, C. (1975) *Management Development: Theory and Practice*. Bradford, Management Bibliographies and Reviews.
4. Ashton, D. and Easterby-Smith, M. (1979) *Management Development in the Organization: Analysis and Action*. London, Macmillan.
5. Ashton, D., Easterby-Smith, M. and Irvine, C. (1975) *Management Development: Theory and Practice*. Bradford, Management Bibliographies and Reviews.
6. Morris, J. (1971) 'Management development and development management'. *Personnel Review*, **1** (1), 30–43.
7. British Institute of Management (1969) *Management Development and Training: A Brief Survey of the Schemes used by 278 Companies*. London, British Institute of Management.
8. Buckley, J. and Kemp, N. (1987) 'The strategic role of management development'. *Management Education and Development*, **18**(3), pp. 157–174.
9. Ashton, D. and Easterby-Smith, M. (1979) *Management Development in the Organization: Analysis and Action*. London, Macmillan.
10. Leggatt, T. W. (1972) *The Training of British Managers: A Study of Need and Demand*. London, HMSO.
11. Mumford, A. (1987) 'Using reality in management development'. *Management Education and Development*, **18**(3), 223–243.
12. Housing and Construction Statistics, HMSO, 1989.
    Institute of Personnel Management (1983) *A Positive Policy for Training and Development*. London, Institute of Personnel Management.
13. Construction Industry Training Board (1989) *Annual Report, 1989*, HMSO.
14. Williams, R. (1987) Management Training for Civil Engineers in Mid-career. Unpublished MSc Thesis, Brunel University.
15. Ashton, D., Easterby-Smith, M. and Irvine, C. (1975) *Management Development: Theory and Practice*. Bradford, Management Bibliographies and Reviews.
16. Barrett D., Hayzelden K. and Tagg J. (1989) 'Personnel development' in *Managing People*, Mattin, A. and Grover, F. (eds.) London, Thomas Telford.
17. Aboobucker, M. (1987) Personnel Appraisal Schemes in the Construction Industry, Unpublished MSc Thesis, Brunel University.
18. Ashton, D. and Easterby-Smith, M. (1979) *Management Development in the Organization: Analysis and Action*. London, Macmillan.
19. Mumford, A. (1987) 'Using reality in management development'. *Management Education and Development*, **18**(3), 223–243.
20. Ascher, K. (1983) *Management Training in Large UK Business Organization: A Survey*. Harbridge House Europe.

21. Koudra, M. (1975) *Management Training: Practice and Attitudes*. London, British Institute of Management.
22. Mumford, A. (1987) 'Using reality in management development'. *Management Education and Development*, **18**(3), 223–243.
23. Mangham, I. L. and Silver, M. S. (1986) *Management Training: Context and Practice*. Bath School of Management, University of Bath.
24. Kenney, J. and Reid, M. (1986) *Training Interventions*. Wandsworth, Institute of Personnel Management.
25. Peel, M. (1984) *Management Development 1983 and Training: A Survey of Current Policy and Practice*. British Institute of Management.
26. Pepper, A. D. (1984) *Managing the Training and Development Function*. Aldershot, Gower.
27. Ascher, K. (1983) *Management Training in Large UK Business Organization: A Survey*. Harbridge House Europe.
28. Fryer, B. G. (1979) 'Management development in the construction industry'. *Building Technology and Management* (11 May) pp. 16–18.
29. Mphake, J. (1988) Construction Companies Investment in Management Development. Unpublished MSc Thesis, University of Bath.

9

The effects of culture on the management of organizations

Monir Tayeb

Introduction

How would you feel if you became ill and were admitted to a hospital, and your manager came to visit you with a bunch or flowers as soon as he or she could? Angry? Delighted? Or would your manager never do such a thing! Yet this is precisely what some managers in Japan do; and their subordinates approve of it. Many people in other parts of the world might find this disturbing to say the least, and might assume that their manager was spying on them to ensure that they are actually ill. These two different interpretations of the same action reflect different value systems, assumptions and meanings, in other words different cultures.

This chapter explores the possibilities of cultural influences on organizations and on their members' relationships with each other and with the outside world.

The chapter consists of five parts. Section 1 defines culture and examines its likely origins. Section 2 concerns the ways in which culture influences organizations from 'without', through social institutions such as trade unions, political economic structure, consumers and other interest groups. Section 3 discusses the cultural origins of employees' work-related attitudes and behaviour, and the implications of these for an organization's policies, management style and structure. Section 4 examines the management of culture, which includes strategies, ranging from cultural synergy to a building organization's own cultural identity, which aim at suppressing cultural characteristics that may have been carried over from outside the organization. The chapter concludes by drawing attention to some of the non-cultural factors which have significant implications for organizations.

1. Culture and its scope

Culture may be defined as historically evolved values, attitudes, and 'meanings' which are learned and shared by the members of a given community and which influence their material and non-material way of life [1].

This is not to say that all members of a community think and behave in the same way or hold the same values and attitudes. There are, of course, variations among people from the same culture, but there is also a discernible general pattern of values, attitudes and behaviour which distinguishes one cultural grouping from another. For instance, although not all Indians are alike, one can always tell an Indian person from, say, a person from Sweden, not only by their physical differences but also by the differences in their world views and other invisible attributes.

2. Origins of culture

It is difficult to pinpoint the origins of culture accurately, even more so because of the interconnection between various institutions and factors, which may be said to be responsible for the creation of a culture, and the two-way reinforcement processes between these institutions and culture itself. Table 9.1 illustrates factors and institutions which play the most significant role in these processes.

3. Culture and organizations

Culture can influence organizations either from without, through social and political institutions, or from within, through employees' work-related attitudes and values.

3.1 Influence of culture on organizations from without

There are many institutions and elements 'outside' an organization which are influenced or created by culture and which in turn have implications, in varying degrees of magnitude, for the organization. The following outlines some of these. It should be noted that some of these factors are heavily 'mixed up' with politics, both at national and international levels (e.g. the role of the superpowers in suppressing economic developments in some less powerful countries); and the role of culture in the processes must therefore be treated with caution.

3.2 Technology

There are three fundamentally different philosophies of human relationships with their physical environment, on the basis of which all cultures can be broadly categorized. These are mastery over environment, subjugation to environment and harmony with environment.

Table 9.1 Origins of culture

Factors	Likely implications
1. Ecology, physical environment	
Example I:	
• harsh and hostile climate	• aggressive
• severe cold or hot seasons	• tenacious
• land difficult to cultivate	• non-hard working
• scarce natural resources	• 'fighters'
Example II:	
• fertile lands	• passive
• mild climate	• easy-going
• abundant natural resources	• non-violent
2. Family	
Example I:	
• hierarchical	• large power differentiation
• role differentiation between sexes	
• patriarchal	• male dominance
• severe discipline	
• deference to seniors	
• emotional dependence	• collectivism
Example II:	
• egalitarian	• small power differentiation
• little or no role differentiation between sexes	• little or no male/female dominance
• no deference to seniors	• individualism
• emotional independence	
3. Religion	
Example I:	
• God is Almighty to be feared and obeyed	• large power differentiation
• strict codes of conduct	• little or no opportunity to experiment
• male dominance sanctioned	
• obedience to seniors a duty	
Example II:	
• God is merciful	• small power differentiation
• codes of conduct open to interpretation	• experimentation encouraged
• no male dominance	

Factors	Likely implications
4. Education	
Teaching style	
Example I:	
• one-way teacher–pupil relationship	• large power differentiation
• memorizing textbooks	• unable to cope with new and uncertain situations
• challenge and innovation discouraged	
Example II:	
• learning based on experiments and trial and error	• small power differentiation
• teaching based on two-way discussions and arguments	• able to cope with new and uncertain situations
• challenge and innovation encouraged	
Value system	
Example I:	
• middle-class value-based	• 'gentleman's' culture
• emphasis on arts and pure science	
Example II:	
• non-class-based value system	• 'enterprise' culture
• emphasis on technology and applied science	
5. Political system	
Example I:	
• intolerance of opposition	• large power differentiation
• hierarchical	
• little or no participation by the masses	
• centralization of power	
Example II:	
• tolerance of opposition	• small power differentiation
• egalitarian	
• mass participation	
• decentralization of power	

The first philosophy, which underlies Western civilization, emphasizes the power of human beings over 'nature'. It is basically a challenging and non-fatalistic view of the world. Natural resources are there to be exploited, animals to be tamed and forests to be felled to provide us with more land and timber. The kind of technology that one expects a culture based on such a philosophy to 'produce' is inherently an aggressive one. It is a tool in the hands of human beings, used to conquer 'the world out there'. It is therefore not surprising that major technological innovations, especially in the past two hundred years, originated in Western cultures.

The subjugation to environment philosophy regards human beings as less powerful than, and at the mercy of, the elements. Eastern cultures, with their mostly fatalistic religions, are generally based on this philosophy. Natural forces, symbolized in the will of God, are too powerful to master. The extremely low level of technological innovations in these cultures seems to reflect this type of world view. When was the last time an Eastern society came up with a major technological breakthrough?

A third view, which has been developed in recent years and is increasingly gaining support, argues that the survival of human beings in the long run depends on a benign and sustainable relationship with their environment. Unless they harmonize their activities with those of nature this life support system will be irrevocably damaged, and with disastrous consequences. The type of technology which the proponents of this view envisage is one which will economize the use of non-renewable natural resources and will allow nature time to recover from the effects of exploitation.

3.3 Economic advancement

The level of economic advancement and industrialization of a country may also reflect the cultural attitudes and values of its people. For instance, it has been argued (Weber, 1930) that the driving force behind capitalism, and indeed the Industrial Revolution in eighteenth-century England, was the English people's high degree of individualism, encouraged and reinforced by Protestantism.

In a technologically and economically developed country, organizations have better access to advanced technical know-how and infrastructures. They can recruit from a pool of professional managers and a highly skilled labour force, which would be utilized to create and maintain a competitive edge in the market over those in the less developed societies.

3.4 Trade unions

Labour movements and trade unions are institutions which are encouraged and flourish in some cultures and which are repressed in others. The nature of the ideology and activities that unions might adopt also differ from one society to another. For instance, in France unions are highly political and engage in the class struggle; in Britain they are more pragmatic and have no intention of overthrowing or to challenging the authority of management, but they do fight for jobs and for better working conditions.

There are differences, too, in the nature of industrial relations in different countries. In Britain, the management–worker relationship is hostile and is charcterized by a 'them and us' division. In Japan the unions, which are plant-based, recruit both management and workers. The two 'sides' of the industry cooperate with each other and see themselves as striving to achieve the same goals. The Japanese culturally rooted national unity and consensus are clearly reflected in that country's industrial relations practices.

3.5 Pressure groups

Pressure groups other than trade unions can also be more successful in some cultures than in others, both in terms of their numbers and their influence on policies, which in turn have implications for organizations. These groups can aim their activities at various levels, namely, national, regional, local, industry and firm. Antipollution and other environmental groups try to influence government policies through changes in legislation, or even direct action (e.g. Greenpeace). Some pressure groups may focus their attention on increasing the general public's awareness about certain issues, such as the harmful effects of some food additives, the dangers associated with the nuclear power industry, and food contamination in, say, egg production. Changes in legislation and consumer awareness force companies to adopt new policies and take appropriate actions.

3.6 Influence of culture on organizations from within

In order to explore the ways in which culture influences employees' work-related attitudes and behaviour, and the bearing that these might in turn have on organizations, one must study organizations at a level which is more likely to be brought face to face with culture. The decision-making process in organizations may be an appropriate point to look for this face-to-face encounter.

At the heart of any action taken by organizations are decisions regarding issues of what and how to produce, what sort of employees are needed to carry out the business of the organization, who the likely customers are, what geographical markets to serve, what pricing policy to adopt, and so forth.

Decision processes in an organization obviously involve more than one person. This brings us to the issues which might arise out of the formal and the informal interpersonal relationships which are a crucial part of life in a work organization. These issues are concerned with power and authority relationships, risk-taking, coping with uncertainty, delegation, dedication, commitment, motivation, communication, consultation, control, discipline, rules and regulations.

The attitudes and values that managers and other employees hold with respect to these issues and relationships determine to a large extent the form that the decision-making processes take. There is evidence that these attitudes and values are heavily influenced by the cultural upbringing of the members of an organization [3].

3.7 Attitude towards power and authority

In a culture where people respect their seniors and are even afraid of people in positions of power, it is less likely that as employees they will challenge their superiors, and decisions tend to be taken by a few senior managers and carried out by subordinates. Iran is an example of this type of culture [4]. In cultures where people are brought up to share power with others, organizations may also be more decentralized, managers may delegate their authority lower down the hierarchy and there will be more consultation and communication among employees. The United States and the United Kingdom, to a large extent, belong to this cultural category.

3.8 Tolerance for ambiguity and uncertainty

This cultural dimension is especially relevant to the risk-taking aspect of decision-making in an organization. Social institutions such as family, religion and education could encourage or discourage risk-taking and accepting responsibility for one's own action. The ability, or inability, to cope with uncertainty can thus be inculcated in people as a cultural group. This trait can then be manifested in their behaviour within the work organization.

Employees who have less tolerance for uncertainty and are unwilling to face ambiguity and risk are more likely to avoid either making decisions on their own without direction from above in the form of procedures and regulations, or sharing responsibilities with others [5]. Hofstede attributes the Japanese organizations' practice of collective decision-making, *ringi*, to the Japanese people's high uncertainty avoidance. Fromm [6] argues that the rise of Nazism in Germany earlier this century could be attributed to the German people's relatively low degree of tolerance for ambiguity. Even now West German organizations are more centralized than those in many of their fellow European countries [7, 8].

3.9 Individualism, collectivism

These concepts do not easily lend themselves to clear-cut definitions. Individualism, for instance, can be interpreted as self-interest and selfishness, and collectivism as self-sacrifice [9]. It is argued here that an individualistic culture is generally characterized by a high value placed on one's independence, autonomy, privacy, belief in one's own worth, and confidence in one's own ideas and opinion. In a collectivist culture the group to which one belongs, such as family, community, or even work organization, takes priority over one's individuality. The United Kingdom and many Western European cultures are considered individualistic cultures, as defined here, and India and Japan as collectivist ones.

The relationships between employees and their work organizations reflect their cultural background in this respect. Japanese employees, for instance, consider their workplace as an extension of their family and are highly committed to its goals and objectives. Their commitment is reciprocated by the organization. Managers, for example, may become involved in their employees' personal difficulties and try to help them out. In an individualistic culture, such as the United Kingdom, this is far from the case and may in fact be regarded by employees as managers' intrusion in their privacy [10].

In individualistic cultures the relationships between employees and work organizations are on the whole less emotional, and are sometimes even downright hostile. Compare, for instance, the industrial relations scene in Britain with that in Japan. The former is characterized by mutual hostility and distrust and the latter by harmony and cooperation.

3.10 Interpersonal trust

Some cultures are characterized by honesty and mutual trust and some others by distrust. Organizations can reflect this trait. In low trusting cultures, such as Iran, decisions are more centralized, key positions are allocated to trusted people who are usually friends and relatives of the owners and senior managers; control and discipline are tight and rules and regulations are accompanied by close personal supervision [11]. In high trusting cultures, such as the United Kingdom, there will be a relatively higher degree of delegation with control being more impersonal and less severe.

4. Managers and culture

If you were a manager of a multicultural organization or a company in a country other than your own, how would you handle the issue of culture?

One option for a manager placed in this situation is to ignore employees' diversified cultures and treat them as if they were from a homogeneous background, concentrating instead on issues such as market share, competition and technological changes, which have more immediate relevance to the organization's success. To do this might indeed be easier, but it may not necessarily be a more useful course of action, in terms of, for instance, employees' satisfaction and productivity. There is evidence that some cultural characteristics, such as attitude to power and authority, can be dysfunctional [12]. It has also been argued that some cultures set limits on the extent to which organizations can respond and adapt to their environmental demands [13].

For instance, if a firm operates in a volatile environment (rapid technological change, fierce competition or rapid change in customers' preferences), senior managers may have to delegate authority to employees lower down the hierarchy (i.e. decentralization) in order to enable them to respond promptly to situations as they arise, and to make necessary decisions. In the case of organizations operating in more stable and certain environments with predictable changes (e.g. civil service), a highly centralized and formalized management style might be more appropriate and efficient. Employees of the former firm are required to have a more positive attitude to power (be willing to accept and challenge power), to be able to make decisions on their own, to cope with new and uncertain situations and to be trustworthy. The latter organization's employees are likely to be happier working under seniors' direction and close supervision, feel more comfortable in clearly defined job territories and less able to face new situations on their own.

Some cultures, such as that of the United Kingdom are more able to provide both types of people who are able to operate under the two different circumstances. Some cultures, such as Iran and India, generally tend to encourage attitudes and behaviour capable of dealing only with the second type of situation. In this case, even organizations operating in volatile environments might end up having a fairly centralized and formalized management system, which may be dysfunctional, inefficient and ineffective.

The second option is to take employees' different cultural backgrounds into consideration when devising authority structures, control strategies and inducement policies, and to recognize and utilize employees' diverse attitudes and behaviour. This could in turn result in higher satisfaction for employees and more effective management of organizations. For instance, if employees come from a culture where people generally work better under constant direction and guidance from superiors than when left alone with only overall task objectives at hand, then their managers could design a system which would facilitate the flow of detailed information and instruction between superiors and subordinates. Alternatively, these employees could be assigned the tasks which are routine and predictable, and for which a manual of detailed instructions can be prepared.

A relevant question is how managers can measure and assess culture, or, more specifically, their employees' work-related attitudes and values. Multinational corporations such as IBM conduct periodic attitudinal questionnaire surveys among their employees worldwide. This kind of survey can provide managers with information about the cultural and non-cultural characteristics of their employees.

Another course of action would be to create a cultural synergy [14]. There are many aspects of cultures which can be beneficially incorporated and utilized in the management style of a multicultural organization. For example, group-orientation of employees from a collectivist cultural background could be turned into a high degree of commitment to the workplace. Also, employees from a trustworthy culture could be put in charge of jobs which, by their nature, cannot be subjected to constant direct supervision by senior managers.

A further way of dealing with employees' diversified cultural background is to build a strong organizational culture in order to create a more or less homogeneous value system to which employees would be encouraged to subscribe. Formal and informal communication channels can be utilized to foster the company's own philosophy and 'way of life'. Selection procedures can be devised to recruit new employees with the kind of values and preferences that are compatible with the organization's prevailing culture, or the culture it would wish to have.

On becoming a manager of a Western company's subsidiary within a developing country, the recognition of the socio-cultural characteristics of the host country will enable the manager to devise management systems which are more authentic and appropriate to the particular circumstances therein, instead of importing and applying unmodified management practices from countries with different sets of values, socio-economic conditions and political ideologies.

5. Non-cultural factors and organizations

The effect of culture on organizations should not, however, be exaggerated. For example, Japan's so called 'lifetime employment' system was first identified for western readers by Abegglen [15] who regarded it as a near-absolute moral commitment which was culturally inspired by the ideals of earlier feudal eras. Subsequent investigation, while not necessarily denying the element of cultural continuity, tends towards the conclusion that lifetime employment was instituted by large oligopolistic firms between 1910 and 1930 approximately, in the light of politico-economic factors. In a period of growing labour militancy and high labour turnover, oligopolistic firms could attempt to secure labour commitment through offering job security and regular upward progression within a pay hierarchy. These firms were in a position to protect themselves from the risk of shouldering this overhead cost in times of poor trade by exporting any adjustment of employment levels to large numbers of small, highly dependent external sub-contractors [16, 17]. The important point is that this dual labour market policy is comparable to that pursued by oligo-polistic firms in many other countries, including the United States [18]. It has also been argued that the desire of workers to remain with a single employer offering favourable conditions is not a particularly Japanese cultural characteristic [19].

There are also some aspects of an organization which are less open to the influence of culture than others. The core technology which is used for the production of goods and services is one such aspect, which managers can seal from intervention by 'outside' actors [20]. For instance, in car manufac-turing firms using assembly line production technology, the lay-out of the equipment, type of machinery needed, technical know-how and expertise and other related requirements, are more or less the same everywhere.

Furthermore, there is evidence [21, 22, 23] that other factors such as a company's market share, size, age, ownership and control may play an equally important role in its structure and management style. For instance, in most societies, organizations in the public sector tend to be more centralized than those in the private sector (because of the former's greater degree of accountability to the public). Also, older companies use standard rules and regulations gleaned from their accumulated experience and knowledge more than do newer companies. Family-owned-and-managed organizations tend to be more centralized than those owned by general public shareholders and run by professional managers due to the professionalism of these managers.

6. Conclusion

It is abundantly clear that culture plays, to varying degrees, an influencing role on the business organization. Cultural influences may impinge on organization structures and strategies from the external environment. However, the internal sub-systems concerned with leadership and management styles, power and authority, for example, are also areas of the organization to which attitudes, values and beliefs bring their influence. The effects of culture on organizations in the international construction industry is explored further in Chapter 12.

References

1. Tayeb, M. H. (1988) *Organisations and National Culture*. Sage Publications, London.
2. Weber, M. (1930) *The Protestant Ethic and the Spirit of Capitalism*. George Allen & Unwin, London.
3. Tayeb, M. H. *op. cit.*

4. Tayeb, M. H. (1981) 'Cultural influences on organisational response to environmental demands'. *University of Aston Management Centre Working Paper No. 215.*
5. Hofstede, G. (1980) *Culture's Consequences.* Sage Publications, California.
6. Fromm, E. (1942) *The Fear of Freedom.* Routledge & Kegan Paul, London.
7. Maurice, M., Sorge, A. & Warner, M. (1980) 'Societal differences in organizing manufacturing units: A comparison of France, West Germany and Great Britain'. *Organisation Studies,* **1**, pp. 59–86.
8. Child, J. and Keiser, A. (1979) 'Organisational and managerial roles in British and West German companies: An examination of the culture-free thesis, in Lammers, C. J. and Hickson D. H. (eds.) *Organisations Alike and Unlike.* Routledge & Kegan Paul, London.
9. Tayeb, M. H. (1988) *op. cit.*
10. Tayeb, M. H. and Smith, P. B. (1988) *A Survey of Management Styles in Four Capitalist Countries.* Paper presented to the Fifth Workshop on Capitalist – Socialist Organisations. Brdo Pri Kranju, Yugoslavia.
11. Tayeb, M. H. (1981) *op. cit.*
12. Kakar, S. (1971) 'Authority patterns and subordinate behaviour in Indian organisations'. *Administrative Science Quarterly,* **16**, pp. 298–307.
13. Tayeb, M. H. (1981) *op. cit.*
14. Adler, N. J. (1981) *Cultural Synergy: The Management of Cross-cultural Organisations.* Paper presented to the International Symposium on Cross-Cultural Management. Montreal, Canada, October.
15. Abbeglen, J. C. (1958) *The Japanese Factory.* Glencoe, Ill. Free Press.
16. Littler, C. R. (1982) *The Development of Labour Process in Capitalist Societies.* Heinemann, London.
17. Littler, C. R. (1983) 'A comparative analysis of managerial structures and strategies' in Gospel, H. F. and Littler, C. R. *Management Strategies and Industrial Relations.* Heinemann, London.
18. Loveridge, R. and Mok, A. (1979) *Theories of Labour Market Segmentation.* Martinns Nijhoff, Leiden.
19. Marsh, R. M. and Mannari, H. (1976) *Modernisation and the Japanese Factory.* Princeton University Press, Princeton.
20. Kiggundu, M. N., Jorgensen, J. J. and Hafsi, T. (1983) 'Administrative theory in developing countries: A synthesis'. *Administrative Science Quarterly,* **28**, pp. 66–84.
21. Hickson, D. J. and McMillan, C. J. (1981) *Organisation and Nation: The Aston Programme* IV. Gower, Farnborough.
22. Hickson, D. J., Hinings, C. R., McMillan, C. J. and Schwitter, J. P. (1974) 'The culture-free context of organisation structure: A tri-national comparison'. *Sociology,* **8**, pp. 59–80.
23. Tayeb, M. H. (1988) *op. cit.*

—— 10 ——

Organizational change

Robert Stocks

Introduction

'The way large organizations assess the changing economic, business and political environment around them, and formulate and implement strategic and operational changes, is an important input in the equation leading to the maintenance and improvement of competitive performance.' [1] Transition and transformation is a fact of life for the business concern within its environment of relative uncertainty and risk, and the comparative amount of dynamic activity: 'In an attempt to achieve certain organizational performance objectives, a change of state in the organization's structure and functioning may be required.' [2] The organization and its management will therefore need to make predictions concerning environmental factors as to how they will perform, and thus how they will affect the firm. Management will also be required to control or influence the organization's internal environment in the change process.

Tichy [3] regards change as being involved with organizational restructuring, improving communications, replacing people and altering production and control systems. Three perspectives are involved in the change process; technical problems; political problems; or cultural problems. The mixture of these three forces causes the process to be complex and dynamic to a certain extent.

Strategic change becomes necessary when opportunities or threats arise in the following main areas [4]:

1. *Environment:* pressures from competition, changes in the economy or government influence through legislation are significant examples. The finance and banking industry provides an illustration wherein changes in electronics, communications and competition has recently occurred in its environment.
2. *Diversification:* this move into new areas of business usually involves strategic change, which in turn often requires a change of organizational structure.
3. *Technology:* dynamic changes in technology place new behaviour requirements on the organization and can lead to change, sometimes at the strategic level.
4. *People:* a change in people is seen as a trigger for strategic change. For example, changes in terms of education, expectations or status may be

absorbed into the firm by new recruits, or applied to existing employees.

The three sets of problems (technical, political, cultural) which super-impose themselves on the change processes need to be managed. It is perceived that in the management of change, managers have usually concentrated narrowly on a restricted set of solutions to the change process, due to their view that difficulties with change arise from only one of the three problems.

Tichy takes the view that all three sets of problems need to be managed, and within strategic change the following so-called change levers must be equally available for use [5]. These can be paraphrased as follows:

1. *External interface:* because the organizational environment becomes more dynamic and complex, new forecasting and information process-ing facilities are often required.
2. *Mission:* there must be clear statements of purpose for the organization to follow and be guided by in its strategic decisions. As environmental pressure increases from such factors as economic, political and social systems, this sense of mission becomes vital.
3. *Strategy:* new management techniques and processes are necessary to develop a strategic plan with its multilevel operational objectives.
4. *Managing organizational mission/strategy processes:* as planning and decision-making become more complex, management processes need to be more sophisticated while enlisting all relevant interest-groups.
5. *Task:* changes in strategy may result in the introduction of new tasks and technologies to the organization. This could mean the introduction of new professionals into the firm or a necessary training and develop-ment of existing employees.
6. *Prescribed networks:* in order to deal with new tasks and/or technologies, communications and control networks need to be adjusted to show interrelationships and reporting channels.
7. *Organizational process – communication, problem-solving and decision-making:* because of authority–managerial/professional splits and matrix splits, decision-making lines become indistinct. Managers thus under-stand and utilize the agreed decision-making approaches and conflict bargaining procedures.
8. *People:* because any organizational change entails altering individual behaviour, part of the management of change involves motivating people.
9. *Emergent networks:* a major aspect of organizational change is the management of informal communication and the influence over net-works which exist within an organization. Coalitions and cliques can help or hinder during the change process.

This chapter is concerned with those problems associated with people experiencing strategic change within their organization, whatever the reason for that change. A company may require to know which of the above levers need to be adjusted and which approaches or techniques are available to adjust each of them.

The people aspects of strategic change involve not only motivation but possible changes for the individual in such areas as leadership style, management style, employment roles, training, reward structures, etc. Taken together, these concerns for the individual during strategic change are simultaneously a change in organizational culture for the firm.

1. Organization and management theory

An examination and evaluation of the various schools of organization theory will, in the first instance, outline the context within which change has been, and will be, a continuous aspect of management functions. The administration schools of thought regarding modern business organizations during the early part of this century, evolved from the observations, activities and practices of participating managers. For example, the scientific principles applied to the control of workers by supervisors, were instigated in the pursuit of executing the tasks of the organization in the most efficient manner possible.

A prominent leader in scientific management was the management consultant and engineer, F. W. Taylor [6]. Taylorism portrays the organization studied in isolation with little attention being paid to the influence of the external environment. There are definite and prescribed vertical hierarchical lines of communications, with detailed job content descriptions. The task of an organization is broken down so that managers of various departments exercise their authority over certain key functions, with top management being the supreme coordinating authority. Style of leadership is seen as authoritative and motivation is based on financial rewards with more efficient work techniques improving productivity, thus increasing earnings. Work study, and time and motion practices are instrumental in setting these productivity levels and, hopefully, improved work techniques.

These practices, in effect, remove any discretion which the worker may have in planning, organizing and controlling his own task performance. Time and motion studies provide the standardization of task performance.

Taylor was a product of his time, a time when money was viewed as the prime motivator, there was unity of purpose between management and worker, and control and power resided at the top of the hierarchy.

A manager from this traditional period, the Frenchman Henri Fayol [7], broadened the scope of the theory with an *administrative* or *functional* approach. He showed that organizations contained and comprised interdependent functions which he presented as technical, commercial, financial, security, accounting, and the all-embracing administrative function of management. Fayol's elements of administration are described as follows:

(a) forecasting: appraisal and assessment of needs and resources;
(b) planning: the drafting of operations, i.e. policy;
(c) organizing: the assembling of the work force;
(d) commanding or directing: selection, training, motivating and leading of employees;
(e) coordinating: all of the organization's activities;
(f) controlling: making certain that every activity is carried out according to rules.

In theory at least, the manager has the authority to exert control over subordinates and influence individual job performance.

At the turn of this century a German sociologist, Max Weber [8], with his theory of social and economic organization, put forward the view that there are three styles of authority associated with organizations. Charismatic leadership depends on the personality of an individual, whereas traditional authority is based on heredity, where within a family firm the ownership and management is handed down within the family. Rational–legal authority, on the other hand, pertains to the job and not the person occupying that position. This was seen by Weber as the most efficient style for large and complex organizations, which were development at that time. This bureaucratic form of organization was seen as emerging from the needs of the environment of the time. The commonly perceived characteristics of the bureaucratic organization remain to epitomize the main aim of removing any power which individuals may have vested in themselves.

A hierarchy of authority clearly specifies who is superior to whom within a bureaucratic organization. Work is defined into spheres of activity, each of which is led by one individual who has the authority to carry out the functions of his office. Rules and regulations exist and are formally established to ensure consistency, remove scope for personal bias and remove any effects from changes in personnel.

Problems are recognised in this type of authority structure, one of which concerns the delegation of power and the needs for that delegation to lower levels of the structure for purposes of decision-making by individuals down the hierarchy. Decision-making can also suffer as a result of communication and information requiring to be passed, through forward rules and procedures, upwards and downwards within the hierarchy. Among other bureaucratic dysfunctions, when the organization faces environmental change the rigid inflexibility of its structure is likely to cause problems during the processes of transition.

During the 1920s and 1930s changes were taking place within developed societies, which were mirrored in business organizations. There was a growth in the size of organizations, with increasing specialization. Changing technologies were occurring in communications, transport and production processes. People were becoming more highly educated and at the workplace there 'was an expansion of collective action'.

It was in this setting that new theories arose, and as Taylor and the scientific managers were theorists of their time, the human relations school was likewise. People at the workplace began to be recognized as human beings rather than being treated as machines, or, in Marx's terms, appendages of machines. Studies within a large company by a team of external researchers is an important indication of the changes at this period.

The Hawthorne studies (1927–32) [9] examined individual, small group and intergroup relationships, while recognizing the individual and his or her needs as a human element in production. The attention given to the informal organization, group behaviour and communications networks was significant.

> Communication does not just flow downwards from superiors to subordinates, it flows up, down and across – and in order to cope with the communication problems raised by increasing openness in individual and group relationships, managers will need to acquire a more highly developed interpersonal competence. [10]

Questions regarding control, leadership, motivation, management style, communications and roles are among the organizational factors confronted within the respective frameworks set by the scientific management, bureaucratic and human relations approaches, among others, to organizational behaviour.

A more contemporary view of the business firm regards the organization as any open system in interaction with its environment. An organization can thus be viewed as a system within which there are sub-systems which interact with each other. The primary emphasis in general systems theory is the interdependence of the system's parts, the relationships between these parts and an examination of the system's structure.

The contingency approach, utilizing systems theory, attempts to understand these interrelationships within and among sub-systems, as well as between the organization as a social system and its environment. Many organizational factors, such as tasks, objectives and structure, take on different forms in different organizations and the best form which the company can take will be contingent upon environmental conditions.

A number of studies in the 1960s using [11, 12, 13] the contingency approach highlighted the requirement for different organizational structures and systems of management to contend with particular environmental circumstances.

'. . . an organization is a social system, and management must take into consideration two important variables – the environmental variables and the needs of individuals and groups who are drawn into the system' [14]. Furthermore [15]: 'Contingency theory implies that if an organization's environment is undergoing major change, it is likely to require alterations in its structures, tasks and behaviour if it is to remain responsive and adaptive to that environment.'

2. Organization structure

Structures of organizations have been seen to change, often dramatically, as environmental and other influences have affected organizational operations. The alterations to structure, tasks and behaviour within the pattern of change cannot but affect individuals in the business firm.

'The structure of an organisation is often taken to comprise all the tangible and regularly occurring features which help to shape its members' behaviour.' [16] It is therefore clear, that as the environmental factors for the organization are subject to change, this may cause a change in structure necessitating change in members' behaviour.

In addition to the environment there are a number of influences on structure. The objectives and goals which the organization has set for itself, the size of the organization and the technology utilized by the firm are prime 'determinants' of structure. If the organization is undergoing restructuring or redesigning, important considerations are the history and age of the firm and the style and philosophy of senior management which have been crucial in formulating the culture of the organization. Research carried out by Burns and Stalker can be considered as the first formal attempt to relate the structure of organizations to the nature of the environment.

They 'hoped to be able to observe how management systems changed in accordance with changes in the technical and commercial tasks of the firm, especially the substantial changes in the rate of advance which new interests in electronics development and application would mean' [17]. They were particularly interested in how management systems might change in response to the demands of a rapidly changing external environment.

In general, the study shows the problems of a firm as it experiences technical progress, within the 1950s UK electronics industry, while having to change its style of management in order to contend with these environmental changes. Comparisons are made, within the study's findings, of two fairly distinct methods of management inherent within the firms examined. Many effective organizations operating in stable environments or with stable technologies are characterized by a high degree of formalization, a clear hierarchical control system and strict lines of communications. This system, which corresponds closely to Weber's ideal type of bureaucracy, is termed 'mechanistic' by Burns and Stalker. On the other hand, the 'organic' system is more adaptive and flexible to a changing environment where conditions are relatively unstable. There is more of an emphasis on communication at all levels and joint problem-solving for individuals who do not have such strictly controlled roles. If the organization is confronted by changes in its needs and problems as they arise in the environment, or from other influential areas of operation, then formalized rules and procedures and other characteristics of bureaucracy become outdated and ineffective.

Burns and Stalker found that the necessary change from a mechanistic to an organic system was faced by organizations and their management in varying ways. The transition was either incremental or in a general movement. In some cases it was made in a pre-meditated manner but other firms attempted to return to the position of status quo.

Some firms tried to prevent any move in order to keep existing status, position and rank undisturbed within their management hierarchy. The nature of an organic form of organization tends to cause some managers a measure of distress if they have been accustomed to the structured mechanistic form of 'safety'.

3. People and change

An organization must become adaptive in order to stay alive and thrive; and change must occur within the organization. The internal environment embodies many aspects of structure and organization which directly, or otherwise, affect the individual or groups of individuals.

3.1 Power

Within organizational hierarchies, most problems associated with the firm are handled by application to higher authority or by the exercise of power and influence. Proponents of bureaucracy take the view that the bureaucratic structure is the hierarchy of suitable and acceptable means of distributing power and authority.

Brooks [18], on participative management, points to its part in changing working relations within an organization, and therefore in the functioning of a firm. Furthermore, 'any significant change in human organization involves a rearrangement of power, association and status'.

'While some may benefit by it, others may lose control and influence over resources and other functions.' Power implies the potential ability to exercise one's influence, and the sources of that power are seen in various seats. Handy [19], for example, sees positions of power as follows:

(a) physical power: from superior force;
(b) resource power: the possession of valued resources or rewards;
(c) Position power: legal or legitimate power held by position rather than the person. Assets of this form of power include; information, rights of access to various networks and the right to organize.
(d) Expert power: this is vested in someone's expertise, control over information and access to senior members of the organization.
(e) Personal power: the charisma which resides in a person.
(f) Negative power: the capacity to stop things happening and to delay, distort or disrupt; it is utilized when other attempts to influence fail.

Authority is legitimate power and accrues to the individual by virtue of role and position in an organized social structure. Responsibility is the obligation to use delegated powers for the purpose for which they were delegated.

Organizations depend on the balance of power being maintained, and if the focal concept of organizational change can be considered in terms of uncertainty, effective management of change to authority structures is all-important.

3.2 Leadership

To be effective and to communicate as intended, a leader must always adapt his behaviour to take into account the expectations, values and interpersonal skills of those with whom he is interacting [20].

The earliest approach to research on leadership was to identify and compare characteristics of leaders, with the notion that individuals who are effective leaders have certain traits which set them apart. The view that certain people are born to be leaders saw a brief resurrection of trait theories in the 1960s and effective leaders were seen to tend towards having higher intelligence, initiative, supervisory ability, self-assurance and to perceive themselves as members of high-status groups. Although trait theories are at best generalizations, they have never completely been negated despite the more contemporary views, which see leadership primarily as a function of the environment.

The supervisor of a work group has the two basic roles of task direction and group maintenance; and two basic types of leaders can be identified – autocratic and democratic. A large number of studies have been carried out over the last 30 years or more, examining various aspects of leadership. Throughout, the basic duality of styles has run through such research with the 'labels' changed and descriptions widened. For example, Likert [21] described job centred supervisors as tending to concentrate on having their subordinates employed in a specified work cycle, in a laid-down manner and at a rate determined by time standards. Employee centred supervisors, on the other hand, give primary attention to the human aspects of their subordinates' problems and try to build effective work groups with high-performance goals. From these two basic types Likert expanded his research findings into a four-type spectrum of leadership styles which varied from authoritative to participative.

Fiedler [22], with a contingency approach to research on leadership also identified two basic styles. Relationship motivated leaders are those who achieve their major satisfaction from personal relationships in the work group. Task motivated leaders are more concerned with the job in hand, and their subordinates will have standardized procedures with clear guidelines for task performance. An important expansion of this contingency model is the view that the correct position for effective leadership is where the style of leadership is matched with the situation.

The three situational variables for Fiedler are: the relationships the leader has with his subordinates; the extent to which tasks are defined or structured; and the position power which the leader is perceived to hold. Combining the style of leadership with the favourability of these three situations, he attempted to show whether task or relationship motivated leaders performed more effectively.

However, both types of leaders can be effective depending upon the nature of the task and characteristics of subordinates. Organizational change may necessitate changes in leadership style. The principal contentious issue with Fiedler's study arises when he maintains that it is unrealistic to try to change the leadership style of an individual because it is too deeply rooted and stable. Changing the situation is more feasible and by altering task structure, position power or relationships with subordinates, a situation can be developed in which the style of leadership will be most effective.

4. Communications

The structure, effectiveness and scope of the organization are almost entirely determined by communications techniques [23].

There is, of course, more to communications than correspondence, talks and meetings. The interpersonal aspects of communicating within the organizational structure, vertically, horizontally or diagonally, is a problematical area which may be deeply affected by the process of change. With the many levels which may exist in the large organization, there is the vital need to communicate information and instructions effectively. Higher management within such a hierarchy are far removed from operating problems and direct control over employees. However, 'free' or unstructured communication would only serve to undermine the formal structure and cause resentment by ignoring a superior. There may also be time wastage due to information being received by the wrong people.

The three main elements involved in communication are feedback, a communication's channel and the symbols which are necessary for information in the channel. As the prime objective for management is concerned with inducing people to take action relevant to the tasks set them, both the communicator and receiver will wish to have stability in the three elements above.

Too much in the way of communications can occur when there is a very rigid or formal structure. This situation of information overload may arise as required under the organization's rules and regulations rather than from necessity. However, it can also occur when there are no clear lines of relationships and rules to follow, also when there is unnecessary communication and information which is irrelevant.

Communication is supposed to follow the lines of authority laid down by the formal structure. Change in the organizational structure, no matter the cause, thus creates problems for the firm's employees.

5. Roles

Role theory provides a link between theories of individuals and those of organization. Any social organization exists from participants assuming, or having been allocated, roles and interacting with each other [24]: 'The concept of Role relates to the activities of an individual in a particular position. It describes the behaviour he, or she, is expected to exhibit when occupying a given position in the societal or organizational system.' [25]

One individual may hold multiple roles, often in various organizational locations. When the individual is uncertain as to his role at any given time, he may not know what he is to do because of a lack of clear guidelines and terms of reference in a job, and there exists a state of role ambiguity. Job descriptions rarely give a clear description of organizational roles. At the lower levels of the hierarchy, job descriptions are more detailed and nearer to a full role description. At higher levels there is less job description detail, and the individual's role becomes more ambiguous.

An individual occupying positions concurrently, which involve conflicting roles and consequently conflicting demands, is in a situation of role conflict. Likewise, the person occupying a single position which is involved with a number of conflicting role expectations can be said to experience uncertainty.

There are different types of role conflict. Role overload occurs when the individual is unable to complete tasks from his number of different roles simultaneously. The different roles which one person has becomes too much for him, although this is not a description of work overload. Role underload occurs where the individual believes he has the capacity to handle bigger roles or a larger number of roles than he does at present. For Handy there are two types of role stress [26]. People need some form of stress to achieve optimal performance, although too much can be harmful. The difficulty is in knowing how much stress the individual can handle. Role pressure is therefore seen as beneficial stress whereas role strain is harmful stress, such as tension or low morale.

6. Control

Control is concerned with integrating the differentiated activities within an organization which, as departments or sections of the firm, mutually underpin its operations. If there is too much hierarchical control, this will be at the expense of horizontal and lateral integrative relationships. However, large and complex organizations make it difficult to support a centralized top–down approach and long lines and networks of communications require decentralization to varying degrees.

Organizations need to make decisions regarding the relative rigidity of their control systems and the structure required to sustain control. Choices in the following three areas thus have to be made:

1. *Centralization or decentralization:* the degree of delegation which is given for decision-making purposes.
2. *Formalisation:* the level to which procedures and rules are formalized, and the extent to which the organizational structure is formalized or relatively informal.
3. *Span of control:* is either narrow or wide, the relative amount of direct supervision being determined by the number of subordinates for which a supervisor is responsible. A narrow span of 'heavy' supervision is the situation in which a number of subordinates are controlled by a relatively large number of supervisors.

Business organizations have changed and evolved during this century; theories and writers have developed alongside the transition; and descriptions of organizational control have been updated. The traditional view sees organizations controlled through accounting procedures and practices in order that their operations function as planned to achieve objectives. A broader perspective has managerial aspects in that management control ensures efficient and effective use of resources to achieve objectives. Systems theory provides the contemporary definition of control in that [27], control 'involves the definition of what people and units are to do, the establishment of criteria against which the performance of their activities is to be assessed and a feedback of information as to what has in the event taken place'.

Control systems need to be in a position to enable senior management obtain the necessary information for long-term planning, measure job performance and provide feedback to employees about their performance, and increase motivation for subordinates. The hierarchical chain of command and authority relations, formal rules and regulations and control procedures allow the organization to function in the pursuit of its objectives. Changes which affect people, changes in the social organization of work, will affect not only these people but also the structure and functioning of the firm. The style of control systems implanted within the organization therefore mirrors the management style which operates therein, and which may require to be altered as the firm undergoes transformation.

7. Motivation and satisfaction

As previously noted, the Hawthorne studies were concerned with informal groups, individuals and communications. The impact of social factors on performance and job satisfaction was particularly noted by the study team. Burns and Stalker's mechanistic system, likened to the bureaucratic structure, as well as being inflexible to change, is seen to be 'unresponsive to individual needs' [28].

An organic organization, on the other hand, is characterized not only by its structural aspects but by the following factors which also affect the individual's potential for job satisfaction:

1. Control, authority and communication operates within a network structure.
2. There is an interaction between individuals towards a continual adjustment of work tasks.
3. There is a commitment to the organization as a whole.
4. Interaction takes a lateral as well as vertical direction.
5. Communications are in the form of advice rather than orders.
6. Any sanctions involved are concerned for the organization as a whole and flow from all organizational levels, both equals and superiors.
7. Jobs are not formally defined.

People must be motivated to achieve optimum work performance, and an essential task for management is to arrange organizational conditions and methods of operation to enable individuals to achieve their own goals while directing their efforts towards achieving organizational objectives. Motivation and job satisfaction is the joint spur in this respect. Furthermore, 'when management wants change, such as introducing a new set of work processes – workers must be induced to invest energy in new behaviours' [29].

Scientific management makes the assumption that money is the prime, if not the only, motivator. Many theories have been constructed since the peak of scientific management in the 1920s, to show that this is of course not the case. Maslow's [30] hierarchy of needs, McClelland's [31] achievement needs, Porter and Lawler's [32] expectancy model and Herzberg's [33] framework, which helps delineate between motivation and satisfaction, are important examples of the research into job satisfaction.

In the late 1950s two philosophies, signifying two differing sets of managerial assumptions, were put forward as purely theoretical accounts of human motivation at work. Theory X is McGregor's [34] set of managerial assumptions about workers which existed before the human relations school questioned scientific management principles. These assumptions set out by McGregor comprise three propositions of the conventional conception of management's tasks:

1. Management is responsible for organizing the elements of productive enterprise: money, materials, equipment and people in the interest of economic ends.
2. A process of directing the efforts of people, motivating them, controlling their actions, modifying their behaviour to fit organizations' needs.
3. Without this active intervention by management, people will be passive to organizational needs. They must therefore be persuaded, rewarded, punished, controlled and activities directed, i.e. managing subordinates.

4. (a) The average man works as little as possible.
   (b) He lacks ambition, dislikes responsibility and prefers to be led.
   (c) He is inherently self-centred and indifferent to organizational needs.
   (d) He is by nature resistant to change.
   (e) He is easily led and not very bright.

Additionally there are the following widespread beliefs which management have to consider when having subordinates carry out organizational tasks:

1. Management is responsible for organizing the elements of productive enterprise: money, materials, equipment and people in the interest of economic ends.
2. People are not by nature passive or resistant to organizational needs. They have become so as a result of experience in organizations.
3. The motivation, potential for development, capacity for assuming responsibility and the readiness to direct behaviour towards organizational goals are all present in people. Management does not put them there but it is responsible for making it possible for people to develop these human characteristics.
4. The essential task of management is to arrange organizational conditions and methods of operation so that people can achieve their own goals best, by directing their own efforts towards organizational objectives.

Because people's needs are more than basic, it is irrelevant whether management takes a hard or soft line of control and supervision. It is management's attitude towards the human element at work which determines management style. Whereas Theory X signifies external control of human behaviour, McGregor's Theory Y points towards self-direction to some extent, and the harmonization of organizational and individual goals. The assumptions from Theory Y, including a later extension by McGregor, are as follows:

1. The average human being learns under proper conditions not only to accept but to seek responsibility.
2. The capacity to exercise a relatively high degree of imagination, ingenuity and creativity in the solution of organizational problems is widely, not narrowly, distributed in the population.
3. Under the conditions of modern industrial life, the intellectual potentialities of the average human being are only partially utilized.
4. The expenditure of physical and mental effort in work is as natural as play or rest.
5. External control and the threat of punishment are not the only means of bringing about effort towards organizational objectives. Man will exercise self-direction and self-control in the service of objectives to which he is committed.
6. Commitment to objectives is a function of the rewards associated with

their achievement, e.g. the satisfaction of ego and self-actualization needs can be direct products of effort directed towards organizational objectives.

A few pertinent implications from McGregor's model are concerned with management style, control and change. The style of management and control based on assumptions in Theory X appear inappropriate for the organization of today.

The commitment, self-control and the wish for responsibility by employees in today's work environment, as put forward in Theory Y, creates the necessity for forward planning in the change process.

People do not resent change, they resent being changed. McGregor, and others, recognized the validity of participative management but the levels of, and conditions for, participation are only two problems associated with this style of management.

Job-design changes, in the form of job enrichment by enlarging one job, or rotating the individual from one job to another, are aimed at motivating workers. However, there are problems in this area of motivating employees, and during the processes of organizational change this should be considered and remembered.

8. Pressures for change

Organizations are altered and transformed in order to pursue their goals and objectives better, while ensuring their survival in a more effective manner within their respective environments. Change may be required by events and changes in the environment, from areas such as technology, competition or innovation. Size and technology are seen as major influences on structure, so that innovation of new technology may necessitate a change in not only organizational structure, but also in the processes and interactions within that structure.

Competitive pressures which bring about expansion through diversification, and other corporate activities will result in structural changes. The activities associated with mergers, acquisitions, and diversification in general, bring about an increase in size for organizations. This major determinant of structure entails changes in the operations of people within firms which become large and complex.

Technological change, as a catalyst, is an incremental process which is seen to affect the distribution of power, and thus the decision-making procedures within the firm. Most technological advances, such as computerization, tend to enhance the number and importance of specialists who require to be integrated into the authority structure. Product innovation into markets of increasing competitive pressures involves expansion and change. Additionally, government legislation, as an environmental factor with varying degrees of influence for industries, may encourage and allow expansion.

Firms may instigate change because of certain basic problems; sales are down, operating expenses are too high, market share is slipping.

In any event a firm is judged on its performance, reputation, growth prospects, correct market placing and on being up to date.

With the recognition of these pressures and reasons for change, the consequences for people within the organization can be condensed thus [35]: 'A strategic review may launch a new business strategy or new acquisition but may miss the fact that these new initiatives undermine important values that have guided a company for years and years.' It is, therefore, these values which are inherent in the company and also in the individuals within it, which can be summated in one word, culture. Culture is *the* barrier to change, but there are situations, such as those listed below, when culture should be changed:

(a) when the environment is changing;
(b) when the industry is competitive;
(c) when the company is mediocre;
(d) when the company is about to become very large;
(e) when companies are growing very rapidly.

Deal and Kennedy take the view [36] that in most other situations companies should not undertake large-scale cultural change.

9. Implementation and transition

There are internal considerations which have to be recognized, and emerging organization design factors to be taken into account before attention is given to change: 'In this respect we can't use the organization of the 1890s to solve the problems of the 1980s'. [37].

The traditional organization design factors of the 1890s to 1920s can be seen as follows:

(a) uneducated, unskilled temporary workers;
(b) simple and physical tasks;
(c) mechanical technology;
(d) mechanistic views, direct cause and effect;
(e) stable markets and supplies;
(f) sharp distinction between workers and managers.

On the other hand the emerging organization design factors of the 1960s to 1980s are seen to have drastically changed, as follows:

(a) educated, sophisticated career employees;
(b) complex and intellectual tasks;
(c) electronic and biological technologies;
(d) organic views, multiple causes and effects;
(e) fluid markets and supplies;
(f) overlap between workers and managers.

Firms faced with internal considerations and external factors require the capacity to adjust and adapt. The process of assessing environmental change, and its implications for new strategies, structures and cultures in the firm is a massive human process. In this situation differentials, perceptions, leadership, chance (opportunity), building support for, and then implanting, change, all play their part [38].

9.1 Approaches to change

Organizational change can be introduced through a number of methods, either singly or in combination. Some emphasize the content of what is to be changed while others stress the process of how change is to be accomplished. Leavitt [39] describes the following three 'what' approaches to change:

1. *Structural:* introduce change through new formal guidelines and procedures, such as organization charts, budgeting methods, rules and regulations.
2. *Technological:* emphasize rearrangements in workflow achieved from new physical layouts, work methods, job descriptions and work standards.
3. *People:* stress alterations in attitudes, motivation and behavioural skills which are accomplished through new training programmes, selection procedures and performance appraisal schemes.

The 'how' approaches to organizational change are categorized by Greiner [40] into three types of power, within which are identified seven approaches which may be utilized by management.

9.1.1 Unilateral power

1. The decree approach: takes the form of an announcement from an individual in a position of high authority directed towards those in lower positions.
2. The replacement: individuals in one or more key positions are replaced by other individuals within the organization.
3. The structural approach: the structure of organizational relationships is changed for subordinates without the injection of new people, or decrees.

9.1.2 Shared power

4. The group decision approach: group members will participate in selecting from several alternative solutions specified in advance by superiors. This involves neither problem identification nor problem-solving, but emphasizes the achievement of group agreement to a particular course of action.

5. The group problem-solving approach: problem identification and solving by group discussion.

9.1.3 Delegated power

6. The data discussion approach: organization members are encouraged to develop their own analysis of data presented by change agents within the firm. Data is presented in the form of case materials, survey findings or data reports.
7. Sensitivity training approach: managers are trained to handle small discussion groups while being sensitive to the processes of individual and group behaviour. This approach focuses on interpersonal relationships initially, and then moves towards improvements in work performance.

Management, when executing change, needs to utilize the approach, or combination of approaches, which best anticipates potential problems. The concept of looking at change as an evolving series of stages is useful in this respect.

Lewin [41] puts forward three stages of change which are necessary for attitudinal and behavioural transformation, unfreezing, changing and refreezing.

1. The unfreezing stage represents the first step in stimulating people to perceive the need for change. A challenge is necessary to motivate the individual to find relief from the anxiety and uncertainty which change may cause.
2. Changing involves the introduction and application of new methods and guidelines for change. The desired new set of behaviours and attitudes are also introduced, and individuals should begin to recognize them in other people while displaying them themselves.
3. There is a necessary reinforcement stage to ensure the permanent adoption of new behavioural attitudes. Without this stage of augmentation, these newly acquired behaviours and attitudes would not be sustained. This model serves as a basis of any examination into the various phases involved in change and also into the relationships between these stages.

9.1.4 Resistance to change

With pressures for change, there arises resistance to such change from groups who may feel their interests are threatened. At all levels, if change breaks up established informal social groups this will be perceived as threatening social relationships.

A positional threat is seen from the realignment of formal authority levels. Job security and promotion prospects may also be seen by some to be put in jeopardy by organizational and structural change. Enriching the jobs of subordinates may be viewed by a manager as a threat to his authority and a narrowing of differentials. The process of change itself may simply be seen as an unwelcome disturbance to the well-established routine and status quo.

All people who experience change and are affected by it experience some emotional disturbance and encounter some loss or uncertainty. Individuals can react very differently to change 'from passively resisting it, to aggressively trying to undermine it, to sincerely embracing it' [42].

A wish not to lose something of value, misunderstanding the change and its implications, a belief that the change does not make sense for the organization and a low tolerance for change are the most common reasons why people resist change.

An individualistic self-interest of one person or group, in conflict with the best interest of the organization, may result in the machinations of organizational politics.

Managers need to examine and clarify misunderstandings openly and to create trust between themselves and subordinates.

People undergoing change processes are likely to assess the situation differently from those managing change. Also, 'the difference in information that groups work with often leads to differences in analyses, which in turn can lead to resistance' [43].

Individuals' low tolerance to change arises from their fear of perhaps being unable to develop the new skills and behaviour which they will require. The speed at which change occurs is important in this respect as some people are required to change too quickly.

These are seen to be a number of ways of dealing with resistance to change; Kotter and Schlesinger note the following five:

1. *Education and communication:* educating people before change occurs is one of the most common methods used in overcoming resistance. The transmission of ideas assists people to see the need for, and logic of, change. If people are in possession of inaccurate information, an education and communication programme will be a valuable exercise.
2. *Participation and involvement:* managers may be strongly in favour of, or strongly opposed to, participation by potential resistors to change, and both attitudes can create problems for a manager because neither is very realistic. Participation, while it generally leads to commitment for successful change, can be time consuming. When change has to be quickly initiated, it can take too long to involve others.
3. *Facilitation and support:* support can be given to employees from in-house education and training programmes, although they can be expensive and time consuming.
   Emotional support from internal counselling is most helpful when fear and anxiety are experienced by resistors to change.
4. *Negotiation and agreement:* this is relevant when it is seen that someone will lose from change, but the individual can strongly resist. Incentives can therefore be offered, such as a higher wage rate in return for a work rule change, or an increase in a person's pension benefits in return for

early retirement. Negotiated agreements can be a relatively easy, but expensive, way to avoid major resistance.

5. *Manipulation and cooptation:* This 'normally involves the very selective use of information and the conscious structuring of events' [44]. An individual or group, represented by a leader, can be coopted into a desired role in the design or implementation of change. This is not participation as it is only the coopted member's endorsement which is sought. If a manager is perceived as a manipulator, his ability to use the other approaches in dealing with resistance may be undermined (6).

6. *Explicit and implicit coercion:* people may be threatened with the loss of their jobs or promotion prospects in order to force them to accept change. People resent forced change, but coercion may be the only option when speed is essential and the changes are bound to be unpopular, no matter how they are introduced.

Successful organizational change requires the application of a number of the above approaches, often in different combinations. 'However, successful efforts share two characteristics: managers employ the approaches with a sensitivity to their strengths and limitations and appraise the situation realistically.' [45]

Common mistakes are, first, to use only one approach or a limited set of approaches, regardless of the situation; second, to approach change in a disjointed and incremental way which is not part of a planned strategy.

9.1.5 Planning change

The managers of change make strategic choices with regard to the speed of the process, the amount of pre-planning, the levels of involvement by others and the approaches used.

Change may be clearly planned with a very speedy implementation which calls for little involvement by others. This relatively more coercive approach charges over any resistance to change. On the other hand, a participative approach results from a strategy which calls for a much slower change process, with a less clear plan and the involvement of many other people. Part of this strategy is concerned with reducing resistance to a minimum. An attempt towards quick implementation without pre-planning, or one which involves much participation, tends to founder. In the former situation unanticipated problems arise and, in the latter, well-intentioned participation tends to falter.

How relatively slowly or quickly is the change process to be? Management should consider the following four factors [46]:

1. The amount and kind of resistance which is anticipated: the greater the amount anticipated, the relatively more coercive will management require to be in order to reduce some of that resistance.

2. The position of the change initiator in relation to the resistors, especially with regard to power: the more power the initiator is perceived to hold, the less coercive he needs to be, and conversely so.

3. The person who has the relevant data for designing the change and the energy for implementing it: initiators of change must be more participative if they are aware that they require information and commitment from others, to assist in the design and implementation of the change, which in any event is time consuming.
4. The stakes involved: the greater the short-run potential for risks to organizational performance and survival if the present situation is not changed, the more coercive managers need to be.

If these factors are ignored there is the probability, if not the inevitability, that problems will arise. For example, some managers may move too quickly with insufficient information and yet not involve others to any extent. However, it could be said that a manager perceived to have little power is required to initiate change very quickly, in which case if he cannot increase his power base he is faced with compromising his strategy for change.

Management of change, in order to be effective in processing that change, should therefore have a programme which: (a) conducts an organizational analysis of the current situation, problems and sources of problems; (b) the above analysis of factors relevant to producing the change; (c) selects a change strategy based on that previous analysis; (d) monitors the implementation process.

When sufficient is known about the problems and their determinants, management essentially decides on the overall goals for change, selects the basic approaches to reach these goals and plans the detailed steps for the implementation of the chosen basic approach or approaches. In order for organizational change to take off a plan must be initiated. Much depends on interpersonal skills when using any analysis or diagnosis aimed at the instigation of any plan. However, even the most impressive interpersonal skills will not compensate for a poor choice of strategy, planning and tactics.

10. Case study

The Finance Act of January 1987 meant that building societies, and other financial bodies, were able for the first time to provide services which until that time had been the prerogative of banks. Additional activities, such as diversification into estate agencies and building development, were also strategies widely followed by financial concerns such as insurance offices and building societies.

In order to try to corner a part of this, now highly competitve, financial market a large number of mergers have been taking place during the past three to four years. One such merger between two building societies was monitored over a period of six months pre-merger to eighteen months' post-merger. During these two years' a regional manager of one of the merged societies, who retained his position in the merged firm, was interviewed at regular intervals, and also provided this observer with the occasional apposite literature concerning the new, now very large, organization.

Both organizations planned for change in advance of merging, setting up a programmed timetable leading to the merger and for three years' post-merger. For example, guarantees were given that for three years after merging there would be no redundancies enforced, and job descriptions and responsibilities were to be more sharply defined than had previously been the case.

At the point of merger in autumn 1987 the view was that 'an exercise is being carried out to establish what is going to happen and to reassure staff – because the biggest problem is the staff's perception of the future'. From an organizational culture perspective, 'the them and us attitude is likely to last a long time', signifies the changes in attitudes and behaviours which are required in the change process.

It was perceived that the merged organization would have larger resources and greater financial strength to perform successfully in a more competitive environment, with an increase in combined market share from 4% to 10% in the short term.

Post-Finance Act and post-merger, two 'sets' of employers and two organizational structures and cultures were joined and faced change in many areas:

1. *Competitors:* the two or three larger societies, all banking institutions, insurance companies and brokers.
2. *Technology:* in new computer technology, building societies are seen to outstrip most financial institutions apart from a major bank. A majority of the merged organizations were faced with the latest technology in this area.
3. *Government:* has a great influence, e.g. Finance Act 1987, and there is now an ombudsman for the industry.

However, the behavioural aspects of this enlarged, changed organization were many and varied. Changes in structure itself affected at least some of these key areas, which included the following:

1. Communications
2. Roles
3. Training and education
4. Management style.

1. With a policy of no redundancies for three years, the structure was at the outset, overstaffed at the top of the hierarchy. There was also a congestion of communications within a hierarchical structure, within which span of control was narrow and layers of management were many. Within a year of merger, one layer of management was taken out of the structure with a resultant improvement in communications: 'The decision to remove assistant regional managers should have been made on the first day of merger but it is always difficult to see every

implication of the merger.' After the merger was consolidated the organization would adopt a three-year corporate plan.

At the outset, however, because of the dynamic nature of the environment and the necessity for change, the organization adopted a one-year plan.

2. Because of the new services being offered to the public, changes in relationships with customers at branch level were initiated. Staff at this level assumed new roles as customer advisors rather than simply collectors and dispensers of cash. They also took on, in effect, the role of salespersons when a payment-by-results system was launched as part of employee remuneration.
3. Whereas in the past, new entrants to both pre-merged organizations were placed immediately into branches to learn 'on the job', changes in training methods were brought in at merger. Before being placed in branches, new starts undergo a three- to five-day course giving a broad overview of their jobs with a programmed learning mode of training. Existing staff now attend training and education courses.
4. Management style changed dramatically for all due to the merger. The two respective management philosophies were quite different, and both experienced the changes when a self-control style of management was immediately introduced on merging.

The classical organizational approach is a basically inflexible, mechanistic set-up, as in the bureaucratic form, in effect management by control from the top of the hierarchy. Management by self-control, or management by objectives (MBO) was the vitally important change in management style which occurred on merger. MBO asks for agreement with managers at all levels on their individual targets.

An organizational climate is provided which encourages self-development, self-control and an easy flow of communication, and is supported and shown in McGregor's Theory Y. As stated in interview, 'it is definitely MBO style but not hierarchical'. There are seen to be both benefits and dangers with an MBO style, but in any event the behavioural aspects of this change was experienced by all employees. Other aspects of change which affected people within the merged organization were as follows.

A 'corporate plan' was presented to all employees, with details of the timetable for change. A large management development department existed or training development and monitoring of career structures. Roles, greatly changed, were also now clearly defined and branches were now self-marketing with rewarded selling targets. Despite knowledge of corporate planning and pre-merger work, subordinates showed a high level of uncertainty for approximately a year after the changes brought about by the merger and the Finance Act.

Some uncertainty still existed after a year's post-merger, although it had diminished. Eighteen months after merger there was still a great deal of stress being experienced by branch staff. This arose from the initial uncertainty, having hopes dashed of early expectations of substantial salary increases and harmonizing in attempting to merge into one unit. An integration policy had been adopted in that all branch offices would in time contain a mixture of staff from the respective pre-merged organizations: 'It will take the second and probably the third year before we're thinking "Smith/Jones".'

11. Conclusions and summary

Strategic processes are sometimes now accepted as multilevel activities and not just as the province of a few, (or even a single) general managers. However, the behavioural, political and individual aspects of change still remain to be solved if and when they become a problem. 'Strategic changes takes place over a fairly long period of time and can make a considerable difference to the way in which an organization operates.' [47]

The process of implementing strategic change causes a great deal of uncertainty within an organization, and individuals as well as groups of individuals have to try to cope with this through political activity.

Within the culture of the organization are sets of values pertaining to the organization itself, to groups within the organization and also at the individual level. Strategic change upsets the balance, and although this may be short-lived it is an important factor.

In order to manage the impact of strategic change on people, both at the personal and at the political levels within the organization, certain actions and activities should be implemented [48].

At the political level, acceptance of change can be gained by the following:

(a) information being provided to secure groups to convince them of the need for change;
(b) insecure groups being reassured about the consequences of change;
(c) widening the involvement of people to ensure easier implementation;
(d) implementing those changes where agreement can be found and deferring others within an incremental approach;
(e) waiting until circumstance make particular strategies more politically acceptable.

The personal implications of change call for the following actions, which may be taken to ensure a match between strategy and people's personalities and capabilities:

1. people's roles are reassessed;
2. people's capabilities may be a constraint on certain strategies while they are better suited to other strategies;
3. training programmes may be needed;
4. recruitment of new people may be the best way to obtain new, required skills;

5. redeployment or redundancy may be the only means of coping with certain people within the organization;
6. a transition period may be necessary before more changes are considered.

It is therefore clear that people will be affected by strategic change and there are situations when the culture surrounding these people will be affected by strategic change and there are situations when the culture surrounding these people should be changed.

References

1. Whipp, R., Rosenfield, R. and Pettigrew, A. (1988) 'Understanding strategic change processes: some preliminary British findings', in Pettigrew, A. (ed.), *The Management of Strategic Change*. Basil Blackwell, p. 15.
2. Brooks, E. (1980) *Organisational Change: The Managerial Dilemma*. Macmillan, p. 73.
3. Tichy, N. M. (1983) *Managing Strategic Change: Technical, Political and Cultural Dynamics*. John Wiley & Sons, p. 5.
4. Tichy, N. M. *op. cit.*, p. 18.
5. Tichy, N. M. *op. cit.*, p. 6.
6. Taylor, F. W. (1964) *Scientific Management*, Harper.
7. Fayol, H (1949) *General and Industrial Management*. Translated by Constance Stoors. Ritman.
8. Weber, M. (1947) *The Theory of Social and Economic Organisation*. Free Press.
9. Mayo, E. (1949) *The Social Problems of an Industrial Civilisation*. Routledge, Kegan Paul.
10. Brooks, E. *op. cit.*, p. 37.
11. Burns, T. and Stalker, G.M. (1977) *The Management of Innovation*. Tavistock Publications.
12. Woodward, J. (1980) *Industrial Organisation: Theory and Practice*, 2nd edn. Oxford University Press.
13. Lawrence, P. R. and Lorsch, J. W. (1979) *Organisation and Environment: Managing Differentiation and Integration*. Harvard University Press.
14. Brooks, E. *op. cit.*, p. 57.
15. Brooks, E. *op. cit.*, p. 59.
16. Child, J. (1977) *Organisation: A Guide to Problems and Practice*. Harper and Row, p. 9.
17. Burns, T. and Stalker, G. M. *op. cit.*, p. 4.
18. Brooks, E. *op. cit.*, p. 139.
19. Handy, C. B. (1980) *Understanding Organisations*. Penguin, p. 116.
20. Fiedler, F. E. (1967) *A Theory of Leadership Effectiveness*. McGraw-Hill.
21. Likert, R. (1961) *New Patterns of Management*. McGraw-Hill.
22. Fiedler, F. E. (1967) *A Theory of Leadership Effectiveness*. McGraw-Hill.
23. Barnard, C. I. (1938) *The Functions of the Executive*. Harvard University Press.
24. Handy, P. 53.
25. Kast, F. E. and Rosenzweig, J. E., Organisation and Management: A Systems and Contingency Approach 4th Edition: McGraw-Hill 1985, p. 307.
26. Handy, C. B. *op. cit.*, p. 63.

27. Child, J. *op. cit.*, p. 119.
28. Tichy, N. M., *op. cit.*, p. 43.
29. Tichy, N. M. *op. cit.*, p. 86.
30. Maslow, A. H. (1977) *The Farther Reaches of Human Nature.* Penguin.
31. McClelland, D. C. (1951) *Personality*, Sloane, cited in *Management and Motivation'* V. H. Vroom and E. A. Deci (eds.) (1970), Penguin.
32. Porter, L. W. and Lawler, E. E. (1968) *Managerial Attitudes and Performance*: Dorsey.
33. Herzberg, F. (1968) *Work and the Nature of Man.* Staples Press.
34. McGregor, D. (1983) *The Human Side of Enterprise*: McGraw-Hill.
35. Deal, T. and Kennedy, A. (1988) *Corporate Cultures: The Rites and Rituals of Corporate Life.* Penguin, p. 158.
36. Deal, T. and Kennedy, A. *op. cit.*, p. 161.
37. Kanter, R. M. (1985) *The Change Masters: Corporate Entrepreneurs at Work:* Unwin, p. 42.
38. Pettigrew, A. (1985) *The Awakening Giant: Continuity and Change in ICI.* Basil Blackwell.
39. Leavitt, H. (1965) 'Applied organisational change in industry: Structural, technological and humanistic approaches', in J. G. March (ed.) *Handbook of Organisations.* Rand McNally.
40. Greiner, L. E. (May/June 1967) 'Patterns of Organization Change', *Harvard Business Review.*
41. Lewin, K. (1947) 'Group Decision and Social Change' in *Readings in Social Psychology*, New York, Holt, Rinehart and Winston.
42. Kotter, J. P. and Schlesinger, L. A. (1979) 'Choosing strategies for change: *Harvard Business Review*, **57**, March–April, p. 107.
43. Kotter, J. P. and Schlesinger, L. A. *op. cit.*, p. 108.
44. Kotter, J. P. and Schlesinger, L. A. *op. cit.*, p. 110.
45. Kotter, J. P. and Schlesinger, L. A. *op. cit.*, p. 112.
46. Kotter, J. P. and Schlesinger, L. A. *op. cit.*, p. 112.
47. Johnson, G. and Scholes, K. (1984) *Exploring Corporate Strategy.* Prentice Hall, p. 313.
48. Johnson, G. and Scholes K. *op. cit.*, p. 316.

—— 11 ——

Industrial relations in the UK construction industry: a sociological and organizational analysis

Robert Stocks and Steven Male

1. Introduction

This chapter is an exploration of industrial relations in construction within the framework provided by both a sociological and organizational analysis. The first half of the chapter highlights the main concepts involved in the analysis. The final half discusses the industrial relations framework in the UK construction industry, sub-contracting and labour-only sub-contracting in particular, making international comparisons where appropriate to assist in clarifying issues; it concludes by drawing together concepts from the earlier part of the chapter with the themes raised in the sections on construction to provide a comparative assessment.

2. The division of labour

The division of labour and its allied industrialization increased production and led to problems at the workplace. In a wider sense the division of labour is seen as a major determinant of social structure, wherein structured inequality develops as a result of that division and additional factors.

The productive activity within industrialization requires cooperation for the production of goods and services, but there is a simultaneous competition between the parties involved within the production process, particularly management and labour.

Hill [1] points to the locus of employment where a conflict of interest exists: 'Since wages are costs which affect profits and profits can be raised at the cost of wages those whose interests lie in maximising wages are in competition with those concerned to raise profits.' Thus, as management and labour are involved in the necessary cooperation to achieve their respective aims, they are at the same time on differing courses in competitive pursuit of these benefits.

This divergence arises when it is seen that within the system, one of the parties does not retain the profits gained as a result of its work efforts. Capitalism, as one economic system resulting from industrialization, is an example of one party to the production process appropriating the profits from that process. Two participants attempting to gain the maximum from the modern economic organization create this destabilizing effect, as competition and cooperation coexist.

Structured inequality within society is seen by Marxist theory as the exploitation of one class by another arising from the production processes of capitalism. Class, in this respect, is defined by owning, or otherwise, the means of production. Exploitation follows from the separation of workers from ownership, as the owner appropriates a value which is surplus to costs of production, in the form of profits: "Because value can only be created by labour in production, then by definition, any surplus must result from the expenditure of that labour.'[2] A contrasting view would state that labour carries no more weight in the economic processes than land, capital and the enterprise of business owners or their managers.

State socialism is also a situation in which profits are taken by someone other than the producer–labourer. However, within the capitalist mode of production are seen two groups with unequal power, whose interest at times conflict. In terms of capital, because of competition in markets it must attempt to increase profit by making producers make more, or by decreasing wages. On the other hand, labour attempts to increase wages and improve conditions, thereby increasing costs for the capitalist business owner, or his extension the manager. Wages are costs which affect profits and profits can be raised at the cost of wages.

3. Conflict

Within capitalist industry therefore, is the structure of opposing interest of those who appropriate surplus value and those who sell their labour power while being subjected to the control of the former.

'Within the context of antagonistic relations of production industrial conflict cannot be fully understood except in terms of the opposing strategies of those whose interests, and hence whose underlying orientations and objectives, are themselves in opposition.' [3] A strike, overtime ban or work to rule on the one hand, or greater control over the labour process, on the other, are only a few examples of strategic actions from opposing sides in the conflict. Emile Durkheim dealt with the same issues as Marx but with different explanations of the social processes of industrial society. Society comprises individuals with different values, beliefs and attitudes, and with groups representing these differences. The question is concerned with how society is therefore possible in the first instance and, given the ever present threats of conflict, how it binds together. For the industrialized society where differentiation is an aspect of the division of labour, an analysis of social solidarity examines the bonding together of society. Durkheim's analysis for all societies is to look at moral regulation and authority – the social rules which make up solidarity. There are a number of systems of moral authority in modern society and, for Durkheim, one large formal system which integrates the many.

Durkheim presented a model of two 'ideal' types of society. The mechanical society is a pre-industrial society with a social bond in existence, with similarities rather than differences and held together by a universal legal system. There is also cultural uniformity of values, ideals, beliefs and morality in the mechanical form. The division of labour is seen to disrupt this form, with specialization breaking up the uniformity of society. Mechanical solidarity breaks up as its sources no longer hold and a new form arises. Within the organic form, the second 'ideal' type of industrialized society, with its complex systems from the division of labour, differences are highlighted. Functionally different units are held together as a whole, through interdependence; although there is more chance of conflict through differentiation within organic solidarity. Society itself determines the collective conscience, rather than the holding together of each individual conscience experienced in mechanical solidarity.

Whereas Marx viewed the division of labour as leading to social divisions and class conflict, Durkheim saw it as a social system based normally upon cooperation rather than conflict. Conflict is explained in terms of an abnormal division of labour. Hyman [4] outlines the view concerning normal conflict essential to the maintenance of the system, and dysfunctional conflict which is not only not essential, but is destructive. Clegg and Dunkerley [5] however, point out that what Durkheim described as abnormal about the early capitalist society that he examined, was in fact the norm.

Anomie is seen as a state of society in which disagreement exists over appropriate norms, that is to say patterns of expectation concerning behaviour. Durkheim's notion of anomie has been adopted into industrial relations research. Fox [6] describes the problems associated with variations in the commitment of employees to the shared values of industrial organizations, values which uphold the procedural norms of decision-making relationships between management and labour. Depending on the level of commitment to these values, the subordinate will respond in different ways and varying intensity to organizational procedures. Fox sees three levels of conflict between individual aspirations and shared norms. Individuals may accept organizational norms but on occasion break those which they find specially irritating, or which they can easily avoid. At this first level, sanctions which punish the culprit may be seen by management as necessary to avoid any further breakdown in normative behaviour. The transgressor, in perceiving the legitimacy of the organizational norms, may also view the sanctions as legitimate. A second situation is one of normative conflict where the individual response to shared values is such as to break his commitment to the values underlying these norms. If there is no way of adjusting the overall normative system while maintaining the aspirations of both superior and subordinate, sanctions may be used to impose existing norms. Subordinates in this instance are no longer legitimizing relevant organizational norms and therefore will perceive sanctions as illegitimate. If this situation continues to exist over a long period, even beneath the exercise of management power, the commitment to shared values may disappear completely. This may eventually lead to

Fox's third level in which management cannot strengthen the value commitment of employees to procedural norms because those employees are ideologically opposed to the organization's procedural norms. Although there may be few individuals within this extreme group, their role as leaders may be of great practical importance in some situations. Only by the use of managerial power can such behaviour be controlled.

It is important for management to perceive correctly which of the three situations they are being confronted with, in order that the conditions are correctly handled. Durkheim took the view, in respect of anomie, that if a set of people are in complete disagreement they cannot be perceived as a society. The organizational culture is viewed in similar terms by writers such as Fox. However, as Hill points out [7] 'both Durkheim and later sociologists argued that a new form of moral order, based on the sense of belonging to an industrial social community, would provide a solution to this normative disorder and the frustration of needs'.

Where the collective conscience cannot reduce individual bias there exists an anomic situation. It requires an integration of 'individuals into occupational groups on the basis of professional ethics which do not merely integrate each group within itself but which also relate to the totality of groups in the wider society.'[8]

4. Control

'The simplification and standardisation of tasks, together with managerial intervention in work coordination, laid the foundations for the greater control of labour by management.' [9] At the beginning of this century, scientific management principles were seen at the forefront of development in management control systems. An increased division of labour, work study methods and payment-by-results schemes were aspects of F. W. Taylor's scientific management, wherein management control was used to increase the individual's productivity level by making the individual work harder and more effectively. Administration of work has been affected by Taylorism up to the present time. Work study and time and motion studies retain the same form as when introduced originally by scientific management. One of the assumptions made by scientific management was that the worker was, at the very least, highly motivated by the acquisition of money. This cash nexus was intrinsic to incentive schemes being set up to increase work performance and productivity while simultaneously allowing workers to maximize their own wages. Incentive schemes in varying forms have been utilized by management since that time, and are still seen in operation notwithstanding their deficiencies in effectiveness. Whereas scientific management concentrated on the structural level of production organizations, bureaucracy 'provided a normative basis to, and justification of, managerial authority'. [10] The bureaucratic division of labour did not, in scientific management, de-skill the work process by maximum task fragmentation, but established work roles which were specialized and required a significant level of expertise. Bureaucratic forms of organization developed in the early part of this century and created an employment relationship which continues to exist. Max Weber, the German sociologist, in describing the bureaucratic form as a rational–legal style of authority structure, was concerned with how organization members come to be controlled and directed, and the manner in which tasks, authority levels and product types are regularized. Commitment by employees to the organization, allied to integration and involvement, is achieved by the formalization of rules and regulations and the contractual organization of career prospects for all occupants of position within the bureaucratic structure. Fox [11], in identifying levels of trust within organizations, takes the view that managers do not trust their workers to work effectively for, or in the best interests of, their firms. It is also assumed that the interests of workers are in conflict with those of management. Management control within scientific management is seen to show a situation of low trust, compared to the higher level of trust existing within bureaucratic principles of work organizations.

Clegg and Dunkerley [12] indicate that the major opposition to scientific management came from trade unions growing in power during the early part of this century. The main area of distrust lay in the decline of craft skills and loss of control which workers previously had over their own work. 'Employment based on the cash nexus, the commodity status of labour and the play of market forces still magnifies the opposition between the interests of employers and employees.' [13] As a result of employment relations, low trust principles are firmly rooted in work organization. Fox [14], in examining the bases for management authority, indicates that by entering into a contract of employment, the worker authorizes the employer's actions of directing and controlling employees' activities. In addition to this legitimization of time, place, content and method of work, the use of sanctions by the employer to achieve the necessary compliance is likewise perceived as authoritative. In any event, as Hyman [15] posits, capitalist management establishes an authoritarian hierarchy wherein work processes are of a collective character where labour power is relinquished to the employer. Management therefore requires to coordinate activities towards the collective processes of production, but also carries out the control procedures of the organization and its structure. The struggle by workers for job control 'involves a confrontation with a managerial hierarchy which itself controlled from above, constitutes a hostile totality' [16].

5. Power and authority

Employees will dispute certain aspects of managerial authority even if accepting the right of management to manage. Because managerial authority is insufficient, it needs to be supplemented by power. As Hill [17] points out, the contract of employment, while establishing the prerogative of management to plan and command, does not confirm the solid details of this command. As a result of their positional power and authority, managers are able to design and implement control systems in pursuit of employee compliance. Collective action on the shop floor is a growing indication of the questioning of ways in which managerial power is exercised. There are a number of situations in which management, having recourse to sanctions, are perceived by subordinates to be exercising power. 'Managers discover that even in the most favourable circumstances they cannot rely on normative agreement alone to support the hierarchical relations which they perceive as necessary.' [18] The necessary utilization of power is often confronted with negative responses, and therefore management resort to the strengthening of authority relations. As planned and predictable behaviour is required for organizations, the leaders of these organizations see the necessity to, at least as a last resort, use power to enforce such behaviour.

It is within the area of normative conflict that various power-plays are seen to operate. When individuals find their aspirations are not being met by the norms which are established within the organizations, they will try to substitute norms of their own choosing by changing the normative system and corresponding aspirations of other individuals or groups. The possession of power enables one individual or group to impose the change of norms on another.

Fox [19] provides three illustrations of the dynamics of the process. First, such behaviour as high absenteeism, bad time-keeping, excessive time off or sickness and poor work performance, are examples of the individual substituting his own norms to replace those defined by management. Some degree of power is needed by the individual, even to display this withdrawal behaviour. If there are alternatives for employment because of low unemployment levels, or the individual possesses scarce skills, management may be deterred from punishing such withdrawal behaviours.

A second example is of a group with collective power which substitute their own norms in place of organizational norms. The group may be able to impose unilaterally its norms on the appropriate level of management if the manager believes that if he resists the group can use its power to prevent him pursuing his own goals, which in turn may be at odds with top management. He therefore substitutes the work group's norm for the organization's, although he will not be committed to the situation or the norm imposed upon him.

The third example is the situation which is historically the most common. Management exercises power in imposing its own normative system on lower members of the organization who must accept change, whether wishing to or not, because they are unable to challenge these superiors. They may use their power to force employees to change their behaviour if, for example, unacceptable norms such as restrictive practices are inherent in the organization. Having not agreed to this change situation, employees may attempt to evade or change whenever the opportunity arises, or resort to withdrawal behaviour if no such opportunity presents itself.

Individuals may hold sufficient power to achieve change independently although most lower-hierarchical-level employees have to activate it through collective organizations. The whole purpose of the collectivity is to shift the balance of power and to a great extent the processes can be understood only with this in mind. The sale of labour power and the control of the labour process are the interdependent elements of industrial relations processes, the balance of which is crucial for those involved with bargaining and compromise.

Within the framework of power and authority relationships which pervade the organization, there will be resistance to orders which are perceived as unreasonable. This position 'is increased by the fact that legitimacy is too strong a concept to apply to most workers' conception of management' [20]. Given these authority relations within industrial organizations, subordinates are seen to accept them with a low-key level of acquiescence. Hierarchical control as a feature of employment relationships is accepted as natural and inevitable by subordinates. It is only when requested to perform some extraordinary task that the possibility of disobedience arises. It is at the limit of disobedience, where the individual questions the authority of management to command, that coercive power is exercised. Workers obey orders because managers issue orders which workers find reasonable, and this situation will exist until some outside influence alters the position of stability. However, 'occupational groups clearly vary considerably in respect of the sanctions and resources at their disposal, and also in terms of their readiness to mobilise these in opposition to the power of management' [21]. This and other influences help shape the power balance through which relations at the point of production are negotiated. The reason why people in organizations conform to orders and follow laid-down standards of behaviour is, for Etzioni, summed up in the term 'compliance', which is 'a relationship consisting of the power employed by superiors to control subordinates and the orientation of subordinates to this power' [22]. Organizations are classified into three basic types, according to the types of power found within them. The coercive, remunerative and normative typology has many critics.

6. Collectivities and institutionalization

6.1 Trade unions

Workers as individuals can exert little meaningful control over their work environment; only by submitting to collective principles and decisions can they share in more significant influence over the conditions of their working lives but, 'in subordinating part of their individual autonomy to collective decision-making processes they create an institution which can pursue objectives which diverge from their own interests' [23].

Unionism appears to require acceptance by government and major employers and the paradox is created whereby unions both attempt to limit industrial conflict while at the same time express, and may even stimulate, their members' consciousness of grievances.

Trade unions, as the historical products of the relationship between labour and capital, are among the vital mediating institutions between labour on one side, and on the other management as representatives of capital in industrial organizations.

The role of trade unions is the ambivalent one of being opposed to capitalism while at the same time being a part of it. However, they exist because conflict prevails between the two components of capitalism and it is only through organized collective action that labour can bring pressure to bear on capital in the form of owners or their managers. A trade union operates within the confines of the existing social and economic systems, not only the power distribution between employers and employees but also between different groups of workers, and different sexes or races. Contemporary trade unions are therefore seen as coming to terms with the power of capital rather than overthrowing it. 'Collective bargaining is a process of defensive accommodation to the existing external power structure and involves the relief or suppression of immediate grievances rather than any attempt to tackle the underlying cause of workers' problems.' [24] Trade unions provide the formal channel wherein workers may have their interests represented and rights protected. It is therefore the case that unions not only organize conflict but also manage conflict, with the result that this management reduces the threat to the stability of the existing social and economic order. Furthermore, unions have achieved few significant concessions on control of the labour process itself. 'Trade unions do not challenge the existence of a society based on a division of classes; they merely express it.' [25] In any event, trade unions are not cohesive class organizations uniting all workers behind one collective aim. Although class opposition constitutes the basis of work relations in capitalist society, this is superimposed and often hidden by differing forms of work processes and practices, and with group interests. Union objectives appear to be confined to the negotiation of limited improvements within the framework of capitalist work relations. As Hyman states, 'the basic character of capitalism exerts a pervasive influence on the nature of industrial relations, most crucially through the way in which it shapes the structure, actions and objectives of trade unionism' [26].

An additional contradiction for trade unionism is that while trade unions unite workers, they also divide them. Within trade unionism are many diverse union organizations which are often in competition with each other. With each union containing specific categories of workers as members, other groupings are excluded. There has also traditionally been conflict between the officers and representatives of unions and their members. This has particularly been the case since the innovation of national collective bargaining procedures, and also as a result of union organizations at times becoming bureaucratized.

6.2 Employers

In the short term at least, the interests of trade unions and employers conflict. However, employers will wish to emphasize the need for cooperation and will set up procedures aimed at the resolution of conflict. Fox argues that the acceptance of collective bargaining or other institutional arrangements for the settlement of industrial conflict, 'is an example of the use of the ideology of pluralism in which gross inequalities of power are obscured by the illusion of balance between competing interest groups' [27]. The role of unions is legitimized by management in certain areas in order that employers achieve their business objectives, 'not by opposition to representative institutions but by collaboration with them' [28]. Employers may also act either as individuals or as a collectivity. However, employers are seen as less unified as a social group than are workers. Organizations will differ in size, organizational structure, technology, managerial style, organization culture, etc. Furthermore, employers are involved with product markets in addition to labour markets, and 'different conditions in product markets give rise to different interests that are likely to reflect also on the interest of firms in industrial relations' [29]. Competition in these product markets also limits cohesion and unity of employers. However, economic crises increase competition between firms, weaken trade unions and foster government action which is seen to favour business organizations.

6.3 The state

The state plays an important part in determining the nature and effectiveness of employee representation. Public sector employment itself comprises a large proportion of the United Kingdom's workforce. Additionally, all parties in government would wish to maintain stability and productivity for business organizations as part of the national economy; industrial relations are therefore affected.

Government policies, as well as social and economic programmes, create the environment within which industrial relations are enacted. Because the state affects industrial development and profitability, it helps to structure social relations and the balance of power within industry. Furthermore, industrial relations policies propounded by government have a direct influence on conflict even if these policies are not converted into legislation. The nature and extent of direct state involvement in industrial relations varies from the individualistic philosophy of *laissez-faire*, which sees the state separated from other groups in the economy, to corporatism, which presupposes the existence of representative organizations, and in terms of industrial relations tries to achieve workers' cooperation and avoid conflict by involving both unions and employers' organizations in the formulation and implementation of state policies. Workers are subordinated, not through individualism, but through the very fact of belonging to collectivities, and these organizations which represent them also regulate them [30]. As with *laissez-faire*, there are few examples of 'pure' corporatism.

A pluralist view is one in which the state is perceived as autonomous within its complex institutions, politically neutral and external to structurally determined social forces. The political system rather than the state is therefore seem as the major agent of policy formulation.

The Marxist view sees the state as the tool of the ruling class, assisting capital, and the state as shaped by the requirements of capital. 'Both the pluralist and Marxist approaches view the state as essentially a reactive mechanism to pressure generated within civil society.' [31].

Pressure and influences can include: different organs of the state pursuing different strategies; influence of the working class on government policy; the relationship between political parties and the labour movement; public opinion; and the state of the economy.

The ability of different interest groups to affect state activity and the ability of the state to influence industrial relations are allied to the features of existing structure and the economic context within which state activity occurs.

7. Perspectives

Farnham and Pimlott [32] describes a number of perspectives by which industrial relations can be understood, and these differing models can be outlined as follows:

7.1 The unitary perspective

This theory derives from the notion that every work organization is an integrated and harmonious whole, existing for a common purpose. It makes the following assumptions:

(a) Each employee identifies with the aims of the enterprise and with its methods of operation.
(b) Managers and managed are part of the same team and, therefore, are complementary partners.
(c) Management of this team comes from the top of the organization.

As a result of these premises, team spirit and individual management authority coexist to the benefit of all, with mutual cooperation and harmony of interest between management and managed. Any disruption to this unity is seen to be caused by personality conflicts, misunderstandings about aims and methods of achieving these, a failure to grasp the communality of interest, and the work of agitators.

7.2 Industrial conflict perspective

Within this theory the following two views of contemporary society are interrelated:

1. Post-capitalist society contains the situation where political and industrial conflicts have become institutionalized. Industrial conflict is less violent because it has become an accepted part of society and is socially regulated.
2. Industrial and work organizations become microcosms of society. Industrial relations between employers and unions are expressions of power relations as they exist in society itself.

The institutionalization of conflict in industry takes on the following features: organizations of conflicting interest groups; the establishment of parliamentary negotiating bodies; an institution of mediation and arbitration; a formal representation of labour within the organization; and tendencies towards, and institutionalization of, worker participation in management. Conflict between manager and employee is therefore regulated by trade unionists, employers' organizations and collective bargaining, with additional involvement from local shop stewards. Arbitration is available, with all its services, for difficult problems. This post-capitalist perspective is very closely related to the pluralist perspective where the central feature of industrial relations is the potential conflict which exists between employer and employee, manager and managed. Unlike the unitary perspective, however, trade unionism is accepted as having both a representative function and an important part in regulating this conflict, rather than causing it. Collective bargaining is seen as the institutional means by which industrial conflict is regularized and resolved.

7.3 Systems model

This perspective takes the view that an industrial relations system is a separate and distinctive sub-system of the wider society. However, it partly overlaps the economic and political institutions and interacts with them. An industrial relations system has its own rules and procedures, either written, oral or from custom and practice. The three main groups of actors, or active participants in the system are as follows:

(a) a hierarchy of managers and their representatives in the form of supervisors;
(b) a hierarchy of non-managerial employees and their spokesmen;
(c) any specialized third-party agencies, from government or private sources, concerned with workers' enterprises and their relationships.

There are seen to be features of the environment which affect actors and their roles. The technological characteristics of the workplace and work community is an influence because of the way in which technology can affect the form of management and employee organization, and the problems posed for supervisors. Market and budgetary constraints can influence the ease with which products can be sold; therefore labour availability and wage increases are influenced in the same situation. The distribution of power within the industrial relations system will be affected by, and responsive to, the larger society with its locus and distribution of power.

8. Collective bargaining: the standard model

The state has secured the role of an economic manager, which necessitates it having an influential role in the results of collective bargaining. Government encouragement and tight markets have meant that employers have taken the initiative in the field of industrial relations: 'The formalities of collective bargaining remain but its scope and effectiveness are severely restricted.' [33] It cannot be assumed that collective bargaining is the major form of job administration in the United Kingdom.

There are differing aims and authority relationships between employers within organizations and a resultant level of conflict of interest exists. Beaumont therefore puts forward the view that 'collective bargaining as a means of establishing and regulating the terms and conditions of employment can only be judged in relation to possible alternative mechanisms' [34]. These would include informal work group arrangements, government legislation and unilateral human resource management. However, despite its critics, the existence of collective bargaining arrangements is one of a number of formal considerations concerning the potential conflict between management and their individual employees. The introduction of an institutional organization, trade union representation, means that conflict can then arise from and involve interpersonal, intraorganizational and procedural sources.

Notwithstanding the criticisms levelled against collective bargaining, compromise agreements negotiated through collective bargaining have become the standard pattern governing some of the most central relationships between employer and employee. Negotiating relationships vary widely, with differing levels of distrust showing the failure of full integration. Fox [35] describes the 'standard' model of collective bargaining which is 'grounded firmly on the explicit or implicit acceptance by both negotiating parties of the pluralistic conception of the organization'. A distribution of power exists which is unbalanced, but not to the extent that either party perceives it is being coerced. Management holds a view of the areas in which it has a monopoly in decision-making, and those other areas in which unions and work groups may demand participation.

In this respect economic and political issues have until recently been separated within the industrial field. Employers and managers 'will strike bargains on financial issues and conditions of employment, whereas they will resist concessions on control, while unions react to this state of affairs by negotiating where they know that they have some chance of success' [36]. The separation of economic and control issues, with the former taking centre stage, are essential pre-conditions of the institutionalization of conflict.

Many unions have shown a willingness to negotiate over, and agree to, systems of job evaluation and work measurement, payment by results systems based on work study alone, productivity schemes which allocate a range of decisions over the labour process to managerial initiative or formalized collective bargaining. Flanders [37] points out that these developments 'strengthen managerial control over pay and work through joint regulation'.

Under the 'standard' model of collective bargaining the employee collective conforms to existing hierarchical authority relationships and division of labour, while management modifies its position to accommodate its subordinates. However, the fundamental work situation, and relationships between manager and managed, remain the same.

In conclusion, industrial relations strategies of employers should be linked to the overall long-term strategy of the firm. Corporate strategy is invariably concerned with, and affected by, change. Flexibility is required by the organization in order to deal with changes in its environment and to assist in coping with the uncertainties involved. These uncertainties are seen to be linked to the strategic decisions of others, including trade unions.

Industrial relations between capital and labour have been shown to be concerned with aspects of power and authority, conflict and control, negotiating and bargaining. However, in their pursuit of profits, the firm's aim may be primarily interested in increasing control over labour in order to secure these profits.

Perhaps the cynic would doubt the validity of the statement that 'overall corporate strategy may formulate aims for, say, technology, corporate organization, product range, and so on, that reflect market opportunities rather than being directly geared to labour control' [38]. The following section takes the preceding issues and discusses them in the context of industrial relations in construction.

9. Industrial relations in the UK construction industry

Industrial relations in construction have a chequered history. The focus of much of this activity has been concerned with, first, the non-unionized labour-only sub-contract workforce (the 'lump') and, second, the consolidation of bonus payments into the wage contract'. Austrin [39] has indicated that violent strike action, such as the 'National Building Strike' of 1972, and passive non-union activity can coexist easily in construction. Strikes have not, however, been a major problem in the industry [40].

Working rule agreements (WRA) are supposed to form the industry-wide stipulation of employment conditions for operatives but in practice, depending on the type of operative employment, these can be modified at the construction site. This has already been alluded to in Chapter 2 dealing with site management and the modifications to bonus payments. Furthermore, the industrial relations structure in construction, with respect to employer and trade union associations, is fragmented. There are three major industry sectors concerned with industrial relations in construction – building, civil engineering and specialist trades. There are four trade unions and three major employers' associations aligned with the building sector. In civil engineering there are three trade unions and one employers' association. And in the specialist trades sector there are nine trade unions, two major employers' associations and 17 other employers' associations that could be involved depending on circumstances [41].

9.1 The labour force in construction

One of the major defining characteristics of the labour force in construction is the presence of differing skill levels. Skill is a social construct and signifies differing degrees of [42]:

(a) status;
(b) earning capacity;
(c) industrial power;
(d) exclusion;
(e) task capability.

The relative balance of operatives within the construction industry and their skills levels are as follows:

1. General labourers form the largest group of operatives within construction. They account for 25–30% of the workforce in building and over 40% in civil engineering [43]. There is also a marked difference between the skilled labour required for building and civil engineering projects [44].
2. Of the 70% of skilled operatives in the industry, the four trades of carpenters and joiners, painters, bricklayers and mechanical plant operators account for over half the workforce [45], with the latter employed to a greater extent in civil engineering projects. In comparison to unskilled operatives, the majority of skilled workers have spent most of their working lives in construction [46].

Other important facets of the workforce in construction are that, first, the single most important distinguishing characteristic of the manual workforce in construction, compared to other industrial sectors, is its age distribution. In 1981 64% of the blue collar workforce in construction were less than 40 years old, 28% of the workforce in construction were under 25 [47]. Allied with this is that age is the single most important factor associated with mobility in construction. Forty per cent of those aged between 25 and 35 years will have had four or more jobs. Furthermore, there is a high degree of mobility among general labourers in comparison to skilled workers. Young labourers are the most mobile and experience 'enormous amounts' of unemployment. In addition, the unskilled, in general, suffer a high rate of unemployment and redundancy [48].

Second, the public sector attracts more older workers in construction; their earning levels are lower but they have greater job security [49]. Third, there is partial evidence to suggest that the labour market for local firms is different than that for regional or national firms. This derives from the empirical evidence which indicates that those working for local firms appear to have similar earnings to those operatives working in local government departments, and locally based operatives appear to enjoy a higher length of service than their counterparts employed by regional or national companies [50]. Fourth, a considerable number of older workers are invalided out of the industry. This is especially prevalent among the unskilled [51]. Finally, self-employment in construction now represents over 50% of the labour force, some 600,000 operatives [52].

In the preceding chapter we indicated that the production process is characterized by different skill requirements, at different stages of the process, often with many organizations working on the same site and with a local industrial relations–labour climate in existence. This is exacerbated on large construction sites where there is a wide diversity of crafts, represented by different unions and with differing employer–union agreements in existence [53]. For example, on the Thames Barrier project, at the peak of working the labour force had escalated from 490 to 1550, with 450 sub-contractors and a total workforce of 2000. Industrial relations problems, primarily surrounding changes to shift patterns and bonus payments, bedevilled the project from the outset [54].

To summarize, in construction there is a high level of labour mobility, skill and status division. From our earlier discussions we can conclude that construction, through the division of labour, can be attributed to considerable social inequality associated with the production process. Social inequality and status differentials are brought sharply into focus in sub-contracting, now a major issue in production and the subject of the next section.

9.2 Sub-contracting

Sub-contracting, as we indicated in a preceding chapter, is demanding in terms of management expertise. It requires a considerable degree of cooperative behaviour between contracts management and sub-contractors. However, contractual responsibilities are a continual source of devisiveness and profitability. In addition, a management strategy of sub-contracting has considerable social costs attached to it, for example the apportionment of responsibility for health and safety, training and the undermining of the apprenticeship system [55]. A strategy of sub-contracting allows main contractor flexibility in response to labour shortages. However, two issues are associated that impact the industrial relations scene in construction. First, due to high-demand conditions, earnings are bid up but are not consolidated through union collective bargaining into wage agreements. Second, from an operative's viewpoint, higher wages decrease any reliance on union membership for collective action and help to foster a climate of self-employment in the industry. A study of self-employment in the industry by Marsh *et al.* [56] revealed that distinct categories of self-employment exist in the industry. These are set out in Table 11.1, which indicates that a strong orientation for independence is present in the self-employed. Three other orientations are present,

Table 11.1 Categories of self-employment in construction

Work for contractors *(N=130, 41%)*	*Work for public* *(N=81, 26%)*	*Work for both* *(N=105, 33%)*
Provide a *labour-only* service and are predominantly carpenters and joiners, bricklayers, and general labourers. Are also well represented by the plastering and tiling trade. Tend to be below 40 years old and a high proportion view earning power in weekly terms. Main reasons for self-employment, of approximately equal importance are independence and money. In addition, the third reason, of lesser importance, is that this is seen as the only way of gaining employment.	Provide *materials and equipment/plant* and are predominantly electricians, plumbers, painters, plasterers and tilers and 'general builders'. They are older, being biased towards the over-40 age group. Over 50% of this group see their earning power in annual terms. Main reason for self-employment is overwhelmingly independence and to a lesser extent as the only way of gaining employment.	Provide *materials and equipment/plant* and to a lesser extent *labour-only* services. This group are represented by 'general builders', carpenters and joiners, electricians, plumbers, painters, mechanical equipment operators, plasterers and tilers. These trade skills are spread approximately equally through the sample. Over 50% of this group see their earning power in annual terms. The main reason given by this group for self-employment is independence and, to a lesser extent, money. The issue of this being the only way of gaining employment is not seen as of great importance

Source: Adapted from Marsh *et al.*, 1981.

but to different degrees. These are, first, a concern with earning potential – viewed in weekly terms by the labour-only group and more predominantly in annual terms by the other two groupings; second, self-employment as the only way of gaining employment; third, age – the labour-only group are younger and have a stronger orientation for earning potential. The following sub-section looks more closely at labour-only sub-contracting.

9.2.1 Contractual issues in sub-contracting

There are five significant contractual issues, as follows, associated with the employment of sub-contractors that impact the employer–employed relationship [57].

1. Onerous payment conditions by the main contractor – the 'pay when paid' clauses. In essence this means that the contractor writes into the sub-contract that the sub-contractor will only receive payment for work done when the main contractor has received payment from the client through the monthly valuation process. As Gray and Flanagan point out, the issues for the sub-contractor are being able to determine when the main contractor is paid, the inherent risk that the client or main contractor may go bankrupt and the fact that withholding payments may mean that the sub-contractor has a negative cashflow, in effect providing finance to the main contractor.
2. The main contractor makes a contra charge against the sub-contractor for failing to meet the full sub-contract conditions.
3. The sub-contractor is held responsible by the main contractor for protecting and making good work, regardless of when it was installed or damaged.
4. The presumption is that the sub-contractor knows the detailed conditions of the main contract. In practice, the main contractor will only provide those sections of the contract documents relevant for the sub-contractor to tender and insert a 'catch all' clause into the sub-contract documents. In essence the main contractor is operating a 'need to know' policy and while the sub-contractor has the opportunity to inspect the full contract documents at the main contractor's office, Gray and Flanagan point out that there is usually insufficient time in the sub-contract tender stage for this to occur.
5. The sub-contractor, where there is a substantial design aspect, is held responsible for coordinating his design with other sub-contractors, especially where there are multiple specialists.

The foregoing indicate clearly that contractual obligations as between main contractor and sub-contractor place the former in a considerable position of power and control over the latter, depending on the size of the sub-contractor. This is especially true in the case of labour-only sub-contractors (LOSC) an issue that is taken up below.

9.3 Labour-only sub-contracting

LOSC allows market forces to directly control the regulation of wages without the intervention of trade unions, and the state's main attempt at intervention in this area has been through legislation to prevent or reduce tax evasion [58]. LOSC is not a new phenomenon and has been evident in the UK construction industry since the nineteenth century. The early trade union movement recognized the potential threat posed by LOSC and the emerging problem was given official recognition by the Royal Commission on Labour in 1895. In 1968, the Phelps–Brown Report [59] estimated that the highest levels of LOSC were to be found in bricklaying, carpentry and joinery, plastering, roofing and plumbing.

There are four different forms of LOSC, as follows [60]:

1. Individuals.
2. Small firms.
3. The gang system under a labour master: in this instance members of the gang are all self-employed but the labour master bears a responsibility to find work and pays each member of the gang on the basis of a mutual agreement.
4. Labour agencies, where workers are paid an hourly rate and are contracted out by the agency to a contractor: the contractor pays the agency which, in turn, pays the sub-contracted men. In a sense this legitimizes LOSC through legal status.

The 'informal economy' caused by LOSC is viewed by contractors as a serious threat to the stability of the industry in two ways, as follows [61]:

1. Genuine firms are constantly being undercut for 'cash-in'hand' payments to LOSC operatives, with the consequence that companies are no longer tendering for particular types of work.
2. No training is carried out and skilled workers are attracted away from genuine firms and direct labour organizations, either for higher rates of pay or for cash-in-hand.

In addition, LOSC 'lump' workers have caused a crisis in unionism in construction. Operatives have ignored trade union membership and have opted for negotiating their own wage contracts and conditions of employment rather than fighting for union regulated work through collective action [62]. LOSC operatives have conducted, therefore, individual bargaining of employment conditions at site level and have fragmented the underlying wage structure of the industry set by wage agreements. In reinforcing this point, two significant events occurred in the mid- to late-1980s that highlight the fact that LOSC had become a significant issue in the construction industry, especially for the trade union movement:

1. In late 1986 the Federation of Brickwork Contractors (FBC) was launched with the primary aim of becoming a trade association representing bona fide LOSC firms offering high-quality brickwork. Shortly

after, the FBC opened negotiations with both the Union of Construction Allied Trades and Technicians (UCATT) and the Transport and General Workers' Union (TGWU).

2. At the 1988 UCATT conference, delegates effectively gave official sanction to 714 Certificate (self-employed) labour when they voted by a clear majority to abandon their opposition to the recruitment of this type of labour into the movement.

In a case study analysis of LOSC, Waterfall concluded that from the employer's point of view, a strategy of LOSC has three distinct advantages for improving cashflow [63]:

1. Depending on the firm, interim payments to sub-contractors can vary between two and four weeks.
2. Retentions of up to 5% may be held against LOSC work.
3. LOSC final accounts may take between four and twelve weeks to finalize.

This sub-section has highlighted the fact that LOSC has undermined trade unionism in the UK construction industry and threatens to destabilize increasingly the structure of the industry in the future. It is interesting to note that LOSC is not permitted by law in France and Germany [64]. State control in the United Kingdom in this area has only addressed the issue of tax evasion. However, it cannot be denied that as a labour strategy it has distinct financial advantages for the employer. The following section discusses operative attitudes to these issues.

9.4 Operatives' attitudes in construction

There is a commonly held view in the industry, across all trades, regions and types of employment, of dissatisfaction with the wage structure [65]. Operatives are prepared to work hard to get the job done, especially where deadlines are concerned, but are not prepared to do so at the expense of safety. The primary motivation is a desire for overtime or bonus rather than coercion from management [66].

NEDO [67] suggests that operatives' orientations are primarily towards short-term task attainment. They have only a broad appreciation of the overall project completion times and it is primarily through informal methods that this information is obtained rather than from site management, who are reluctant to communicate project completion dates. Two types of attitudes towards project completion dates are prevalent within the directly employed workforce: a minority attitude, held especially by those with a long association with an employer, that completion dates are important to ensure that the company's reputation is maintained or enhanced; a majority held attitude is that continuity of employment is of paramount importance and with a greater concern that the longer the project continues the better. Finally, operatives have particularly strong views about supervision. They see overcontrol by site management as detrimental to productivity, and prefer a degree of autonomy. In addition, operatives respect site supervisors who are able to control the work rather than leave it to the operative [68].

Cheetham [69] also investigated operatives' viewpoints in his site studies. Empirical results indicate that operatives, first, see and accept mobility and redundancy as a normal part of working in the industry. Many leave contracts voluntarily in anticipation of redundancy, especially since they will not receive redundancy payments for short periods of employment. Second, chasing bonus or overtime is seen by operatives as a perfectly acceptable attitude and they justify the lack of commitment to an employer on the grounds that the latter shows a smaller lack of commitment, especially where operatives are often given short notice of dismissal. Third, basic rates of pay were seen as unacceptable for the work done and skills offered and, when coupled with the motive to maintain or enhance earnings, added to the impetus for bonus chasing. However, it must also be added that many operatives enjoyed the independence afforded by site work, supporting the evidence reported by the OPCS survey [70].

The following sub-sections break down operative attitudes into different categories.

9.4.1 Directly employed operatives

Directly employed operatives resent LOSC for the following five reasons [71]:

1. Their greater earning potential.
2. The devaluation of the status and work of the directly employed.
3. The marginalization of the directly employed into effective LOSC support.
4. An apparent reduced concern by the LOSC worker for safety; the evidence to support this contention is, however, mixed [72].
5. The blame for fragmentation of the workforce in the industry.

In addition, directly employed operatives:

1. Are very disgruntled about the hourly wage rate.
2. Are looking to bonus and overtime payments to make up their wages. However, these are also the focus of discontent. Bonus payments are often viewed as arbitrary, especially where site agents decide on spot bonuses, and overtime often caused friction between management and operatives where it was intermittently available.

9.4.2 Craftsmen

Attitudes exhibited by craftsmen include the following [73]:

(a) Obtaining considerable satisfaction from the exercise of their skill.
(b) A strong sense of pride in their jobs and the motivation to take responsibility for the quality of the finished product.

(c) That in some situations management are forcing them to forsake quality in the interests of high output.

9.4.3 Labour-only sub-contractors

LOSC workers see themselves as follows [74]:

(a) being forced to take this type of work due to difficulties in finding direct employment;
(b) highly productive;
(c) expected to be attended by main contractor labourers;
(d) having to work harder to obtain adequate levels of pay because piecework rates had been driven down recently.

The following section draws together the conceptual foundations of the early part of the chapter with the themes from the sub-sections specific to the industry to reach a set of conclusions about industrial relations in construction.

10. Conclusions

Division of labour, one of our pre-requisites for organizational structure, introduces structured inequality into any social system, namely, the workforce. In addition, since labour and management are bound together in a profit-making organization through the production process, a paradox is created. The focus of this paradox is the need for simultaneous cooperation and competition between the workforce and management – competition in the sense that management want to maximize profits and the workforce want to maximize their earnings. Cooperation is at the same time essential because both management and labour have to cooperate in order for the production process to proceed relatively smoothly and allow profits to be generated in the first place. This simultaneous need for cooperation and competition between management and labour can create tensions which can eventually erupt into conflict. One type of conflict remains within the boundaries of legitimized managerial control but normative and ideological conflict directly challenge the legitimacy of management. In construction, the production process is also characterized by the tension of cooperation and competition between management and labour. However, the waters are muddied by the fact that there are many different types of employment practice in construction, from directly employed operatives, through to sub-contractors and labour-only sub-contractors. Management in construction faces this paradox internally within the organization with its own direct employee operatives. However, by using considerable levels of sub-contracting this problem has been externalized to the marketplace by confronting the paradox through the effective organization and control of sub-contractors. All things being equal, the greater the level of sub-contracting obtained through competition the more fragmented the workforce becomes and the greater the degree of managerial control that can be exercised over the production process to raise profits by controlling costs. The downside of this argument is, however, that when the industry is experiencing a boom, power is transferred to sub-contracted labour where there are skill shortages, labour costs rise and profits become squeezed.

In Chapter 2 we have talked about the employment contract as forming part of the defining characteristics of the internal labour market of an organization. The employment contract, forming part of the formal structure, legitimizes and authorizes the employer to direct, control and sanction the employee. As such, the employment contract will operate normally through the managerial hierarchy, depending on the type of organization, and the creation of a superior/subordinate role is accepted as a natural and inevitable consequence of working in a company. Within the managerial hierarchy the assumption by the workforce is that management has the right to manage. In other words, the workforce accepts the reasonable use of power by management, but where this right is challenged management will exercise coercive power in order to redirect employees' attentions back towards achieving organizational objectives. In construction the focus of the argument over the employment contract is the division between directly employed and sub-contracted labour. Control over directly employed operatives is exercised through their employment contract built around working rule agreements. However, bonus payments and overtime are contentious issues with the directly employed workforce, and the focus of much of this tension rests with the actions of site management. Where labour is sub-contracted out the managerial hierarchy in the contracting firm exercises control through market forces by hiring and firing sub-contracted workers on individually negotiated employment conditions. If we take a wider view of sub-contracting, however, the managerial hierarchy of the main contractor is fragmented into other sub-contractor managerial hierarchies or by the legal status of the self-employed. It is only in the middle line, the strategic apex or the non-sub-contracted-out portion of the operating core that the managerial hierarchy can exist undisturbed. As the level of sub-contracting increases, power and authority in the operating core move from that legitimized by the internal employment contract to that legitimized by contractually based market exchanges. In this instance the strength of this market-based contractual exchange will depend very much on the type of sub-contractor employed.

Trade unions are paradoxical institutions in the industrial relations scene. Unions are at one and the same time a mediating force between management and the workforce, since they organize and manage industrial conflict, and a divisive force within the labour force, since they compete, segregate and organize labour. Employers also face a paradoxical situation. On the one hand, they either individually or collectively legitimize the role of trade unions in order to achieve business objectives. On the other hand, employers are competing in both product and labour markets which tends to constrain their cohesion and unity. Trade union-ism in construction has been under threat by the increasing use of labour-only sub-contracting. The pull of higher wages by becoming self-employed without redress to the collective action of construction unions has meant that operatives have seen little need to become members of these associations. However, it is the unions that have had to make concessions to the self-employed. Employers have benefited from the fragmentation of the workforce through LOSC and sub-contracting in general. It has meant that they have been faced, in general, with an unorganized labour force that has only temporarily been able to upgrade wages in times of boom but is unable to consolidate these gains in working rule agreements. Furthermore, by careful manipulation of cash flows and without taking on board the liabilities of a large direct workforce that stem from employment legislation, contractors have been able to benefit financially from the fragmented, unorganized, non-unionized workforce. One of the major losers in this sense appears to be the unskilled operative, especially in the younger age group, who appears to experience high levels of mobility within and outwith the industry compared to skilled workers, and is often invalided out of construction. On the other side of the coin, however, it must be stated that with over 50% of the workforce in construction opting for self-employment because they are either unable to find work in any other way or overwhelmingly enjoy the independence provided by self-employment, it is difficult to see that there will be any significant change in the employment relationships within the industry. The obvious consequence must be, in the medium to long term, that an industry faced with substantial skill shortages and an inability to upgrade itself because it is unattractive to new recruits due to high levels of structural casualisation and a lack of career prospects at craft level.

Finally, the state has a significant impact on industrial relations: it creates legislation impacting the workplace; is a significant employer of the unionized workforce; and, depending on the ideological persuasion of the political party in power, it creates a balance between employers and employees. The major intervention of the state in construction in the United Kingdom has been through legislation to reduce or attempt to eradicate tax evasion by the self-employed. In contrast to Germany and France, where the state is actively supporting construction industry upgrading through its enabling legislatory role in support of employer–union–employee training activity, the state in the United King-dom has adopted a passive if not negative role towards training in the industry.

11. Bibliography

Aldridge, A. (1976) *Power, Authority and Restrictive Practices: A Sociological Essay on Industrial Relations*. Basil Blackwell.

Edwards, P. K. and Scullion, H. (1982) *The Social Organisation of Industrial Conflict: Control and Resistance in the Workplace.* Basil Blackwell.

Marchington, M. and Parker, P. (1990) *Changing Patterns of Employee Relations.* Harvester Wheatsheaf.

Rueschemeyer, D. (1986), *Power and the Division of Labour.* Policy Press 1986.

References

1. Hill, S. (1983) *Competition and Control at Work.* Heinemann.
2. Hill, S. *op. cit.*
3. Hyman, R. (1989) *The Political Economy of Industrial Relations: Theory and Practice in a Cold Climate.* Macmillan.
4. Hyman, R. *op. cit.*
5. Clegg, S. and Dunkerley, D. (1980) *Organisation, Class and Control.* Routledge and Kegan Paul.
6. Fox, A. (1971) *A Sociology of Work and Industry.* Collier Macmillan 1980.
7. Hill, S. *op. cit.*
8. Clegg, S. and Dunkerley, D. *op. cit.*
9. Hill, S. *op. cit.*
10. Hill, S. *op. cit.*
11. Fox, A. (1974) 'Beyond contract: work power and trust relations', in Hill, S. *op. cit.*
12. Clegg, S. and Dunkerley, D. *op. cit.*
13. Hill, S. *op. cit.*
14. Fox, A. 1974 *op. cit.*
15. Hyman, R. *op. cit.*
16. Hyman, R. *op. cit.*
17. Hill, S. *op. cit.*
18. Fox, A. 1980 (1971) *op. cit.*
19. Fox, A. 1980 (1971) *op. cit.*
20. Fox, A. 1980 (1971) *op. cit.*
21. Hyman, R. *op. cit.*
22. Etzioni, A. (1961) *The Comparative Analysis of Complex Organisations.* Free Press.
23. Hill, S. (1983) *op. cit.*
24. Clarke, T. and Clements, L. (1977) (eds.) *Trade Unions under Capitalism.* Fontana.
25. Anderson, P. (1967) 'The limits and possibilities of trade union action,' in Blackburn, R. and Cockburn, A. (eds.), *The Incompatibles.* Penguin.
26. Hyman, R. (1975) *Industrial Relations: A Marxist Introduction.* Macmillan.
27. Fox, A. (1973) 'Industrial relations: a social critique of pluralist ideology', in. Child, J. (ed.), *Man and Organisation.* Allen and Unwin.
28. Fox, A. (1974) *Beyond Contract: Work, Power and Trust Relations.* Faber.
29. Streek, W. (1987) 'The uncertainties of management in the management of uncertainty: Employers, labour relations and industrial adjustment in the 1980s', *Work, Employment and Society,* **1** No. 3, p. 282.
30. Crouch, C. (1982) *Trade Unions: the Logic of Collective Action.* Fontana.
31. Beaumont, P. B. (1990) *Change in Industrial Relations: the Organisation and Environment.* Routledge.

32. Farnham, D. and Pimlott, J. (1983) *Understanding Industrial Relations*, 2nd edn. Cassell, 1983 pp. 51–64.
33. Hyman, R. (1989) *op. cit.*
34. Beaumont, P. B. *op. cit.*
35. Fox, A. (1985) *Man Mismanagement*, 2nd edn. Hutchinson.
36. Hill, S. (1983) *op. cit.*
37. Flanders, A. (1970) *Management and Unions*. Faber.
38. Streeck, W. (1987) *op. cit.*, p. 284.
39. Austrin, T. (1980) 'The "Lump" in the UK construction industry', in Nichols, T. (ed.), *Capital and Labour: Studies in the Capitalist Labour Process*. Athlone Press, London.
40. Fellows, R., Langford, D., Newcombe, R. and Urry, S. (1983) *Construction Management in Practice*. Construction Press, London.
41. Advisory, Conciliation and Arbitration Service (1980) *Industrial Relations Handbook*. HMSO.
42. Ball, M. (1988) *Rebuilding Construction: Economic Change and the British Construction Industry*. Routledge, London.
43. National Economic Development Office (1978) *How Flexible is Construction*. HMSO, London.
44. March A., Heady P. and Matheson, J. (1981) *Labour Mobility in the Construction Industry*. Office of Population Census and Surveys, HMSO.
45. NEDO (1984) *op. cit.*
46. Marsh, A., Heady, P. and Matheson, J. *op. cit.*
47. Marsh, A., Heady, P. and Matheson, J. *op. cit.*
48. Marsh, A., Heady, P. and Matheson, J. *op. cit.*
49. Marsh, A., Heady, P. and Matheson, J. *op. cit.*
50. Marsh, A., Heady, P. and Matheson, J. *op. cit.*
51. Marsh, A., Heady, P. and Matheson, J. *op. cit.*
52. National Economic Development Office (1988). *Faster Building for Commerce*. Millbank, London.
53. National Economic Development Office (1970) *Large Industrial Sites*. HMSO. 1970.
54. Morris, P. W. G. and Hough, G. H. (1987) 'The Thames Barrier', in *The Anatomy of Major Projects*. John Wiley and Sons, Chichester.
55. Buckley, P. J. and Enderwick, P. (1989) 'Manpower management', in Hillebrandt, P. M. and Cannon, J. (eds.), *The Management of Construction Firms*. Macmillan, London.
56. Marsh, A. Heady, P. and Matheson, J. *op. cit.*
57. Gray, C. and Flanagan, R. (1989) *The Changing Role of Specialist and Trade Sub Contractors*. Chartered Institute of Building, Epsom.
58. Austrin, T. *op. cit.*
59. Phelps-Brown, E.H. (1968) *Report of the Committee of Enquiry Under Professor E. H. Phelps-Brown into Certain Matters Concerning Labour in Building and Civil Engineering*, HMSO, Cmnd 3714.
60. Austrin, T. *op. cit.*
61. London Research Centre (1987). *Skills Shortages in the London Building Industry*. Report by the Economic Activities Group.
62. Austrin, T. *op. cit.*
63. Waterfall, M. H. P. (1989) The Profitability of Labour Only Sub Contracting. MSc Thesis. Heriot-Watt University.
64. Hillebrandt, P. M. (1959) 'Summary and conclusions', in Construction Industry

Studies Group (ed.), *Proceedings of Construction Training in the 1990s and Beyond: A Policy Conference. Warwick University. 13–15 December 1989.*
65. NEDO (1988) *op. cit.*
66. NEDO (1988) *op. cit.*
67. NEDO (1988) *op. cit.*
68. NEDO (1988) *op. cit.*
69. Cheetham, D. W. (1988) 'Labour management practices', *Construction Papers*, **V1**, No. 3,
70. Marsh, A., Heady, P. and Matheson, J. *op. cit.*
71. NEDO (1989) *op. cit.*
72. Waterfall, M. H. P. (1989) The Profitability of Labour Only Sub Contractors. MSc Thesis. Heriot-Watt University.
73. NEDO (1988) *op. cit.*
74. NEDO (1989) *op. cit.*

— PART III —

International business strategy in construction

The chapters comprising Part III of the book are concerned with construction in an international perspective. Some chapters are devoted to developing in-depth insights into particular international construction industries, Cannon and Hillebrandt on the United Kingdom, Flanagan on Japan and Mathewson on North America. Other chapters – Smith on the EC and Walker on the Asia Pacific Rim – take a broader perspective, mapping out the operations of construction in a number of nation states. The chapter by Male acts as an introduction to this group of chapters by providing analytical models and theoretical insights into competitive advantage internationally. It has been suggested that competitive advantage in the international construction industry is only an issue during periods of declining demand and in this context isolating competitive advantages becomes a more difficult analytical undertaking since the identification of superiority over competitors takes on a wider dimension. Competitors in this instance comprise not only home-based construction companies operating overseas but also those from other nations, together with those present in the host nation. The analysis is further complicated by the fact that governments also have a major influence, as well as the diffuse effects of 'nation state heritages' on competitive advantage.

In Chapter 12 Male provides an introduction to international business strategy in general and then proceeds to discuss and integrate, for analytical purposes in construction, two models of international competitive advantage, drawing on insights from construction where appropriate. The Middle East, a well-documented and analysed international construction market, is then used by Male as a case study to explore theoretical issues in a more practical context, from economic, organizational and cultural frameworks. Chapter 13 explores construction within the different nation states of the European Community (EC), focusing particularly on civil engineering. Here, Smith discusses in outline the operations of the UK construction industry within an EC comparative framework, and this compliments and reinforces aspects raised in earlier chapters. In Chapter 14 Cannon and Hillebrandt develop issues raised in the preceding and earlier chapters and detail the results of their empirical investigations of the operations of larger UK contractors, both in a domestic and international context. In Chapter 15 Walker discusses the construction markets comprising the Asia Pacific Rim, the barriers to entry, opportunities that have been and could arise including highlighting national distinctions. He discusses in outline the operations of the Japanese construction industry, a theme developed in more detail in Chapter 16 by Flanagan. Finally, Mathewson outlines the operations of the North American construction industry in Chapter 17, an international market where British and Japanese contractors have been particularly active.

─── 12 ───

Competitive advantage in the international construction industry

Steven Male

1. Introduction

This chapter draws together work from a number of different authors [1] on the international construction industry and highlights the major themes. Readers are advised to consult individual texts for a more in-depth analysis. A brief overview of the issues associated with competing internationally is provided initially. Two major analytical models for developing strategies within international construction are reviewed, synthesized and integrated to produce a conceptual model for analysing competitive advantage in international construction. Finally, a number of issues highlighted in the earlier sections are discussed in the context of a series of small case studies of operations undertaken in the Middle East market – one that brings into sharp forces the problems of operating and managing internationally in a multicultural environment.

2. Competing in an international business environment for construction

The international business environment can be considered a special case of the general and task environments of the company. Its main characteristics are as follows [2]:

1. It is more competitive.
2. It is more heterogeneous.
3. It is more complex due to differing:
   - societies;
   - cultures;
   - educational practices;
   - legal frameworks;
   - economic and political systems;
   - business ideologies.
4. Additional features also present include:
   - government to government relationships;
   - company to government relationships.

In addition to the above, the international construction environment possesses added characteristics – some of which are found domestically and others only internationally – which, in combination, make it unique. These characteristics are as follows [3]:

1. A fragmented industry structure.
2. Large geographically.
3. Decreasing demand and hence a buyer's market.
4. The provision of 'soft loans–credit–subsidized finance' to secure work, that is, the provision of long-term loans, in one form or another, at preferential interest rates.
5. High levels of risk in addition to those identified earlier include:
   • climatic conditions;
   • exchange rate fluctuations;
   • profit repatriation;
   • early abortive tendering.
6. The probable legal requirement for a host country partner with local market knowledge and contacts.
7. The use of countertrade in goods as a method of payment.

A major consideration in competing in the international construction environment is the requirement for a high turnover to absorb critical market research and entry costs. It has been estimated that it can take up to 15 months to win the first contract and between three and four years to obtain larger contracts [4]. The following section reviews models of competitive advantage for use in international construction.

3. Analytical models for assessing competitive advantage in international construction

Two models have been developed, both from an economist's viewpoint, that can be utilized for analysing competitive advantage in construction. The first is the 'national diamond' proposed by Michael Porter [5]. The second model is the eclectic paradigm formulated by Dunning [6] in analysing the multinational enterprise (MNE). The theoretical perspective of the MNE stemmed initially from manufacturing but has been used in an analysis of international construction by Seymour and Enderwick [7].

3.1 Porter's National Diamond

Building on his earlier work on competitive strategy, competitive advantage and competition in global industries, Porter has now conducted a major analysis of the competitive advantage of nations [8]. Part of this work deals with international competition in services, and engineering and construction services in particular. The following provides a brief insight into the key concepts that can be used for analysing international construction.

Porter argues that the creation and sustenance of international competitive advantage involves a company in constant change and internationalizing competitive processes that have their roots in domestic industries or industry segments. In this latter instance it is in the home base that a company's strategy is developed, core product and process technologies are created and maintained, and the most advanced skills located. Using our earlier ideas about the external environment faced by a company, one of the key issues, according to Porter, appears to be how a company operates in and handles the pressures from its task environment and how the perceived environment is transformed into an organizational structure that creates and sustains competitive success in the long term.

Porter contends that international success in a particular industry is attributable to four basic mutually dependent national conditions – the 'national diamond' – comprising;

(a) factor conditions or factors of production;
(b) domestic demand conditions;
(c) related and supplier industries;
(d) company strategy, structure and rivalry.

Porter identifies two other important variables that influence the national diamond as follows:

1. Chance: chance events creates discontinuities and therefore allow shifts in competitive position. We can consider chance events as those that burst onto the national or international scene relatively unannounced, for example the exact date Britain joined the European Exchange Rate Mechanism, the Iran–Iraq war, the Iraqi invasion of Kuwait, the reunification of Germany and the dissolution of the Communist State of the USSR. An important point here is the distinction between the perceived and actual environment. Chance events, depending on their nature, at a national and/or international level, may be experienced by all or only a small group of a company's key competitors. However, senior managements' perceptions of such events will differ. Some will see these chance events as opportunities while others will see them as threats. These differences in perception will follow through into a company's strategy in handling such events and subsequently into organizational behaviour.
2. Government: government can influence the four determinants of national competitive advantage. Governments play a particularly active role in international construction [9] where they can provide financial and technical assistance, become active in the trade promotion of contractors and also assist in developing a strong domestic industry. These are direct benefits stemming from government involvement. Indirect benefits for contractors accrue from current and historical political ties between governments.

One important clue as to the importance a government places on construction is the presence, in one form or another, of a Ministry of Construction. For example, Japan and South Korea both have Ministries of Construction. The absence of a clearly delineated Ministry is an indication of a lack of interest in promoting that sector at a national level [10]. Countries that fall into this latter category include the United Kingdom, Germany, the United States and those governments comprising the Scandinavian countries. In addition, governments can vary in their degree of intervention in their international construction industries. Countries that have highly interventionist governments include Japan, France, Italy and Korea.

Active government support can also be obtained in assisting contractors deal with project payments through countertrade. Active support in this area is found from the governments of Italy, France, Japan, Korea and Brazil; the German and UK governments act in an advisory and facilitatory role and the government of the United States has a *laissez-faire policy*.

3.2 The eclectic paradigm and international construction

The theoretical perspective utilized in this model for analysing international construction is that of the economics of the multinational enterprise (MNE) – a company that is involved in foreign direct investment (FDI) to set up a production base in a country other than the home country of registration [11].

For FDI to take place in international construction three necessary conditions must be met, as follows:

1. The company has competitive or *ownership advantages* over indigenous companies and also over other international competitors. Ownership advantages are derived from country specific, industry specific and firm specific advantages. In international construction, ownership advantages stem from a combination of country specific advantage – either the home and/or host country – and firm specific advantages – derived from the actions of the company itself.

2. Ownership advantages are *internalized* and exploited by the company rather than exploited externally by selling or licensing to other companies. An example of externalization in construction would be the licensing of the company's name to another contractor who would be responsible for undertaking construction of a facility for a client. Sub-contracting is an additional example of externalizing part of the production process, as discussed in Chapter 2.

3. On the assumption that the preceding two conditions are met, the third necessary condition is that it is more profitable to undertake production internationally than domestically and then subsequently exporting, i.e. there is a *locational* advantage. Locational advantages are immobile and

must be exploited at source. Seymour notes that since contracting production is client led and pre-demanded, contractors, in order to exploit locational advantages are involved in a process of *demand searching*, judging themselves against competition from foreign and indigenous competitors. Porter [12] adds that for a globally coordinated firm competitive advantages can be separated out into those that are derived solely from location (nations) and those independent of location – system-based advantages – deriving from the company's network of activities. In the case of location advantages Porter argues that these can be derived either from the home base or from nations within which the firm wishes to locate. The global firm will utilize home-based advantages to penetrate overseas markets or locate overseas to augment home advantages or offset home disadvantages.

An MNE, as an organizational form, is created when firm specific advantages are internalized across national boundaries [13]. Taking our analytical framework from Chapter 1 where we define a company as a business and social entity that is involved in both contractual and psychological exchanges and where it is the latter that delineates what is internal or external to the company, in these terms an MNE would be created when firm specific advantages are exploited internally within the psychological boundaries of the company across nations. In an international construction environment, the question of multinationality and the exploitation of firm specific advantages internally, as opposed to externally through licensing, becomes one of where the managerial hierarchy is truncated to form an administrative adhocracy.

3.3 A synthesis of competitive advantage in international construction

By way of introduction to this sub-section and the model for analysing competitive advantage in international construction, it must be emphasized that there are similarities and overlaps between the eclectic paradigm and Porter's 'national diamond'. However, a number of comments are necessary when considering both as a basis of analysis in international construction. First, country specific advantages distinguish domestic from international construction [14]. Second, international construction is increasingly being dominated by the exploitation of country specific advantages, namely, historical and political links and the level of financial and political support from the home country [15]. Isolating country specific advantages is a major analytical source for understanding how competition has emerged in international construction [16]. Third, firm specific advantages are generated from country specific advantages. Fourth, competitive strategy in construction is achieved through a combination of firm and country specific advantages to achieve differentiation [17]. We would also add that these act in tandem with price. Fifth, the final necessary condition for FDI to take place – locational advantages – implies a coordinated global strategy by management when seeking profit potential, i.e. to locate in one international market as opposed to another because it is advantageous to do so. There is evidence to suggest that UK contractors do not undertake a coordinated global strategy in construction [18]. This view is also supported in a wider international context [19]. Construction internationally appears to have a closer parallel to Porter's [20] notion of a 'multidomestic' industry where competition in each nation is independent and there is little opportunity for learning opportunities for the firm across nations due to differences in national buyer needs and local business conditions. This works against a coordinated global strategy in international construction, essentially due to the project-based nature of the production process. We have already raised the issue of what is the basis of an MNE in the preceding section. Therefore, the extent to which international contractors move away from being multidomestic competitors to MNEs will depend on the degree to which linkages exist between choices of strategies to compete domestically and between markets internationally. These linkages would primarily occur in information exchange, management transferability and the global procurement of material inputs into projects [21]. In this sense they are systems-based advantages. Sixth, there are conflicting views on the nature and form of research and development in construction – a firm specific advantage – that have an important bearing on determining competitive advantage internationally. Seymour contends that R & D in construction (and unlike manufacturing) provides no significant advantage. Enderwick, on the other hand, views training as equivalent to research and development of human capital. Human capital is critical in construction, both domestically and, more importantly, in international construction. Finally, the relevance of the eclectic paradigm to a service rather than manufacturing industry has been questioned [22]. Based on the foregoing, in the writer's view, the 'national diamond' provides a framework that is more intuitively appealing to managers when considering competitive advantage internationally. It has also been used to analyse international competition in services. However, when placed with the context of the eclectic paradigm, both act together to provide a powerful tool for analysing competitive advantage in international construction.

The following discussion draws together the work of Porter's 'national diamond', discussing it in the context of construction, and Seymour's and Enderwick's work on international construction. The components making up the 'national diamond' are introduced first and then subsequently their linkage with the eclectic paradigm is established for a model of competitive advantage in international construction to be established.

3.3.1 Factor conditions

Factor conditions or factors of production are the inputs required by a company to compete. Table 12.1 sets out the different categories of factors. Additionally, Porter discriminates between different types of factors. These are set out in Table 12.2.

Table 12.1 Factor conditions affecting national competitive advantage

National factor condition	Comments
Human resources	The quantity, skills and costs of labour and management. These are particularly important in construction
Physical resources	Climatic conditions can be viewed as part of a nation's physical resources. Geographic and geological conditions can also be included as a physical resource since they form part of the land factor. Climatic, geographic and geological conditions have an important impact on construction because it sets part of the domain of domestic knowledge and skills of contractors for subsequent application in overseas operations. In this respect physical factors impact the generation of advanced and specialised factors in construction
Knowledge resources	The nation's stock of scientific, technical and market knowledge in goods and services.
Capital resources	The amount and cost of capital available to finance industry. This is a non-homogeneous factor with different terms and conditions attached to each form of capital. Access to cheap finance has become an important competitive issue for different countries in international construction. The French, Italians and Japanese are the most active in pursuing international construction services through subsidized finance. The USA is the least supportive of this approach
Infrastructure	A broad-based factor of competition that includes the transportation, postal, health and other like systems affecting business and the quality of a nation's living and working environment. In international construction this is likely to have a more important impact in the host as opposed to home country

Source: Adapted from Porter, 1990 [1].

3.3.2 Domestic demand conditions

Three broad attributes of home demand are significant according to Porter. These are set out in Table 12.3 including comments on their place in construction.

3.3.3 Related and support industries

Porter argues that internationally competitive domestic industries providing inputs into a company can also provide it with an opportunity for

Table 12.2 Factor types

Type	Comments	Examples
Basic factors	Usually provide unsustainable advantages	National resources, climate, location, unskilled and semi-skilled labour, debt capital
Advanced factors	The most important for competitive advantage. They lead to product differentiation and proprietary technology. Their development requires large and sustained investment in physical and human capital	Modern digital communication infrastructure, highly educated personnel, university research institutes in advanced technologies
Generalized factors	Can be utilized in a wide range of industries and are usually available in a number of nations. They support rudimentary advantages	Road and other communication networks, supply of debt capital, a well-motivated workforce with a general education
Specialized factors	These are more scarce, require investment, and have a narrow or limited range of application. They provide a more decisive and sustainable basis for competitive advantage and are integral to the process of innovation. They may stem from generalized factors. They are necessary at the company's domestic base and less effective in a foreign location	Narrowly skilled personnel, infrastructure with specific knowledge bases

Source: Adapted from Porter 1990 [1].

gaining international competitive advantages. The mechanisms through which this can work are as follows:

1. Competitive advantage in supplier industries through:
   - preferred or early access to cost-effective inputs that are utilized effectively;
   - on-going coordination linking into value activities;
   - through the process of innovation and upgrading via close working relationships.

There are abundant examples of this effect in construction. Design consultancies may favour home contractors, specify domestic components and use home-based procedures. For example, UK contractors are

Table 12.3 Domestic demand conditions

Demand attributes	Characteristics	Comments
Home demand conditions	Segmented demand structure	Impacts task environment. Highly visible segments with global possibilities
		Demand in construction is highly segmented. One of the keys to international competition in construction lies in identifying domestic segments that are demanded internationally. This implies, from our earlier analysis, segmented technological competition by project type
	Sophisticated and demanding buyers	Pressure for higher standards and quality
		The UK construction industry, for example, is coming under increasing pressure from buyers to improve standards. However, there is a range of client types with differing degrees of industry knowledge and their reasons for procuring the construction of facilities are diverse. Particular buyer types can be highly demanding, high-tech companies requiring controlled internal environments, for example
	Anticipatory buyer needs	Home buyer needs anticipate foreign market needs
		Market structure in construction – speculative or contracting – is characterized by two demand types. Speculative construction can anticipate foreign demand. Contracting stems from derived demand from buyer needs.
Size of demand and demand growth patterns	Size of home demand	This leads to economies of scale and learning through investment in fixed assets, technological developments and methods to improve productivity. We would also add, from our earlier discussion, investment in developing human capital in construction through training and management development in company and contracts management

Table 12.3 cont'd.

Demand attributes	Characteristics	Comments
		This relates to the relative development of the construction sector in terms of skill base, size of firm and nature of expertise in constructing the final product. Enderwick argues that international construction is concerned with supplying human capital and comparative advantages appear through the nature and skills of the contractor for different types of project available to a national group of contractors. In international construction the follow through of the impact of the size of the domestic market may not be of importance except in developed countries
	Number of independent buyers	Creation of environment for innovation and industry investment
		In the UK, for example, construction innovation is primarily in 'organization' and 'finance' to cope with a diversity of different buyer types and production processes. The segmented structure of demand has considerable short-term variability in the private sector and a long-term decline in public sector. This necessitates investment in 'organizational methods' to improve strategic flexibility in the long term.
	Rate of growth of home demand	Pressure to adopt new technologies. The two major market structures in construction lead to different patterns of growth and hence different pressures in UK construction, for example to adopt new corporate organizational forms
Internationaliza-tion of demand	Mobile or multinational buyers	Reduces risks for other companies considering overseas expansion when domestic buyers internationalize
		Examples in construction include the internationalization of UK, Japanese, German and US contractors who have followed their nation's clients overseas

Demand attributes	Characteristics	Comments
	Domestic influences on foreign need	Domestic needs and desires transmitted to foreign buyers
		The push for 'industrialization' by Third World countries has created significant demand for construction internationally in diverse market segments. The impact of political and historical ties is particularly important in internationalizing construction services

Source: Adapted from Porter 1990 [1], Enderwick 1989 [1], Seymour 1987, 1989 [1].

reported to benefit from international UK consultant engineering and architectural companies [23]. German companies are reported to derive similar benefits from their design engineers. Another example would be Japanese contractors involved in a European turnkey contract utilizing domestic internationally competitive equipment suppliers to produce an 'intelligent building', an area where the Japanese are known to be investing heavily in research and development [24]. Finally, German and Scandinavian contractors benefit because they are involved in constructing some of the most advanced manufacturing plants in the world for their nations' clients operating internationally [25].

2. Competitive advantage in related industries providing opportunities for informations flows and technical interchange: this occurs where companies can coordinate or share activities in the value chain when competing internationally, or have access to complementary products. Examples in construction would be consultant engineers or architects operating in a joint venture (JV) with a contractor to design and construct a facility for a foreign client. In this instance the JV would benefit from the technical interchange between the consultants in design and contractors in production. A further example is that of Japanese contractors, who benefit from their relationship with the Sogo Shosha or trading houses who act as sources of information on international construction contracts [26].

3.3.4 Firm strategy, structure and rivalry

This sets the context within which firms compete, structure and restructure themselves, as well as undertake innovation. Other issues considered important by Porter within this aspect of the national diamond and we see as impacting construction are as follows:

1. The influence of national prestige, goal priorities and the ability of particular industries to attract talent: we have already highlighted differences between national priorities given to construction. Other examples include the fact that the UK, German and French construction industries, for example, have a lower recruitment status than other industrial sectors. Taking a broader international example, the Japanese government has targeted construction as an important industry but it also appears to have low recruitment status [27].
2. Sustained commitment of capital and human resources to an industry: in the United Kingdom, for example, construction has a high labour mobility and low recruitment status. Construction companies are also seen as risky investments. Construction is unlikely, therefore, to attract sustained commitment in terms of capital and human resources in the long term for industry upgrading, except in as much as construction companies can become cash generators for other industrial groupings [28]. Germany and France, as indicated in Chapter 2, are moving towards a sustained commitment to upgrade their construction industries status and skill base.
3. A high level of domestic competition pressures companies to innovate and upgrade towards advantages that are high-order and thus sustainable. Contrasting examples can be found internationally in construction. Japanese companies invest heavily in technical system R & D as compared to their Western counterparts [29]. This is primarily due to intense competitive rivalry between companies in Japan and a shrinking skilled labour force [30]. We have argued that the pressure to innovate in the UK construction industry is in new organizational forms and hence the manipulation of the relationships between the social and technical systems. This appears also to be the case in France and Germany.
4. The level of new business formation, which feeds the innovative process: taking the case of the UK contracting industry, new business formation has been identified in Chapter 1 as primarily occurring in the small company sector for tax reasons. In addition, growth, as a business objective of small contracting companies, is of secondary importance compared to issues of family momentary security and a need for independence. In the United Kingdom, for example, new business formation as part of the innovative processes for upgrading the construction industry are limited.

The next sub-section outlines some of the major issues associated with variables in the eclectic paradigm.

3.3.5 The eclectic paradigm

Table 12.4 sets out the major variable (and ancillary comments) comprising the application of the eclectic paradigm in international construction.

Table 12.4 The eclectic paradigm in international construction

Advantage			Construction related comments
Ownership advantages	*Country specific advantages*	Demand for related consultancy services	Source of differentiation
		Home government support	Source of direct and indirect differentiation
		Nationality of company	Only exploitable by the companies of a nation
		Size of domestic market	Source of differentiation
	Firm specific advantages	Size of firm	Access to cheaper finance, better production resources, bidding on larger projects, access to more competent labour, diversified service provision
		Human resources and specialisms	Stems from factors conditions. Basis of reputation. Training, management development and team knowledge important, especially for overseas projects. Specialisms provide high-order factor advantages
		Service offered	Source of differentiation
		Firm's name	Source of differentiation. Embodies and represents reputation, expertise and historical competencies
Internalization advantages			Internalization is favoured where ownership advantages have a high 'intangible' component such as reputation, expertise, brand name and company image. Examples of internalized market servicing includes FDI and/or exporting of labour to cope with demand peaks. Another example of the use of exporting in international construction is the Japanese in steel and fertilizer process plants

Table 12.4 cont'd.

Advantage		Construction related comments
		Externalization involves market servicing by selling or licensing ownership advantages. Quality control is a major problem with externalization. Enderwick notes different types of market servicing have been used in international construction. Externalizing has been used for example with management contracting in industrial plant and heavy civils projects; licensing is used for process plant projects where proprietary technology is available
Locational advantages	Previous two conditions of advantages met	Overseas production becomes more profitable than domestic production and exporting. The major reasons for UK contractors locating overseas, for example, include the presence of large markets and the need for a permanent presence to maintain competitive advantage. Little weight appears to be given to integrating overseas operations into a global strategy or through difficulties of handling licensing or other contractual arrangements

Source: Adapted from Seymour 1987, 1989 [1], and Enderwick 1989 [1].

3.3.6 Competitive advantage in international construction

Figure 12.1 draws together both the eclectic and national diamond to present our conceptual view of the major forces impacting competitive advantage in international construction. Porter's 'national demand' provides the basic building blocks upon which country specific advantages are built. It also allows a comparative assessment of other nations' advantages in international construction. The eclectic paradigm draws attention to the fact that country specific advantages, acting through the 'national diamond' are focused and modified through firm specific advantages to produce a competitive strategy for an individual company. Finally, locational advantages act as a pull to enter a specific international market due to home or host country advantages or to overcome home country

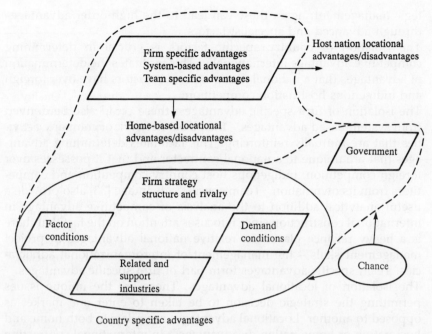

Figure 12.1 *Competitive advantage in international construction (Adapted from Porter (1990), fig. 3.5, p. 127.)*

disadvantages, and where the company has to assess itself against other foreign and indigeneous competitors.

In drawing this section to a conclusion, we can state the following about competitive advantage in international construction;

1. The internationalization of engineering and construction services is heavily influenced by early demand, advanced and demanding local buyers and demand surges in international success [31].
2. Competitive advantage in international engineering and construction services is influenced by linkages between related and support industries [32].
3. Porter has argued that factor conditions have an impact through the education system and for low wage countries. We would also add from our earlier analysis that other important factor conditions are the quantity and quality of human resources in construction – both managerial and operative – in the long term; national physical resources, especially land and climate, since these two have an important impact on the knowledge domain for construction in generating high-order advantages through advanced and specialist factors; access to capital resources – these are particularly important in international contracting for offering financial packages to assist in differentiation; finally, the relative development of knowledge resources in design – the architects and engineers; production methods – on site production technology and contracts management; surveying; commercial and business skills – estimating, bidding, materials and plant/equipment procurement; stra-

tegic management; again these can lead to the high-order advantages through advanced and specialist factors.

4. The isolation of country specific factors is crucial in determining competitive advantage internationally. This facilitates the determination of advantages that a national grouping of contractors have over foreign and indigenous host nation competition.

5. The isolation of firm specific advantages: these could also be derived from system-based advantages – the global network of company activities that are mutually reinforcing. This facilitates determining advantages that are unique to a national contractor and that it possesses over foreign competition, indigenous host country competition and competitors from its own nation. 'Team specific' advantage [33] also provide a useful analytical addition to the analysis of competitive advantage in international construction since it focuses attention on the fact that there is a heavy reliance placed on relative national advantages in project management skills – the management of interorganizational adhocracies. Team specific advantages form part of firm specific advantages.

6. The isolation of locational advantages. These are the unique issues permitting the strategic decision to be taken to enter one market as opposed to another. Locational advantages can relate to both home and host nation or home nation disadvantages. In international contracting these primarily relate to potential market size, political and historical links and political stability.

7. Governments have a substantial impact on the operations of international construction.

8. A number of market servicing mechanisms exist in international construction – FDI and/or exporting, licensing.

9. Competitive advantage in international construction may not be important in growing markets but will determine the survivors in declining markets [34].

The following section explores some of these issues in the context of a case study of the Middle East.

4. Problems of international construction: production strategy in a multicultural environment – the case of the Middle East

This section sets out a framework for considering the exporting of construction services and the setting up of a production base in another country. A series of case studies on the Middle East are used subsequently to explore a number of different issues that can affect international business strategy in construction.

Porter has identified three pure types of service provision and these are set out in Table 12.5. The difficulty lies in the fact that competition in international service delivery, unlike production for manufacturing, has a

Table 12.5 Types of international service provision

Service type	Description and comments
Type I	Mobile buyers travel to a nation to have services performed. The problem of classification here is that unlike domestic production for manufacturing the service is being consumed and presumably paid for by the foreign buyer at the point of domestic production. It is unusual in international construction unless for reasons of training or management development
Type II	Firms from a nation provide services in other nations using domestically based personnel and services. This type of service provision is common in construction and usually involves the movement of labour internationally to staff up a temporary project structure in a host country
Type III	A nation's firms provide services in other countries via foreign service locations staffed with either expatriate or local nationals. This type of service delivery can also be common in construction where a contractor has a permanent office set up in another country

degree of intangibility of delivery attached to it with respect to international trade and FDI.

Porter argues that service types I and II (pure export) are classified as international trade, while service type III is FDI and suggests that trade and FDI are closely intertwined in many service industries to produce hybrid forms of service delivery. This situation is common in international construction and Figures 12.2–12.5, derived from fieldwork undertaken by Seymour [35], indicate possible variations that may occur in practice. Figure 12.2 is an example of pure FDI or service type III where an autonomous subsidiary is set up. Figure 12.3 is an example of service type II. Figures 12.4 (page 320) and 12.5 (page 324) are a hybrid of service types II and III.

In terms of the 'national diamond', Porter has argued for the following influences in competition for international services:

1. Factor conditions. Their importance is dependent on the type of service sold. Factor conditions are important for service types I and II but of lesser importance for type III. For service type III competitive advantage is more dependent on techniques, technologies and service features

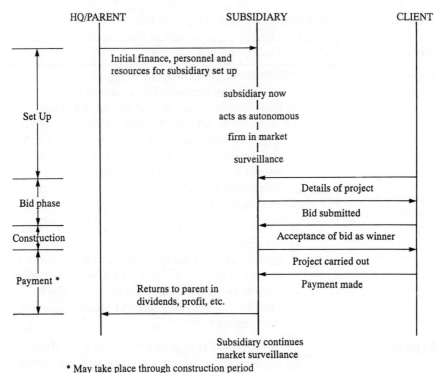

HQ/PARENT   SUBSIDIARY   CLIENT

Initial finance, personnel and
resources for subsidiary set up

subsidiary now

Set Up   acts as autonomous

firm in market

surveillance

Details of project

Bid phase

Bid submitted

Construction   Acceptance of bid as winner

Project carried out

Payment *   Payment made

Returns to parent in
dividends, profit, etc.

Subsidiary continues
market surveillance

* May take place through construction period

Figure 12.2 *FDI subsidiary operation in international contracting – service type III (Source: Seymour (1987), fig. 6.1, p. 182. Reprinted with permission.)*

developed domestically, where demand conditions and related and support industries are critical. Low-order factors such as domestic labour costs can be critical in construction. This was one of the main competitive weapons of Korean contractors [36] but proved to be unreliable for Brazilian contractors [37]. High-order technical skills are important in international construction services (consulting and contracting) where UK and US firms are known to have an advantage [38].
2. Porter contends that demand conditions are currently the most powerful determinant of international competitiveness in international services. Demand segmentation is important for competitive advantage if it is large domestically but small internationally.

4.1 The Middle East market

The Middle East construction market of the 1970s provided an important opportunity for international construction companies to expand rapidly and make substantial profits. By the early 1980s, however, the boom was over and international contractors refocused much of their attention back towards domestic markets. The Middle East markets do, however, provide

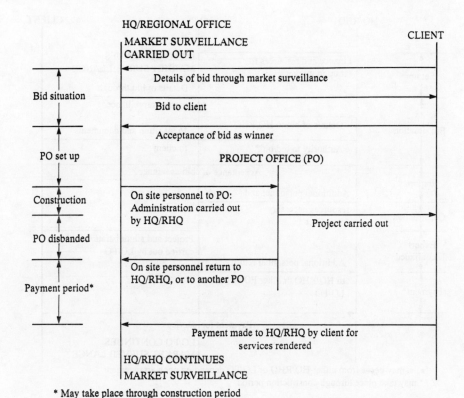

Figure 12.3 *One-off project office in international contracting – service type II (Source: Seymour (1987), fig. 6.2, p. 183. Reprinted with permission.)*

considerable future potential for contractors. For example, following the cessation of the Iran–Iraq war it was estimated that the rebuilding cost of war damage in Iraq would be $US30 billion and $US80 billion in Iran [39]. In addition, once civil war in Lebanon has ceased and the political situation eventually resolved, substantial rebuilding work can be expected in that country. However, the current annexation of Kuwait by Iraq (1990) has plunged the Middle East back into political turmoil.

Table 12.6 sets out the advantages and disadvantages that international contractors have seen as important when considering entering the Middle East market.

4.2 Diversity within the Middle East markets[a]

Seymour's [40] empirical investigations of the reasons why contractors entered the Middle East belies a uniformity within the market that does not exist in reality. Table 12.7 sets out a view of the Middle East that suggests considerable diversity in terms of culture, religion, politics and

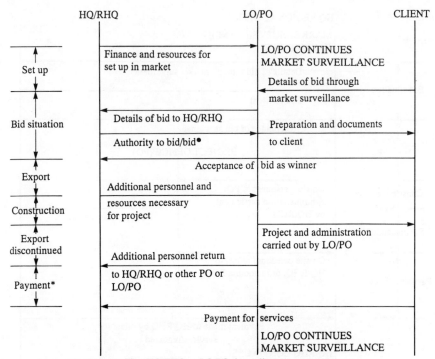

| HQ/RHQ | | LO/PO | CLIENT |

| | Finance and resources for set up in market | LO/PO CONTINUES MARKET SURVEILLANCE | |

Set up

Details of bid through

market surveillance

Bid situation — Details of bid to HQ/RHQ — Preparation and documents

Authority to bid/bid● — to client

Acceptance of bid as winner

Export

Additional personnel and

Construction — resources necessary for project

Export discontinued — Project and administration carried out by LO/PO

Additional personnel return

to HQ/RHQ or other PO or

Payment* — LO/PO

Payment for services

LO/PO CONTINUES MARKET SURVEILLANCE

●i.e. may come from either HQ/RHQ or LO/PO depending upon arrangement
* may take place through construction period

Figure 12.4   *Simultaneous export and FDI in international contracting – service types II and III (Source: Seymour (1987), fig. 6.3, p. 184. Reprinted with permission.)*

relative degree of political stability. It should be noted that columns 3–5 represent an impression only.

Faced with such cultural diversity, the following section discusses issues surrounding establishing a contracting production base in the Middle East.

4.3 Problems of international production in construction

4.3.1 The Bandur Khomeini Petrochemical Plant in Iran

Stallworthy and Kharbanda [41] set out the major influences that led to the demise of a Japanese funded and built petrochemical plant in Iran. The major issues surrounding the project are as follows:

1. The initial idea for the project came from a senior executive of the Mitsui Group in 1968. Feasibility studies were undertaken from 1973 onwards and construction for the world scale ethylene cracker was commenced in 1976 with the project due for completion in 1979, at their

Table 12.6 Locational issues associated with the Middle East

	Advantage	*Little or no effect*	*Disadvantage*
Host country conditions			
Chance events			Possibility of revolution
Social conditions		Language. English is in widespread use in Middle East. A country specific advantage for UK and US contractors	
		Expatriate social and living conditions	
		Distance from home country	
Market	Size of regional market		
Competition		Number of home country contractors	Number of foreign contractors
			Number of local contractors
Systems-based advantages			
Company corporate support relationships and other allied issues	Proximity to: offices providing services necessary to company, other subsidiaries of the firm	Proximity to: corporate HQ	
		Travelling costs of executives	
	Long association of firm to region		

Table 12.6 cont'd

Host government	Expatriate work permits		Expropriation of firm's assets
	Personal tax level		
	Corporate tax level		
	Availability of host government incentives		
	Attitude of host government to company		
	Controls on capital, imports, dividend remittances		
Trading freedom (a government issue)	Tariff and import controls, immigration regulations	Non-tariff barriers such as host government procurement policies	
Buyers (clients)	Attitudes towards company		
Factor conditions			
Manpower quality and availability	Local professional/ technical	Local executive/ managerial	
	Local labour		
	Local imported labour		
Manpower costs	Local skilled/ unskilled	Local executive/ managerial	
		Local professional/ technical	
		Manpower cost regulations	
Home/host government relationships	Mutual government agreements		

Table 12.6 cont'd

	such as single taxation		
	Home/host government political links		
Related and support industries	Number of home country companies (not construction) in region	Proximity to offices of companies providing similar services	
	Availability of financial and consulting services		
Home government		Home government incentives	

Source: Adapted from Seymour, table 6.7, pp. 200–202. (Reprinted with permission.)

    time of writing. Stallworthy and Kharbanda indicated that the project had still not been completed in 1984.
2. Mitsui was to provide the initiative for the project, the technology, the finance and substantially underwrote the marketing of the final product. The project was economically viable at the outset with the majority of the product for export. In addition, the Japanese were keen to invest in the plant in order to obtain supplies of crude oil.
3. The cost escalated from an initial $US600 million to $US5.6 billion following considerable political upheaval in the wake of the Iran–Iraq war and subsequent disruption to on-site production.
4. The massive cost and time overruns on the project led to considerable financial embarrassment for Mitsui and involved the Japanese government effectively in a rescue attempt on a project in which they had not been originally involved. In addition, the project became non-viable because other world scale ethylene cracking plants were either coming on stream or in the planning stages.

Stallworthy and Kharbanda conclude that the political situation could not have been predicted because during the feasibility stages and up to virtual scheduled completion Iran was politically stable. Stemming from the preceding, they also suggest that risk analysis is valueless in the face of political uncertainty and that the only way to deal with such an issue is by the use of intuition.

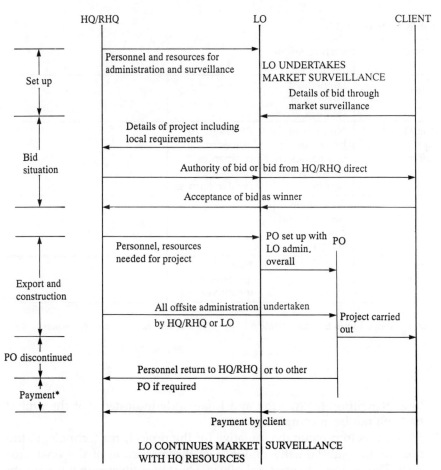

Figure 12.5 *Simultaneous export and FDI in international contracting – service types* II *and* III *(Source: Seymour (1987), fig. 6.4, p. 185. Reprinted with permission.)*

4.3.2 Market entry in the Middle East – the experience of a medium-sized UK contractor

Try and Rush [42] detail the motivating forces and issues behind their company's move into Saudi Arabia. In 1975 the company was reviewing the situation it faced in the UK market and considered that more opportunities were available overseas than domestically. At the time two potential markets were investigated, Nigeria – subsequently rejected on the grounds of problems associated with profit repatriation – and the Middle East. The

Table 12.7 Examples of cultural diversity in the Middle East

Country	Sectarian religious mixes	Government power base	Stable versus unstable	Major issues
Turkey	Majority religion is Islam (Suni Sect). Minority religions include Christianity and Judaism	Military government, result of coup. Parliamentary elections. President elected for life	Probably unstable	Kurdistan, Armenia, Cyprus. NATO country
Iran	Religion is Islam (Majority Shia sect, minority Suni sect). Other religions include Christianity, Judaism and Zoroastrianism	Islamic Revolution. Parliamentary elections. Elected President	Probably unstable due to volatility of religious leaders' power bases	Kurdish and Shia refugees from Iraq. Rebuilding country following Iran–Iraq war
Iraq	Majority religion is Islam (55–60% Shia Sect, Suni Sect). Minority religions include Christianity and some Judaism	Political power mainly wielded by Suni moslems concentrated in Revolutionary Command Council and Baath party	Unstable	Kurdistan. UN economic embargo. Shia opposition to government. Rebuilding country following Gulf war
Syria	Religion is Islam (majority Suni Sect). Minority moslem sects and religions include Alawite (and Shia, Druse), Christianity and Judaism	Power concentrated in Arab Socialist Renaissance (Baath Party)	Probably unstable	USSR influence decreasing. Strong diplomatic relations with the West following the Gulf war
Lebanon	Majority religion Islam (60% Shia Sect, 40% Suni and Druse Sect).	Parliamentary and Presidential elections. President must	Heading to stability	Rebuilding country after 15 year civil war. Leaning towards West

Table 12.7 cont'd.

Country	Sectarian religious mixes	Government power base	Stable versus unstable	Major issues
	Christianity (Catholic, Maronite and Armenian, Greek and Syrian sects, Protestants)	be from Christian Maronites. Prime Minister from Suni sect and Leader of Parliament from Shia Sect		
Jordan	Religion Islam (majority Suni sect, minority Shia sect), Christianity	Kingdom. Elections for Parliament	Unstable	70% of people are Palestinians and only 30% Jordanian. Drawn into West/Iraq problem. Caught in a dilemma initial leaning to West but underlying population trends ensure that Iraq has some influence
Israel	Majority religion Judaism. Minority religions Islam (Suni Sect) and Christianity	Elected government	Unstable	Palestinian problem. Pro-West.
Saudi Arabia	Majority religion Islam (Majority Suni Sect, Minority Shia Sect)	No political parties	Stable	Pro-West
United Arab Emirates (Dubai, Sharjah, Abu Dhabi, Ajman,	Religion Islam (Majority Suni-Sect, Minority Shia Sect), Christianity, Hinduism	President	Stable	Pro-West

Country	Sectarian religious mixes	Government power base	Stable versus unstable	Major issues
Umm al Qaiwan, Fujarah, Ras-al-Kaimah)				
Kuwait	Religion Islam (Majority Suni Sect, Minority Shia Sect), Christianity	Sheikdom Amir	Now stable	Rebuilding country
Qatar	Majority religion Islam (Majority Suni Sect, minority Shia Sect)	Sheikdom Amir	Stable	Pro-British
Bahrain	Majority religion Islam (Majority Shia Sect, Minority Suni Sect)	Sheikdom Amir	Stable	Pro-British
Yemen	Religion Islam, Suni and Shia sects	Elections for Parliament	Republic founded in May 1990	Border, tribal and religious conflicts. Communism
Oman	Religion Islam (Majority Suni Sect), Hindus	Sultanate	Stable	Pro-British

This data for the Middle East countries referenced in Table 12.7 was compiled by Avan Ibrahim, research assistant, Department of Building Engineering and Surveying, Heriot-Watt University.

Note: [a] The term 'elections for Parliament/President may not necessarily refer to a multiparty situation

processes leading to market entry in the Middle East included the following:

(a) talking to construction contacts in the United Kingdom and collecting both soft and hard factual data
(b) undertaking a three-week fact finding mission to the Middle East, covering the countries of Saudi Arabia, Qatar, Oman and three of the UAE states – Abu Dhabi, Sharjah and Dubai.

The conclusion reached by the company was that of the countries they had visited, Saudi Arabia appeared the most promising because it was the largest construction market, was the least well served by both international and local contractors and the company was at less of a disadvantage as a newcomer compared to entering other potential markets. Saudi Arabia was, however, potentially the most difficult to operate in due to physical conditions, poor back-up in terms of hotels, telephones and port facilities and had the least developed infrastructure. The other Middle Eastern countries visited were more preferable but the volume of work was smaller and competition was well established, especially in terms of UK contractors.

Try and Rush report that a large number of contractors had set up offices in Saudi Arabia for anything up to two years before they reaped any benefits from this high investment. Faced with this level of investment the company obtained work initially in the United Kingdom through UK consultants, and their first project in Saudi Arabia, while unusual, had the following characteristics:

1. The superstructure was relatively simple in concept and was to be supplied and erected largely by a Swiss sub-contractor.
2. The company's responsibility was for the provision of foundation and floor slab work, considered to be reasonably uncomplicated.
3. The project of two years' duration and worth approximately £11 million at 1977 tender prices was considered to be of the right size for bonding and obtaining interim finance.
4. The company utilized management personnel from within the UK company rather than recruit those with a knowledge of the Middle East but unknown to the company. This approach was also confirmed by Skinn in a case study analysis of five UK contractors operating in the Middle East [43].

Try and Rush concluded that at the time of writing their paper (1984) the entry potential into the Saudi Arabian market for medium-sized UK construction companies had passed. Local contractors were able to cope with medium-sized construction projects in the value range up to £10 million and perhaps even up to £20 million. The company had developed this view in a relatively short space of time, some nine years, from initial market surveillance in 1975 to market entry in 1977 to Try and Rush's conference presentation in 1984. In their view, the paper's authors suggested that foreign companies were then subsequently adopting niche entry strategies.

4.2.3 The managerial and operative production hierarchy

Figures 12.6 and 12.7 set out the project organizational structures for two contracts undertaken in the Middle East [44]. Figure 12.6 is the project structure for a civil engineering contract valued at £40 million (1979–80 prices) and forming part of a larger complex. Figure 12.7 sets out the

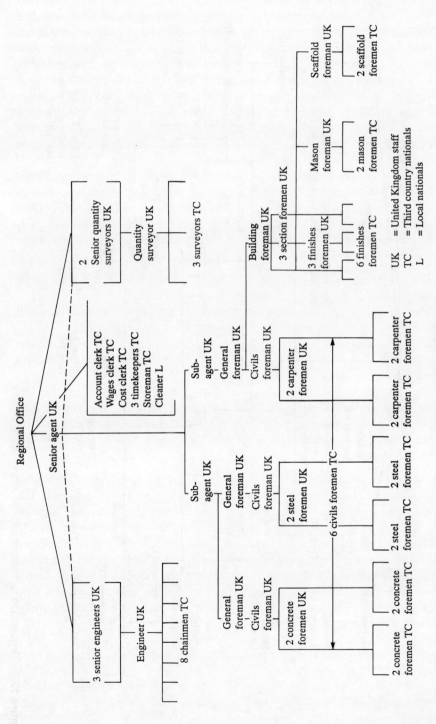

Figure 12.6   *Organizational structure for large civil engineering 30 storey project*

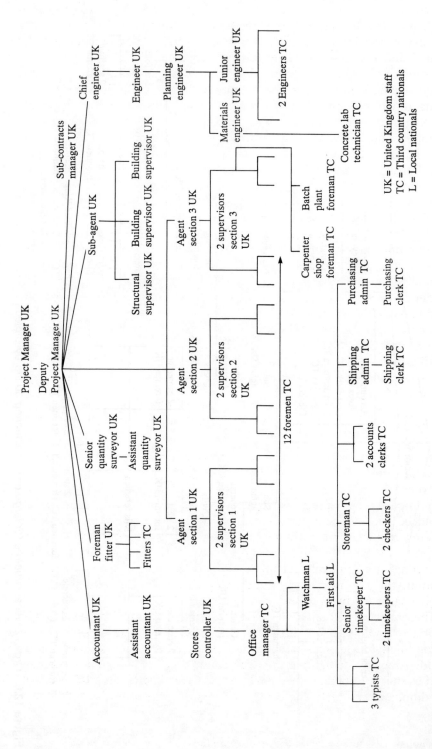

Figure 12.7 *Organizational structure for 30 storey office project*

structure for a 30 storey office and hotel complex, valued at £44 million (1979–80 prices). The site organization was under the direction of a regional office. However, its involvement on project administration was limited and revolved primarily around projecting the company's operations in the marketplace, seeking future work and assisting site operations when required. Both project structures indicate clearly that as one proceeds down the hierarchy the incidence of Third Country Nationals (TCNs) increases. National examples of skilled and unskilled labour imported into the Middle East, primarily due to a lack of supply of local skill, included Pakistani, Indian, Yemeni, Phillipino, South Korean, Turkish, Portuguese, Egyptian, Thai and Sri-Lankan operatives [45]. The operating core of the international contractor has to cope not only with those issues identified as part of the project life cycle in a domestic context but has the added dimension of cultural complexity. A recent empirical study [46] of site managers operating in the Middle East indicates a relative unawareness of cultural differences by production management. This is attributed to the low level and number of training programmes related to managing multicultural work forces in construction. Empirical evidence reported by Enshassi and Burgess indicated that most site managers did not receive any form of cross-cultural training. Furthermore, while managers appreciated the *need* for modifying their managerial styles to accommodate differences in culture, in *reality*, however, they did not modify their style to take account of the more culturally complex organizational situations they faced on site. There was a more consequent reduction in managerial and operative performance.

4.3.4 The problems of managing a multicultural workforce[1]

The case study presented below is derived from data on a project in Riyadh, Saudi Arabia. It is used to demonstrate how the interplay between a multicultural workforce and the required level of supervision may impact project progress. It raises the question of whether hard data could be used to determine a suitable mix of expatriate to total labour where a multicultural workforce is involved. It also reinforces the question raised by Enshassi and Burgess above concerning the need for contractors operating in a multicultural production situation to consider specialized training for site management in order that they can understand the problems posed by such an environment.

The project, a £50 million (1981 prices) mixed commercial development contract, had a project team comprising a UK quantity surveyor on secondment to a Japanese architectural practice, a German contractor and a Saudi Arabian client. Business was conducted in the English language under the International Federation of Civil Engineering Consultants conditions of contract. The contractor's work force comprised Phillipino,

[1] This case study was prepared by Mr Tim Whitworth, Department of Building and Surveying, Glasgow College, Glasgow, Scotland.

Pakistani, Indian, Thai, UK and German operatives. Cultural difficulties were experienced in two areas. First, between the client, consultant and contractor interfaces since a considerable amount of time was spent in face-to-face negotiation. Different cultural traits came to the fore as interpersonal relationships developed involving negotiations over contractual and technical issues. Second, due to varying cultural mixes at operative level workforce problems were reflected in varying levels of output. This particular case study is concerned mainly with the second cultural issue at workforce level.

In the earlier stages of the contract, Portuguese labour was employed for structural steelwork and was found to be very efficient. Mechanical and electrical work was carried out with Philippino and Thai labour. It was considered that the quality of work was good provided there was adequate levels of supervision from the German supervisors. At one stage in the contract a number of German contractors were demobilized and the level of TCN labour increased dramatically. The consequent result was that output fell and after a few months the contractor had to increase the number of supervisors with a subsequent rise in output.

An analysis was carried out to investigate the slowing down of output on the finishing trades, mechanical and electrical engineering services for the project. The data were collated from interim valuations and the contractor's daily labour returns. It was hoped that the results obtained would give an optimum cultural mix of labour on the project which would result in satisfactory progress. Figure 12.8 shows a series of graphs all related to a base of 100 in September 1983. The indices for subsequent months were all related to the base index. This procedure allows a variety of data to be plotted on the chart and the impact of changing the cultural mix of the labour force can be clearly seen. The following graphs were plotted:

Graph 1. interim valuations.
Graph 2. expatriate labour, German nationality.
Graph 3. third country national labour, that is labour other than German.
Graph 4. Average output per labourer (both German and TCN). The data
for this graph were obtained by dividing the amount paid in the
valuations for finishing trades and services by the number of man
days worked in that month

The gross valuation in November 1983 soared, reflecting the increase in labour from 347 men (both TCNs and German) in September to 459 men in November. This was the gross labour force working on finishings and service trades on both phase 2 – the project in question – and the adjacent phase 3 scheme. The contractor had stated that he would transfer all labour working on phase 3 to phase 2 in December, since phase 3 was handed over to the client in November. However, instead, 78 German operatives were demobilized during December, resulting in a dramatic slump in output and reflected in the change in monthly valuations. It should be borne in mind that the amount of TCN labour was being increased but with little impact on output. During the period December 1983 to March 1984

(1) Histogram of work executed each month excluding structure
(2) Expatriate labour
(3) Third Country National labour
(4) Average output per labourer

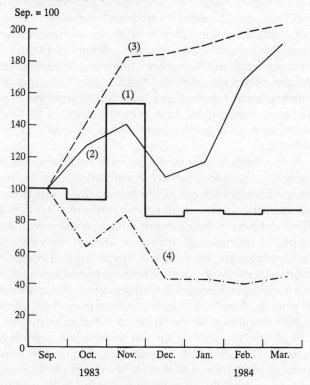

Figure 12.8 *Cultural mix of workers in the operating core*

the contractor took steps to reverse the fall in output by increasing the number of German operatives from 28 to 51. At the same time the number of TCNs increased from 332 to 367. From April to May 1984 output, and hence interim valuations, increased significantly. As a rough guide, the data available suggests that a suitable mix of expatriate to total labour on this project is 51/418 × 100 = 12%. It should also be noted that, whereas demobilizing expatriate labour had an immediate effect on output and interim valuations, the mobilizing of new expatriate labour does not significantly increase output and valuations for about two months.

5. Conclusions

In our discussion on international construction, we highlighted the fact that competition internationally has characteristics more akin to competing in multidomestic industries rather than through an integrated global strategy. The extent to which international construction companies can be classified as multidomestic or multinational enterprises, competing with coordinated global strategies, depends on the extent to which internalized advantages are integrated and used to compete across national boundaries. In our view this would require integrated strategic decision-making comparing opportunities domestically with those internationally. Major UK contractors are primarily domestically oriented, with the majority of their turnover coming from UK markets. Internalized advantages are likely to be exploited internationally in construction through information exchange, management transfer and materials–equipment procurement, i.e. Systems-based advantages. However, the pull is towards a multi-domestic orientation due to the nature and diversity of construction activity.

Two economic models were introduced – the 'national diamond' and the eclectic paradigm – and subsequently integrated to produce an analytical model of competitive advantage in international construction. The inter-play between country specific, firm specific and team specific advantages were identified as being of major importance in competing internationally in construction. A number of forms of market servicing operate in international construction, internalized mechanisms through FDI and/or exporting and externalized mechanisms through licensing and sub-contracting, for example. Competitive advantage in international construction was not seen as important in an expanding market but of considerable importance in determining the survivors in a declining market.

Exploration of the case studies for the Middle East market identified a number of issues. First, the problems encountered on the construction of the petrochemical plant indicated that there are high risks associated with overseas projects, especially where national politics are involved. In this instance, this geographic region is bedevilled by political uncertainties and, as in the case of Iran (and more recently the annexation of Kuwait by Iraq), political stability can change to instability very quickly. The project suffered massive cost overruns and could potentially have led to the destabilization of a company. Risk analysis, in a situation of high uncertainty, may best be undertaken using the intuitive–emotional style of decision-making at senior management level.

The case study of the UK contracting firm indicated that senior management went through a process of comparative demand searching, taking account of relative market size within the region, an assessment of competition – both national, international and in the host country – and the relative importance of the host country infrastructure. Contrary to Sey-mour's [47] findings, this particular company also took account of other UK competition when deciding on which market to enter in the Middle East. This suggests that size was a firm specific disadvantage relative to other British contractors. Having decided to enter the market the company chose to use home-based contacts in related and support industries to obtain a contract they felt was within their capability, in this instance an unusual but relatively straightforward project. To staff up the project the company used UK-based personnel on secondment, that is, they exploited a firm specific advantage in order to develop a team specific advantage for the project. Using Porter's service typology the company was utilizing a service type II approach to serving the market. Finally, this case study also demonstrated senior management's perception of the relative speed of development of indigenous contractors to compete on equal terms, seven years from initial market entry by the company.

The case studies on production strategy indicated the problems associated with cultural complexity in the operating core of an international contractor. These case studies highlighted the fact that site management is given insufficient training in the operating core to deal with complex social situations overlayed with technical and contractual issues. This detracts from the development of team specific, and hence firm specific, advantages. In addition, these case studies also suggested that the cultural mix on a project can affect output levels and the consequent degree of supervision required.

Finally, if we take the Middle East case study as a whole it demonstrates that the relative attractiveness/unattractiveness of entering a country or geographic region in international construction depends on market size, the level of competition, the joint influences of home and host governments, chance events, factor conditions in the host nation – especially labour supply and also the influence of related and support industries in both the home and host country. Seymour's data indicated that cultural issues were not seen as a major item by international contractors but the data presented above indicates a wide variety of potential impacts through differing government persuasions, and political ideologies, and deep within the operating core in the production process.

References

1. Seymour, H. (1987) *The Multinational Construction Industry*. Croom Helm, London. Seymour, H. (1989) 'International contracting', in Hillebrandt, P. M. and Cannon, J. (eds.), *The Management of Construction Firms: Aspects of Theory*. Macmillan, Basingstoke. Porter, M. E. (1990) *The Competitive Advantage of Nations*. Macmillan, London. Ball, M. (1988) *Rebuilding Construction: Economic Change in the British Construction Industry*. Routledge, London 1988. Strassman, W. P. and Wells, J. (eds.) (1988) *The Global Construction Industry: Strategies for Entry, Growth and Survival*. Unwin Hyman, London. Enderwick, P. (1989) 'Multinational contracting', in Enderwick, P. (ed.), *The Multinational Service Firm*. Routledge, London.
2. Jauch, L. R. and Glueck, W. F. *Business Policy and Strategic Management*. McGraw-Hill, Singapore, 5th edn.
3. Strassman, P. W. and Wells, J. (eds.) *op. cit.* Enderwick P. *op. cit.* Hillebrandt, P. M. (1984) *Analysis of the British Construction Industry*. Macmillan, London. Seymour H. (1987) *op. cit.*
4. Hillebrandt, P. M. (1984) *op. cit.*
5. Porter, M. E. (1990) *op. cit.*

6. Dunning, J. H. (1981) *International Production and the Multinational Enterprise*. George Allen and Unwin, London.
7. Seymour, H. (1987) *op. cit.*
8. Porter, M. E. (1990) *op. cit.*
9. See country chapters in Strassman, W. P. and Wells, J. (eds.) *op. cit.* and Seymour, H. (1987) and (1989) *op. cit.*
10. Strassman, P. W. and Wells, J. 'Conclusions: Comparisons and analysis', in Strassman, P. W. and Wells, J. (eds.) *op. cit.*
11. Seymour, H. (1987) *op. cit.*
12. Porter, M. A. (1990) *op. cit.*
13. Enderwick, P. *op. cit.*
14. Seymour, H. (1987) *op. cit.*
15. Seymour, H. (1987) *op. cit.*
16. Seymour, H. (1987) *op. cit.*
17. Seymour, H. (1989) *op. cit.*
18. Enderwick, P. *op. cit.*
19. Strassman, W. P. and Wells, J. 'Introduction', in Strassman, W. P. and Wells, J. (eds.) *op. cit.*
20. Porter, M. E. (1990) *op. cit.*
21. Enderwick, P. *op. cit.*
22. Enderwick, P. *op. cit.*
23. Hillebrandt, P. M. (1984) *op. cit.* Ball, M. *op. cit.* Strassman, P. W. and Wells, J. 'Conclusions', *op. cit.*
24. Bennett, J., Flanagan, R., and Norman, G. (1987) *Capital and Counties Report: Japanese Construction Industry*. Centre for Strategic Studies, University of Reading.
25. See country chapters in Strassman, P. W. and Wells, J. (eds.) *op. cit.*
26. Bennett, J., Flanagan, R. and Norman, G. *op. cit.* Hippo, Y. and Tamura, S. Japan, in Strassman, P. W. and Wells, J. (eds.) *op. cit.*
27. Hasegawa, F. and The Shimizu Group (1988) *Built by Japan: Competitive Strategies of the Japanese Construction Industry*. John Wiley & Sons, New York.
28. Cannon, J. and Hillebrandt, P. M. 'Diversification', in Hillebrandt, P. M. and Cannon, J. (eds.) *op. cit.*
29. Bennett, J., Flanagan, R. and Norman, G. *op. cit.*
30. See Roger Flanagan's chapter on Japan in this book.
31. Porter, M. E. (1990) *op. cit.*
32. Porter, M. E. (1980) *op. cit.* Enderwick, P. *op. cit.* Seymour, H. (1987) *op. cit.*
33. Enderwick, P. *op. cit.*
34. Strassman, W. P. and Wells, J. 'Conclusions', in Strassman, W. P. and Wells, J. (eds.) *op. cit.*
35. Seymour, H. (1987) *op. cit.*
36. Porter, M. E. (1990) *op. cit.* Chang, D. W. 'The Republic of Korea,' in Strassman, W. P. and Wells, J. (eds.) *op. cit.*
37. Verillo, J. Brazil, in Strassman, W. P. and Wells, J. (eds.) *op. cit.*
38. Strassman, W. P. and Wells, J. (eds.) *op. cit.*
39. *World Oil Publication*, September 1988, p. 25.
40. Seymour, H. (1987) *op. cit.*
41. Stallworthy, E. A. and Kharbanda, O. P. (1985) *International Construction: The Role of Project Management*. Gower.
42. Try, H. W. and Rush, M. A. F. (1984) 'The experiences of a medium sized construction company in the Middle East', in *Management of International*

Construction Projects, pps. 137–147. *Proceedings of a Conference held at the Institution of Civil Engineers. 14–15 November 1984.* Thomas Telford, London.

43. Skinn, A. (1980) International Business Strategy: A Study of the Staffing of International Construction Projects. MSc Thesis. Heriot-Watt University.
44. Skinn, A. *op. cit.*
45. Strassman, W. P. and Wells, J. (eds.) *op. cit.*
46. Enshassi, A. and Burgess, R. (1990) 'Training for construction site managers involved with multicultural work teams', *International Journal of Project Management*, **8**, No. 2, pp. 95–101.
47. Seymour, H. (1987) *op. cit.*

—— *13* ——

Competition within the EC and the Single European Market in 1992

Nigel Smith

1. Introduction

The member states of the European Community (EC) have pledged to introduce in 1992 the Single European Market, an area without internal frontiers in which the free movement of goods, persons, services and capital is ensured. The construction industries in the EC states are directly affected in terms of design standards, construction procurement, the use of construction products and the free and fair competition for EC public works contracts.

This chapter initially reviews the construction industry in the United Kingdom, and examines the competitive processes for obtaining work in the domestic and international markets. This is compared with the current structure of the construction industries in the other EC states, concentrating on the civil engineering sector. The basis for the formation of the Single European Market in 1992 is outlined and the strategic implications in terms of UK domestic market position, new internal EC markets and international competition outside the EC are discussed.

2. The UK construction industry

United Kingdom: Population 56 million; Area 230 000 square kilometres; GNP per capita $US7 920 [1]; Construction market £26.2 billion [2]. (Note: Statistics for the United Kingdom and all other EC member states see references 1 and 2.)

The construction industry underwent a recession between 1973 and 1983, during which time a reduction in output of 19% occurred. There are about 170 000 contracting companies, many of which are medium and small-scale builders and sub-contractors, although the top 100 contracting firms are responsible for 25% of construction work. Half of the total expenditure is on repair and maintenance, with civil engineering and building accounting for 20 and 30% respectively.

Over the last 40 years the industry has retained the same basic structure. The civil engineering sector consists of a small number of mainly public sector clients, contracting companies ranging from multinational contractors to small specialist firms and a large number of relatively small consulting engineering partnerships. In building work which is divided into housing and building structures, there are both private and public clients, a number of architectural practices and designers and a range of contractors and builders.

The conventional UK contract strategy is based upon the rigid separation of design and construction. The competition for both design and construction work is largely based on restricted, or selected, tendering practices for the major contracts and open tendering for the minor works. With the exception of a few major public sector projects of recent years, the competition for this work has been between UK firms or UK subsidiary companies. However, there has been some penetration into the construction market in the specialist skills areas where non-UK companies familiar with new design techniques, novel construction processes or new materials have proved to be cost effective.

Conventionally, consulting engineers compete on the basis of fee competition for a contract to prepare a complete design and the associated contract documents. The consultant is usually retained to supervise the construction work on site. A number of contracting companies are then subjected to pre-qualification in order to assure the client that a number of competitive, reasonable and easy to evaluate bids from suitable and experienced contractors would be obtained from the tender list. Under an admeasurement contract the completed design is defined by the contract drawings, and the permanent materials to be included in the works are itemized in the bill of quantities, (BOQ). At tender the contractors price the BOQ and hence produce a tender sum for the works, including the temporary works, overheads and profit margin. The returned tender bids are then checked for compliance and mathematical errors prior to evaluation, and the current practice is to accept the lowest priced bid, unless there is good reason to do otherwise.

The admeasurement contract does not inform the client of the final price. The permanent works are remeasured and payment is based upon the final quantities for each of the priced BOQ items. Hence the BOQ fulfils two functions: it has to have a low total price to be successful in competition and it also has to maximize the financial return to the contractor by careful pricing. Variations to the works and claims made under the contract which also affect the final price are an accepted part of the UK industry. This has given UK contractors a reputation for disputes, and of financial overruns for international clients more accustomed to fixed-price lump-sum contracting.

There have been significant fluctuations in the national economy over this period, and the level of public investment in the construction sector has been used as a regulator. This has produced periods of boom and recession which have directly affected the competitiveness, profitability and value-for-money of work in this sector, and has influenced the international outlook of the UK industry. This background, together with the relatively small volume of UK construction work and the market's irregularity, have led major construction companies to diversify by working outside the United Kingdom, or by becoming engaged in non-construction activities.

3. International aspects of the UK construction industry

The growth in world population, the higher expectations and demands for infrastructure and services, the aid programmes related to establishing agriculture and commerce, all contribute towards an increasing demand for construction services. However, many countries are unable to meet the financial consequences of this demand and the major construction activity in recent years has been concentrated in countries showing growth in gross national product (GNP) per capita.

The United Kingdom has a significant share of the international construction market, second only to Italy in the EC member states. In 1986, the United States was by far the most important market for UK construction companies working overseas, with £408 million out of a UK overseas new works total of £1471 million. In joint second place each with about £190 million, were Oceania, Africa and the Middle East, while EC work accounted for £93 million [3]. The United States has been seen as the major market because a small increase in market share could result in huge increases in profit.

To compete successfully for international work requires knowledge of conditions, working practices, cultural differences and climatic conditions. Many of the most potentially profitable contracts are for complex and expensive projects which also have the greatest financial and technical risk for the contractor. Increasingly, many countries insist that local firms are employed on all contracts. Hence many UK construction firms have formed temporary or semi-permanent joint ventures or consortia with local firms, or have appointed local sponsors. In addition, arrangements have been made with other UK or EC or international firms to acquire the necessary expertise and to share the risk of the project. The majority of this competition is not based on the UK system and experience of fixed price contracting has needed to be acquired.

The upturn in the UK economy during the mid- to late-1980s attracted non-UK firms to conduct similar arrangements in the United Kingdom. Several construction firms have now been acquired by non-UK firms or have undergone mergers. A second attraction would be an established outlet inside the Single European Market prior to 1992. These effects, and others, are causing changes in the structure of UK consulting practices and contracting businesses, which in turn place great demands upon the conventional contractual procedure.

4. Competitive change in the United Kingdom prior to 1992

Despite a number of reports and investigations into the UK construction industry between 1950 and 1980, the basic structure of the industry has remained largely unchanged. However, significant changes in the balance between public and private sectors have started to take place in the last ten years. Several public sector clients have been, or are in the process of being, restructured and privatized. Public sector clients have a duty of public accountability to ensure free and fair competition for new contracts and to demonstrate value for money. This is reflected in the adoption of the current competitive tendering procedure. Privatization usually involves the blending of commercial requirements with certain restrictions and statutory duties which result in the privatized company behaving as a hybrid organization. Purely private organizations are profit-making enterprises and thus have a prime responsibility to their shareholders.

For over 150 years, consulting engineers have operated as partnerships. A partnership has unlimited liability. Many consultants are engaged on large and complex projects, and the threat of financial ruin is raised by the increasing numbers of clients, contractors and members of the public who resort to litigation to resolve disputes. To overcome these problems a number of consulting partnerships have become part of larger multi-disciplinary consulting firms, while others have merged to form larger limited liability companies.

Contracting companies are relatively low-cost, high-risk businesses, and during the recent recession in the UK economy many of these companies became attractive targets for acquisition or merger. In 1987 over two thousand UK companies were acquired with a market value in excess of £28 billion [4], including many in the construction sector. Acquisition is basically a choice between development or modification of an in-house facility, and the purchase of an already operating facility. There are capital costs and operational costs associated with acquisitions, and to be successful there must be the possibility of a significant improvement in economic performance. This trend has resulted in many contractors becoming part of large national or multinational corporate organizations owned by UK, EC and non-EC parent companies.

These organizational and business changes have resulted in changes to the conventional contract strategy. The conventional system is not seen as placing sufficient emphasis on time and cost performance. There is also pressure for forms of contract strategy which facilitate buildability, reduce the risk to the client, allow client involvement in management and permit early starts. Two increasingly popular strategies are the management contract and the package deal. Under a management contract the work is divided into discrete contracts, each of which is administered by the management contractor. The management contractor is appointed on the basis of fee competition and acts as the client's agent. The package deal has three basic forms, design and build, turnkey and build-own-operate-transfer, which involve detailed design and construction, complete design and construction and design, construct and finance respectively. Contractors are appointed after competitive tender on a lump-sum, fixed-price contract.

The resultant effect of these changes is that new parameters form the basis for competition in the industry. The privatized client is concerned with identifying a competent and experienced contractor who is likely to perform on site and also act as a working partner. This commercial emphasis supersedes lowest price as the dominant competitive variable. Equally, the reorganization of the contracting sector has produced companies with the size and capability to tackle very large projects, and to compete with the major contracting firms in other world markets. Longer-term commitment to these package deal strategies could provide the major construction contractors with the incentive to invest in new technology and staff training, hence providing larger and financially stronger firms with superior financial, technical and operational expertise. The numbers of firms might be reduced, but the competition is more diversified, a wider range and type of work is available to the contractor and the company has a greater capability to offer a client a complete service.

5. Origins of the European Community

At the end of the Second World War, in 1945, the economies of the European countries were largely in ruins and Europe itself became divided into two spheres of influence: Eastern Europe and Western Europe. This weakness made cooperation and interdependence between the countries from each of these two groupings a necessity. The current EC member states are all countries from the Western European group.

The few years following 1945 saw a proliferation of international organizations and charters to put these ideas into practice, largely with the backing of the United States. In 1946, at Bretton Woods, the International Monetary Fund and the World Bank were formed to help re-establish the European currencies. A year later the 'Marshall Plan' was proposed by the United States, whereby aid was provided without political obligations, on the condition that the European countries prepared an integrated programme to relieve poverty and encourage industry. This led to the formation of the Organisation for European Economic Co-operation (OEEC) in 1948. Also in that year the General Agreement on Tariffs and Trade (GATT) was signed. This provided for customs duties on certain items to be harmonized, and was initially operated by more than 20 countries, providing the basic ideas for trade within the future Single European Market.

In 1948 three European countries decided to cooperate more closely on trade and tariffs by having no charges on internal trade, and common rates for all other countries. Belgium, Holland and Luxembourg (Benelux) strengthened this arrangement with further agreements in the 1950s which permitted the movement of capital and labour, and subsequently benefited from a massive increase in internal trade and an improved performance in external trade. Some of these ideas were later incorporated into the Treaty of Rome.

After lengthy negotiations the French announced the 'Schuman Plan' in 1950, which was a proposal that the French and German production of coal and steel should be controlled by a single authority, to which other countries were invited to join. This resulted in the Treaty of Paris in 1951 when France, Germany, Italy, Holland, Belgium and Luxembourg agreed to form the European Coal and Steel Community, which was the first really supranational organization.

At this time the United Kingdom was supportive of these developments in Europe but did not express any desire to participate. The United Kingdom was also involved in unsuccessful attempts to establish a European Army. However it was not until 1956 and the Suez affair that the United Kingdom first seriously considered a role in Europe, rather than acting independently as a world power.

The moves towards closer integration of the European countries continued and in 1957 the two Treaties of Rome were signed creating the European Economic Community (EEC) and the European Community of Atomic Energy (EURATOM). The member states of the EEC were the same six countries which had formed the ECSC six years earlier. The EEC was the most important of the three communities and was primarily responsible for economic integration, which provided the basis for the Single European Market.

In 1959 the United Kingdom was instrumental in the establishment of the European Free Trade Association (EFTA), which also involved Austria, Denmark, Norway, Portugal, Sweden and Switzerland. This response to the EEC was moderately successful but three of these countries subsequently joined the EC.

The three communities have undergone a degree of rationalization and have admitted new member states between 1973 and 1986. There is now a single Council and a single Commission to deal with all aspects of Community business. The first Treaty of Accession was drafted in 1972 as a result of discussions with the United Kingdom, Denmark, Eire and Norway. Norway decided against joining but the other three were admitted in 1973. Greece followed in 1981 and most recently, in 1986, Spain and Portugal were admitted to bring the EC up to 12 member states, illustrated in Figure 13.1.

The Act leading to the creation of the Single European Market for the 12 member states came into effect on 1 July, 1987 [5]. It is based on the principles of the free movement of goods, services, capital and people between member states, and the creation of a single market of 320 million people. The Act will modify the three community treaties at the same time. There will still be major differences between each of the member states but this Act is a major step forward towards closer integration and greater monetary and political links within Europe.

Figure 13.1 *Membership of the European Community in 1986*

6. The construction industries of the EC member states

Despite comprising countries which already have a developed infrastructure, roughly 10% of the EC GNP is spent on construction, which
accounts for a quarter of the world market.

Procurement methods vary between the member states, but there are
three standard methods of tendering for construction work which are used
in the majority of member states: open tendering; selective tendering; and
negotiation. Sometimes, particular works require specialized skills and
clients have adopted the package deal, or management contract. Unlike the
United Kingdom many EC member states do not tender on the basis of
precise quantities, which places a great deal of emphasis on the preparation and clarity of the written specification.

An outline of the current basic structure and contractual procedures in each of the other EC member states is given below. These descriptions are not detailed and provide a background against which to assess the implications of competition in the Single European Market.

6.1 France
Population 54 million; Area 543000 square kilometres; GNP per capita $US11730 [1]; Construction market £36.6 billion [2].

There are a small number of major construction firms with an important share of the domestic market and a consistent record of success in the international construction business. However, between 1980 and 1985, there has been a decline in construction output of about 22%. Domestic construction work is undertaken by one of these majors, or by one of the approximately 290000 small firms employing less than 20 people.

Three main tendering procedures are currently in use. The first 'adjudication', is conventional open-tendering which is adopted for simple supply contracts only. The *Appel d'offre* is the most common procurement method. It is based upon competitive tendering with open or restricted tender lists, against a detailed specification. The work is offered to the most attractive bidder in terms of the overall cost, the technical value and the likely duration. About 60% of all construction work is awarded using selected tendering procedures. Finally, there will be a limited number of contracts where, for a variety of reasons, negotiated tendering is adopted. In some cases the client may insist on pre-qualification before negotiation.

Public works contracts are usually announced by public notice and are tendered competitively, with restrictions for the major contracts. A deposit, *cautionnement*, of 5% has to be paid. The contract documents usually include a specification, conditions of contract, drawings and sometimes a BOQ. When tenders are submitted they are usually accompanied by variations since alternatives to tender documentation are encouraged. The tender bids are opened in the presence of the tenderers and the lowest bid is accepted. The tenderer has 24 hours in which to accept, and may withdraw if a payment equal to the difference to the next lowest bid is made. For building work in particular, fixed-price lump-sum contracts are quite common.

6.2 Germany
Population 61 million; Area 248000 square kilometres; GNP per capital $US13590 [1]; Construction market £64.3 billion [2].

The industry in Germany is based upon a small number of major regionally based contractors with about 50000 very small specialist trades contractors. The major companies compete around the world and have a significant market share in the Middle East, Africa, South America and

Australia. Germany is the major EC economy, and spends about 50% of construction expenditure on building, 10% on civil engineering and 40% on repair and maintenance. The smaller companies cooperate to execute contracts and about 30% of all construction is undertaken by joint ventures. The public sector is the largest client area and is also responsible for the majority of design work. Consequently, most German consultants concentrate on overseas markets.

The eight local authorities, *Lande*, and the two city states administer the public sector contracts usually under the *Verdingungsordnung fuer Bauleistungen*, (VOB), regulations. The VOB are in three sections: Part A deals with the method of tendering; Part B with the general conditions of contract, the specification and other documents; and Part C includes the 49 'DIN' standards and notes on measurement. The majority of public works are procured by advertisement and open competitive tender, whereas private sector work uses the method of invitation and negotiation. The most common form of contract is the fixed-price, lump-sum contract based upon a specification and approximate BOQ. The award is not necessarily made to the lowest. Winning tenders are evaluated on the basis of a price-to-performance ratio, but details of how this assessment will be calculated are not provided to the contractor. In certain circumstances restricted tendering is used.

Other EC states' contractors can compete for work, but must conform with 'DIN' standards which can involve lengthy certification procedures, and demonstrate the ability to meet fast delivery requirements or the need for spare parts. Currently about 5% of work is awarded to other national contractors, which is one of the highest figures in the EC.

6.3 Holland
Population 14 million; Area 33 948 square kilometres; GNP per capita $US11 470 [1], Construction market £14.2 billion [2].

The major Dutch contractors have established an international reputation for specialized hydraulic, marine and offshore construction works. There are about 20 000 contracting companies but most employ less than five people. The market underwent a recession between 1981 and 1983 since when there has been a slight recovery. Repair and maintenance accounts for about 50% of the construction work, with the remainder divided 40% building and 10% civil engineering.

In Holland most private sector, and public sector civil engineering contracts, use the Ministry of Public Works Contract in conjunction with a BOQ. There is no special administrative law applying to contracts with the state. The *Rijkswaterstaat* tender regulations mean that work is awarded to the most acceptable tenderer. A small proportion of work is awarded by open tendering, or negotiated tendering, but the majority of work is awarded on the basis of selective tendering. In addition, each commissioning body has its own regulations. Returned competitive tender bids are opened in public and contracts are awarded to the tenderer whose bids appears to be the most acceptable, and not necessarily the lowest. However, in about 98% of cases the contract is awarded to the lowest priced bid. For building works the specification and drawings rather than quantities are used as the basis for a tender and the *standard contracte administrative voorwaarden voor de uitvoering von werken* (UAV) is usually adopted.

There has been some privatization in recent years and this has encouraged the use of design-and-build contracts and negotiated tendering procedures. Some of the larger contractors have formed permanent or semi-permanent ventures, with banks or financial institutions, to strengthen their international competitiveness.

6.4 Belgium
Population 10 million; Area 30 000 square kilometres; GNP per capita $US12 180 [1]; Construction market £2.6 billion [2].

The Belgian market suffered a short recession during the early 1980s but has staged a small recovery. There are about 1 600 contracting companies of which about 15 have over 500 employees. The construction industry is almost equally divided between civil engineering, building, and repair and maintenance work.

Approximately 93% of construction work in Belgium is awarded by competitive tendering and most of the remainder by negotiation. The majority of public works contracts are awarded on the basis of open competition. The object of the competitive tendering system is to determine the most competitive price, which is regarded as the lowest fair price. There is no standard contract but there are three main types of strategy currently in use. The *marche a forfait absolu* is the standard form of fixed-price, lump-sum contract with no variations permitted. There is a modified contract which incorporates variations and price fluctuations. This is known as the *marche a forfait relatif*. Finally, there is a contract based on a schedule of rates, the *marche a borderaux de prix*. Private sector work is less formal and invited tendering and negotiation are widely used.

A unique aspect of the Belgian market is that there is organized collaboration between the contracting firms: the 'Charpo' system. Therefore, although open tendering procedures are used, the final price of the lowest priced bid includes a sum decided by the contractors themselves, to avoid suicidally low prices being submitted.

6.5 Luxembourg
Population 0.36 million; Area 2 580 square kilometres; GNP per capita $US14 510 [1].

Luxembourg is not a major construction market. There are a few small contractors but much of the work is done by Belgian or French companies. Open tendering is adopted for any public works contracts.

6.6 Italy
Population 56 million; Area 301 000 square kilometres; GNP per capita $US6 480 [1]; Construction market £29.7 billion [2].

The Italian construction industry consists of a few large state owned construction organizations, a number of medium-sized private sector companies and about 260 000 small constructors and builders employing less than five people. Much of the construction work is carried out by consortia, or temporary associations of firms arranged for individual contracts. Almost half the construction work is in building, with civil engineering and maintenance accounting for about 25% each. Internationally, Italian contractors have been very successful and currently have the biggest share of the world market of any EC member state. Construction in Italy is well below the levels of the 1970s and although there has been some recent recovery, output is well below the EC average.

There is a high degree of regulation of public works contracts. The *asta pubblica* is an open tendering procedure in which the contract is awarded to the lowest bidder. The *licitazione privata* is the closest method to UK practice, except for the fact that the contract is not always advertised. Bidders have to undergo a pre-qualification process and generally the lowest priced bid is awarded the contract, although delivery, operating cost and technical merit are all assessed in the evaluation procedure. A variation on this approach is the *appalto concorso*, which is similar but usually contains detailed specifications and is used for complex projects. A proportion of work can be awarded by negotiated tender or *trattativa privata*, which requires no advertising or competition.

The use of the design and build package is very popular and this is frequently used for public works contracts on a fixed-price basis. Often, tender bids are priced on the basis of a downward adjustment of the client's estimate. Most construction materials and products are available within the domestic market.

6.7 Denmark
Population 5 million; Area 43 000 square kilometres; GNP per capita $US12 950 [1]; Construction market £6.9 billion [2].

There are no major contracting companies in Denmark, although construction accounts for about 6% of all public expenditure. The work is carried out by about 20 000 small-sized trade contractors. Various companies are assembled under the guidance of an architect to coordinate the work for each contract. Denmark suffered a general recession in construction from 1979 to 1983 but there has been an increase in the building sector recently.

There are standard procedures for the award of public works contracts. Work is advertised and tenders are invited in open competition which is largely based on a compliance specification rather than on detailed quantities. The majority of work is awarded on the basis of fixed-price, lump-sum tendering, where the lowest acceptably priced bid is successful.

Some public sector work, and some private work, is awarded using both cost-reimbursable and negotiated contract strategies.

6.8 Eire
Population 4 million; Area 68 000 square kilometres; GNP per capita $US4 880 [1]; Construction market £1.7 billion [2].

The workload in Eire declined by over 50% between 1979 and 1985 due to cuts in both public and private sectors. Recently, a small recovery has been possible, due to funding provided by the EC to assist in the development of the infrastructure. This has resulted in many skilled construction workers returning to work in the domestic market. There are four or five medium-sized companies but most of these are jointly owned ventures with firms from overseas. The remainder of the sector consists of small builders and sub-contractors.

The basic contractual procedures are very similar to those of the United Kingdom. All public works contracts are advertised and awarded as the result of competitive tender to the lowest evaluated bid. The private sector clients use a wider range of contract strategies including management contracting and complete design, build and finance packages.

6.9 Greece
Population 10 million; Area 131 000 square kilometres; GNP per capita $US4 520 [1]; Construction market £1.0 billion [2].

Contractors in Greece are licensed and the classification of the licence depends upon the previous technical and contractual experience of the firm, and on the qualifications and professional expertise of the staff employed. There are about 400 contracting firms of small-to-medium size and a large number of very small trade contractors undertaking small jobs and sub-contract work. The domestic market suffered a period of recession from 1978 until 1984 but the improvement in 1985 was largely in building work and not across the entire construction industry.

All public works contracts are advertised. However, only contractors with the appropriate classification of licence are able to respond. Tendering is competitive and an award is made on the basis of the lowest acceptable price, although technical considerations are often included in the bid evaluation. In building work, the price would be broken down into rates, and for most civil engineering the tender sum would show a percentage saving compared to the client's estimate. The bidder is responsible for quantities, and tenders are subjected to the *omalotita timon* which restricts adjustment.

The private sector is less regulated and contracts can be awarded by negotiation. There is also no need to comply with the strict licensing requirements. Greece has a strong market in construction materials and products and is a net exporter of cement.

6.10 Spain
Population 38 million; Area 492 000 square kilometres; GNP per capita $US5 350 [1]; Construction market £17 billion [2].

Spain joined the EC in 1986 and full membership will be achieved over a ten-year integration period. Construction is a major employer in Spain, with about 10% of the workforce employed in 35 000 companies. There are a few large contractors undertaking major infrastructure development, tourism and residential housing developments. The industry suffered a severe recession between 1974 and 1984 when construction output fell by 25%, but recent public investment and an increase in housing work has slightly improved the market.

Most major contracts are awarded to general contractors who subsequently employ sub-contractors as required. The public works contracts are subject to regulation but the basic principle is that contractors compete for work on the basis of the lowest acceptable tender figure. The *subasta* is a system of open, competitive tendering. The contractor has to calculate the detailed quantities and submit a price below the client's estimate. *Concurso* is a method of qualified tendering under which the record, experience, staff and the technical capabilities of the firm are considered, in addition to the tender price. This approach is often used for design and construction work. The *subasta con admision previa* is a form of selective competitive tendering whereby the tender list is narrowed down prior to the submission of bids. The return bids are then assessed on the basis of lowest price. There is a form of negotiated tender, the *contraction directa*, which is used for a minority of contracts.

Private sector work is not as heavily regulated. Architects play a key role in private design and construct contracts, occasionally including arrangements with Spanish banks. Spain has an active construction materials and supply sector, which satisfies most construction requirements. Many firms from other EC member states are already working in Spain, particularly on housing and building projects.

6.11 Portugal
Population 10 million; Area 91 000 square kilometres; GNP per capita $US2 350 [1]; Construction market £1.1 billion [2].

The construction market has a very small proportion of repair and maintenance, about 10%. The dominant factor is new building and residential works which accounts for about 60% with civil engineering works taking the remainder. There are a large number of very small trade contractors in Portugal and from approximately 18 000 companies only about 18% have more than ten employees.

Public works contracts are awarded using one of the three official procedures. The *concurso publico* is a form of open competitive tendering under which public advertisements are placed requesting tenders from all suitably qualified contractors. The award is usually made to the lowest priced bid. A variation of this approach is the *concurso limitado* which restricts the tender list to contractors selected by the client. Usually, a minimum of three contractors must be invited. Finally, there is a negotiated form of tendering the *do a juste directo*, which can be used for certain types of work.

Payment for the works can be by unit price but this is not always the case. In some contracts, payment might be specified by total value or by percentage of the work completed. It is possible to have a combination of methods of payment for different sections of the work under the same contract. Private sector contracts are not subjected to the same degree of regulation but they tend to follow similar procedures.

7. 1992 The Single European Market

The concept of the Single European Market is the creation of a free space which permits the free movement of goods, people, services and capital. It has the aims of furthering the internal economic integration of the member states and of unifying the relationships of the EC with other countries. This is a natural development of the basic tenets of the three aforementioned communities and these four freedoms are referred to in the articles of the Treaty of Rome. There has already been some progress made towards the implementation of the first three freedoms but progress on monetary integration has been very slow.

The Act leading to the creation of the Single European Market came into effect on 1 July, 1987 and envisages some 300 legislative acts to be formulated, translated into national law, and enforced. The Single European Market will remove internal tariffs and procurement restrictions which will reduce costs. It will also remove restrictions on competition for public sector works contracts, thus further reducing costs and providing better value for money for clients and a more efficient and expanded market for contractors [6]. Currently only about 2% of construction work in the EC is undertaken by non-national companies.

The 12 separate domestic markets will be transformed into one internal market. There will be a need to harmonize industrial practice within the member states but this will be a gradual process rather than an instantaneous change in 1992. The basic framework will be established in 1992 but it would not be practical to expect the complete integration of 12 independent countries with their sovereign identities, different practices, traditions, wealth, and public and private sector industries.

The strength of the Single European Market will lie in its increased internal trade which will generate more employment, higher internal investment, and in its approach to the rest of the world. Individually, most of the member states do not have the resources for either investment in research and development or in market penetration to match such major industrial powers as the United States and Japan.

The EC has the power to issue internal legislation of three main types: Regulations, Directives and Decisions [7]. Basically, Regulations are obligatory acts which are binding upon all the member states. Directives are binding in as far as the results of the Directive have to achieved, but precisely how this result is achieved is left to the discretion of each of the member states. Most of the legislation relating to the construction industry is in the form of Directives. Finally there are Decisions which are binding upon specific parties which could be states, companies or individuals.

8. Harmonization

Harmonization is the process of removing the physical, technical and fiscal barriers by adjusting the community, law, taxes, markets and procedures of the 12 member states, to conform to agreed Community standards. It is estimated that harmonization should produce a 5–6% increase in internal trade, which would be worth about $US250 000 million. In the short time between the publication of the Act in 1986 and the creation of the Single European Market, from 1986 to 1992, it will not be possible to complete all the necessary arrangements. Therefore, the main objective of harmonization is not to remove all national diversity, except when the diversity is perceived as a barrier to the four freedoms of the Single European Market.

The EC construction industry is primarily affected by four key Directives, dealing with public works contracts, compliance, construction products, and public supply contracts. However, significant penetration of non-domestic construction markets requires the additional harmonization of design techniques, insurance and liability and professional qualifications. Ultimately, national design codes will be replaced by Eurocodes. Until these codes are operational the national codes of member states will be acceptable. The Eurocodes 1–9 are intended to be available from 1 June 1992 to cover about 95% of all structures built in Europe. Work is being carried out on the insurance and liability aspects of construction. The four main areas of concern are: providing insurance for building defects ten years after completion; a five-year guarantee for civil engineering work either by contract or in law; latent defects insurance; and a clearly defined standard civil liability insurance policy. Harmonization will also apply to education, training and professional qualifications. All EC member states have recognized procedures to allow engineers to become professionally qualified.

9. EC public works contracts

Civil engineering and building work account for about 30% of all EC public procurement, most of which should be awarded by competitive tender. The public works Directive [8], contains strict proposals for advertising public works contracts and guidelines for open, restricted and negotiated tendering. Advertising is needed to ensure fair competition throughout the Single European Market. There are proposals regarding the time periods to be allowed for tendering and award. The time periods will be longer than would be usual for domestic competition, which would slightly delay work but this should be off-set by the increased competitiveness of the tendering process. The Directive is required to overcome some of the restrictive practices currently in operation. These include the complex procedures for admission to approved lists, the acceptance of domestic standards only, the requirements for licensed offices in the member states and the necessity of using a high percentage of local labour or materials. This should encourage competitive tendering across national boundaries.

Public works will also include those industries which have been privatized and, in the United Kingdom, will consider themselves to be in the private sector. The objective is to ensure equal access for EC firms irrespective of nationality. The original Directive is to be supplemented by a second Directive extending these principles to the energy, transport, water and telecoms sectors.

To accompany both the public works Directive and the public supply Directive, a compliance Directive [9] is being drafted. Programmed to come into effect in 1991, this Directive provides for the payment of damages to companies unfairly treated by member states. It allows the Commission to intervene in the award of a contract and, if necessary, to suspend the award. Post 1992, the public works sector of the EC will be competitive in terms of competition for design, in terms of competition for work and in terms of the use of materials. The biggest market is likely to be in the supply and distribution of construction materials and products.

10. Construction materials and products

The construction products sector is more flexible than the construction services sector. Products are manufactured at a specific location within one of the EC member states and then require transportation and distribution to site. The distances involved within some EC member states are comparable with cross-national-boundary travel. Work on the harmonization of product standards has been progressing slowly over many years.

The EC established the Central Europe Committee for Standardisation (CEN), which is required to produce an estimated 4000 EC standards before 1992. The construction products Directive [10], which is due to become operative in 1991, will ensure that every permanent product complies with EC standards. No member state will be able to veto a product conforming to CEN standards, or conforming to national standards recognized as meeting the essential requirements of the directive, which when incorporated in a structure will meet certain essential requirements. Products satisfying the Construction Products Directive will bear an E mark and will then be deemed to satisfy all national regulations.

The supply Directive [11] will apply to contracting authorities who will be required to specify products which meet agreed conforming standards. This will apply to basic commodities such as cement, sand and aggregate, as well as to sophisticated construction products. However, it should be noted that there could be problems with products which deteriorate many years later; thus there has been some pressure to allow products to be prohibited if there are good reasons for suspecting them to be faulty. The Directive ensures that companies can compete outside their national boundaries, with further provisions to limit the use of single tendering by requiring greater advertising, increased time limits and justification for negotiated tendering.

11. Opportunity and competition in 1992

In 1992 the creation of the Single European Market will offer new opportunities for competition inside the Community. There will be increased competition in each of the domestic markets and opportunities to compete in the domestic markets of the other EC member states. However, no major penetration into other countries' markets is likely until the products, materials and design approaches have been harmonized. Domestic market penetration by other EC member states is currently very low with most states having less than 2% of work executed in this way.

In all 12 member states the construction sector is showing varying degrees of recovery from a period of major recession. The civil engineering sector is particularly depressed, and the recent upturn has been largely in the building structures and housing sectors. The UK market has experienced some reorganization as a result of major contracting companies which used to work overseas now concentrating on the home market. Consequently, there has been an identifiable trend for a rationalization of the market, as a number of medium-sized companies have been acquired or have taken part in mergers. The structure in most EC states is that of major companies and small specialist sub-contractors and builders. The same process has applied to a lesser extent with consultants, and the existing UK trend for restructuring of consulting firms is likely to continue.

The majority of EC states are accustomed to fixed-price, lump-sum packages, some without variations. The EC is also divided into relatively well-developed countries, with large construction sectors and a high proportion of annual expenditure on maintenance, and some less well-developed countries with major EC funding for infrastructure development. To compete in these markets UK firms are unlikely to seem attractive without making significant changes. The biggest detractors for UK competitiveness are the lack of local knowledge, experience and organization, and the reputation for disputes and higher final costs.

To overcome the difficulties of local contact, UK companies would probably try to identify slightly smaller firms in a specific EC market as potential targets for merger or acquisition. The target firm should be reasonably successful, have a good reputation for quality and performance and enjoy a key share in the market, probably in the housing sector. The UK firm would supply the ideas, the capital and certain key staff to dominate the operation, while fully utilizing the long-established trading goodwill and local knowledge of the target firm. In this way the UK company would be able to offer a simpler client package which would need to be fixed-price, lump-sum, possibly offer incentives on time or financial arrangements, and would demonstrate proven quality assurance and project management skills.

A similar process is also likely to happen to medium-sized UK firms with predator companies from other member states and from non-EC based countries. The United States, Japan and Scandinavia have all expressed interest in obtaining a domestic market position in the United Kingdom and other member states, and this would act additionally as an access to the Single European Market. If the United Kingdom does not compete in other member states, the end of the building boom would leave a large overcapacity in construction and the need for further rationalization.

Considerable concern has been expressed by both UK government ministers and industry leaders about the industry's apparent lack of preparedness for 1992. An important factor for UK construction companies is the identification of the knowledge and skills needed to compete in the new environment. In addition to the local presence and simplified client package, the UK firm requires a greater market awareness, a reorientation of the business to the target areas within the Single European Market, access to finance and more education and training in technical, financial, project management and linguistic skills.

12. Development of competition after 1992

It is always difficult to predict the future but it seems likely that the Single European Market could be the first step towards an integrated European state. The most rapid progress is likely to be made in these sectors in which integration has already become established. This would indicate that the construction products sector would be one of the first to take advantage of the new conditions. The trend for mergers and acquisitions is likely to continue as European companies slowly begin to emerge. The collaboration inside the EC is likely to lead to collaboration within world markets and in competition with major US and Japanese contractors. The Single European Market will inevitably result in more, rather than less, competition. The EC member states' economies are buoyant, but the construction sector is merely average and most of the heavy civil engineering industries are well down on output performances of ten years ago. UK firms will require to offer EC clients a simpler fixed-price, no claims package, and be able to integrate design, construction, financing and project management skills across the market. This will require collaboration, investment and staff education and training.

References

1. J. Paxton (ed.) (1984) *The Statesman's Year Book* 120th edn. Macmillan Press
2. Davis, Langdon and Everest (eds.) (1988) *Spons International Construction Cost Handbook*. E & FN Spons.
3. *New Civil Engineer* (1987) 'US and Europe up as overseas incomes slip', 7 August, p. 8.
4. Sandler, R. (1989) *Making Mergers and Acquisitions Work*, Management 89 Inc., Henry Stone & Son.
5. Commission of the European Communities (1987) *The Single Act – A New Frontier for Europe*, Bulletin of the European Commission.
6. *Europe Without Frontiers – Completing the Internal Market* (1987) Office for Official Publications of the European Communities (English Language), L-2985, Luxembourg.
7. Lasok, D. and Bridge, J. W. (1987) *Law & Institutions of the European Communities*, 4th edn. Butterworths.
8. *Public Works Contracts Directive* (COM(89)141), April, 1989.
9. *Compliance Directive* (COM(87)134 FINAL), 1987.
10. *Construction Products Directive* (COM(86)FINAL 3), 1986.
11. *Public Supplies Directive* (COM(88)42 FINAL), 1988.

Recommended reading

Griffiths, F. (1989) 'Project contract strategy for 1992'. *International Journal of Project Mangement*, 7, No. 2, May, p. 69. Butterworths.

Le Moniteur, *EC Special*. 30 Septembre, 1988, Paris.

Fisher, N. (1986) *Marketing for the Construction Industry*. Longman, Harlow.

Cecchini, P. (1988) *The European Challenge – The Benefit of the Single Market*, Gower.

The Cost of Non-Europe for Business Services, Peat, Marwick and McLintock, London, 1987.

Single European Act, European Commission No. 12, 1986, HMSO, Cmnd. 9578.

——— 14 ———

UK contractors in national and international markets

Jacqueline Cannon and Patricia M. Hillebrandt

1. Introduction

This chapter focuses on the strategic behaviour of large construction firms. The reference to construction firms rather than contracting ones is deliberate, for all large firms operate in markets other than contracting, and this feature of their structure also applies to their international businesses. It is therefore important to underline the relationship between contracting and other types of operations, as well as the reasons for the particular structure of both large construction firms and of corporations which include contracting firms in their portfolio of businesses.

The major source for the arguments developed in this chapter is a research project undertaken by the authors for Reading University and funded by the Science and Engineering Research Council [1].

The chapter is divided into eight sections. Section 2 establishes the range of activities undertaken by large construction firms, their organization structure and their approach to strategic decisions. It provides the frame-work for the following five sections which deal with selected policies: overall planning and finance; growth and diversification; international contracting; marketing and bidding; and the management of human resources. The last section draws together particular issues raised earlier in the chapter.

2. Business organization

Most of the large UK contracting companies have broadened their operations to include many other construction related activities, notably house-building and property development, but also production of building materials, plant hire and merchandising. Several are also now operating in completely different industries, such as mining and instrument manufacture. With one or two minor exceptions, diversification has been the result of a deliberate policy. It is discussed fully in Section 4 below.

Most of the top 30 companies have at some time operated abroad and most are still doing so. However, by no means all of their operations overseas are construction related, let alone contracting related. In the process of diversification construction companies have acquired or developed businesses in a number of industries in the United States, Europe, Australia and other countries. Almost none of these are contracting operations. When they are construction related, they tend to be housing or property development rather than contracting. Nearly all companies are prepared to operate anywhere in the United Kingdom. The breadth of their activities within contracting normally embraces both building and civil engineering, although only some undertake more specialized types of engineering. Their activities are concentrated on large projects. Even regional offices would not normally be engaged on very small works or repair and maintenance, although almost all the large contractors undertake major rehabilitation schemes.

Except where they have a subsidiary company specializing in a particular trade, for example scaffolding or joinery, they operate as main contractors sub-contracting most of the specialist trades to supply-and-fix contractors, and they increasingly sub-contract to labour-only sub-contractors.

Five features specific to construction affect the division of work between that carried out by the contractor and that which he contracts out. They are: the finite construction period of projects; the wide geographical spread of location of projects; the uneven demand for specific skills during the execution of the project; the wide diversity of required skills; and fluctuations in demand for particular types of work. These features taken together make it difficult to guarantee continuous employment or to guarantee the availability, in-house, of required skills.

For all large projects, some work is sub-contracted to specialist firms and there is virtual agreement among large firms that sub-contracting some services is the efficient solution to the problem of discontinuity in the use of skilled manpower. It is also the rule that local site managers have discretion as regards the type and extent of sub-contracting on individual sites, as they are expected to be monitoring the demand and supply conditions of the local labour market closely.

Both main contractors and supply-and-fix sub-contractors use labour-only sub-contractors. This type of relationship, at present prevalent in the south, is now becoming more widespread in northern regions.

When compared with direct employment, the main advantages of sub-contracting to large firms are seen in terms of reduced costs, increased efficiency and speed of work.

The main disadvantages are related to the adverse impact which reliance on sub-contracting may have on the availability and level of skills and risk and lack of control over sub-contractors. A particular worry concerns training, especially for trades and at supervisory levels.

The patterns of ownership of contracting companies are very varied, even among the large companies in the industry. In the first place some of them are part of a conglomerate. Second, a large number are family controlled, surprisingly so because it is generally unusual for any industry to have a high proportion of very large family-controlled firms. The reasons are largely financial and are described in Section 3. In many companies the current family member in control is about third or fourth generation. This means that the shares may be held by distant relations who may not wish to retain them in the long run (unless they have no option because they are in trusts). There are also difficulties in providing for succession and therefore doubts as to how long these family controlled firms will be able to survive.

In addition to those firms where the family has financial control, there are those which are publicly owned but still managed by people who are related to the original founders. It seems that because the industry is very 'people intensive', long associations between manager and managed, or in some cases owner and managed, are very important.

There are also one or two management buy-out companies among the largest construction firms. Thus, after allowing for the conglomerates, the family controlled and family connected firms and the very few management buy-outs, there are left those 'ordinary' companies, about a third of the total, most of which are mainly in construction but some of which have diversified into other businesses.

There is a great variety of organizational structures to take account of the diversity of business interests. It is usual to have each separate type of activity represented at main board level, for example UK building and civil engineering, housebuilding, property development and overseas work, as well as the functional representation which always includes finance. The personnel function is sometimes represented on the main board but one of the shortcomings of the companies examined seemed to be that, although all acknowledged the importance of people as the principal asset of the contracting business, they did not always pay sufficient attention to training, management progression and succession planning. Representation of the personnel function on the main board would help to correct this deficiency.

Below board level, companies are divided into operating units which are either divisions or subsidiary companies – the choice being largely historically determined. However, there are financial and marketing advantages in having limited liability companies for distinct work types, especially when operating abroad. Frequently, the division is the umbrella organization for a number of limited companies. Each division is either directly or indirectly represented on the main board and in many cases has a board of its own. Regional offices in the United Kingdom are also often run as quite separate organizations with their own boards. In some cases the regional offices are companies which have been acquired to obtain a fully geographical spread, and some companies prefer to retain the identity and name of the local company. They find this has advantages in marketing, and in giving the local management an identity which is good for both morale, and as a work incentive. Indeed, one of the advantages of a structure based on companies rather than divisions is that managers can enjoy director status. Unfortunately, in a few cases this has led to over-large, or too many, boards.

Companies vary considerably in the degree of centralization of service functions. In some there are strong head office services departments which the divisions are required to use. This may be linked to a detailed central control of the way sites and offices are run. In other companies all service functions are an integral part of the divisional or regional set-up, but the level of autonomy of the site itself varies greatly from company to company.

There are similar differences in the extent of formal consultation in committees. Some companies have a myriad of committees and meetings. One company, by contrast, is proud that it has no committees at all. Communication, apart from that in committees and meetings, could be by telephone, by messages on linked computers or by personal contact. These differences have substantial consequences for the attitudes of managers and form part of the 'culture' of the company, or of its philosophy. The company culture is important in all firms, but because the efficiency of individual sites is partly due to the quality of the relationships within short-lived management teams, culture is an important facet of companies' behaviour. Committees as formal meetings in which people can be brought together are one way in which the culture can be nurtured and subtly directed by the managers. They may also be helpful in getting the ultimate long-term objectives of the business across to the managers.

3. Strategy and planning

Three levels can be distinguished in the determination of strategy. The first is the mission of the business which is where the board members would ideally like the firm to be in the long term. The second level is the objectives which are finite goals expressed quantitatively and within a certain time frame. The strategy does not include the objectives, but is about the means of achieving them.

There is often a blurred line between mission and objectives and in many companies the mission is called an objective. Examples of mission are to achieve excellence in quality of performance and profit or to become a truly international contractor. In many companies so-called objectives are imprecise and lack a time frame which hinders the development of a coherent strategy.

Objectives vary according to the types of company. Family firms tend to have a wide range of objectives with some *acceptable* level of financial achievement combined with more social objectives including the welfare of the workforce, reputation and good relations with the workforce. In some cases companies also refer to modernization of the company, or development of new areas of activity.

Other companies place more stress on financially related objectives. The objectives of a company which is part of a conglomerate tend to be imposed upon it by the board of the conglomerate, and are almost purely financial.

Planning is the process whereby an agreed strategy is translated into more detailed targets and required actions which have to be completed within a fixed time frame. It is concerned with the achievement of objectives. The latter may or may not require action at levels below the company board, although it will require the board's agreement. For instance, the negotiations leading to acquisition of a company in the United States may be vested in a single member of the board, although the final sanction can of course only be given by the board itself.

Planning has a different role in contracting firms than in manufacturing firms. In the latter, planning in the short-term is constrained by the finite capacity of the production units. It is limited by the efficient use of the capital assets of the enterprise. Contracting companies are not capital intensive, but labour intensive, and hence planning is essentially concerned with ensuring that the required labour and management inputs are available in the necessary numbers, at the desired time and in the right place. Planning in this case is, therefore, a more dynamic function than in other industries. The ultimate capacity of the contracting firm is determined by the availability of the managerial skills which are required to ensure the successful completion of the projects that the company wishes to undertake. Contracting involves different relationships with the purchasers of construction products than those which other industries have with their clients. There are other aspects of the product of constructing which increase the complexity and uncertainty of planning in construction firms. These are the immobile nature of construction products and their one-off nature. There are inherent risks attached to the latter in terms of problems and delays arising from unanticipated events, such as different soil conditions from those which had been revealed in surveys.

Planning is also concerned with the efficient use of finance. Contracting firms should be able to generate a positive cash flow. There are four reasons for this. The first is that they receive payments for preliminaries in advance and thereafter on monthly certificates as the work progresses. Second, they can weight the bill of quantities so that they get higher rates for items at the earlier stages of the project. Third, many companies choose to pay sub-contractors only after they themselves have been paid, and in this process there may be delay. Last, they receive credit on purchases of building materials.

One of the aims of companies is thus to maximize their positive cash flow and to ensure that it is used to best purpose. In the case of construction companies which do not require extensive physical assets in their operations, the acquisition of land or property assets to bolster balance sheets is an important element of financial policies. How they achieve this aim is discussed in Section 4.

In a number of companies, the uncertainty attached to the future overall level of demand for construction products implies a greater degree of uncertainty about their prospects which results in shorter-horizon planning than is probably common in capital intensive industries. This applies more specifically to the future level of demand in the geographical areas where firms are able to operate and for the particular types of construction in which they have the necessary expertise. In manufacturing, the inevitable lags between the decision to expand facilities and the commissioning of additional capacity can span several years. In contracting, a few large projects may account for a high proportion of a firm's turnover and the difficulties in correctly assessing the rate of success in the bidding process favours a shorter planning horizon.

It is thus unusual for firms to extend formal planning processes beyond three years. The budget is the first input into the three-year analysis and, by definition, the most detailed. The larger the firm, the larger the average size of contract and the longer the construction phase; therefore the easier the three-year planning exercise becomes.

Where the firm's strategy involves a fundamental change in its range or type of operations, it may need to extend its planning horizon beyond the usual three years to up to five years. Those firms which consider two further years, will obviously tend to do so in less precise terms than in the shorter time horizon. In a few cases planning is not an independent feature of the firm's behaviour but is imposed on it by the corporation which owns it.

Objectives require actions which should be expressed in strategic terms, and detailed operational plans which should be fully understood by all those involved in their implementation. This process is not carried out with the same degree of care and attention in all companies. Correct downward dissemination may be lacking, or the board may be insufficiently aware of the objectives which subsidiaries or divisions have set themselves.

The elaboration of the planning process is not handled in similar fashion in all firms. In some cases, the process is one which involves detailed discussions between the board and the divisions of the company in a two-way exercise. In others, the process is handled within the company board and then imposed on the various parts of the business.

The goals of the planning exercise are not necessarily the same across a range of companies. In some they are expressed in terms of achieving a specified increase in total turnover and in profits. In others the contracting business is required to perform to certain standards expressed in a range of indices which, additionally, may include cash flow projections. With low capital assets, return on capital as an index of performance is of little use in the purely contracting business.

In an industry where the importance of skilled labour is crucial, it is interesting to note that the planning of human resources is not generally accorded the status and focus which it deserves relative to its other major resource – finance.

Within the range of policies which are linked together in the planning strategy of construction firms, the financial policy stands out as that which emphasizes the major differences between the process of contracting and that of manufacturing. In those businesses which are primarily contracting, the financial policy will include the use to which the cash flow from contracting could be put, that is, the excess of cash flow over and above that which is required to finance work in progress. If, as all firms intend, turnover and hence work in progress, are planned to increase, there will be a requirement for an increase in the use of cash flow. Given that there is a positive net cash flow, contracting firms will be keen to use it to acquire assets. In a contracting business the most likely outlets are land and housebuilding, or land and property development, with building material production as another possible outlet. The ownership of fixed assets is advantageous to those firms which will require to borrow to fund expansion programmes.

Given that an adverse outcome from a single large contract can have a very harmful impact on the firm, financial institutions may be reluctant to lend to construction firms which lack a firm asset base. Diversification may also be hampered if firms lack the necessary finance for the proposed acquisition.

The situation from the point of view of a corporation which owns a contracting firm is quite different. Modern corporations with a diversified range of activities welcome the contribution to the group's cash flow from its contracting subsidiary, and it is this particular feature which is the contracting firm's major appeal for predators.

The relatively low requirement for fixed assets may be the major reason for the large number of family-owned or controlled contracting businesses. Expansion of those firms, unlike that of more capital intensive ones, does not necessarily require the injection of additional funds necessitating the use of external capital and hence the dilution of the family shareholdings.

4. Growth and diversification

As suggested in the preceding section, the acquisition of a fixed asset base on its own provides justification for diversification by contracting business into other types of activity. However, the growth objective is often the main trigger for diversification and further growth in some form or other, and is the clear aim of large firms.

In construction firms, even in those well diversified into capital intensive activities, growth objectives tend to be stated in commercial terms based on profit rather than turnover, or on a larger asset valuation.

Where there are few prospects of higher profits through greater efficiency, the alternatives are internal or external growth. Firms will consider both methods, but they appear to plan for internal growth in a more controlled manner than when seeking expansion through external means. In the latter case, some firms seem content to have suitable opportunities drawn to their attention rather than pursuing them in a deliberate and purposeful fashion.

Growth of the contracting business should improve cash flow and hence feed the expansion of the capital-hungry parts of the company. An additional benefit from growth is that of increased opportunity for promotion, or other rewards, for managers.

Yet another reason for seeking external growth is the opportunity it offers to expand the company's managerial strength. This process may be a faster route to acquiring necessary skills and expertise, or for developing a different mix of related activities than might be achieved by internal growth. Conversely, underemployment of managers may be a spur to seeking expansion.

Other reasons for external growth of contracting activities include a desire for a wider geographical base, a change from regional to a national coverage, or from a national to an international enterprise. Personal ambitions of board members also have a part to play in the search for growth.

Growth can be achieved either by increasing the level of current activities or by diversifying into new types of activities, either horizontally or vertically. Horizontal diversification may be related to the existing business or be a move into a totally different sector. Vertical diversification can either be forward or backward. Backward vertical diversification implies extension of the existing business into that of its suppliers. Forward vertical diversification is defined as the extension into businesses to which the diversifying firm itself is a supplier.

Vertical diversification of both types leads to a greater degree of integration of the construction activity, or a more extensive role for a business in the construction chain.

All large construction firms, without exception, are now diversified to a lesser or greater extent, or are themselves part of diversified groups.

As with growth, firms can achieve diversification either by internal or external means. If they choose the internal route they have to recruit new skills, develop expertise and establish production facilities. This route will be slower than the purchase of a business. Risk of failure may also be greater in the former case, for instance where barriers to entry may have been incorrectly assessed.

The external route also has disadvantages. The most thorough investigations of acquired businesses may fail to uncover some adverse facts which would make commercial success less likely.

If management is a crucial element in the eventual success of the purchase, there is an added risk to the acquisition since those with the essential specialist know-how may leave the new owners. This problem was recognized by more than one company as a reason for exercising extra care when purchasing new businesses, and also for granting specialists a largely independent existence.

The particular financial circumstances of a diversifying company will dictate how the purchase will be made, that is by cash, by the issue of shares or a combination of both. A cash settlement may be preferred by companies with a large cash-generating contracting section of their business, and even more so by family-controlled firms keen to avoid the dilution of their shareholdings. For corporations, diversification is more likely to be financed by a share issue.

The scope for diversification by a contracting business is considerable and, as we have already seen, the majority of large firms have diversified into housing and property development. The direction and pace of diversification are not by any means uniform across the large construction firms, nor are those firms similar in the implementation of diversification policies, either in terms of why or how strongly they are pursued. In a few cases the reason may be historical, although elsewhere it may be accidental. One firm referred to its policy as 'evolutionary'. In another firm its diversification policy may appear relentless to outsiders.

Vertical and horizontal diversification are seen as capable of offering the right solution to a number of problems faced by contracting companies [2]. It has been suggested that there are two major reasons for selecting vertical integration. These are uncertainty and market failure, where the requirements of the industry are not available at the right place, time, price, quality or quantity. There are also two major justifications for horizontal diversification, the secular decline of parts of the market and the reduction of risks through the ownership of a business in a market where demand is relatively stable.

Reasons for diversification given by large construction firms corroborate the above positions. Broadly, they include an increase in profitable growth through new activities over and above increases available through the expansion of existing businesses, the means to greater efficiency in the use of in-house resources, an outlet for excess cash, and greater security. Increased efficiency may be achieved through the ownership or control of essential sources of materials, or by acquiring sub-contractors. Financial efficiency includes the most profitable use of cash flow. More than one company mentioned that interest earned was an important source of profit, but it will be obvious that companies will seek outlets which hold the promise of returns higher than ruling interest rates and which enable the acquisition of physical assets.

The unavoidable cyclical nature of contracting, at regional level even if not at national level, compounded by fluctuations in public sector demand in the past two decades, has led contracting firms to seek diversification into businesses where cyclical features are far less pronounced. Spreading operations outside the domestic market may also help to counteract these harmful cyclical movements.

There may also be extraneous reasons for diversification, including the acquisition of a business which is part of the purchase of another company.

5. International contracting

The market in international contracting has changed substantially over the last 20 years or so. World demand for construction work has fallen over the last decade or more, because of the fall in oil revenues which had been used to finance construction projects, and also because of the decline in aid from international agencies. The market has also changed in terms of the areas of demand, while work carried out by UK contractors abroad has shifted geographically. Very prominent is the rise and fall of markets in the Middle East, Asia and Oceania, and recently, Europe, with the fall in the Americas followed by a recent rapid rise.

There has also been a change in the types of operation of UK contractors. They no longer undertake so many one-off contracts sponsored by international organizations. There are two reasons for this additional to the decline in volume referred to above. The first is that these contracts are generally let in competition with a very large number of tenderers as in World Bank projects, for example, where it is not unusual to have 40 tenderers. The second reason is that there has been a dramatic upsurge in the ability of contractors from semi-industrialized countries to undertake major contracts abroad, and who are generally able to quote low prices either because they have low manpower costs or because they are receiving some form of subsidy from their governments.

While UK contractors continue to seek work all over the world they now tend to undertake only selected one-off contracts. This is especially so: where specialist expertise is required; where they are able to use some other special market advantage such as assistance with the provision of finance; or where they wish to nurture their connections in a specific area of the developing world; to ultimately generate a continuing flow of work there.

The United Kingdom has lost some of its comparative advantage in world markets. Its expertise and management may well be as high in quality as before but a number of other countries have also developed equivalent expertise.

UK contractors feel strongly that they should receive more assistance from government overseas missions and relevant government ministers in obtaining contracts abroad. They compare the assistance they receive with that of other European countries, notably France, where it is common practice for ministers to give active support to French contractors, by visiting the potential clients for example. Contractors are critical, too, of the way in which ECGD (Export Credit Guarantee Department) insurance and certain grants are administered. It has been suggested that the administration of export insurance would be better handled by a bank rather than by ECGD, even if no more money was made available. In these areas, too, it is claimed that European countries give considerably better terms for guarantees and insurance cover. Thus the overall failure of government to give adequate support is seen as a comparative disadvantage.

However, contractors regard the wide use of the British legal and contractual systems and the building regulations and specifications as a continuing advantage. In addition the high repute in which British consulting engineers are held, and the design contracts they obtain, sometimes facilitate the employment of British contractors.

Specific firms need to be large to carry the risks of working abroad and to bear the high costs of breaking into new markets. This normally takes a year or more, with the presence of a representative of the company in the territory in order to obtain the first contact. The cost of keeping a man abroad in these circumstances is over £100 000. Costs of estimating are two or three times those in the United Kingdom and the size of the initial project needs to be in excess of about £5 million before the costs of working there begin to be recovered.

With the inclusion of financial packages within contracting work, firms also need a large capital base. Diversified companies and those which are parts of larger groups are seen to be sound in this area.

Contractors increasingly have to differentiate the product they are selling abroad, and the ability to offer very specialized services helps in this respect, with the provision of financial packages as an important part of this operation. They are also starting to offer management contracts, which has an advantage for the client country in that the arrangements permit training for local contractors, although in the long run the UK contractor will suffer a further decline in his market from this approach.

Risk is an important element in working abroad because of unfamiliar environments, greater difficulties in controlling a project, different conditions of contract and the increased possibility of not being paid all that is due. Contractors who work continuously in a territory may be able to reduce some of these risks by increased familiarity with the environment.

For very large projects, a contractor will prefer to work in joint venture with another contractor so that the risks are spread and, in any case, some contractors have established a maximum size of contract which they will undertake alone.

The calibre of manager required to operate abroad is very high. He must be able to take decisions on his own, and deal with all the administrative and political problems as well as the actual running of the job. He is usually expected to prospect for further work while he is there. At the same time he must be completely loyal to his company and have good judgement of when to request help. It is not surprising, therefore, that those going abroad are often those with most drive and ambition. It is interesting that companies with a high degree of head office control over their UK sites have difficulty in finding the right personnel to operate abroad.

Successful overseas managers may find it difficult to readjust to UK conditions and the company may have problems, in the short run, of fitting them back into the UK business. Some return to work abroad. However, the skills which overseas managers require for work abroad make them particularly suitable candidates for ultimate promotion in the company, to the very highest levels.

6. Marketing and bidding

Marketing has not been well developed in contracting. During the long period in the post-war period, until 1973, the rise in the workload of the industry was such that firms did not need to market themselves to expand their activities, and the tendering system made marketing less important than with other means of contractor selection. Change came with the fall in domestic demand in the 1970s, with a move away from traditional methods of contractor selection and contractual arrangements, and with the need for sophisticated marketing in the expanding markets of the Middle East.

Although marketing is still not fully understood, most contractors are now actively trying to develop their own marketing policies. There are three aspects of marketing. First, the process of selection of which markets the company wishes to operate in is part of overall marketing strategy. It should be considered as part of the overall strategy of the company, or of the group as a whole. In most companies it is now considered as such and can lead to takeovers and mergers as well as to internal development of markets. Once the broad markets are determined it is for the individual operating units to refine the process and decide in which parts of various markets it wishes to develop its involvement most and, in some cases, from which markets it wishes to withdraw.

The second aspect is market research. This can either be linked to the process of determining what markets to be in, of deciding if more information is required for that decision, or to aid entry into selected markets. It must be linked directly into the market selection process.

The third component is that of selling, which involves a proactive approach of finding potential clients *before* they have formulated their ideas, and a reactive one which responds to a definite client requirement.

Companies experience great difficulties in integrating their marketing functions into their corporate strategy and in locating them correctly in their organizations. Traditionally, marketing has been one of the functions of operations managers. It is still so in some companies and it is important that they should continue to be involved in some way. However, it is increasingly being recognized as a separate function and most large companies now have someone in head office with marketing somewhere in his title. The role of that person varies from trying to develop all three aspects of marketing to simply producing publicity literature. Moreover, marketing is not given a sufficiently high status in most companies. It should be at sufficiently high level that the marketing manager has access to all relevant board papers concerning their markets, including the strategic plan which should be the point of departure for marketing work. This is certainly not always the case.

The move away from competition on price to differentiation of product (see Section 2) has led to the development of a number of new product packages. They may be divided into four types. First, most large contractors offer a range of different ways of management of the project and of contractual arrangements, for example management contracting or fast track construction. Second, they may extend the construction phase backwards into design with some form of design and build package in which they either provide the designer services themselves or commission others to do so, but in fact manage the process. Third, they may extend the process back beyond the construction phase into provision of financial packages. This is a particular aim of the large contractors operating in a substantial way internationally and where the edge provided by the provision of finance is important. Last, they may extend the process forward to furnishing, maintenance of the building and management of the facility. This is carried out by some firms, but is less important than the first three.

Bidding is in the hands of the operating units with reference to board members only if the contracts are especially large or risky. The decision on whether to tender for a particular project is dependent first of all on the company having the necessary skills to undertake the work, including estimating and management capacity at the appropriate time. The company then has to be satisfied with proposed payment arrangements, especially when operating abroad, and ensure that it is not bidding against too many competitors. Companies may decide not to bid because of some unsatisfactory experience in a particular area. Further disadvantages of a project may be taken care of in the bid price, including, for example, unsatisfactory past experience with client or designer, inadequate information and other reasons for high risk.

In determining their bid price, contractors take into account not only the actual outgoings on a contract, together with the risks involved, but also whether they might be better served by retaining their resources for use on another, possibly more profitable, contract by considering its opportunity cost. Their mark-ups on cost will be higher if they have much work, and also if their competitors are in the same situation and therefore likely to put in a high tender price. All contractors have a fairly clear knowledge of the identity of competitors and their order books, either from memory or from detailed records.

Risk is of course an important element in determination of price. Many types of risk have been mentioned above as reasons for a higher tender price. There is also the technical risk of the job, the danger that the company itself makes an error or manages the project badly, or that their sub-contractors do not perform well.

The problem is that the risks bear little relation to the size of the contract, so that it is difficult to express them in percentage terms. Although risks are less dangerous to the company if it has a large number of small contracts, there are many instances where one large contract, especially if overseas, has had a very damaging effect on the performance of the company as a whole.

The policies concerning risk carried out by the various companies in the industry vary widely, not only in bidding but also in the degree of volatility of the markets in which they are prepared to operate. Some companies take the line that contracting in particular, and construction in general, is a risky business and that to make good profits it is necessary to take risks. Others are averse to risk and prefer work with lower margins carrying less risk, rather than potentially profitable but more risky work.

7. Management

Efficiency in contracting is determined by the quantity and quality of managerial resources available to the firm. In contracting, the role of management has a special importance, due to some of the characteristics of the industry. These include: the one-off character of each project; the labour intensiveness of the production process; the range and variety of inputs into the process; the practical problems of ensuring timely delivery of materials and equipment and presence of labour; and the uncertain nature of projects due to weather and ground conditions. Each operating unit brings together representatives of different client and professional organizations. Finally, the wide geographical dispersion of activities often calls for decisions by managers without the ability to refer to, or seek counsel from, head office.

Because of the importance of quality management for success in the construction process, management planning and ensuring that the right type of managers are in place at all times is a more crucial aspect of company policy than in other processes.

Each new project is short-term compared to the typical manufacturing process, and each new site requires its own management team. The function of management planning is to ensure the smooth transfer of managers to form new teams, or to join existing teams at relevant times and at all levels of the organization. It is concerned with promotion and recruitment from outside the company to ensure that the company's operational plan will not be jeopardized by lack of management resources of the right calibre. Training is an important element in the development of managerial resources and is increasingly recognized within the industry.

Management planning in construction is thus an essential part of a company's strategy, and in this respect is different from that of other industries where it is possible to raise the level of output by increasing overtime without necessitating any change in the managerial capacity or the structure of the firm.

There are various types of promotional hierarchy within companies. These may be divided into those where a specialist rises through the specialist department to take control, or those in the general contracting management hierarchy where the progression follows the pattern of site manager to contracts manager, thence to regional or head office management function, and finally to the main board. While there are problems in the first category of a need for more management skills as well as technical knowledge, in general the specialist progression presents fewer problems than that of the main contracting stream.

The first stage of promotion, from site to contracts manager, implies a loss of direct physical control over the construction process and a loss of identity with a specific project. The contracts manager is managing site managers rather than sites. At the same time he will become involved in more office work, in report writing and financial control, and in different relationships to participants in the construction process, for example clients and the design team.

At the next stage of promotion to general policy-making, similar difficulties arise because what are essentially required are business skills. Many recently promoted senior personnel feel themselves deficient in some areas, most notably financial understanding.

There is considerably variety of practice and attitude to the question of internal promotion versus external appointment. Where vacancies arise, companies prefer promotion to external recruitment, and family firms in particular show strong support for internal promotion. Where external recruitment occurs, the main reason for it are: growth of the group; greater degree of specialization in the industry; growth of particular forms of contracting; the contribution from outsiders to innovative thought and better practice; a useful test of conditions of employment and remuneration on offer; a remedy for gaps in management development; and unforeseen increases in workload.

Some companies have now adopted a policy of filling approximately one third of new appointments through external recruitment. Considerable caution is required in this approach because of the importance of integrating new staff into the existing management teams. There is therefore a preference either for recruitment of staff known personally or from 'head hunting' or advertising. There may be an opportunity to acquire a management team through the purchase of another company.

Whether posts are being filled through internal promotion or external recruitment, some training will be required for new appointees. All major companies, of which data are available, undertake some form of training for managers and express their commitment to it. In practice, however, the implementation of policy in this area is very patchy.

Training takes place on the job, by moving personnel from one job to another in order to obtain experience, or by internal and external courses. In one company studied, there was a 'shadow board' set up to enable high-flyers learn the skills required for membership of decision-making boards.

At trainee level various experiments are taking place in addition to the usual approaches of taking in school leavers with 'O' and 'A' levels and training them to ONC and HND, or recruiting young building civil engineering or surveying graduates. In one company, its northern region recruits and trains staff for all areas because the supply is greater there, with costs being lower. Another company employs graduates of subjects unconnected with construction and trains them in construction work.

Monitoring of the size and age structure of the managerial force, and the selection, training and nurturing of high-flyers should be an integral element of management planning, but this function is not equally well developed in all large firms. One of the reasons for this may well be the low average status of personnel managers. Although in a few companies there is a personnel director on the main board, in general the personnel function is not in the mainstream of activity. In many companies personnel decisions are taken at subsidiary or regional level so that the group personnel manager has a peripheral advisory or informational function. This is regrettable in an industry which acknowledges that its main asset is its human resources.

8. Conclusions

There is no correct answer to the question of how contracting companies should be structured; what markets they should be in; or how they should be managed. Certain observations can, however, be made.

Firms are very dissimilar in their organization and structure and when attempts are made to relate particular types of organization and structure to performance, it is not possible to conclude that any one form is better than another. Tight central control on the one hand and devolution of authority on the other can both be found in successful companies. Companies with many committees and consultative arrangements can be equally as successful as those with few. What is important is that within a company the organization and structure should form a coherent system so that the various parts of the organization dovetail into each other and the communication system matches the organization.

An efficient planning system seems to be very beneficial to the performance of companies. There are examples where companies which apparently do not plan well have been fairly successful. However, those companies which had not performed well were also those that had an inadequate strategic plan or processes for its implementation. Improvements in the determination of objectives, in the strategic plan and in the planning process would seem possible in a number of companies. Also, in the field of personnel management, succession planning and marketing policy are two of the most obvious deficiencies.

Despite certain weaknesses, however, the overall impression gained from the research on which much of this chapter is based is that firms have greater concern with tight management and improved levels of efficiency than at any time in the post-war period. Those shortcomings which do exist are often recognized within the firms concerned but they do not necessarily know how best to deal with them. As firms have developed an awareness of the need for tighter management and improved efficiency, their knowledge of the best methods to achieve these will hopefully follow.

References

1. Hillebrandt, P. M. and Cannon, J. (1990) *The Modern Construction Firm*. London, Macmillan.
2. Ramsay, W. (1989) 'Business objectives and strategy' in Hillebrandt, P. M. and Cannon, J. (eds.), *The Management of Construction Firms: Aspects of Theory*. London, Macmillan, p. 19.

— 15 —

The Asia Pacific Rim – market opportunities for contractors

Anthony Walker

1. Introduction

The Asia Pacific Rim is a vast and diverse region. Using the limited definition of the region shown in Figure 15.1, the scale of the countries ranges from the third largest in the world in terms of land area and the largest in terms of population – China, to one of the smallest – Brunei. From the wealthiest in terms of GDP per capita – Japan, to one of the poorest – China. But these illustrations are deceptive. China appears poor on the basis of GDP per capita but on the basis of 'quality of life indicators' China really does not look like a developing country.

An examination of these indicators given in Table 15.1, helps to put the Asia Pacific Rim into perspective. It has a giant of modern industrialization in Japan; it has the 'newly industrialized countries' (NICs) – Hong Kong, Taiwan, Singapore and South Korea, those countries which could be classified as developing countries (although that is a term which is not well defined) and, finally, China – the enigma.

To generalize about the Asia Pacific Rim is to be in great danger of arriving at unsound conclusions; to compare it with other regions of the world is difficult. For example, Hong Kong now has a GDP per capita which is greater than that of the United Kingdom. But it is possible to note trends, some of which are established, some of which it is not known where they will lead. For example, Japan is economically dominant in the region. It has vast investments in all the countries and any country's disproportionate growth relative to its neighbours is likely to be as a result of Japanese investment. The developing countries of Indonesia, Thailand, Malaysia and the Philippines struggle to maintain consistent growth and, interestingly, the newly industrialized countries are all predominantly ethnic Chinese by origin. What sort of message does that situation have for the rest of the world in the context of China's struggle with political and economic pressures? What will be the long-term effects on China and the rest of the region from the events of June 1989 when the forces for democracy in China were curtailed by the Peoples Liberation Army?

Table 15.1 Quality of life indicators

Country	Population (millions) mid-1986	Population growth rate (%) 1980–86	Infant mortality rate (%) (per 1000 live births) 1986	Daily per capita calorie supply 1985	Life expectancy (years) 1986	Urban population (%) 1985	Literacy rate (%)	Cultivated[a] land (%) 1983	Per capita GNP (1986 $US)
China	1054.0	1.2	34	2620	69	22	65	41	300
Hong Kong	5.4	1.2	8	2692	76	93	77	9	6910
Indonesia	166.4	2.2	87	2476	57	25	67	18	490
Japan	121.5	0.7	6	2695	78	76	100	14	12840
Malaysia	16.1	2.7	27	2601	69	38	58	13	1830
Philippines	57.3	2.5	46	2260	63	39	83	41	560
Singapore	2.6	1.1	9	2696	73	100	83	11	7410
South Korea	41.5	1.4	25	2806	69	64	88	23	2370
Taiwan	19.7	1.8	---	2800	72	60	89	25	4989
Thailand	52.6	2.0	41	2399	64	18	88	38	810

Note:
[a] The Taiwan figures are the nearest available to the captions.
Sources:
World Development Report (1988), Oxford University Press, Oxford.
The New Geographical Digest (1986), G. Phillips, London.
The World in Figures (1987) compiled by *The Economist*, G. K. Hall & Co., Boston.

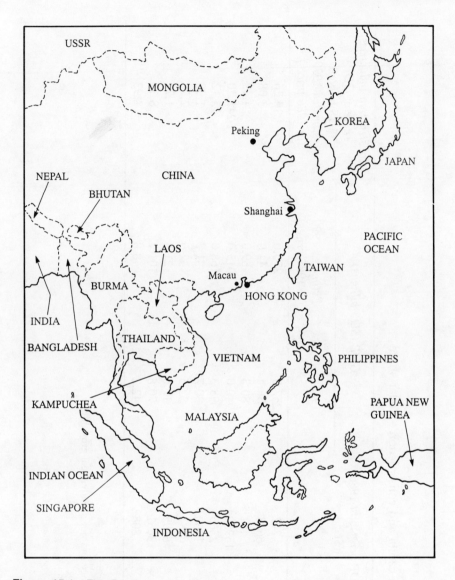

Figure 15.1 *The Far East*

2. The construction industry

The Asia Pacific Rim is powered by Japan's burgeoning economy and the rate of expansion of the region is much greater than the older established economies of Europe and North America. The construction industry is playing a leading role in this expansion, both benefiting from the developing commercial and industrial base and contributing to it by attracting investment from countries both within the region and outside it.

Table 15.2 GDP in total and per capita and construction's dollar share

	GDP per capita 1986 ($US)	GDP ($US billions)		Construction industries share of GDP ($US billion) estimated 1990 (at 1986 prices)
		1986	Estimated 1990 (at 1986 prices)	
China	242	257.0	270.0	10.26
Hong Kong	6618	36.4	44.0	3.08
Indonesia[a]	481	80.3	69.0	4.49
Japan	15980	1940.0	3015.0	241.20
S. Korea	2365	98.3	168.0	15.12
Malaysia	1930	30.7	31.7	1.90
Philippines	584	32.5	32.5	2.76
Singapore	6795	17.6	21.4	1.71
Taiwan	3661	70.8	101.2	8.10
Thailand	808	42.2	48.8	2.93

Note:
[a] Decrease due to depreciation of currency and not negative real growth.

Construction's share of gross domestic product (GDP) in percentage terms is given in Figure 15.2, with the dollar value of construction's contribution given in Table 15.2. These figures give a sense of the size of the market for construction work in the region. It can be seen that, generally, the more developed countries have a greater percentage of GDP devoted to construction, but in absolute terms even countries with a relatively small percentage of GDP devoted to construction have a large construction market in dollar terms, e.g. China. The strength of the construction markets in the NICs is well demonstrated, as they exceed those in much larger and more populous countries.

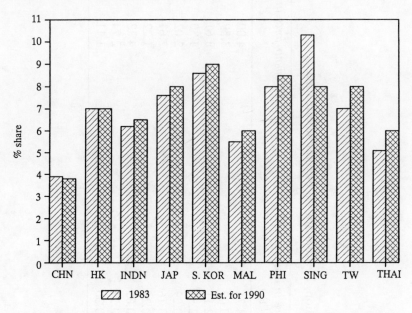

Figure 15.2 *The % share of GDP taken by construction (1983 and estimated for 1990)*

The size of the construction labour forces, as shown in Table 15.3 shows the enormous size of the industry in China. It also shows the larger percentages of labour involved in construction in the more developed countries, as a result of greater capital investment, both public and private, arising from their more wealthy economies. The feature is also reflected in the size of the industries as shown in Table 15.2, particularly the outstanding performance of Japan.

Such global figures can only give a sense of scale, structure and comparison of construction in the economies of the various countries. Such statistics are often unreliable, invariably produced rather late, and the bases on which they are compiled are often not compatible. The distinctive features of the industry in each country will now be discussed, using these overall figures as a backcloth for the region. The available data varies

Table 15.3 Labour force in construction, by total and % of total labour force

	Total labour force in construction (million)	% of total labour force in construction
China	18.74	4.00
Hong Kong	0.09	3.59
Indonesia	2.11	3.61
Japan	2.51	4.30
S. Korea	0.29	2.02
Malaysia	0.16	2.61
Philippines	0.23	1.22
Singapore	0.05	4.13
Taiwan	0.21	2.74
Thailand	0.30	1.11

considerably between countries in terms of amount, quality and reliability but the trends expressed are those generally accepted in the region.

2.1 China

The People's Republic of China (PRC) is the only communist country covered in this chapter. That in itself distinguishes China from other communist states in the Far East as China has presented opportunities for foreign contractors. No other communist state in the Far East, or perhaps for that matter in the world, is open to foreign contractors. However, in practical terms it is not as open as at first seems apparent, particularly since the suppression of the democracy movement in 1989 and the developed-world's reaction.

Significant changes in the last decade, led by the open door policy, had focused attention on China as an emerging major economic and political power. Yet it should not be forgotten that China is one of the more ancient of human civilizations, with a recorded history of thousands of years and one of the most volatile, as illustrated by the clamp-down on the democracy movement in 1989. Some parts of its technological base are highly sophisticated, as evidenced by the advanced satellite programme, but many are not. There is now a clear intention on the part of China to acquire and develop new technologies as part of its drive to modernize its economy.

The development and construction industry has ambitious targets to meet by the year 2000. The need to improve urban housing, for example, will mean that 3.3 billion square metres of new housing must be constructed, at an average rate of 200 million square metres per annum, about double the present rate. Tens of thousands of small towns will accommodate the vigorous development of the rural commercial economy.

In order to meet the new demands, the PRC has recognized that it must change many of its approaches. It was stated at the Sixth National People's Congress in Beijing in 1984 that the Chinese development and construction industry has for many years been plagued with such problems as long construction cycles and poor quality. It called for a reform of the industry, focusing on quicker construction times, improved quality, increased returns on investment, and the introduction of a public tendering system. The changes of the past decade have had three significant impacts on the construction market although in post-1989 it is not clear how they will develop.

First, the freedom was given to enterprises to make investment decisions and to raise funds which led to an increased proportion of construction work being financed outside the state budget, for example by domestic loans and self-raised finance. The resulting increase in demand for construction work produced shortages of building materials and generated higher prices. To counter this trend, restrictions on funds for extrabudgetary projects were introduced in the mid-1980s and access to loans was limited.

Second, foreign investment as a result of foreign investment joint ventures was increasing. It is still a relatively small proportion of the total but it does represent a large market in absolute terms. In 1987 the value of construction in joint ventures was Rmb 13.9 billion. Post-1989 there will be a significant reduction in investment from the Western economies.

Third, many major construction projects in certain regions can now be bid by competitive tender among construction companies. To a western contractor, competitive tendering may not seem a major step, but Chinese contractors have been used to projects being allocated to them.

A cornerstone of this policy is to attract foreign investment, technology and expertise, through joint venture arrangements with foreign parties. Since 1978, over 6000 firms have been involved in direct investment in China. This has invariably been achieved through joint venture companies comprising a partner from China and one or more foreign partners. For foreign investment joint ventures to be successful they must have efficient buildings in which to conduct their operations, whether these buildings be power stations, factories, offices or hotels.

In principle, foreign investment can be undertaken almost anywhere in China. However, the PRC has designated a series of economic zones in order to develop foreign economic relations and trade and in particular to encourage foreign investment through joint ventures. Special arrangements exist within the economic zones regarding taxation, import levies and such charges as are designated to provide strong incentives to foreign investors. So far, over 20% of China's total foreign investment has been in these zones. Investment from Hong Kong has amounted to 80–90%.

Fourteen coastal cities, together with the five special economic zones (SEZs) in Guangdong and Fujian provinces and the three open economic zones (OEZs) have been designated. They are:

The fourteen coastal cities

Beihai
Dalian
Fuzhou
Guangzhou
Lianyungang
Nantong
Ningbo
Qingdao
Qinhuangdao
Shanghai
Tianjin
Wenzhou
Yantai
Zhanjiang

Special economic zones

Shantou
Shenzhen
Xiamen
Zhubai
Hainan Island

Open economic zones

Fujian Delta
Yangtze River Delta
Zhujiang Delta

The SEZs have led the economic development of China but the 14 cities have vigorously competed for investment. In 1986, the government decided to concentrate attention on the best-placed cities of Dalian, Tianjin, Shanghai and Guangzhou and give them priority in funding and increased autonomy. About 60% of industrial and enterprise units in the coastal city areas are located in these urban areas and they produce over 75% of industrial value.

Some of the PRC's construction companies act as general or main contractors and others as specialist trade contractors. There are three types of ownership for construction companies in China.

First, state owned enterprises under the State budget are those enterprises under the direct management of the government's financial budget. They may be construction companies which are owned by ministries, for example the Ministry of Railway's various construction companies' annual work output in 1987 was Rmb 6 billion, which represented about 10% of the total output of state owned construction companies.

Second, collective owned enterprises not under the state budget but owned by the people as a whole (but in reality owned by the state): for instance, the provinces, municipalities and cities have local construction corporations which report directly to the local construction commission. A construction corporation oversees a number of construction companies within its municipality and is responsible for allocating resources to them. The role of the corporations is to coordinate the work of the companies under their control. The corporations are also responsible for various building associated organizations, such as component manufacturers. The nearest Western equivalent of a construction corporation would be a holding company. For example, the Shanghai Municipal Construction Commission oversees the Shanghai Building Construction Corporation which, in turn, comprises six construction companies.

Third, true collective ownership of construction companies through rural construction teams, although an increasing amount of work is being undertaken by collectively owned enterprises in the urban areas: the means of production are collectively owned by the workers, they can be run by villages, cities, towns and neighbourhood committees. The collective sector has grown rapidly since 1982. It operates almost entirely outside the state planning system.

In 1987, there were nearly 19 000 000 workers and staff members employed by 87 474 construction enterprises of whom:

- 6 392 000 work in 3 788 state owned enterprises;
- 4 059 000 work in 9 837 collectively owned enterprises in cities and towns;
- 8 284 000 work in 73 849 rural construction teams

Although the rural construction teams represent a large percentage of the total number engaged in construction, they are made up of small groups of people in house building and other small, simple projects for the local community with limited plant and equipment. They tend not to have highly skilled engineering staff; indeed many of their workers are unskilled and work mainly on the land. Sometimes they act as subcontractors on major projects, for example building workers' housing on a large factory project.

The larger construction companies employ as many as 25 000 people and work on major construction projects. In 1987 the total output of state owned construction companies alone was over Rmb 66 billion.

Within this framework, construction companies are licensed and classified into four categories in terms of the size of project which they are allowed to construct. The classification is based upon their fixed assets, expertise, and previous experience. Apart from the national contractors, they will normally undertake work only in the municipality or province to which they belong. However, they may work in other regions but need to obtain permission from the construction commission in the area in which they wish to work. Permission to work overseas can be given only by the state authorities.

The PRC has strict rules about the involvement of foreign general contractors in its construction industry. Foreign general contractors have worked mainly on some foreign investment joint ventures, foreign aid projects, World Bank, and special high technology turnkey projects such as power stations or chemical plants. Increasingly, they are discouraged from undertaking foreign investment joint venture projects in order to provide local construction companies with the opportunity to construct them.

Foreign general contractors are rarely employed on *local* projects because of the following:

1. China wishes to maximize and develop the use of its own labour and skills.
2. Foreign contractors have higher operating costs which, in general, result in their prices or tenders being higher than those submitted by indigenous companies.
3. Foreign companies will be paid in Renminbi for local projects. The Renminbi is not an internationally convertible currency.

The same discouragement does not apply to foreign specialist contractors which are encouraged for technology transfer. Also, foreign general contractors often act in a management role only, for similar reasons. Restrictions do not apply to consultants, although they are required to work in conjunction with a PRC design institute.

For a joint venture company which needs to build there are, in theory, four options available for construction, although the last two are rarely approved:

(a) the employment of a PRC construction company or a number of companies undertaking different sections of the project;
(b) the employment of a PRC construction company together with a foreign construction company which acts in a management role only;

(c) the employment of a PRC construction company together with a foreign construction company in a joint venture construction company;

(d) the employment of a foreign construction company.

A preparatory office may be used as coordinator when a number of separate PRC construction companies are employed for different sections of the work, and even when one acts as general contractor. Traditionally, a preparatory office has been established for local projects to handle procedures and submissions for approval, transportation, liaison with fire services, utilities and similar agencies, procurement, post-contract payments and final accounts, and to coordinate contractors and materials supply. This office acts as the 'client's representative' to ensure that the project progresses. It is mainly involved during the construction stage but its work does overlap the design stages in so far as procurement of construction is concerned. It is staffed by specialists who are responsible for ensuring that all the tasks which are commonly seen to be project management, are carried out. The specialists, e.g. engineers, are often permanent employees of the client's organization.

Alternatively a foreign project management organization may be used, which could be part of an overseas contractor's organization.

Construction can be organized in collaboration with a foreign construction company with whom the PRC construction company enters into an agreement. Generally, this option is allowed only when advanced technical and managerial skills are required for major complex joint venture projects, for example nuclear power stations. It is impracticable for a foreign general contractor to work in the PRC without the collaboration of a PRC construction company because of the problems encountered in obtaining local labour and materials and in dealing with the many parties and government agencies involved. Hence in many cases foreign general contractors provide only a project management service when working with a Chinese construction company.

However, foreign general contractors have been employed independently in the PRC, most frequently on 'high-tech' turnkey projects, but the PRC discourages their employment as main contractors. There remain exceptions, of course, as for instance the China World Trade Centre joint venture project in Beijing, the contract for which was signed in 1986. This is a $US231 million hotel, office and apartment complex which was awarded to a leading French general contractor, Societe Auxiliare d'Entreprises (SAE). One of the obligations of the contractor is to employ Chinese workers and provide technical training to the Chinese specialist trade contractors.

The China market is subject to political and economic uncertainty. Due to rising inflation and concern over the validity of the open door policy, 1988 saw a significant reduction in expenditure on construction. The reduction of plans for infrastructure development cut Rmb 50 billion from the budget and resulted in an easing of the chronic materials shortages of previous years.

Concern about quality of construction has resulted in a large number of Chinese construction companies working in Beijing and outside their own provinces being sent back. It was claimed that they were ill-managed or manned by farmers-turned-construction-workers with little experience.

As referred to earlier, the long-term effect of the huge student demonstration in 1989 is still unknown. It has led to caution on the part of investors with adverse effects on the construction market. It illustrates the greatest disincentive to working in the PRC – political uncertainty. It is likely to be many years before foreign involvement in the construction industry reaches the levels of the past.

2.2 Hong Kong

Hong Kong's construction industry has been faced with high demand since the recovery following the property slump in the early 1980s. It has faced unprecedented work loads as a result of its highly active economy. Hong Kong benefits from its unique geographical position, an industrious, intelligent and adaptive workforce and an entrepreneurial spirit. When these fundamental attributes were given the opportunities presented by China's modernization, the economy went into overdrive. The result is that there are now as many people working for Hong Kong firms in Guangdong Province in the PRC, over the border from Hong Kong, as there are in Hong Kong itself.

For many years it has been felt that, if China continued its drive to modernization Hong Kong would continue to prosper, and its construction industry with it. As well as its manufacturing base, Hong Kong is the commercial centre for all firms dealing with China and in addition it is now the gateway for Taiwan into China. The property market has been booming and there is plenty of government revenue for public sector projects.

Hong Kong now faces considerable political uncertainty, and it has resulted in a decline in confidence of both the Hong Kong people and the business community which may take a long time to reverse, but Hong Kong is a resilient and adaptive place.

Huge public sector projects are planned. The recently established Land Development Corporation is charged with the redevelopment of Hong Kong's neglected urban areas. New projects coming on stream include: a new airport and associated port facilities estimated at a staggering $HK30 billion, with the existing airport expected to reach maximum capacity by 1992–93, and even though Hong Kong has the busiest container terminal in the world a shortfall will occur from 1994; a third university – the Hong Kong University of Science and Technology – with a total estimated development cost of $HK2 billion; a third cross-harbour tunnel will be needed by the early 1990s and the government plans to spend $HK12–15 billion by 1997 on waste treatment and other environmental projects. A huge reclamation is due to take place in the harbour which will incorporate major new roads and a subway line and will provide central business district land for commercial expansion. These are just some examples of the public sector projects which are realities in addition to the normal expenditure on the more mundane infrastructure projects needed to develop the territory.

Illustrative of the private sector is Hong Kong's position in early 1989 as the fourth most expensive in the world for office space. This is due to a significant suppressed demand which is leading to the development of secondary commercial areas and also for mixed industrial and commercial use, something which is new to Hong Kong. The industrial sector is not under quite the same pressure due to relocation to China, but this may change. The residential market has remained buoyant in spite of the 'brain-drain' of young middle class families overseas looking to obtaining a passport as an insurance against China's mishandling of Hong Kong after 1997; and this may well accelerate. The private sector is characterized by companies which are developer/contractors for which profit is to be made on the development rather than solely from construction activities.

Access to the market is not restricted for foreign contractors. Hong Kong's free market economy provides the conditions which allow overseas contractors to establish in the territory. However, they may find the structure and organization of the industry difficult to cope with. The industry depends on a large number of small sub-contractors and most general contractors employ very little direct labour, but act mainly as a management organization. This does mean that they need to know intimately the miriad of sub-contractors and their capabilities. In such conditions delivery quality can be a problem. Local Chinese staff are necessary, or joint venturing with a local contractor could be a more viable way into the market.

A large number of overseas contractors are established in Hong Kong. While the Japanese dominate the group, the Koreans also have a large presence and there are French, German, British, Australian and many others. Some have been established in Hong Kong for over 30 years and could now hardly be called foreign.

Alongside them are a number of sophisticated local contractors, though the majority are relatively unsophisticated, local family-based firms. But while demand may be high, satisfying that demand is not easy. With opportunities comes competition, labour shortages and increased costs.

Despite bringing a rapid surge in demand, Hong Kong's spectacular economic growth has intensified the competitiveness of the construction market due to the influx of foreign contractors attracted by the contracts on offer. It is felt by many local contractors that the objectives and policies of Japanese and Korean contractors give these firms an advantage. The Japanese make most of their money in their domestic market and take overseas work because it enables them to obtain orders in Japan. Whenever possible, South Koreans bring their own staff, who are cheap by Hong Kong standards, particularly in the current labour shortage situation.

The construction boom brought a serious labour shortage problem to Hong Kong's industry. It is estimated that there is a shortfall of 100 000 workers, resulting in higher wages being paid, which has led to an escalation in construction costs. This situation is restricting the growth of the industry as a 25% annual growth may represent as little as 5% in real terms.

The government has resisted, until recently, the suggestion to import labour, due to the fear of creating adverse social effects. However, a first allocation of 3000 foreign workers was allowed in 1989, through this was for all sectors of the economy. The use of mechanization as a substitute for labour is a long-term policy and it is difficult to change the thinking and practices of the labour force. It is suspected that illegal practices by contractors to secure foreign workers has been taking place. The labour shortage was so chronic that the public sector housing authority had to reduce its annual target from 40 000 to 36 000 flats per year in 1989. A resultant problem is the reduction in quality of workmanship as a result of the labour shortage.

A recurring complaint of contractors in Hong Kong is the inhibition of technological change in the industry which is induced by government through its bureaucratic, and in many cases archaic, building regulations. Such procedures mean that technologically advanced construction techniques and materials are slow to be adopted and, even worse, designers and contractors do not bring them forward because they expect them to be rejected. It is thus easier to stick to the old methods.

Recent events have seen the completion of the Light Rail Transit System, the Hong Kong Convention and Exhibition Centre, the breaking through of the Eastern Harbour Crossing, the construction of container terminals 6 and 7 at Kwai Chung, the 70-storey Bank of China building (the PRC bank!), the Cultural Centre, the New Standard Chartered Bank and Pacific Place. These are just the spectacular buildings and there are many hundreds more which could be added to further if China continues to modernize.

2.3 Indonesia

Indonesia is a developing country of more than 17 000 islands in an area of two million square kilometres stretching more than 5000 kilometres. Its population of 175 million is growing at 2.18% annually, one of the world's greatest growth rates. It is expected to reach 216 million by the year 2000; 55% of its workforce are employed in agriculture, forestry and fishing and only 22% of its population live in urban areas.

The major problem for Indonesia is meeting the basic needs of its population: food; health; education; clean water; housing and a healthy environment. It has a pressing need to complete its economic infrastructure for land, sea and air transportation, communications and energy.

Indonesia's oil resources have provided the core of the country's income but rapidly falling prices have required Indonesia to quickly develop the export of non-oil products. As a result, drastic measures had to be taken by government to produce a balanced budget, which means that there were no government funded construction projects in 1988. To help achieve a restructuring of the economy, Indonesia is welcoming foreign investors and measures have been introduced to attract foreign investment. Sectors currently being highlighted are the tourist, agriculture, infrastructure, mining and energy industries.

Indonesia's economic recovery is taking place within a reasonably stable political environment, with the government's landslide victory in 1987 reiterating the stability of the military-backed government.

The construction industry is not buoyant, particularly for foreign construction companies, unless they are part of a package delivering foreign investment and technology. For example, it is reported that an Italian construction company has signed a $US208 million contract with an Indonesian–Hong Kong consortium to build a steel plant in Java. The plant is expected to have an annual capacity of 300 000 tonnes of seamless pipe used in oil rig construction. It is reported that Indonesia's state oil company, Pertamina owns 30% of the consortium, and that 39% is owned by Bakri Brothers, the country's leading non-Chinese private industrial concern. The state-run PT Kralatau Steel holds 4.9%, PT Encona Engineering 6.1% and the Hong Kong based Asia Pacific Pipe Investment 20%.

Areas which are more likely to provide projects are agriculture, tourism and housing. There is a continuing emphasis on low-cost housing but this is handled by local contractors who are more economical, as most components and materials can be obtained locally and they rely on traditional methods.

The scale of the housing programme is impressive. Indonesia needs some 780 000 units of houses annually, according to a recent report presented by Soernarjobo Danoedjo, Director General of the Public Works Ministry. The Jakarta city government has set a target of about 70 000 units a year for the next 11 years, when the population of the capital is expected to grow from 7.5 million today to about 12 million. Other big cities such as Medan, Surabaya, Semarang and Bandong, each with a population of 2 million, have a big demand for medium- and low-cost houses. The major factor in achieving these targets will be opening up new sources of finance to reduce dependency on government subsidy.

Hotels may be in demand but the tourist hotels in the resorts tend to be built using local contractors, materials and techniques, and demand in Jakarta is producing occupancy rates of about 70%.

Foreign aid is provided from a number of sources and foreign contractors have been involved in projects arising from such sources. It is often required that joint ventures be formed with local contractors but this has not always been viable.

There is, however, no shortage of skill among Indonesia contractors and developers for handling large projects. In response to the government's increasing tendency to opt for localizing major projects, eight Indonesian companies joined forces to undertake a most challenging toll-road project.

The group, comprising financial institutions, cement and steel manufacturers as well as contractors, have been given three years to complete 12 kilometres of elevated highway over a busy ring road and another 4 kilometres of highway at grade level. The group, through its joint-venture company PT Citra Marga Nusaphala Persada, is to recoup the investment by toll collection for 18 years under the terms of the concession agreement signed with the government. Total value of the project is estimated at Rp291 billion, making it the biggest road project currently underway in Indonesia.

Foreign construction companies are not allowed to be established and can only enter the market in joint ventures with local companies, which in any case is in the best interests of both parties. Interestingly, at least one construction company exists which is wholly foreign but this is an anachronism since overtaken by new legislation.

The office, retail and industrial markets show no widespread opportunities, although there is some demand in all areas. For example, a Korean contractor was responsible for the structure and finishes of Wisma D Larmala Sakti, a 24-storey prestigious commercial/office building in Jakarta, under a construction management arrangement.

It is in the long term that Indonesia may present an attractive market as there are plans to build a mass rapid transit system in Jakarta, and for further toll-roads. Foreign companies are attracted to Indonesia to establish manufacturing bases because of low labour costs and the availability of raw materials.

The position of Indonesia was well stated by Henry Boldrick of the World Bank [1]:

> Indonesia is currently one of the more successful examples of structural adjustments in the developing world, having reacted swiftly and decisively to the effects of the oil price slump with a comprehensive economic reform programme beginning in 1983 which has brought public sector spending under control and is stimulating the non-oil industrial sectors.
>
> The Government has indicated its willingness and ability to continue to adjust with last year's measures. While the adjustment process involves hardship and this process is not yet complete, by making the hard decisions early, Indonesia has avoided the extreme suffering being experienced by many countries.
>
> Structural adjustment has involved constriction of the construction sector, and necessarily so, as oil which has long been the driving force of both the public and private sectors' expenditures of Government and business had to be brought into line with revenues.

2.4 Japan

Japanese contractors' penetration of construction markets in other countries has been dealt with elsewhere in this book. What this section will consider is the scope for foreign contractors to obtain work in Japan's domestic market.

Until the agreement in May 1988 between the Japanese and US governments, designed to facilitate foreign companies' access to the Japanese market, such opportunity was extremely restricted, in sharp contrast to the opening up of overseas markets to Japanese contractors. Although the US construction industry and government were the prime movers behind the agreement its provisions are not limited to US companies, and all foreign contractors are eligible to benefit from its terms.

It is predicted that South Korean contractors, who now have surplus capacity and cultural and geographical advantages, may be the most successful at breaking into this difficult market. It is felt that Korean firms will take a long-term approach and turn to Japanese sub-contractors of Korean descent for a competitive advantage, in contrast to profit-taking US companies. By late-1988, six Korean firms had been licensed to construct in Japan and seven more applications were pending, with one US firm having been licensed and one pending.

However, the ability of US firms to offer advanced technology and Korean firms' inability to import cheap labour, may give the US companies an advantage over the Koreans, but both of them will find it difficult to compete with the Japanese in their own market. For example, the Trans-Tokyo Bay Highway Corp has chosen 12 Japanese construction companies in preliminary bidding for part of the ¥1.5 trillion Trans-Tokyo Bay highway project.

Rejected applicants included 40 Japanese firms and the South Korean firms – Hyundai Engineering & Construction Co. and Samsung Construction Co. In December 1988 one US and three South Korean companies were among bidders for shore-protection construction work on one of two man-made islands that are part of the project. No foreign firms were chosen in the preliminary bidding for that work either. The company, however, has chosen the US Bechtel group to act as consultant for a project to build one of the two man-made islands.

By any standard the Japanese domestic construction market is huge, five times as large as the rest of the Asia Pacific Countries combined. Moreover, government spending on public works in Japan is on the increase, and with Japan's new prosperity a number of megaprojects are being planned to improve infrastructure and the quality of life.

Japanese contractors, having become distinctly less competitive in bids for overseas work, due to the present high level of the yen, are enjoying the boom at home where margins are excellent, and they are looking to increase their own activities in the domestic market, and more so as the megaprojects come along. On the other hand, access by foreign contractors to the Japanese market has in the past been very restricted. It is perhaps not surprising, therefore, that the issue of participation by overseas contractors in the Japanese construction market should have become a trade issue with the United States and the EC.

The one-trillion-yen Kansai International Airport project, in particular, has been at the forefront of recent intergovernmental trade discussions on the liberalization of the Japanese market. Much of the debate over such projects as the Kansai airport has been generated by the 'designated bidding system' used to award public works contracts in Japan. This involves the listing of 'approved' companies from whom candidates are selected and then invited to tender for the work. It is claimed that the system ensures that smaller companies are given an opportunity to secure government contracts in circumstances where only the larger construction companies might succeed if an 'open tender' system was used. Critics of the system argue, however, that, in effect, it excludes overseas contractors who, although possessing relevant experience in other countries, do not have an existing track-record in Japan.

In addition, non-competitive (illegal) fixed bidding (a process known in Japanese as 'dango') is widely thought to be practised by contractors in Japan, even though such measures are outlawed by the Japanese Anti-Monopoly Act and the criminal code. Indeed, the chairman or the Japan Institute of Architects was recently quoted as reporting to the US Trade Representative's Office that the actual bidding procedure in Japan was a mere official formality and a 'sham'. However, prosecution of those alleged to be involved in dango practices is rare.

Thus, against this background, in May 1988 the Japanese and US governments concluded the agreement designed to facilitate market entry into Japan by overseas companies. It is to be noted that the agreement does nothing to lift the almost total ban which exists on the entry of foreign labour into Japan, in spite of the reported shortfall of around 100 000 workers in the construction industry. Japanese immigration laws are in this respect some of the toughest in the world despite Japan's claim that it is trying to 'internationalize' its outlook. However, what the agreement does is to permit foreign companies involved in the construction industry (whether as contractors, consultants or suppliers) to become qualified to bid for certain defined major public works in Japan, without regard to their prior experience in the country.

These 'special measures' (which are outlined below) are intended to overcome the 'chicken and egg' problem facing many foreigners who want to operate in Japan but who do not have the Japanese work experience required to qualify in the first place. The agreement is not without its critics, however, both in Japan and elsewhere, who claim that it is insufficient to overcome other 'non-tariff barriers'. These include not only 'dango' but also the Japanese system of sub-contracting, where it is feared that the threat of 'blackballing' by the big Japanese main contractors will deter Japanese sub-contractors who might otherwise contemplate working for a foreign contractor.

The public works projects listed for implementation, in accordance with the agreement, are Phase III of the Tokyo (Haneda) Airport expansion plan, the new Hiroshima Airport, the Akaski Kaikyo Suspension Bridge over the Seto Inland Sea, the Ise Bay Highway, the Yokohama 'Minato Mirai 21' International Conference Centre and the Kansai Science Park. The Japanese government has confirmed that the agreement does not detract from the right of foreign companies to seek participation in other public projects not listed in the agreement (although application of the special measures is limited to the designated projects).

The special measures themselves differ slightly, depending on whether the foreign company is seeking to provide consulting services, construction services or goods. However, in general terms, they set up a procedure whereby prospective tenders may register their interest in a particular project or projects in advance of the designation process, which will then notify those companies who are to be invited to tender.

Registration of interests are to be accepted three times a year, or more frequently if considered necessary. In the case of construction companies seeking registration, the agreement states that they may be required to provide evidence that they are duly licensed under Japanese law to carry on construction business in Japan. This licensing procedure is discussed further below. On a practical level, it clearly makes sense for foreign contractors wishing to participate in projects under the agreement to obtain the necessary contractor's licence before seeking registration for a particular project.

Once interested parties have been registered the agreement provides for each applicant to be ranked by reference to nine specified criteria. These include turnover, issued capital, staff numbers, financial ratios, number of years in business, and safety and welfare records. Different factors carry different weightings and the agreement contains a formula to be used to calculate an applicant's final ranking. It is expressly laid-down, however, that in examining a foreign firm's credentials, experience overseas will be treated as equivalent to experience in Japan.

As to the designation process itself, the agreement requires that initiation of the process for each project is to be advertised in the (Japanese language) trade press, together with relevant details of the contract including pre-qualification requirements, contact points, date of explanatory meeting, etc. Details of the specification and contract terms and conditions, will also be made available to registered applicants during this period. While certain specified information (e.g. addresses for contact points) is required to be in English, it is to be assumed that all other documentation will be in the Japanese language.

The agreement stipulates that designation of those companies to be invited to tender will follow within 30 days of advertisement. In deciding whether or not to designate a foreign construction company, the agreement provides for such factors as 'business conditions, results of its previous construction works and its technical competence' to be taken into account. Presumably, a company's previously determined ranking will also be a relevant factor, although this is not expressly stated in the agreement.

Unsuccessful applicants are to be told the reason for their non-designation. The agreement also provides for a further 40 days to elapse before bidding takes place, with contracts to be awarded to the lowest bidder below a specified ceiling price.

However, the agreement does anticipate that the procedure may not always be appropriate and provides that the whole designation process may not be applied 'in cases where urgency is required, where high confidentiality is involved, where no alternative is available or where proprietary rights are involved'.

In addition to the public projects referred to above, the agreement identifies a number of projects in the private sector where the Japanese government will 'actively encourage' employers to take steps to ensure that their procurement policies provide competitive opportunities for both foreign and Japanese companies without discrimination. These projects include terminal construction at the new Haneda, Hiroshima and Kitakyushu Airports as well as the Tokyo Teleport and Osaka Technosport projects.

Among the steps which the Japanese government expects private sector employers to take are the provision of technical information to foreign firms, giving foreign companies the opportunity to discuss technical requirements and allowing tenderers a reasonable time in which to submit their bids. In the past, some foreign contractors have felt that such pre-contract matters have been conducted in a way that effectively excluded them from participating.

US contractor Schal Associates Inc., in joint venture with eight Japanese contractors, was successful in securing one of the listed projects, a ¥17.95 billion contract on the Minato Mirai 21 development in Yokohama, and other contracts are expected to follow.

The agreement itself is to be viewed by both governments after two years to see whether the arrangements are serving the intended purpose of facilitating foreign access to the Japanese construction market. Depending on the results of the proposed review, the measures covered by the agreement may be adjusted. It is therefore to be hoped that there will be sufficient foreign interest in the current list of projects to justify a renewal of the present agreement when it expires.

Market opportunity apart, Japanese law requires that all contractors must obtain a contractor's licence, as specified by Construction Business Law, if they wish to engage in construction in Japan. This applies to both Japanese and overseas contractors. Contractors' licences are obtained from the Ministry of Construction if it is intended to have business premises in two or more prefectures. However, if it is intended to set up an office in one location only, then the application is to be made to the local government of that prefecture. A further licence is required if the contractor wishes to sub-contract more than a specified amount of work.

The requirements which have to be fulfilled in order to obtain a construction licence are detailed and the Japanese Ministry of Construction has produced an outline guide (in English) to assist overseas contractors in this respect. In essence, however, the authorities will need to be satisfied that the following four requirements are met:

1. The applicant has experienced management with at least one full time director who has five or more years' experience in managing a construction company;
2. The staff of the local office in Japan will include a full-time qualified engineer;
3. The company will be able to fulfil its obligations under the contracts which it intends to enter into;
4. The company exhibits a sound financial basis, by reference to defined criteria.

Management experience and professional qualifications obtained overseas can be recognized if comparable to those obtainable in Japan, although such matters are examined by the Ministry of Construction on a case-by-case basis. All applications must be completed in Japanese and filed with supporting documentation to the prefectural or central government office as appropriate. Once licensed, a contractor who wishes to participate in bidding for a public works project is required to submit details of his previous experience, etc., to the prefectual or central government for examination.

One American company, Pacific Architects and Engineers at one time held the only construction licence granted to a foreign enterprise for some years. In 1987 Bechtel was licensed, and recently Fluor-Daniel also from the United States, obtained a contractor's licence. More licences can be expected, and in addition several joint venture tie-ups are being made between Japanese contractors and foreign contractors to carry out work in Japan and to conduct research and development.

This section has drawn very heavily upon an article in Building and Construction News *dated 26 April 1989 by Richard Curl, who is an English solicitor also qualified to practice in Hong Kong and in Japan as a registration foreign lawyer* (gaikokuho jimu bengoshi). *He is a resident partner in the Tokyo office of McKenna & Co (known locally as the Richard A. Eastman Richard J. Curl Law Office) and has over 12 years' experience in the fields of building and engineering law and practice both in the United Kingdom and the Far East.*

2.5 Malaysia

After a number of years of stagnation the property market has recently shown signs of activity, although the uptake of an oversupply of office and hotel space will require a number of years' growth. The recent private sector activity has been in the residential, agricultural and industrial sectors.

The oversupply of office space resulted in 2.2 million square metres of the 5.04 million square metres available in Kuala Lumpur being empty in 1986 and this increased by a further 1.8 million square metres in 1987. The situation has been exacerbated by the movement of tenants from purpose-built office blocks to lower rental space in the upper floors of shophouses, and has worsened in 1988 and 1989 with further space coming onto the market. The hotel sector occupancy rates have been down and a number of projects have been abandoned.

For the construction industry Penang has been the most attractive location. The demand for industrial property has been high to satisfy electronics and manufacturing industry, but an oversupply of office space exists. The KOMTAR project covers 27 acres and is being developed in phases. Phase 1 constitutes a 65-storey office tower and a 484-room hotel. It will be constructed in five phases which could take until the late 1990s to complete. Residential demand is expected to rise in Penang and some ambitious reclamation projects are planned.

The public sector is likely to be more productive for contractors, with housing and infrastructure projects being the most promising and a housing target of about 120 000 units per year. The $M3.4 billion North–South Express Way is an example of the infrastructure development needed. This project is headed by United Engineers Malaysia teaming up with a number of foreign contractors and it is expected that contracts worth about $M4 billion will be awarded annually for the next few years. This compares with the peak of $M6 billion in 1982.

A number of projects have been shelved or abandoned, including hydroelectric schemes and housing projects, in addition to hotels. The easing financial situation may see some of them revived and it was expected that the construction sector would record a 2.5% growth in 1988, and that reasonable levels of activity should be achieved during the early 1990s.

There are certain restrictions on foreign contractors operating in Malaysia which reflect the 'Bumiputra' policy of the government. This policy is designed to give advantage in business and other walks of life to native Malays, working not only against foreign companies, but also against other ethnic groups who are Malaysian citizens, such as the Chinese.

The three measures applying to public sector construction projects are as follows:

1. The restriction of civil engineering projects below $M50 million to local contractors.
2. Civil engineering projects over $M50 can be tendered by local firms and locally incorporated joint ventures between Malaysian and foreign contractors. These joint ventures must, however, operate on a permanent basis and not on a project-by-project basis.
3. All projects for building works (as opposed to civil engineering), irrespective of value, are restricted to local firms only.

It seems that for the civils projects over $M50 million, 30% of the work should be undertaken by 'Bumiputra' companies. Firms would normally wish to do this in any case for reasons of economy and logistics. Such regulations are laid down in Treasury circulars and built into tender documents.

Such restrictions to not apply to private sector projects, but nevertheless it is valuable in terms of establishing relationships for foreign firms to 'look local' by taking a local partner. It is also good business sense to gain knowledge of, and access to, the local industry.

Japanese construction companies are the largest foreign group, they are in all Far Eastern countries, constituting 30% of the estimated 93 multinational construction companies operating in Malaysia.

In common with many South-East Asian countries Malaysia has its political tensions and volatility and it pays to monitor the situation and gauge future directions.

2.6 Philippines

After many years of uncertainty and inactivity, the Philippines' property and construction industries are showing signs of activity. However, foreign contractors are still reluctant to develop a high profile in what is still a politically uncertain environment.

The future may be brighter for the Philippine economy, which grew by 5.7% in 1987, largely fulled by domestic demand. The growth is expected to be higher in future because of increased foreign and local investments and robust spending by urban dwellers.

Construction activity is highly visible in three areas: the Makati Financial Centre; the site of the new Asian Development Bank (ADB) in nearby Pasig town; and the Chinatown district in Central Manila. The Philippines' tallest structure is the 43-storey Pacific Plaza, a 750 million peso prestige development.

In Chinatown, high-priced condominiums are also going up amidst the small shops, food stalls and two-storey buildings which date back to early post-World War II years. A fully furnished three-bedroom unit in the Pacific Plaza selling for 6.3 million pesos approaches European and US standards.

The largest activity is in the Pasig area where South Korea's Hyundai Construction Company built the new headquarters for the ADB, a 47-nation institution that makes low-interest loans to Asia-Pacific countries. A nine-storey main building comprises 1200 rooms for up to 4000 employees. The $US171 million building has a floor area of 131 000 square metres.

There is a feeling, therefore, that the construction industry may be set for a major injection of work, following growth during 1988. The number of registered contractors in the Philippines rose to 4370 in 1988 and the forecast is for further growth.

Though mining is the spearhead of the economy, the construction industry is the fastest growing sector at 14.8% and this growth is anticipated to increase further when the government infrastructure programme is up and running. The road system in the Philippines is in great need of upgrading as rural roads are few and far between, and for the most part in poor condition.

Despite the fact that hundreds of thousands of Filipinos are working throughout the world in the construction and other sectors, the local industry is very labour oriented with a rich supply of labour.

As well as major government expenditure through loans from the World Bank and the Asian Development Bank, private investment in the construction sector increased by 15% on the 1987 figure.

One major infrastructural project which appears, after more than 20 years, to be leaving the drawing stage, is a huge dam about 60 kilometres outside Manila. The project is aimed at alleviating some of the water problems faced by the city as its water table continues to fall.

Joint ventures are being initiated with valuable incentives being provided. For example, Republic Glass Corp. and Asahi Glass Corp. of Japan have obtained Board of Investments (BOI) approval for a $US100 million joint venture in float glass manufacture. The glass venture is the second largest joint venture in the country, next to the $US220 million petrochemical plant by two Taiwanese companies, USI Far East and China General Plastics. Republic Glass is to have a 60% majority stake in the project.

The BOI has granted the project a six-year income tax 'holiday', and other incentives such as duty-free capital equipment imports and tax credits on domestic capital equipment and raw materials and wharfage duty exemption. However, the board has required the joint venture to put up an equity of at least 970 million pesos in advance of its commercial operation, which has been set for 1991.

A particular aspect of the construction programme in the Philippines is US Armed Forces construction work. In 1989 the US House of Representatives approved almost $US46 million as follows:

Navy

Public Works Centre, Subic Bay	$27.8
Power Plant	

Air Force

Clark AFB

Aircraft Operational Apron	$5.0
Dormitories	$5.2
Flow Through Shelters	$4.2
Intelligence Facility	$2.2
Security Police Operations Facility	$3.2
SOF-Hangar/Nose Dock	$2.1
SOF-Helo Maintenance Facility	$4.1
Family Housing – 260 units	$19.9

The Pacific Preference gives US contractors a 20% bid preference on military construction projects over $1 million in US possessions and former trust territories in the Pacific, provided that the low bid by a qualified US firm is within 20% of the lowest qualified bid by a foreign company. For example, Turner International Industries Inc. was awarded an $US8.2 million contract to construct a commissary mall at the US naval base in Guantanamo Bay, Philippines.

The Philippines is the most westernized of the Far Eastern countries, due principally to the influence of the United States. It has a rather bureaucratic system and has yet to attract great activity from foreign contractors but its potential is undoubtedly high, given political stability.

2.7 Singapore

Singapore as a city state of just over 620 square kilometres in area, with a population of about $2\frac{1}{2}$ million, has limits therein on the size of its construction industry. Its topography works against civil engineering projects, as it is relatively flat and there is a well developed infrastructure, particularly with the recent completion of the Mass Rapid Transit rail system. It is certainly a developed, if not 'overdeveloped', country. The housing problem has been solved with 85% of Singaporeans living in the more than half a million flats built by the Housing Development Board. Three-quarters of occupiers own their flats.

Following a number of years of sustained slump in the construction industry, 1989 saw a turn to growth in new and retrofitting construction work. In 1989, the industry expected to exceed $S4 billion in new and retrofitting projects, at least 20% more than 1988's estimated figure of $S3.3 billion. The optimism was due to the upturn in the local property market and the prospect of about $S7.6 billion in public sector projects coming on stream over the following three years. In the private sector, planning approvals totalled $S1.6 billion in the first nine months of 1988 compared with $S1.5 billion for the whole of 1987.

The biggest problem confronting contractors is how to counter the effects of the slowdown in the various government building activities, especially the Housing and Development Board's public housing programme. The industry has traditionally relied on the government for most of its work. During the boom years in the early 1980s, public sector construction contributed to two-thirds of the total workload, growing to 90% in 1986.

Most of the infrastructure works initiated in the past few years have been completed. The Housing Development Board, by far the largest developer in Singapore, has reduced its annual building target from a peak 60 000 units to a current 20 000 or less. As a result, work from the public sector only reached a monthly average of $S167.9 million in the first five months of 1988, down almost 30% against 1987.

The Ministry of National Development data show that the monthly average for work in the private sector was $S145.5 million in the first five months of 1988. Most of the new projects launched were for residential developments, followed by factories and warehouses. The volume of industrial projects showed a marked increase, in line with the recovery in the manufacturing sector. Jurong Town Corporation awarded a total of $S25 million work in the first quarter of 1988 compared to the $S4 million awarded for the same period in 1987.

In the private sector, the jump in demand was due to the $S223 million spent on residential construction, which represents a 73% increase over the volume of housing construction work awarded by private developers in the first quarter of 1987.

For private commercial and industrial buildings the volume of work increased to $S66 million from $S57 million in the same period in 1987.

The rapid development of Singapore, and the consequential slow down in new property development, has seen the development of maintenance and retrofitting as a significant part of the construction industry's workload as it became economically viable to rehabilitate older properties. Such work, valued at $S845 million in 1987, about 21% of total construction work, was up 26% on 1986 and was projected to reach $S1 billion in 1990. As a result, government is studying the possibility of bringing forward the upgrading of older public housing estates to provide a greater workload for the industry.

Even with its relatively low demand for construction work, Singapore suffers from a labour shortage in the industry. This is particularly so as the upturn in the industry has coincided with the expulsion of more than 10 000 illegal Thai immigrant construction workers. It is suggested that they may be replaced by Malaysian workers attracted by the higher pay in Singapore, which could produce a shortage of labour in Malaysia as opportunities for work increases there. It is also suggested that many Thai workers will return legally. The shortage exists in spite of the Construction Brigade Scheme which has trained some 5000 men enlisted in Singapore's National Service. An estimated 25.2% have remained in the industry since the scheme was revised in 1985, and another 7.3% are employed in building-industry-related works.

Although there are no legal restrictions on foreign contractors becoming established in Singapore, and there are no real problems of importing staff, it is considered to be a tough market in which to earn money. There are a large number of foreign contractors active in the market and there are regulations which favour local firms. These local preference rules change frequently but an example is where local firms which are 50% or over Singaporean gain a 5% bidding advantage with a maximum $S5 million discount. There is a sliding scale of advantages depending on what percentage of the firm is Singaporean owned. Joint venture arrangements which are acceptable are usually specified in public sector tender documents.

The difficulties facing foreign contractors are illustrated by local construction companies having successfully tendered 93% of the public sector jobs in the first quarter of 1988, which is their best quarterly performance.

Local contractors won 85% of public construction contracts in both 1985 and 1986, and attained 87% in 1987. However, local contractors received only 46% of the mechanical and electrical work in the first quarter of 1988.

With regard to public building contracts, in the first quarter of 1988 local contractors won $S152.7 million worth of jobs, including two worth more than $S20 million each for building public flats in Hougang New Town. In contrast, foreign firms' market share of building contracts has consistently been below 11%, ranging from 0.2% in 1986 to 10.8% in 1984. In civil engineering works, all the $S39.2 million worth of public sector engineering projects went to local construction firms.

Foreign companies took a huge share of the major mechanical and electrical projects at about 90% of contracts above $US10 million. Most large projects involved supplying and installing sophisticated machines imported from abroad.

2.8 South Korea

Until recently, South Korea was a relatively closed country to exporters. Import liberalization has become a centrepiece of the South Korean government's open door policy, although what opportunities this will provide for foreign contractors is unknown.

South Korea has a large construction market, second only to that of Japan on the Asia-Pacific Rim, but it also has a large number of effective contractors and has for many years been a leading exporter of construction.

South Korea's edge in the market is found primarily in cheap labour and a good level of construction expertise, which may be difficult for foreign contractors to compete with on the Koreans' own ground, even if they were allowed to. However, it is just possible that there may be some opportunities in connection with projects with a high technology content.

The demand for construction is certainly high, due to a large current account surplus and resultant liquidity. A real estate boom has developed, centred almost exclusively around Seoul. In addition, extensive redevelopment projects have been initiated by the city authorities to improve the living conditions in Seoul. The demand for infrastructure work is huge, only 54% of roads are paved, and two new towns are planned to relieve the pressure on the capital.

2.9 Taiwan

Taiwan is one of the newly industrialized countries and its growth reflects that status. In the last decade Taiwan has experienced an increase of nearly 300% in the gross national product, which is the consequence of a remarkable development of its export-driven economy.

By the end of 1988 the GNP achieved a 7.07% growth, and total export trade has broken through the $US100 billion mark. Foreign exchange reserves are set to exceed $US70 billion and unemployment is less than 2%, while per capita income stands at a record high of $US6,000. The executive, Yuan, announced a forecast of 7% growth in 1989.

Good export performance has generated huge trade surpluses (about $US11 billion in 1988) and increased pressure for the continuing appreciation of the NT dollar which could affect domestic inflation, which has been successfully kept at a low level.

In response, the government has adopted a policy to liberalize and internationalize the economy. The measures have attracted foreign firms in the service sector such as banking, insurance, fast food, etc. While this policy shows that long-term prosperity can only be achieved through integration into the world economy, it is still a difficult market for foreign developers and contractors to penetrate. The vast majority of property developers are Taiwanese, although there are some joint ventures, but even in these cases the majority share is with the Taiwanese partner. A very similar position exists with contractors. A further reflection of the still 'closed' nature of the market is that foreigners are not permitted to buy property.

Reliable figures on the property market are impossible to obtain at present but an indication of its buoyancy is given by the office sector in Taipei which saw an exceptionally good demand for space during 1988. Space was available for both sale and lease, resulting in an average occupancy rate of approximately 90%, with Grade 'A' office buildings in better accessible locations enjoying occupancy levels in excess of 95%, while some buildings were in full occupancy.

In the public sector, infrastructure needs dominate government spending. In 1988 over 25% of the government budget was allocated to capital expenditure on infrastructure. From time to time the government announces a number of key infrastructure projects designed to make substantial progress in bringing the infrastructure up to date. The latest group, of 'Fourteen Key Projects' were announced in 1985 and include energy projects, subways and railways, highways, reservoirs, and flood prevention. Practically all are progressing satisfactorily.

The most dominant infrastructure project is the Mass Rapid Transit System (MRT) aimed to ease Taipei's chronic traffic problems. With Taipei's population expected to increase by 45% to over 6 million by 2001, and with vehicle ownership by 400%, the need for the MRT is apparent.

The government came to a decision to implement the project, estimated to cost $US6 billion, in 1986. The initial phase is for a 33.1 kilometre line with the whole system being 70.3 kilometres long and due to be completed by 1999. The lack of experience of Taiwanese contractors in such work has meant that the government has had to offer the work to foreign contractors, and construction of the first phase is being undertaken by the French company Matra. Many parts of the first phase are still to be tendered. The MRT Authority signed a two-year contract in 1987 with the US company ATC to provide overall consultancy services.

In 1987 there were 2467 registered contractors and 543 developers in Taiwan, with all the large developers having established their own construction firms. Due to the booming economy, local construction workers are being attracted to other industries, and the shortage of labour within the industry only helps to create a concern for a resultant loss of quality.

The construction industry is administered by the Department of Construction and Planning Administration under the Ministry of the Interior. All contractors are licensed and classified as Class A, B or C.

1. A Class 'A' contractor is one:
   - with capital of over $NT9 million;
   - that has been a Class B contractor for five years and has undertaken contracts amounting to $NT72 million and above within the same period;
   - that has a full-time registered engineer with minimum five years' post-qualification experience.

There were 919 Class A contractors in 1987.

2. A Class 'B' contractor is one:
   - with capital of over $NT3 million;
   - that has been a Class C contractor for five years and has undertaken contracts amounting $NT36 million and above within the same period;
   - that has a full-time registered engineer with minimum two years' post-qualification experience.

There were 426 Class B contractors in 1987.

3. A Class 'C' contractor is one:
   - with capital of over $NT1.2 million;
   - that has a full-time registered engineer with minimum 1 year's post-qualification experience.

There are 1122 Class C contractors in 1987.

Among the class A contractors there are three government construction companies – The Retired Servicemen Engineering Agency, The BES Engineering Corporation, The Tang Eng Iron Works.

For foreign contractors to operate in Taiwan, on both public and private projects, they need a licence, except for work on the Mass Rapid Transit system. Licences are difficult to obtain. Class C licences are of no real interest to multinational construction companies and contractors do not qualify for Class A or B on the grounds that they have not constructed projects in Taiwan. It is possible to buy a licence from a Taiwan company which no longer uses it, but the problem with this arrangement is that the purchaser also inherits the liability for previous projects associated with the licence. As there is no way of finding out what these liabilities are, the risk involved can be high.

Joint ventures cannot be established on an enforceable legal basis in Taiwan, and although they can and are formed, if something goes wrong there is no recourse in law. The Japanese have entered such joint ventures with local companies based solely on trust. If each party needs the other sufficiently, and given an eastern culture and way of doing business, then the system is viable. This is particularly so if the foreign party is providing capital investment for, say, the manufacturing activity for which the building is being provided.

In the Western world such an arrangement would need justifying to higher authorities, such as the Board and shareholders, who would be unlikely to have a cultural background that would find it acceptable.

2.9 Thailand

Thailand is the latest of the Asia Pacific Rim economies to enjoy boom conditions and the years following 1987 have seen substantial construction activity. In the public sector, infrastructural developments are important, with plans for the government to spend $US1.6 million on road and bridge construction in Bangkok during the next five years.

Infrastructure projects to come on stream include the 41.7 kilometres Second Stage Expressway System (SES) and construction of the B22 billion Mass Rapid Transit System (MTS). Some B9.5 billion will be spent on construction alone, but the scheme has been on the drawing board since 1970.

The development of toll-roads is being encouraged by the government, which has approved two at a cost of B20 billion. The first is a 73.5 kilometres highway linking Rangsit and Saraburi and estimated to cost B4 billion; the second is an elevated highway from Bang Na to Chan Buri at a cost of B16 billion. Kumagai Gumi of Japan has been awarded a contract to build an expressway in Bangkok on a 30-year concession basis by Bangkok Expressway Co. Ltd. The project is to be built using the building–operate–transfer (BOT) method.

Until recently, Thailand's property market received little international attention, but now substantial foreign investment, the recent growth of the manufacturing and service sectors, increased liquidity, lower interest rates and regular remittances from Thai workers in the Middle East have combined to provide more spending power. The development of the property industry in Thailand is well documented by Mary Seddon and this section draws heavily on her paper [2].

These forces led to a boom in house construction and a government survey shows that some 40 000 units were constructed in the Bangkok area alone during the first nine months of 1987. A majority of these new homes are individual houses rather than flats.

The high-income residential market still appears to be suffering from an oversupply problem resulting from the condominium construction 'boom' of the early 1980s, arising from the belief that both foreign and local demand existed for high-rise flats close to the city centre, but the demand never materialized as a major influx of foreign workers did not occur.

High-rise office development was initiated in 1960 with the construction of the seven-storey Sibunruang Building on Siloni Road. Since then a large number of high-rise office complexes have been built, providing some 1.1 million square metres of floor space, although there is not yet a definable central business district in Bangkok.

The lack of any comprehensive government land-use planning has led to the development of a city where commercial, residential and industrial premises are to be found side-by-side. This has led to severe and uncontrolled urban sprawl. Commercial developments tend to locate near major distributor roads, taking advantage of the relatively cheap land prices of such locations. However, the government understands that such a situation cannot continue indefinitely, and is now considering the introduction of zoning controls.

The lack of any preferred location for office developments has contributed to rents being charged as a reflection of the design, layout and management of the office building itself rather than its location, with rents ranging from B200 to B280 per square metre per month for buildings standing adjacent to each other.

In the overall scheme of things, the importance of land to the Thai people is clearly demonstrated by the administrative codes which control its ownership and transfer. This is exemplified by regulations prohibiting freehold ownership of land by aliens, and by the mortgage controls which permit land to be mortgaged independently of the buildings on it.

One of the 'restrictions' on aliens entering the property development market means that they are not at present able to own land although they are able to freely lease land and construct and own buildings. A 'promoted' alien company under the Investment Promotion Act may be granted the right to own the land necessary for carrying out its activities, subject to possible conditions specified by the Board of Investment. However, the amount of land that an alien can own is restricted by the land code.

Hotel development is responding to Thailand's growing reputation as an attractive and important destination for tourists. The country's very successful 'Visit Thailand Year' boosted tourist arrivals in 1987 by some 21% to an estimated 3.4 million people. Tourism is Thailand's largest foreign exchange earner, having generated revenues of B37 321 million in 1986, and the increase in visitor arrivals has sparked a mini boom in hotel construction.

Until 1987, average room occupancy rates were around 60% in Bangkok and in 1988 they were around 90% in the city's deluxe–first-class hotels, reflecting the enormous increase in tourist arrivals, and cheaper hotel rates. In 1988 there were some 4000 additional rooms under construction and a further 2000 at the planning stage. These include a 400-room hotel at the Mah Boonkrong Centre, a 400-room hotel as part of the World Trade Centre development, the 600-room Royal Cliff, a 200-room extension at the Airport Hotel and 400 rooms at the Beaufort International.

Aside from the tourist industry, Thailand's most notable development has been the rapid growth of the manufacturing sector. Over the past decade annual growth has averaged 6.9%, and since 1970 it has averaged 7.2%. The country's cheap labour market and relatively stable political climate make it a very attractive place for foreign investors and manufacturers.

In 1987 the Board of Investment attempted to encourage decentralization of the industrial base from Bangkok by offering promotional incentives to investors willing to set up factories in provincial areas. Despite these measures, however, the most extensive industrial development is still taking place in industrial estates around Bangkok, including Bangpoo and Bangplee.

The major 'competitor' to industrial growth in Bangkok will be the development of the various Eastern Sea Board Projects associated with the deep-sea port of Laem Chabang. The Bangkok Basin is currently very congested and although take-up of industrial floor space in the Sea Board Projects has to date been slow, the completion of the container port is likely to act as a catalyst in encouraging relocation of industries from Bangkok.

Under the Land Code any limited company in which over 49% of the share equity of capital is owned by aliens, or where more than half the partners are aliens, is deemed to be 'alien'. As indicated by these codes, land is an extremely important 'commodity' in Thailand. Nearly all 'families' have a landholding varying in size from small agricultural lots to larger lots, the latter of which are usually owned by wealthy families, large institutions or government organizations such as the University or state railways.

Despite the restrictions governing aliens, it has been rumoured that the Japanese have also been acquiring land in areas deemed to have good development potential by being adjacent to major transport infrastructures or tourist zones. Although corporate entities, in which foreigners hold up to 49% of shares, can own land in Thailand, the country's Government–Parliament Coordinating Committee is pushing for a new land law that would curb extensive alien ownership of land.

An indication of Thailand's widely recognized economic boom has been investment from Hong Kong in construction and real estate development. In early-1989 Citibank reported 'Over the last six months 40 per cent of the total corporate business in Citibank Thailand has been in the construction lending business, and a big chunk of the investment is from Hong Kong.'

Citibank attributes this to a number of factors: 'Land and housing development is very attractive in Thailand compared to Hong Kong. It is relatively very cheap to buy land here, the labour and materials are very competitively priced, and there is little need to import construction materials, as almost all are made locally to high quality specifications. Basic costs can be cut by 20–25 per cent by the savings in time and raw material expenses through this.'

Mindful of national interests, the Thai government has imposed strict controls on the proportion of foreign investment possible in any one project. Equity participation is restricted to a 49% ceiling, and is carefully guarded. This restriction has not stemmed the tide of interest, however, and foreign investment has been pouring into this country, which is popularly seen as the best for investment in South-East Asia.

The construction industry was expected to record a turnover of B150–200 billion in 1989, up from B130–150 billion in 1988; but it is felt that it is in danger of overheating. Prices of steel bars, cable, copper, aluminium and timber have all increased recently and calls have been made to lift the 25% import tariff on steel bars. There is also a shortage of manpower, including professionals. Thai labour is widely used in other South-East Asian countries where they are paid more than in Thailand; so it is difficult to attract them to return.

The Thai Contractors' Association reported that government contracts suffered from a lack of bidders in the first quarter of 1989. Of 206 projects, 55 did not attract bidders and those that were awarded involved high costs.

The demand for middle class housing is high, with the private home-building market valued at B15 billion. It is estimated that the accumulated demand of the last ten years amounts to about 200 000 houses in Bangkok and its suburbs. During the first nine months of 1987, 38 000 low-cost houses were built in Bangkok.

Foreign construction companies can only be established in Thailand if the majority of shares in the company are held by Thai citizens. Companies can be established either as local companies or as joint ventures but in both cases 51% must be owned by Thais. It therefore becomes very important for the foreign party to ensure that Thai participation is appropriate, and similarly the Thai partner will want to be sure that the foreign partner will not desert partly completed projects.

Local contractors do not have high technical and managerial skills, thus they welcome joint ventures to which they can bring knowledge of local conditions and appropriate connections, both business and political.

Businesses are expensive and slow to set up in Thailand and while it is possible for a foreign company to set up a branch office in Thailand on a project-by-project basis, the benefits of joint venturing are of course lost.

3. Postscript

The Asia Pacific Rim is not a homogeneous group of countries. Consequently, the opportunities for overseas contractors vary significantly between countries, not only in terms of scale of the economies and the construction markets, but in the political and cultural contexts which in turn determine the reception awaiting overseas contractors.

Markets can appear in the most unexpected places. Burma, for example, is believed to be about to develop oil and gas fields and has received World Bank loans. An Asian Development Bank loan will also fund infrastructure development such as dockyard development, irrigation and telecommunications.

This chapter is essentially about opportunities for overseas contractors in the Far East but it should be remembered that the Far East has some of the most aggressive international contracting companies who are active not only in Europe, the Middle East and North America, but also within other Far Eastern countries. Japanese contractors are building in every country in the region in which it is possible for them to be active. South Korea is likewise ($US3 billion in 1989), and is also active in Japan. Korea has a long and successful history of overseas contracting, as has the People's Republic of China. Singapore has made some inroads ($US355 million in 1988) towards alleviating a declining home market, is receiving some support from its Construction Industry Development Board and is prepared to offer incentives such as training. Malaysia, too, is keen to export construction.

It also comes as a surprise to many that China's construction industry undertakes a significant amount of overseas work. The China State Construction Engineering Corporation (CSCEC) which employs 1 480 000 people has an overseas division which has been involved in 400 overseas projects in 50 countries. Since 1979, China has signed more than 4000 contracts worth over $US6.5 billion with 100 different countries and regions. More than 50 000 Chinese workers from 67 construction companies are employed abroad, in regions as diverse as North America, Latin America, Asia and the Middle East.

Construction companies from outside the Asia Pacific Rim will therefore have to compete not only with the indigenous industry, but with construction companies from other Asian countries which are more familiar with culture and customs.

1. Boldrick, H. (1988). 'Housing finance in Indonesia' *South-East Asia Building*, March.
2. Seddon, M. (1988) 'Property boom in Thailand', *South East Asia Building*. June.

—— 16 ——

The strategy of Japanese contractors in their penetration of construction markets

Roger Flanagan

1. Introduction

This chapter is divided into the following three sections: Section 2 introduces the size and scope of the Japanese construction market; Section 3 examines the culture and some of the special facets of Japanese business; and Section 4 looks at the Japanese construction companies and considers what is special about them and how they differ from Western construction companies.

1.1 A brief summary of the Japanese economy

- intensely competitive;
- dominated by a relatively small number of large companies who are members of industrial groups;
- high GNP per capita, high rate of growth, and high wage economy;
- low interest rate, low annual inflation, and low unemployment;
- well-educated population (37% of all school leavers go to university);
- highly skilled and motivated workforce with low absenteeism;
- strong market inclination, high product quality, on-time delivery, and customer satisfaction;
- lack of natural resources, so dependent upon imported raw materials;
- harmony between the government and industry, politics and economics seen as being interlinked;
- commitment to long-term planning;
- high spending on research and development;
- high rate of savings and investment;
- political stability.

2. Putting Japan's construction industry into perspective

All across the world Japanese construction companies have made their mark. But only since the early 1980s has the world's attention has been focused upon them. Many of the world's largest and most exciting projects have involved Japanese contractors, Japanese technology, Japanese equipment or Japanese finance.

As a result of the impact and success of Japanese companies overseas, great interest has been shown in the structure and size of the Japanese construction industry, and the way the companies and consultants operate in their home market.

Many commentators on Japan have reached the conclusion that Japan has the financial strength to make a global take-over of the world's construction markets. In reality, there is potential for success in the world's markets, but it is a myth that this extends to a global take-over. It is true that the major Japanese contractors rank among the largest in the world, as can be seen from Table 16.1, whether measured by size of turnover or by number of employees, but despite their vast annual turnover, the percentage of work undertake in the international markets is not so large. US construction companies still have the largest volume of overseas business, with Japan now ranking number two in the world, closely followed by France, the United Kingdom, and West Germany. Japan's domestic market is so large that the big firms can become one of the world's giants by operating in the domestic market and by having under 10% of total business overseas.

Table 16.1 The world's largest construction companies in 1989

	Turnover $US millions
1. Fluor Daniel Inc. (USA)	16 647
2. Shimizu Corporation (Japan)	13 152
3. Bechtel Group Inc. (USA)	12 010
4. Kajima Corporation (Japan)	11 940
5. Taisei Corporation (Japan)	11 502
6. Takenaka Corporation (Japan)	11 254
7. Brown and Root Inc. (USA)	10 976
8. Ohbayashi Corporation (Japan)	9972
9. M. W. Kellogg Co. (USA)	9394
10. Bouygues (France)	8500
11. Kumagai Gumi Corp. (Japan)	8034
12. Philip Holzmann AG (Germany)	6498
13. Mitsubishi Heavy Industries (Japan)	6355
14. SGE Group (France)	6077
15. ABB Lummus Crest (USA)	5493

Source: *Engineering News Record*, April 1990.

While the Japanese contractors are very good and very successful, the companies are now facing exactly the same problems as Western companies, as follows:

1. There is declining productivity in the construction industry.
2. The industry has an ageing workforce.
3. There is a lack of skilled workers.
4. The industry is not seen as attractive to school leavers because sites are considered to be cold and dirty places to work.
5. There is more competition in the international construction marketplace from newly industrialized countries.
6. There is more protectionism and nationalism in international markets.

2.1 The Japanese domestic construction market

The Japanese domestic construction market is vast. In 1989 Japan's total construction investment reached 63.6 trillion yen, the largest construction market by value in the developed world, while the US market was 60 trillion yen. The combined EC market amounted to 68 trillion yen. Construction investment accounts for 7.9% of Japan's GDP, and for 4.9% in the United States. It has to be emphasized that the published percentages of the construction GDP varies considerably, depending upon the source and method of calculation. The Japanese Ministry of Construction publishes a rate of almost 20%, but international statistics use a different basis of calculation.

Japan has a lot of civil engineering work, almost 38% of construction investment is in civil engineering projects; in comparison the UK percentage is about 20%. Much tunnelling work is undertaken in Japan due to the mountainous terrain.

While the Japanese market is large it is fiercely competitive. There are no snug niche markets. The construction market was in a state of depression for ten years from 1975 to 1985, during which time the Japanese companies developed new strategies in order to survive. A broad range of services was developed with new technologies and construction capabilities. No longer was it feasible for the contractors to sit back and wait for orders. They had to be creative and be prepared to undertake feasibility studies, design the project, manage the construction, in some cases provide the financing, and often manage the completed facility. Observers of the Japanese construction scene *looking in from the outside* see only success, yet Japan has its failures just as does any free market economy.

Quality has become vital to Japanese customers who are very quality conscious. Quality extends beyond the physical aspects of a project to the contractor's responsiveness and service to the client. Simply put, the Japanese construction industry has grown up with the expectation that it must mould itself to the convenience of its clients and the public.

There are four main reasons for the size of the Japanese industry. First, after World War II Japan embarked upon a major rebuilding programme.

The war cost Japan nearly 3 million lives and approximately 25% of all its buildings and capital equipment. The major cities were all but reduced to rubble. Also, Japan was a late starter as a capitalist nation and the infrastructure was not highly developed, hence a lot of work needed to be undertaken. For example, Japan still needs massive investment in its roads and sewerage systems. The three most concentrated Prefectures in Japan, Tokyo, Osaka and Kanagawa contain 23.1% of Japan's population, in 1.7% of Japan's land area. If the Prefectures in the Pacific corridor are added, 50.9% of Japan's population lives in 12.2% of the total land area. In 1986 the Japanese Ministry of Construction published an international comparison of sewerage diffusion rates which showed that Japan only had a 37% diffusion rate. Development of the sewerage system has lagged behind that of other developed nations. The low diffusion rate is not as startling as it first appears because the low percentage is caused by the small towns and villages in rural areas dragging down the rate in major cities which have over 82% diffusion rate.

Second, up until 1988 Japanese contractors had a protected domestic market with no foreign competition. The marketplace was protected from incursion by non-Japanese companies. The protection did not take any obvious crude form, such as a tariff barrier; rather there existed a range of bureaucratic and cultural barriers that inhibited the ability of foreign companies to compete in the Japanese market. Thus the domestic market provided a solid foundation and buffer for earnings from which the companies could penetrate overseas markets. More recently, the Japanese government came under criticism and attack from the Americans and the Europeans who wanted the barriers to entry to be lowered. The Japanese government responded in 1988 by changing regulations and procedures to facilitate foreign involvement. In most instances, non-Japanese firms work in partnership with a Japanese company because of the difficulty of coping with local customs and the language.

Third, the private sector has held the dominant position in the market with 65% of the total output, and it has been in the office, industrial and housing markets where there has been dynamic growth. Also, there has been a trend towards private sector investment in public sector infrastructure projects, for example in the Kansai International Airport and Trans Tokyo Bay Highway. This pattern of cooperation between the government and the private sector is likely to continue.

Finally, since 1987 the Japanese government has changed its economic policies, switching from an export led economy to a domestic demand led economy. This policy change has accelerated the expansion of the domestic market and contractors have moved from the so-called *cold winter* to a *hot summer*. Industrial companies have been reporting record profits which are leading to huge investments in new plants and facilities. In 1989 capital spending (non-residential fixed investment) was approximately 19% of GNP, almost twice the level in the United States.

2.2 The Japanese construction companies

It is only lately that the construction industry has come into the international spotlight. Yet it is one of Japan's largest industries, three to four times larger than either the car or steel industry.

Seen as a whole the industry is gigantic, yet, looked at in detail, it is made up of incongruously small parts. For example, the top six Japanese industrial companies own 70% of the steel industry, but the top six construction companies own only 10% of the construction industry.

The construction business in Japan is highly regulated and a licence is required to design, engineer, or construct a project. Licences are granted by the Ministry of Construction and the Prefectural Governments. The criteria for licensing are stringent: a construction company seeking to undertake major projects must have at least five years' experience in the relevant work area and must have staff who are competent professional engineers with at least three years' postgraduate experience in the relevant work area.

The Japanese Contract Cosntruction Business Law divides construction business into the following three groups:

(a) general and specialized contractors;
(b) specialist sub-contractors;
(c) equipment installers.

These three groups are further divided into 28 sub-groups. The Japanese general contractors, dubbed 'Zenecons', are the dominant members of the construction industry. The general contractors are further divided by the size of their annual turnover into large, semi-large, medium-sized, small, and civil engineering.

There are 533,000 licensed contractors working in Japan and the construction industry employs 9% of the working population. This percentage is substantially higher than that in the United States, with 6.4%, the United Kingdom with 6.7%, West Germany with 7.3%, and France with 8.9%.

Japanese construction is dominated by six major companies, referred to as the *big six*. They are Shimizu Corporation, Taisei Corporation, Kajima Corporation, Obayashi Corporation, Takenaka Corporation and Kumagai Gumi Corporation. As Table 16.2 shows, these companies turn over a large proportion of their work in building works. Each of the big six has a long history dating back between 150 and 190 years. From a distance all these giants look alike, with their strong emphasis on planning and coordination, research and development, and emphasis on high-quality products.

Comparing profitability with a Western construction company is difficult because of different accounting procedures to those in the West. In 1989–90 Obayashi Corporation announced pre-tax profits of 50.54 billion yen ($US337 million) and Kumaga-Gumi Corporation 41.1 billion yen ($US274 million). The ratio of profit to sales, industry wide, is about 2.5%. Table 16.3 shows a survey of profitability in the construction industry up

Table 16.2 Turnover of Big Six construction companies (1989)

Company	Total orders+ received	Total building+ orders	No. of employees
Shimizu Corp.	16 296	12 838	10 448
Kajima Corp.	16 017	11 369	12 791
Ohbayashi Corp.	15 300	11 700	8836
Takenaka Corp.	15 130	8294	10 207
Taisei Corp.	14 355	10 002	12 101
Kumagai-Gumi Corp.	9126	5948	8143

Note:
+ hundreds of millions of yen.
Source: Building Contractors Society of Japan.

Table 16.3 Ratio of current profit to annual sales

Year	All construction firms	52 member firms of JFCC
1980	2.1	2.7
1981	2.5	3.4
1982	2.2	3.6
1983	1.7	3.3
1984	1.7	2.9
1985	1.6	2.5
1986	1.9	2.4
1987	2.4	2.8

to 1987. Profitability for Japanese specialist contractors tends to be higher ranging between 5 and 8% on sales. Figure 16.1 shows the profitability of some of the contractors from 1983. Between 1983 and 1987 the profit curves were very flat. Since 1988 profits have improved significantly, coinciding with the upturn in workload.

3. Business and culture

3.1 Doing business with Japanese companies

There are four interrelated concepts in Japanese business. These are Nintai (patience), Kao (face), Giri (duties) and On (obligations). They cause the Japanese to be very thorough in everything they do. A great deal of time and effort goes in to ensuring that they tackle every task thoroughly and with commitment. It is very important not to lose face or respect by failing to meet commitments.

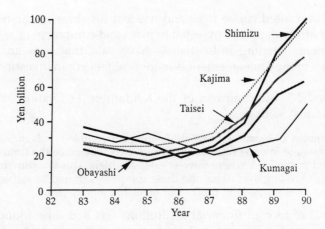

Figure 16.1 *Profitability of Japanese contractors (Source: Shin'nippon Shoken Chosa.)*

Doing business with a Japaense company requires a change in approach for Western companies. There is nothing magical about the Japanese companies, but they do have an Eastern mystique which is embedded in business culture and customs.

Japanese companies show a persistence to win and beat the competition at all costs; persistence is the common denominator, whereas western companies often expect *too much too soon*. This can be partly answered by the long-term view taken by Japanese companies: they have long time horizons unlike many Western companies who are driven by short-term views. Shareholders all around the world want to see profits and growth, but Westerners expect them quicker.

National and corporate culture plays an important part in shaping the success of companies and nations. Culture has been described as the collective programming of the mind that distinguishes the members of one category of people from those of another.

Akio Morita, President of the Sony Corporation, gave a talk in 1987 in Chicago entitled, 'America looks 10 minutes ahead: Japan looks 10 years'. He described how the Japanese plan and develop their business strategies ten years ahead. He referred to a discussion with an American money trader who was asked, 'how far ahead do you plan . . . one week or one year?' The reply was 'no . . . no . . . ten minutes'. American investors do not have the mentality of Japanese investors who are prepared to invest long-term.

Some traditionalists in the Japanese corporate community have stated that profit should be derived from the production of goods and not from financial arbitrage. They insist that finance departments should manage and not produce the company profits. According to this perspective, companies which devote their resources to trading financial instruments are analogous to rice farmers who plant coffee trees in their rice fields when coffee prices are high. When the price of coffee declines the farmer is left with unwanted coffee trees and has lost his share of the rice market. Available funds should be invested in plant and equipment or research and development. Leading industrialists have said that it is an unhealthy notion that money management is more profitable than investments in real goods.

In May 1985, the chairman of the Keidanren (Federation of Economic Organisations) said:

> A number of Japanese firms are floating convertible bonds in Switzerland where interest rates are low, and then they place the funds thus raised in the USA where interest rates are high. This is a pure money game of rolling over debts and these companies should be ashamed of themselves for making profits out of such a money game.

The arrival of foreign financial institutions has had a profound effect on Japanese attitudes. The cultural dimension is still important but the world of competitive finance is now very evident in Japan. Younger members of society are developing many Western views and values – change is on the way.

3.2 Japanese enterprise

From the creation of the modern Japanese enterprise until the present, business ideology has been more pervasive, concerted, and consistent than in other advanced industrial countries. The business philosophy has identified private enterprise with public purpose, which in turn enables members of the enterprise to identify themselves with it. To dismiss corporate philosophy in Japan as irrelevant window-dressing, as it often appears elsewhere, would be a serious error.

People in the enterprise are not bound essentially by contract, but by a common culture of which corporate philosophy is a vital part. Singing the company song, or wearing the company uniform, or exercising with colleagues in the morning, is not something done under duress. People like the sense of corporate identity and they have a commitment to it.

The organization of Japanese enterprises is similar to that of a family-type community. The group generally comes first before the individual, which is contradictory to the individual-oriented Western society.

The central problem of modern corporate enterprise is rooted in the following four basic aims:

(a) between the purpose of the shareholders whose aim is to maximize profits which derives directly from their rights of ownership;
(b) the aim of the managers and workers who see the enterprise as an instrument for maximizing wages and salaries;
(c) the purpose of the firm is to maximize the return on invested capital;
(d) society sees the purpose of the enterprise as being to create wealth.

Two factors conspired over time to give Japan the unifying purpose of enterprise: Japan's economic reality and its family ideology. The absence of natural resources has meant that Japan is dependent upon the wealth created in production. Today, many Japanese are still convinced that Japan is a poor country and that the country's survival depends on the continuous efforts of everyone. Many Japanese don't take their full holiday entitlement, even in government departments, because they believe only hard work and persistence will keep the Japanese machine running.

Workers and managers alike identify themselves with the goals of the enterprise and their most important identification is the name of the company for which they work. They belong to the enterprise in the same sense as they belong to a family. As in the family a series of rewards and obligations binds them to the enterprise.

Managers and workers share equally the sense of identification with the enterprise. Management has not appeared to be in the service of ownership, but rather has been made responsible to all members of the enterprise.

3.3 The Confucian value system of Japanese workers

Today, very few modern Japanese consider themselves Confucian, at least not in the sense that their grandparents were, but almost all Japanese are permeated with Confucian ethics.

Confucianism is not a religion but a set of pragmatic rules for daily life. The following are the four key principles of Confucian teaching:

1. *The stability of society is based on unequal relationships between people:* the five basic relationships are ruler–subject, father–son, older brother–younger brother, husband–wife, and older friend–younger friend.
2. *The family is the prototype of all social organizations:* a person is not primarily an individual, rather a member of a family. Children should learn to restrain themselves to overcome their individuality so as to maintain the harmony of the family.
3. *Virtuous behaviour toward others consists of treating others as one would like to be treated oneself.*
4. *Virtue with regard to one's tasks in life consists of trying to acquire skills and education, working hard, not spending more than necessary, being patient and persevering.*

The Japanese worker translates these in the sense that they are persistent, they order relationships by status and observe that order, they strive for personal steadiness and stability, they respect tradition, they see 'saving face' as being important, they have a sense of shame, and they reciprocate greetings, favours and gifts.

From school, where the Japanese pupil is taught to persevere and have a seriousness of purpose, there is a desire to succeed regardless of the effort involved, and to fear disgrace and failure. Indeed, a growing problem in Japan is the number of school children driven to suicide by the rigid demands of home and school. Many Japanese believe that this is a necessary price to pay to ensure that the majority of children grow into disciplined, hard-working, polite, and helpful members of society.

The ethic of thrift underlies the Japanese way of life. Japanese people have the highest savings ratio, with 16% of disposable income being put into savings.

The lack of adequate public pension schemes for retirement is one of the reasons why people save. Also, education for the children can be expensive. As Japan has become more affluent so the savings ratio has dropped from 26% of disposable income to 16% in 1989.

3.4 The way culture influences the behaviour of a Japanese company

The easiest way to consider this is by comparing some of the attitudes of a Japanese construction company and its workers with those of a Western company:

Japanese	*Western*
long-term view of business	short-term view of business
high respect for clients – 'the customer is king'	clients treated as equals

business objectives in order of priority:
  market share
  growth
  profitability
	business objectives in order of priority:
	  profitability
	  market share
	  growth

hostile takeovers of companies are virtually unknown	hostile takeovers can happen
harmonious labour–management relations	respectful labour–management relations
human relations based business contact with a view to forging long-term relationships	business contact based upon competition on price
decisions made at the top and then reached by consensus and consultation	decisions made at the top and passed down
group orientation by staff	individualism necessary in order to survive
expectation of lifetime employment by workers in larger companies	workers expect mobility of employment – staying with one company is not seen as broadening the work experience
high job security	sufficient job security

Japanese	*Western*
promotion linked to age, length of service and experience	promotion linked to ability
workers have strong identity with the company	workers have identity with the skill or profession
workers prepared to conform with the company by wearing uniform and participating in company organized events	workers see the company as not having a social role
workers conform with accepted practice; they are reluctant to criticize	workers criticize as a way of seeking improvement
shareholders invest for capital growth	shareholders invest for short-term profit and capital growth

The comparison is not intended to show that a Japanese construction company is better than a Western construction company; they are different both in the corporate culture and in the individual's attitude.

Another insight into the differences in the way a Japanese person thinks, as compared with a Westerner, comes from an article in a Japanese newspaper, *Asahi Shimbun*, 29 December 1989. It describes a survey carried out by Dai-Ichi Seimi, a major life insurance company, on the hopes of Japanese parents for their children's careers. In total, 8352 parents of children under 18 years were asked: 'What career do you wish your son or daughter to pursue?' The results were as follows:

For sons
 1. Public officer
 2. Salaried office worker in a private company
 3. Doctor
 4. Professional baseball player
 5. Airline pilot
 6. Engineer
 7. Teacher
 8. Whatever the son wishes
 9. Professional athlete
10. Self-employed.

For daughters
 1. Kindergarten nurse
 2. Office girl
 3. Teacher
 4. Medical nurse
 5. Stewardess
 6. Public officer
 7. Whatever the daughter wishes

8. Doctor
9. Piano instructor
10. Beautician.

The public officer is popular because it promises a stable working life where there is security of employment until retirement. Furthermore, working for a local authority means no regional transfers, allowing the worker to establish a home in one place and concentrate on bringing up and taking care of the family. Interestingly, nowhere in the list are lawyers or accountants, which would rank highly in a Westerner's list.

3.5 Ningen Kenkei

This is a form of social arrangement and web that binds relationships in everyday life and in business. The literal translation is 'human relations', but to the Japanese the term conveys much more. It is tempting to liken Ningen Kenkei to the 'old boy' network that operates in the United Kingdom. However, it is deeper than even that, and basically establishes a relationship which means that within their group, Japanese are honour bound to help one another.

3.6 Japanese companies and litigation

People in Japan do not regard the law as determinant: the legal norm is expected to compromise with the reality of social life. Strict application and execution of law is regarded with disfavour as being unrealistic and too rigorous. As a result lawyers play a much less important role in the conduct of all human affairs in general, and business in particular, than they do in Western countries. Legal departments in Japanese companies are not a recommended avenue to the ranks of top management. In Japan there are only about 13 000 practising lawyers compared with over 500 000 in the United States.

A Japanese company will revert to legal proceedings as a last resort; when a dispute does arise they would prefer to settle any differences in a spirit of mutual respect and understanding. To revert to litigation means that the trust and respect have broken down. However, when working overseas the Japanese companies have been prepared to conform to local custom. For, instance, in South East Asia claims for loss and expense on contracts have been pursued by arbitration and in the courts.

3.7 Labour relations

Japanese contractors have few industrial disputes; the labour relations record is good. There are no industry-wide construction labour unions, and where a union does exist it is common for it to be a staff association or company union to which all workers in the same company belong. The staff association will directly negotiate the wages and conditions with management. An annual wage round, the 'shun to', normally takes place each Spring. Therefore, the usual labour versus management dichotomy does not exist. Since the workers and managers find their common identity in the enterprise, the main concern of labour–management relations shifts from wages, salaries, and working conditions to assuring growth for the necessary lifelong employment for all permanent members and to sustain the seniority reward system.

3.8 Cradle to the grave – lifetime employment and the Japanese

In the major companies it is usual for staff to join a company and to stay throughout their working life; this applies equally to blue and white collar workers. Japanese employers do not poach staff from rival firms, nor do Japanese workers expect to switch employers. Labour mobility between major companies is practically nil. However, in the smaller contracting and sub-contracting firms it is not usual to have lifetime employment for staff.

In the Japanese economy only about 30% of the total labour force is within the lifetime employment cradle to grave group. Moreover, lifetime employment is exclusively male. Single women are expected to retire once they marry. Lifetime employment does not last for life, it ends at 55 years. Retired employees do not receive a company pension; they have to be content with a lump-sum retirement allowance.

Japanese firms back up the guarantee of lifetime employment with a wide range of company-based benefits, which include housing, medicare and sports facilities. The workers' guaranteed lifetime employment shows a high degree of commitment to the firm, a marked reluctance to strike and a willingness to collaborate with management in increasing efficiency.

All this sounds like Utopia to the Western manager, and in a sense it is. But the commitment is not bought for nothing. Company welfare schemes are expensive. The Japanese manager forgoes a wide range of perks taken for granted in the United Kingdom. Company cars are almost unknown and there are no special executive dining rooms or rest rooms. Guaranteeing employees against the risk of lay-offs over a working lifetime is a burden that very few Western contractors would care to assume.

Many observers have studied the Japanese model of lifetime employment and have concluded that the model is 'less the wave of the future than the model of the past'. It is likely to come under threat even in the homeland. Young people are increasingly looking to the Western value system where staff have job mobility.

3.9 Keiretsu – the grouping of companies

One of the mistakes made by foreigners viewing Japanese business is the assumption that business organizations are independent entities. Japanese business is dominated by 16 or so huge cluster companies, each linking vast numbers of complementary industrial and financial entities together into industrial groupings almost totally unique to Japan.

Now referred to as Keiretsu, or informal groups, each of these clusters resembles a massive spider's web with one of the major Japanese commercial banks at its centre. Although each company affiliated with an interest group is ostensibly a separate legal entity, they are bound together in a vast array of informal cooperative relationships.

There are two types of groups as follows:

(a) those that are horizontally connected over a wide spectrum of industries, usually centring around banks and trading companies;
(b) those that are vertically integrated, gathering around their parent company.

Many of the large contractors are associated in very large industrial groups. Understanding how the industrial groupings work is a pre-requisite to looking at the major Japanese contractors. Six major groups – Mitsubishi, Mitsui, Sumitomo, Fuyo, Sanwa and DKB – and two medium-sized groups – Tokai and Industrial Bank of Japan – link together firms, banks, and trading houses with small cross-shareholdings. They have horizontal connections over a wide range of industries. A further ten combine suppliers and subsidiaries of a large firm or a bank. The 18 groups account for a quarter of all Japanese sales. The key aspect is that the groups feel obliged to buy from each other. There is also access to vast financial resources through the relationship with the banks. The six major groups engage in a full spectrum of industrial activities from manufacturing, financing, insuring and trading, to transportation, real estate and other services. Five features that are common to each of the six major industrial groups are as follows:

(a) cross-holding of shares;
(b) intragroup financing to group companies by nucleus banks;
(c) joint investment by group companies;
(d) formation of a presidential council (Shacho-Kai);
(e) use of general trading firms (Sogo Shosha) as nucleus trading arms.

The objective of the cross-holding of shares is to protect each group company from the outside control of threats, thus maintaining independence.

The firms associated with a group use the commercial bank at the core of the group as their main bank. With the ownership of shares, the member companies own small numbers of shares, which seldom exceed 5%. The objective of the cross-holding of shares is to protect each group company from outside control or threats.

There is no central board of directors providing common leadership to the group, but it is customary for the president of each company to meet in a presidential council in order to discuss strategy and to discuss problems of common interest. The presidential council is not the policy-making body for the whole group. The council meets to foster good relations between the companies. Should any individual company associated with a group get into financial difficulty, it is expected that other member companies will come to its aid by extending trade credit, by providing loans, or by giving managerial help. The Keiretsu provides a huge and enormously diversified base over which to spread the risks of launching new enterprises.

The Western idea of the separation of industrial firms and financial institutions does not apply in Japan. The family concept can be seen again with the interlocking ownership structure within the group. The cooperative relationships binding together the members of the industrial group are informal, subtle, and very influential.

A common question is: 'Does this mean if an electronics manufacturer is going to build a plant in the UK, would they use one of the Japanese contractors in the industrial group to project manage the scheme?' Generally, it has been the case that Japanese clients have used Japanese contractors to procure their overseas projects. A large proportion of work undertaken overseas by the Japanese contractors have either been based on Japanese Official Development Aid Projects where the Japanese government have insisted on the project being awarded to a Japanese contractor, or for Japanese clients, or the projects have been instigated by the contractor's own property and development company.

3.10 The financial position of Japanese companies

Perhaps the most striking feature of Japanese companies in the eyes of the Western observer is their high gearing. Risk exposure, almost inconceivable in a Western company prevails in Japanese business finance. It is not uncommon for borrowed funds to exceed owner's equity by a factor of four or five to one. It is tempting to jump to the conclusion that these companies are on the brink of financial disaster, but there are unique financing practices of Japanese companies and Japanese banks.

With the pursuit of growth it is difficult to accumulate sufficient capital out of earnings. Banks tend to be much more closely involved with their borrowers over the long term. The closeness of the lending relationship is reinforced by the banks' holding of bonds and common stocks of the companies to which they lend. It is not uncommon for the banks to send officers directly into the top management of corporate borrowers in financial difficulty.

3.11 Spending Japan's cash overseas

The Japanese economy no longer requires the high levels of savings for its investment, yet the high-savings rule persists. Furthermore, Japan's balance of payments is still showing a large annual surplus. The country has been totally dependent upon its exports. The strength has been based upon importing raw materials, performing high added value operations and then exporting the finished products.

Japan is the world's largest exporter of cash, bigger even than the OPEC countries in their heady days of abundant cash. Japan has targeted specific industries, has invested heavily in plant and equipment, and has been prepared to think very long-term, and when its comparative advantage shifts it has changed its targets. Most importantly, the strategy has worked. Japan has emerged as one of the strongest economies in the world.

The stream of capital to the West has become a tidal wave. The Japanese are estimated to own over £2 billion of commercial developments in the United Kingdom. They have largely avoided the burden of Third World bad debt and have tended to seek low-risk investment opportunities.

3.12 A strategy for construction and property investment overseas

After the 1952 Peace Treaty, Japan agreed to pay repatriation to Asian countries which had been occupied by Japanese forces. Such repatriation offered the Japanese construction industry the first opportunity to work overseas. Kajima provided technological assistance in 1954 to build a hydroplant in Burma. Repatriation projects were less risky because payment was guaranteed by the Japanese government.

Japanese contractors had not previously been active in the international market, but coupled with the massive re-building programme at home after the war, the contractors developed much technical expertise and an ambition to seek new opportunities.

South East Asia was the main market for the contractors. Many opportunities became available in the Middle East after the first oil shock in 1973. Japan was dependent upon Middle East oil and with inflation hitting 20% per annum at home, the Japanese sought closer links with the region. Throughout the 1970s Japanese contractors became increasingly successful at winning projects in the Middle East. The full-scale advance into the international market began after the 1973 oil crisis. At that time Japanese contractors were forced to look outward by a sharp plunge in domestic orders, shrinking profits, and a reduction in government public spending on capital projects. The oil embargo was beginning to affect the economy and contractors saw the need to diversify.

In 1980, 38% of all the Japanese construction firms' overseas orders were in the Middle East. Plunging oil prices led to the reduction in Middle Eastern workload and by 1987 the percentage had dropped to 0.7%.

The 1980s also saw more competition from both indigenous and international contractors in Asia. The Japanese contractors looked for less vulnerable markets and they found them in the industrialized West: the United States, Australia, and the member countries of the European Economic Community.

The power of the family grouping also helped the Japanese contractors. As manufacturing and service companies went overseas and built new plants, so they used the construction companies to help procure their projects. There was phenomenal growth in the value of overseas orders between 1975 and 1985, fuelled substantially by orders from Japanese corporations investing overseas.

The move into the developed markets was also fuelled by a rise in the value of the yen which, over the last few years, has almost doubled against the US dollar. This resulted in lower yen revenues from overseas operations if paid in non-yen currencies, but the price of overseas goods became cheaper. Property has been particularly attractive to Japanese investors. Many Japanese companies have bought major landmark buildings. For instance, in the United States Mitsubishi bought 57% of the Rockefeller Group who own the Rockefeller Centre in New York.

There is a great scarcity of good investment buildings in Japan. A consequence of the Japanese seeking effectively to utilize investors' abundance of funds overseas has been the reaction: 'Japanese buying the USA or Australia or Thailand' which has been a familiar catchphrase round the world. The high land prices coupled with the scarcity of prime business sites in Japan has caused investors to look overseas for property.

Proof of the massive increase in land prices is shown in Figure 16.2. In 35 years the index has moved from 100 to 10 887 for commercial land use.

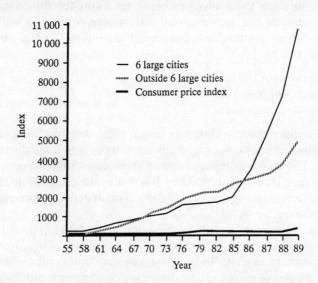

Figure 16.2 *Increase in land prices in Japan (Source:* Indices of Urban Land Prices by Japan Real Estate Institute.)

To put this into perspective, if priced at neighbouring site values the 115 hectares which the Imperial Palace occupies in the heart of Tokyo has been conservatively valued at $US300 billion, which is more than the site value of the whole of California.

The appreciation of the yen and the shortage of suitable real estate investment in Japan has provided the impetus to seek new investments overseas. The net result is that cumulative Japanese real estate investment overseas increased from less than $US5 billion in 1985 to approximately $US50 billion in 1990. The projected potential is over $US200 billion by the end of the century.

The growth in investment has also coincided with an increasing awareness of the possible dangers of having all a company's profit investment placed domestically, with the possible danger of earthquake damage and reduction in earnings. One cloud on the horizon is if the fall in the Japanese stock market values continues through 1990 into 1991, then Japanese banks may become very exposed. They have lent on property against the security of assets valued at Imperial Palace type prices which could leave them very exposed if property prices tumble. They would have to begin to reduce their lending; and they would start by cutting foreign lending.

4. Features of Japanese contractors and construction

4.1 How the contractors describe themselves

The contractors see themselves as being total construction companies, so what are some of the fundamental differences compared with Western contractors? The contractors describe themselves, not as builders or contractors, but as:

- engineering contractors;
- architects, engineers, builders, developers;
- construction engineers.

The term 'builder' has no status in Japan; most construction professionals are described as engineers; even architects are called architectural engineers. The major companies have specialized in achieving excellence in engineering. For instance, they have invested heavily in tunnelling, earthquake engineering, biotechnology, construction robotics, and concrete technology.

There has also been a shift to the contractor–developer. All the major companies are increasingly involved in development. Kumagai Gumi recently commented that: 'In the past, construction companies undertook construction, developers only undertook development and financial institutions arranged finance. Our main policy is to combine these separate businesses into one.'

4.2 The business objectives

As has been described earlier, the business objectives of Japanese companies are market share, growth, and profitability – in that order. The philosophy is towards planning for long-term growth, not short-term profits; this is quite different from Western business approaches. Business relations are based upon trust and human relations, with litigation being seen as a last resort.

4.3 Design and planning

All the large contractors have an extensive in-house multidisciplinary design capability. The size of these design departments is comparable with most of the large Japanese architectural engineering design consultants. Design and build is a major part of a contractor's workload. Little lump-sum competitive bidding is undertaken. The turnkey operation is important to the Japanese contractors, who want to design, engineer, construct and maintain a building, with maintenance management having an increasingly important role. It is also becoming common for the Japanese contractor to arrange the financing and to find the land for the client.

One of the major strengths of Japanese contractors is their meticulous attention to detail and to planning their programme of work. They invest heavily in planning the construction process. Planning and progress meetings are held regularly (often daily) on site with the specialist trade contractors. It is a matter of honour that they meet completion dates.

4.4 Client relationships

Japanese contractors have long-standing relationships with their clients. Repeat business for the client is seen as a deep-rooted part of the Japanese business culture. The expectation is that once the client is satisfied and trust has built up, then a long-term business relationship will follow naturally – they will develop Ningen Kenkei.

Japanese contractors are not complacent, nor are they uncompetitive. The competition for work is fierce and substantial proposals are frequently submitted free of charge. All the contractors believe that a project must be created to become a reality.

4.5 Housing work

In Japan, the major contractors have very limited experience in speculative housing development. Housing work is undertaken by specialist *wooden* contractors. When they have gone overseas, Japanese contractors have been very active in buying household development companies, particularly in the United States and Australia. In the housing business, which is worth about ¥22 trillion per year, a number of textile, steel, and electric-appliance makers have set up home-building operations. For instance, Toyota Motor Co. has a major house building company, including a highly automated pre-fabricated housing facility.

4.6 Workload strategy

There is a planned long-term strategy for the construction industry, both at home and overseas, coordinated by various government departments. The government and contractors work together to build a prosperous industry.

Medium and small contractors are guaranteed a proportion of the public sector workload. The government decides this proportion annually. These contractors are encouraged to form cooperatives to share the risks, to make bulk purchases and to increase their credit worthiness. The cooperatives differ from joint ventures in that they are not involved in just one project. There are various funds and advantageous loan arrangements. For example, the construction industry promotion fund, set up by the Ministry of Construction, guarantees loans given by financial institutions to construction cooperatives.

4.7 Research and development

All the large contractors have research and development centres and are active in developing new technologies. One major difference between Western and Japanese construction companies is the considerable amount of money the Japanese contractors invest in research and development. For example, between 2.5% and 3% of the Japanese contractor's workforce is involved in research and development for the company. Budgets of $US40 million per annum per company are usual. Figure 16.3 shows the expenditure on research and development for four of the major companies. Japanese companies are used to investing in research. Only 21% of Japan's research and development expenditure is provided by the state, which compares with 49% in the United Kingdom and 46% in the United States. This results primarily from the high investment in defence by the United Kingdom and the United States.

Many visitors to Japan express bewilderment at how the large construction companies can afford to operate such impressive research laboratories staffed with high-level research scientists and furnished with the latest scientific equipment which any government or university research laboratory would be proud of.

Visitors fail to understand the complex issues which underlie the need for research and development in Japan; there are five main reasons for its importance, as follows:

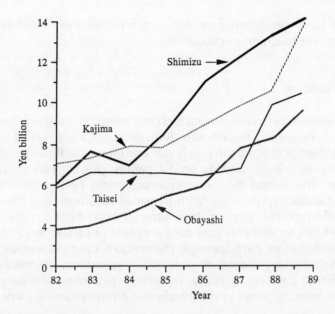

Figure 16.3 *Research and development expenditure (Source: Shin'nippon Shoken Chosa.)*

1. Their culture leads the Japanese to see research as a necessity rather than a luxury.
2. Under Japanese law, constructors must bear more social responsibility than Western contractors. They have a deep-rooted responsibility to the client to maintain a harmonious business relationship. Hence, the contractor has to maintain high technical capabilities.
3. Qualified staff are scarce and the lifetime employment system means that staff do not move jobs. It is therefore necessary to have in-house technical staff to act as problem-solvers.
4. The construction companies need to be at the forefront of new developments and technology and to be seen as such.
5. Companies do not judge their research centres on the basis of profit or loss; a large company without a research facility would be at a commercial disadvantage with its competitors when seeking new business.

One of Kumagai's aims is to produce a completely automated shield tunnelling system for deep tunnels. They suggest that such a system could increase tunnelling speeds by a factor of three. The research and development extends overseas to harness international expertise. Kaijima recently signed an agreement with Pacific Telesis to cooperate on the development of intelligent building technology; not surprisingly, initial development work will be undertaken in Japan.

All the contractors have invested in the development of construction robots. Shimizu have invested heavily in a robotics programme and

Takenaka have developed four different types of robot to improve the placement and finishing of concrete.

4.8 Joint ventures

Joint venturing between contractors on projects, both at home and overseas, is frequently undertaken. Joint ventures are a way of life in the Japanese construction industry. It is not uncommon to find one of the 'big six' contractors joint venturing on a Japanese project with a small local contractor. The reason for joint venturing might be that the client has developed a close relationship with the small contractor and the size and scope of the project is beyond the contractor's capability.

Joint venture agreements may take a variety of forms; there may be as many as six or seven participants in the venture. Contractors may manage their parts as independent or concurrent operations. A balanced and equally shared partnership is also possible, where most of the employees are loaned from the member companies and all equipment is owned by the venture.

4.9 Quality

The construction sites are responsible for cost–time–quality–safety control. The head office fulfils a similar function to a Western contractor's organization. Decentralization of control to the site from the head office is usual and much power and influence resides with the project manager on site.

Quality is vital to all the contractors. Japanese customers are highly quality conscious. Clients are prepared to pay for quality.

4.10 Status and training

Status is important in Japanese society and all the professional tasks in a construction company are undertaken by engineers. The education system is geared towards the training of engineers who will then specialize during their careers.

Japanese construction in general is expensive, and not particularly fast to construct owing to the heavy strictures imposed because of earthquake and typhoon resistant measures.

4.11 Construction contracts

Japan uses a number of standard forms of contract which tend to be short, straightforward and rely upon trust and cooperation. In the General Conditions of Construction Contract, Article 1 embodies the general principles which state, 'the Owner and the Contractor shall perform this contract sincerely through cooperation, good faith, and equality'.

The architect is referred to throughout the contract as the Supervisor. The contract is very different from a Western construction contract because of the lack of definition. In a Western contract every eventuality is covered in a contract condition; there is an assumption that a battle will ensue, whereas the Japanese contract assumes that the project will proceed satisfactorily and it highlights the duties and responsibilities of the parties.

4.12 Specialist and trade contractors

Nearly all building work in Japan is undertaken by specialist trade contractors, who enjoy a paternalistic relationship with the general contractor. They depend on their 'father' contractors for future work. Many of the specialists will have worked for particular major contractors for many years, and in numerous cases they will work for only one contractor.

Japanese specialist trade contractors fall into two categories. First, there are the installation arms of the major electrical, mechanical, component and equipment manufacturing companies such as Toshiba, Mitsubishi, and Hitachi. These companies are also involved in the design and manufacture of a wide range of products from turbines to curtain walling. Second, there are the independent specialist trade contractors ranging in size from the small labour-only gang to the large firm. Most specialist trade work is labour only. Each sub-contractor maintains a core workforce which is supplemented as needed by additional sub-contracted teams, often based on the family unit. It is not uncommon to find husband, wife and children working as a team on a part of the building. The core workforce will be trained in new construction techniques.

The special relationship between contractor and sub-contractor means that at the bid and award stage the general contractor generally stipulates the contract price, instead of letting the specialist estimate the price for the work. The specialist trusts that the contractor will fairly represent his interests. Contractual relationships are more likely to be based on negotiation than on competition. This means that conflicts simply do not arise regarding payment and claims for additional expense, and even when disputes do arise, they are not the subject of litigation. To use the courts would be the last resort in a very lengthy negotiation; because of the need to save face and preserve a long-term relationship, the specialist will negotiate a settlement.

Site management is undertaken by the main contractor using a large site management team that is responsible for all materials, plant, planning and organization. Planning and communication are vital issues with a daily planning meeting at 3 p.m. between the site manager and the key personnel from the sub-contractors. At the start of the shift, there is a *tool box* meeting, at which the site manager and team foremen explain the schedule for the day, highlight any major events or problems and generally make sure that everyone is aware of what is going on. The workforce is very disciplined owing to their cultural background and the need to maintain the highly personal negotiated status and so be able to work on future projects. Payments are negotiated on a weekly basis with the project manager in a bargaining session. There is an absence of quantity surveyors, with cost engineers fulfilling the quantity surveying role.

Quality and time are the ruling disciplines, cost is the variable factor and thus Japanese buildings are relatively more expensive. The pressure of time can be enormous and it is the small and family-based subcontractors who are used to giving the required flexibility of resources. The contractor controls the whole design and construction process and manipulates the design and the resources supplied by the sub-contractors in order to guarantee the timely delivery of a quality product.

Contractors monitor the performance of their sub-contractors to ensure that they are sound and that their performance is steadily improving. Each sub-contractor is required to report his financial performance and work capacity at the end of each financial year. Twice a year the construction firms' project managers evaluate the sub-contractors and their foremen. Sub-contractors face evaluation of the quality of their work, their ability to complete on time, ideas for cost savings, safety record, and quality of management. Foremen are evaluated on their general capability, safety and cost consciousness. These reports are then reviewed by a sub-contractor evaluation committee of senior staff, and some sub-contractors and foremen are commended for their performance. Any failures of performance are discussed at a senior level and such bad reports influence the amount of work given to the sub-contractors.

Japan has been considering the role of its sub-contractors. They believe that in order to achieve an efficient construction industry the specialist contractors must modernize their operations. They must become more independent, reliable builders and stop operating as manpower agents. The general contractors hope that, instead of merely supplying a labour force, the specialists will become equal partners.

5. Conclusion

In a span of 20 years, the eyes of the construction world have focused on Japan's construction industry. Japan's contractors and designers have emerged as major international players. The firms have an enviable reputation for high quality, the quality of the product and the quality of the personnel. Japan will not take over the world's construction markets, but it will be a major player. The companies have gone overseas and they have been successful, and that success is likely to continue.

References

Research Institute of Construction and Economy (1988) *White Paper on Construction*. Ministry of Construction, Japan.

Nomura Research International (1988) *Asian Perspectives*, NRI & NCC Co Ltd, Japan.

Overseas Construction Association of Japan (1990) *Japan's Construction Today*, OCAJI, Japan.

Smith, L. (1990) 'Fear and loathing of Japan', *Fortune*, **121**, 5, February.

Keizai Koho Center Japan (1990) *An International Comparison*. Japan Institute of Social and Economic Affairs, Japan.

Wright, R. W. and Pauli, G. A. *The Second Wave*

Viner, A. (1979) *Inside Japan's Financial Markets*

Suzuki, Y. (1987) *The Japanese Financial System*

Morita, A. (1987) *Made in Japan*. William Collins, London.

Hasegawa, F. (1988) *Built by Japan*. Wiley Interscience, USA.

Mitsubishi Research Institute (1986) *Challenge of a New Construction Industry*. Mitsubishi Research Institute, Japan.

World Economic Forum (1989) *Competition in Global Industries*. Harvard Business School Press, Boston.

Porter, M. R. (1980) *Competitive Strategy*: Free Press, USA.

—— 17 ——

The North American construction industry

Charles Matthewson

1. Construction industry overview

The construction industry in the United States accounts for between 8 and 10% of the gross national product (GNP) and in 1988 over 400 billion dollars' value of construction was put in place [1]. Over $5\frac{1}{2}$ million people, which is just over 6% of the total civilian employment in the United States [2], earned their living working in the industry. Yet unemployment in the industry is high, with over 650000 construction workers unable to obtain work in their skills or crafts. As the largest single industry, changes in construction activities have a significant impact on the economic barometer, and vice versa. In either case, the importance of the construction industry to the economic well-being of the country is an established and acknowledged fact.

The composition of the industry in terms of size of companies follows the traditional pattern of other industries and a very large number of small- to medium-sized contractors complete the major portion of all construction put in place annually. For instance, in 1982 the US Department of Commerce census [3] reported that of the 1.4 million contractors with total collective receipts of 356 billion dollars and employment of 4.2 million people, only 50822 contractors had gross receipts of 1 million dollars or more. Those 50822 contractors accounted for 238 billion dollars, or 67% of the total industry receipts.

The industry supports three general classifications of prime contractors, i.e. residential, general, and engineering (including public utilities). These contractors work in either, or both, the privately funded and the publicly funded sectors of the industry. General contractors normally work within the commercial, industrial, and institutional divisions. Table 17.1 shows the 1988 breakdown of market share of each segment of the industry in the public and private sectors [4].

The building commissioning process in the private sector is primarily based on an architect–engineer (A–E) competitive proposal in response to an owner's brief. The American Institute of Architects (AIA) and the American Consulting Engineers Council (ACEC) both oppose this method

Table 17.1 Market share by sector and division (in billion dollars)

Division	Private sector	Public sector
Residential	201	2
Commercial	62	2
Industrial	14	—
Institutional	15	26
Engineering	36	50
	$330	$80

and actively promote selection of services based on qualification and quality. Since the private owner's money is involved, the competitive proposal method generally prevails. Public commissioning agencies historically employ in-house design specialists but under appropriate circumstances they also utilize the competitive proposal method.

The prime procurement method in the industry is the lump-sum competitive bidding system and approximately 75% of all construction contracts awarded use this method of bidding. The balance is a mix of unit price, negotiated, turnkey and construction-management styles, sprinkled with some owner-idiosyncratic variations.

Construction surety-bonding has become an increasingly attractive option over the last few years in the private sector, due to the high incidence of contractor failure. The public-sector owners mandate the use of bonds extensively, whereas in 1988 the private sector only bonded 25% of all projects bid. In 1986, approximately 7000 general contractors filed for bankruptcy incurring total losses of about 4 billion dollars [5].

Trade unionism has lost its stranglehold on the industry over the last twenty years and, as a consequence, union labour market share has shrunk to about 30% of all construction contracts [6]. Merit or open-shop labour accounts for the remaining 70% and industry opinion suggests this trend will continue.

The industry is served well by several owner and trade associations, three of the most influential being: the Associated General Contractors of America (AGC); the Associated Builders and Contractors (ABC); and the National Association of Home Builders (NAHB). Collectively they organize about 1.7 million member firms and provide a diverse range of support services such as education, labour relations, health and safety, administration and political action committees, through a network of local autonomous chapters. The political action committees (PAC) play a vital role in the industry, by lobbying government officials in an attempt to influence prospective construction-related legislation.

The bid depository process of collecting sub-trade and supplier quotations, touted as a remedy for bid peddling–bid shopping, has yet to significantly impact the industry [7].

Considering the magnitude of the industry, it is relatively free from labour problems, illegal operations and corruption, but public confidence in and perception of the industry is low. Construction in the United States defies the attachment of precise labels to describe its operations, but the national entrepreneurial spirit provides unlimited scope, opportunity and excitement to all its participants, particularly to the innovators.

2. Assessment of contractor types

The US construction industry identifies five main sectors, namely: (a) residential; (b) commercial; (c) institutional; (d) industrial; (e) engineering. The contractors who work within these sectors are either residential, general, or engineering contractors. The matching of sectors with contractors is arbitrary, depending largely on current market activity and contractor flexibility. Residential contractors build either single family dwellings, multifamily units, or work in the home improvement market. Available data indicates that 55% of single family-unit builders complete between one and ten units per year, while only about 2% build over 500 units per year. Apartment builders account for 20%, and refurbishers make up the balance of residential sector contractors. The privately funded residential section produced about half of the 410 billion dollars industry contribution to the GNP, while the publicly funded section produced only 2 billion dollars' worth [8]. Merit and open-shop labour dominates the residential sector and contractor entry into this sector is comparatively wide open. The residential market is a fluctuating mix of custom-built and speculative housing units, influenced by the economic environment.

General contractors (GC), because of their versatility and expertise in many styles of work, are the backbone of the industry. The commercial, institutional, and industrial sectors rely heavily on GCs. Projects as varied as office buildings, hospital and schools and process plant construction are their acknowledged domain. The organizational structure of this sector is triangular in nature, with a vast number of small contractors with an annual turnover of less than 1 million dollars forming the base. The next layer is occupied by contractors with a 1–5 million dollar annual turnover, and progress towards the apex presents large value contracts with a relatively small group of competing contractors [9]. Entry into the general contracting sector is open, particularly at the lower contract value level, but upward mobility within the triangle is subtly controlled by the tacit restraint of financial and construction surety-bonding institutions. Manpower in this sector generally favours merit shop labour for commercial projects, an even mix of non-union–union for institutional projects, and tends toward union labour for industrial projects, because internal plant workers are generally in organized labour unions. Another factor in the merit shop–union selection process is based on the source of finance for the project. Publicly funded projects favour union labour manpower.

Engineering contractors construct non-traditional types of projects and assume either the highway or heavy construction classification. Highway contractors construct roads, bridges and drainage structures, while heavy engineering contractors build service structures such as sewage and water plants, power stations, dams and waterways. Entry into this market demands a high inventory of mechanical equipment, which acts as a natural obstacle to casual entrants. The highway section consists of a large number of contractors, 95% of which have turnovers of less than 1 million dollars, whereas the heavy engineering section consists of a small number of major constructors because of the aspects of multiyear duration, megadollar value and specific area of expertise. Joint ventures and consortiums are not unusual in the heavy engineering section for projects such as transit systems, airfields and power stations. Highway contractors tend to be publicly funded; therefore 'union', heavy engineering contractors generally have a union manpower requirement imposed upon them, unless the project is privately funded. Funding of the engineering sector in 1988 was about 90 billion dollars, of which 50 billion was public money [10].

3. Building commissioning

Commissioning in the construction industry refers to the assembly of building land, capital commitment to cover all financial liabilities and the selection of architectural and/or organizing design professionals. Building commissioning means 'the granting of certain powers or the authority to carry out a particular task or duty' [11], in this case, A–E services.

The two most common selection methods of A–E services are: (a) the invitation and negotiation method; and (b) the competitive proposal method, both of which are primarily based on an owner's or agency's project brief. The brief outlines the size and function of the structure, target costs, target time schedule, services to be performed, and any other instructions deemed relevant to the proposed project.

The invitation and negotiation process is initiated by the commissioning agency selecting one or more A–E firms. The selection is fairly arbitrary and may be based on such factors as industry prominence and recognition for specific expertise, prior professional association or membership of the same golf club. Negotiations take place in informal meetings between representatives of both parties, until a mutually acceptable agreement is reached. Factors such as degree of complexity, scope of project and terms and conditions of contract influence the agreement.

A formal advertisement in a newspaper or a technical journal solicits the services of an A–E in the competitive proposal method, and A–Es respond by preparing a proposal based on the owner's brief. The competing A–Es attempt to convince the commissioning authority of their superior experience and expertise in their submissions, which may include impressive architectural renderings and their company's portfolio. Irrespective of the methods used to attract the owner's attention, the negotiation stage generally revolves around the level of service to be provided and the cost of those services. The fee basis of service reimbursement may be either a percentage of total project costs or a fixed lump sum. Historically the range of fees is 4–6% for architectural services and 6–12% for a total design, including all the required engineering design disciplines.

Most federal, state and local jurisdictions charged with building commissioning responsibilities have access to in-house A–E services; therefore the public sector seldom utilizes either commissioning method except under special circumstances. The private sector, on the other hand, freely uses both methods as circumstances dictate without restriction. Both methods of commissioning culminate in a legal agreement between the commissioner and the A–E. Forms of owner–A–E agreements are available for almost all styles of commissioning currently utilized in the United States, either in an AIA or ACEC approved standard format.

4. Building procurement methods

Procurement involves the two major activities of acquiring the services of construction contractors, and purchasing or renting other materials and equipment required for the construction of a structure. Contractual arrangements and procurement methods are influenced by the project's uniqueness. Two general categories of contract types are: (a) competitive bids which includes lump-sum fixed-price or lump-sum unit price; (b) negotiated, which includes cost plus, design build, turnkey, force account, and construction management.

The competitive bid method of determining the lowest responsible bidder accounts for about 75–80% of all construction contracts awarded in the United States each year [12]. The lump-sum fixed-price bid is most common in the private sector and the lump-sum unit-price bid is used almost exclusively in the public sector. The pros and cons of the US lump-sum competitive bidding system are well documented [13] and the unit-price system used in the United States by public commissioning agencies is a carbon copy of the traditional British procurement method, down to the schedule of quantities, bills and contract remeasurement. In the negotiated procurement sub-categories, cost plus contracts [14] allow maximum flexibility in the cost reimbursement methods available. The plus aspect considers percentage of cost, fixed fee, profit sharing, sliding fee and a whole range of combinations. The particular benefit of cost plus contractors is the flexibility available in meeting variations between the project designed and the physical amount of work done. Design build [15] requires that the design and construction functions are performed by one construction organization. There are two distinct groups of design builders. One group consists of major contractors who design and build heavy industrial projects such as petrochemical and process plants, with multimillion dollar values and multiyear schedules. The second group develops light industrial–commercial estates, normally on a speculative basis. Fast-tracking, a 'buzz' word coined to indicate a schedule compression produced by building a section as soon as it is designed, is a form of design build. When a contractor supplies functional elements such as computers, furniture, telephones, etc., in addition to the design build element, the contract style is termed turnkey, implying that the owner turns the key, opens up the plant and starts production immediately.

The force account [16] approach is also referred to as the owner–builder method of building procurement, because historically government agencies, state, city and county public works departments perform both design and construction functions using their own forces. Some major private sector corporations such as Dupont, Coors and Proctor and Gamble use the owner–builder method with some modifications.

Construction management (CM) is a fairly recent addition to the available procurement methods [17]. Advocates of this method stress the non-adversary relationship between the owner, designer and CM. The owner also has the opportunity to participate fully in the process from concept to completion. This method allows the designer to control the design, and the CM to be solely responsible for all costs, time schedules and the physical construction process.

Generally, all methods of construction procurement used in the US construction industry are available in other parts of the world.

5. Effects of union influence

Union influence in the US construction market is currently at a very low ebb due principally to two specific factors [18]. The first factor is public disenchantment with union labour organizations due to the effect of strikes, secondary boycotts, picketing, costly collective bargaining agreements and low labour productivity. The second factor is the recent strong emergence of an alternative source of construction labour, namely merit or open shop labour. Considering the previous dominance of union labour in the industry, the shift in owner manpower utilization from union to open shop labour is dramatic.

Historically, organized construction workers belong to one of the international unions that form the Building and Construction Trade department of the American Federation of Labour (AFL) Congress of Industrial Organizations (CIO). The AFL–CIO organizes two major types of labour organizations, the craft union and the industrial union. Construction workers are traditionally craft union members. Since the early 1900s legislation such as the Davis–Bacon Act, the Norris–Laguardia Act, the National Labour Relations Act and the Taft–Hartley Act have formed the basis of management–labour relationships in the construction industry and protected the unions' rights [19]. Subsequent enactment of 'right to work' statutes and legislation made labour agreements mandating union membership as a condition of employment illegal. As a consequence, the merit shop labour movement was developed and supported by the ABC. Currently, the merit shop movement, which advocates free enterprise in the construction market place, is strong nationally. The ABC claims that in 1988 merit or open shop labour completed at least 65% of all construction work completed in the United States [20]. Some regions still remain as union labour strongholds, but nationally the construction unions' influence is low. The climate, therefore, in management–labour relations is presently conducive to mutually acceptable harmonious labour agreements. Trade union supporters claim that the national pendulum movement between management and union organized labour will eventually prevail, but construction industry analysts predict that trade unionism may never recover its market share without some drastic changes in their basic antagonist/protagonist philosophy.

6. Different markets for construction

The traditional markets for the industry are in the residential, industrial, commercial, institutional and engineering sectors, but in the last few years several new markets have emerged due to public awareness of the societal impact of pollution. The Environmental Protection Agency (EPA) is the federal agency responsible for protecting the environment, particularly air and water.

As a result of public concern, pollution control and waste management programmes have created a high demand for facilities to handle sewage treatment, soil water treatment, process and toxic waste treatment and disposal, air emission control structures, etc. The removal and disposal of hazardous materials, such as asbestos, has also created a new and potentially lucrative market for a select few licensed contractors.

Preservation of structures with architectural or historical significance is also a growing market, not major in terms of cost but meritorious in terms of its philosophy and change in national attitude. Data on the crumbling infrastructure across the nation, collected over several years, predicted the inevitable collapse of bridges, crumbling of roads, disintegration of major sewer and water mains and other disasters which have occurred. Restoration of the infrastructure, although not a new market, is an emerging multiyear, multibillion dollar project which may lure new entrants.

Different markets for the industry also exist for the implementation of the systems international (metric) measurement system; modular construction component development; prefabrication systems analysis and development; but they appear to be low priority markets as far as any influx of development money is concerned. Different markets for the industry are difficult to predict, but technological advances on earth and in space may create a yet to be recognized market for the industry. As special market funding is allocated, construction contractors will emerge to satisfy the created demand.

7. Problems and opportunities in operating in the United States

The opportunities open to a foreign contractor entering the US construction market are equal to those open to domestic contractors. The US government imposes no restrictions on foreign contractors' rights to bid federal, state, and local public projects. On projects of a sensitive national security nature, foreign contractors would be subject to the same security checks as domestic contractors [21].

The US Department of Commerce provides information to help foreign contractors establish their corporate entity. The federal government in effect invites the foreign contractor to invest in America, to 'hang out a shingle' and start building. Several states require construction contractors to be licensed, where the licences are designed to protect the public's health and safety, and to ensure lawful operation by the contractor.

A major hurdle for foreign contractors concerns the establishment of a construction business and performance track record. Since the corporate records of the contractor are all off-shore, establishing financial and technical credibility becomes extremely difficult. Without access to banking, insurance and bonding, no public work can be undertaken and private work may also be unobtainable.

Other difficulties in operation which must be overcome are (1) cultural differences; (2) practical construction processes and methods; (3) trade union pressure; and (4) 'Build America'.

1. The cultural differences are self-evident and include language, style of dress, standard of living, food, etc.
2. The American construction industry is highly mechanized, and this mechanical aid philosophy has a positive influence on construction processes and methods. Development of a man–machine ratio attitude is essential to ensure contractor competitiveness.
3. Foreign contractors may be pressured to sign collective bargaining agreements, but labour affiliation must be chosen only after prudent investigation and evaluation of the local labour market.
4. 'Build America' is a patriotic slogan which has piqued the country's nationalism. It may be manifested by sub-contractors and suppliers choosing to bid foreign contractors less competitively, if at all.

There may be some benefit for foreign contractors to objectively review and evaluate a construction process or method taken for granted in the United States. Whatever problems or opportunities present themselves a prudent contractor, foreign or otherwise, should prepare a plan and establish strategies to minimize the problems created by a change in geographical location.

8. Potential strategies for market penetration

World observers of the built-environment view the US construction industry as being a highly competitive market. The US Department of Commerce [22] provides some interesting data on market penetration by foreign builders, summarized as follows:

1. The foreign entrants are among the largest construction companies in the world.
2. Their share of the market in 1985 was 3% of the total volume available, accounting for about 8 billion dollars.
3. Foreign company activity was primarily in non-residential construction such as hotels, factories and office buildings.
4. Of the 80 billion dollar foreign contractor share of the construction market, 70% went to foreign acquired US companies and 30% to foreign branch operations or newly established subsidiaries.
5. Factors which have proven to be critical in market penetration are financial strength, technological expertise, and available underutilized professional staff.

The most successful foreign nation in the construction industry is Japan, which favours the branch office approach because of the relatively short distance from Japan to the US west coast. Sensitive public relations work is necessary to resolve branch office staffing by head office personnel, hiring of local industry expertise, labour affiliation selection and local contractor cooperation. An autonomous branch office of a foreign contractor, unobtrusively developed, in time assumes the mantle of the traditional US contractor.

For other nations entering the market, the acquisition of an established company provides the least complicated method. Sound business principles and long-range planning are essential strategies, as are intimate knowledge of the chosen market sector and of the targeted company. Hired US bankers, lawyers and accountants should negotiate the acquisition in accordance with corporate directives. The acquired company remains American except for the source of its funding, while any necessary (astute) evaluation and replacement of the top management on a timely basis makes the acquisition process virtually painless.

In summary, the acquisition or branch office approaches to market entry both apply to foreign contractors at all work-volume and dollar-value levels, but it generally remains the domain of the world's largest construction companies. The acquisition method requires a much larger infusion of capital but with a smaller imported professional staff than the branch office method.

Public and labour organization scrutiny is more intense with the set-up of the foreign branch office, whereas the acquired company remains American.

Regardless of the strategy adopted for market penetration, foreign companies presumably possess astute business acumen for survival in their own countries. Nothing less is required for entry and survival in any other construction environment. Three major elements summarize any business venture, namely research, analysis, and decision. These elements are similarly critical for corporate relocation either across the street or around the world.

References

1. *Value of New Construction Put in Place.* US Department of Commerce, Bureau of the Census, Washington, DC, January 1989.
2. 'Construction economics'. Associated General Contractors of America. *Constructor*, March 1989.
3. *1982 Census of Construction Industries.* Final Report, Industry Series. US Department of Commerce, Bureau of the Census, Washington, DC, July 1985.
4. 'Constructor delivers the industry'. Associated General Contractors of America. *Constructor*, March 1989.
5. *Losses in Private Sector Construction Due to Contractor Failure.* The Surety Association of America and the National Association of Surety Bond Producers. Ardrey Incorporated, March 1988.
6. *America Built and Merit.* Associated Builders and Contractors, Washington, DC 1989.
7. Matthewson, C. (1988) Lump Sum Competitive Building Systems. Heriot Watt University, Edinburgh Master's Thesis (unpublished), October.
8. *NAHB The Voice of America's Building Industry.* National Association of House Builders, Washington, DC, 1988.
9. 'Constructor delivers the industry'. Associated General Contractors of America, *Constructor*, March 1989.
10. 'Constructor delivers the industry'. Associated General Contractors of America, *Constructor*, March 1989.
11. *The American Heritage Dictionary.* 2nd edn. Houghton Mifflin, Boston 1985.
12. *1982 Census of Construction Industries*, July 1985.
13. Matthewson, C. (1985) *op. cit.*
14. Clough, R. H. (1975) *Construction Contracting*, 3rd edn. John Wiley and Sons.
15. Hendrickson, C., Tune, A. V. (1989) *Project Management in Construction.* Prentice Hall, New Jersey.
16. Clough, R. H. (1975) *op. cit.*
17. Barrie, D. S., Paulson, B. C. (1978) *Professional Construction Management.* McGraw-Hill.
18. *Labstat Series Report.* US Department of Labor, Bureau of Labour Statistics, Washington, D.C. February.
19. Clough, R. H. (1975) *op. cit.*
20. America Built and Merit (1989) *op. cit.*

21. *Foreign Builders Target the United States: Implications and Trends*. US Department of Commerce International Trade Administration, Washington, DC, March 1988.
22. *Foreign Builders Target the United States*, March 1988, *op. cit.*

Additional reading

Halpin, D. W., Woodhead, R. W. (1980) *Construction Management*. John Wiley & Sons.

—— *PART IV* ——

Strategic management in construction companies: an integrated approach for achieving competitive advantage

The final chapter draws together a number of the themes running throughout the book. A highly selective approach has been adopted on the choice of themes to include since a wide range of material has been covered in each of the chapters. However, the final chapter has attempted to capture the essence of what the editors see as the derivatives of competitive advantage in construction and how theory, when combined with practical insight, can be used to guide managers' decision-making within the strategic management process to achieve competitive advantage. The four major themes isolated for consideration within the final chapter are as follows:

1. The external environment
    *   industry analysis and market structure;
    *   demand as part of the environment;
    *   types of environmental change and their relationship to strategy.
2. Innovation in construction.
3. The strategic management process:
    *   tools, techniques and methodologies for competitive advantage;
    *   organizational structure and roles;
    *   the marketing function and its contribution to competitive advantage;
    *   production and industrial relations;
    *   the management of change;
    *   management development and operative training.
4. Competitive advantage in international construction.

── 18 ──

Competitive advantage in construction: a synthesis

Steven Male and Robert Stocks

1. Introduction

The construction industry, both domestically and internationally, is large by any standards. It is one of the most important contributors to a nation's economy but one of the least understood and investigated in depth by researchers. The country chapters in this book indicate it has, both nationally and internationally, a poor public image and low-recruitment status. The industry is characterized by a wide diversity of clients, local, regional, national and international, with differing degrees of knowledge of the industry, who range in size from individuals to multinational enterprises and from local to national governments.

This book has brought together a range of material concerning the domestic UK and international construction industries in different nations in order to integrate this into a framework for developing and understanding competitive strategy and advantage within construction. The following sections draw together some of the major themes running throughout the book.

2. Competitive strategy and advantage in construction

2.1 The environmental variables of industry and market structure

The starting point for any analysis of competitive strategy and advantage for a construction firm is the fact that it competes simultaneously in both markets and industries. For analytical purposes it is useful to keep the concept of a market and industry distinct. A market is a demand side concept and is buyer (client) generated. An industry is a supply side concept and is generated by companies through their collective actions in producing either goods or services for purchase by buyers. Both markets and industries involve the actions of the company *and* competitors. In effect, since one is demand generated and the other supply generated, with interactions between both, a *tension* is created involving both strategic and tactical considerations that has to be resolved within the construction company through organizational structure via the decisions of strategists and management.

For a construction company, industry analysis involves the joint examination of the impact of the five competitive forces on the company's position in the industry, namely:

(a) buyers;
(b) suppliers;
(c) interfirm rivalry;
(d) substitute products or services;
(e) new entrants.

Industry analysis takes a long-term perspective and involves the firm's strategists in analysing the actions of their competitors as well as economic, political, social, technological and legal trends. Industry analysis sets up the strategically important structural parameters of competition that flow through into tactical market competition. An industry generates a pool of existing and potential competitors producing goods and services that are demanded by clients in markets. The market organizes the exchange relationship for a mutually agreed price. In a construction context the contracting industry represents those firms that are linked economically, socially and competitively to produce facilities – different types of building or civil engineering structures – for a client via different procurement and tendering strategies and where the various parties are bound together through contractual arrangements. Therefore, embedded within industry structure are contracting markets where clients and their consultant advisers are involved in an exchange relationship with a contractor to erect an edifice by a production process for an agreed price. In this sense, an industry is a long-term structural concept, whereas a market is transient and short-term. Depending on how a firm orients itself to the market place in the short term, either through providing a service or by producing goods, it will lead to industry structure in the medium and long term.

There are two primary market types operating in the construction industry, namely, contracting and speculative work, with different economic forces at play in each. Each market type requires a different set of managerial and commercial skills. In a concentrically diversified construction company these different market types are resolved through organizational structure. For example, in the instance of a concentrically diversified construction firm that is involved in speculative house building as well as contracting, the organizational structure will reflect these differences through some kind of divisional or subsidiary-based organizational configuration. In the case of contracting, demand is derived and price is determined in advance of production. Institutionalized distribution channels are in operation for contractors that diffuse their services through clients' consultant advisers. Contracting markets are heavily influenced by the choice of procurement, tendering and contractual arrangements. In speculative work construction companies are involved in demand creation for their products and price is determined after production. This has a closer affinity to manufacturing industries.

One of the key issues identified in Chapter 1 is the presence or absence of entry barriers in the construction industry. It has been argued that barriers are still yet to crystallize in the construction industry among the top 35–50 UK construction companies since they have been involved in considerable diversification away from their contracting bases over the last 10–15 years. The essence now of any analysis of competition within the construction industry is to determine the different forms of entry barrier that are now present for the diversified construction company. Porter's classification of entry barriers was used to explore their presence, in various forms, within the industry. He identified six different types of entry barrier and each was shown to operate in construction in different ways. For example, in contracting entry barriers are subtle and relate very much to the fact that, first, consultants act as intermediaries between client and contractor and, second, the type, size, project technology and locality of a construction project also have an impact. For the diversified construction company, other entry barriers are related to the degree of fixed assets held by the company and the extent to which these could be bound up with manufacturing type subsidiary operations for example.

The construction industry, at some 'suprasystem' level, was identified as being fragmented for many reasons and the degree of fragmentation was related to the geographically dispersed project-based nature of the industry and the split between the new build and repair and maintenance sectors. In the former where projects can range from the very small to the very large, project type and location have an impact on the extent to which the industry is, in reality, fragmented. For example, on the larger contracts where managerial expertise, technical knowledge and financial stability of a company are seen as important there may be only a relatively small number of contractors able to tender. In addition, pre-qualification procedures on projects mean that the number of firms entering the market for setting up a production base are small anyway. In the repair and maintenance sector where projects have a greater tendency to be small, local firms have an advantage. Therefore, in contracting, tendering strategies create distinct project-based markets where subtle forms of barriers to entry can exist and only a few or many contractors may be able to compete depending on the client tendering strategy adopted. It has been argued that this sets up a vertical project-based market structure in contracting, where project size and technological complexity are the major determinants. Also, location plays an important part since the geographically dispersed nature of demand may favour the local contracting community with local–regional client or consultant contacts. Finally, management and finance were identified as scale economy–learning-type barriers in contracting but some authors consider that the managerial barrier, intrinsically linked to the vertical project market, is easily vaultable. We have argued, however, that since entry barriers are long term in nature, the extent to which 'poaching' of managers from other companies is a long-term solution to vaulting managerial barriers in the United Kingdom is very much dependent on the supply and continued upgrading of managerial talent in the industry over the long term. The available evidence suggests that insufficient management training and development is taking place in construction in the United Kingdom. Coupled with this is the fact that the industry is not seen as a first or even second choice recruitment opportunity for many new recruits entering the industry. 'Poaching' can only be seen as a short-term solution to vaulting managerial entry barriers. Taking a cross-cultural view, the lifetime employment practices of the large Japanese construction companies would suggest that 'poaching' is not a method of vaulting managerial barriers to entry in their domestic market. In their case it would appear that a continued commitment to upgrading managerial and technological capabilities is their only option.

The nation chapters have indicated clearly that the structuring of UK construction into a hierarchical industry of a small number of large firms and large numbers of small firms is also characteristic of other nations' construction industries. Sub-contracting was identified as a major project strategy in the United Kingdom and is equally important in other nations' construction industries, for example Japan. However, the issue identified in the United Kingdom was that labour-only sub-contracting (LOSC) is seriously undermining industry structure in terms of the upgrading of its skill base. A comparison was made with France and Germany where LOSC was illegal. Both nations are embarking on a sustained commitment to upgrading the skill and status base of their construction industry. It could be argued that since construction is an essentially domestic industry with a relatively small international component the actions of other nations in upgrading their domestic skill base is of little concern. However, as Smith noted in his chapter on the European Community (EC), once the Single European Market is in operation there may be significant shifts in the way that construction work is undertaken in the Community, especially with harmonization of standards to meet these new technological demands. Operative flexibility will become increasingly important. In addition, since the United Kingdom has faced serious skill shortages in boom periods the incursion of foreign labour to fill the gaps does little to solve the long-term problems of the industry.

Two other forces are at play to affect the manpower requirements of the UK construction industry. First, the demographic shift will primarily hit the social strata from which the industry draws its skilled and unskilled workforce. This means that the construction industry in the United Kingdom will have to compete with other industries for a diminishing pool of workers. The UK construction industry already faces severe shortages of skilled labour when the economy enters a boom period, and the implications of the demographic shift can only worsen this in the foreseeable future. Second, there is not a track record of high numbers of young people entering the tertiary education sector in the United Kingdom and while the demographic shift will not hit this sector in anywhere near the magnitude that it will hit the skilled and unskilled workforce, it does mean that construction companies are in direct competition with other industries for managerial and technical talent. As indicated above, construction is not a first-choice industry for many potential recruits. It was argued that the industry has, over many years, geared up for structural casualization and the evidence would suggest that the available pool of managerial talent, both from the skilled workforce and from those potential managerial recruits seeking employment across industries, will diminish considerably in the long term unless positive steps are taken to prevent this happening. Some of the larger construction firms are now taking positive steps to attract people from non-construction-related disciplines into the industry. The effect of this can only be considered from a strategic perspective with reference to the balance between current and future needs and the opportunities for employment stability in the industry.

2.2 Demand as part of the environment in construction

We have argued that strategic management is about managing the long-term relationship between the company and its environment. Two factors come into play with construction. First, long-term trends can be discerned both for demand and output in construction and this is a pre-requisite for strategic thinking. Second, demand in construction is highly variable in the short term – a tactical issue – but is no worse than that with which managers in manufacturing industry have to contend. Transposing both of these into our strategic framework of industry and market structures, long-term trends are related to the development of competitive strategy through the industry analysis framework. This is subsequently inverted into tactical considerations for competing in markets where demand variability has its greatest impact. For example, long-term trend analysis may reveal a move away from public sector funded construction of dam structures, a lucrative market at one time in the United Kingdom. A company geared up for this type of work had to make a strategic decision to shift its emphasis away from this type of structure to take on board the capabilities of undertaking other types of projects before the market dried up. A further example is the increasing upward trend for repair and maintenance – accounting for between 40 and 50% of UK construction workload. Any construction firm ignoring this considerable market potential and not gearing itself up with the right managerial operative capabilities to undertake this type of work may place itself at a strategic disadvantage compared to its competitors. It was indicated in Chapter 2 that many construction firms have now set up subsidiaries or other types of operating unit to deal with this type of work.

2.3 Types of environmental change and a hierarchy of strategies

A hierarchy of strategies was identified. Corporate strategy is holistic and concerned with the activities of the whole company. Business strategy is concerned with competing in different markets or industries. Bidding strategy is an example in contracting. Operational–functional strategy is concerned with the operating core or functional departments. A focus on production and the associated processes would be an example in construction.

Two major and three contingent types of environmental change were identified to which a company has to adapt. The first type – recurrent – is incremental and allows an organizational memory to be developed. There is no significant change in the relationship of the firm with its environment. We identified operational change as falling within this type where the focus is internal. In this instance managers could focus their attention in construction on improvements in the production process, i.e. a production-oriented strategy. Managers can use experience to handle this type of change. The second type – transformational – involves a fundamental shift in the relationship of the company with its environment. We identified two additional contingent types of environmental change here. The first type – strategic – is discontinuous, fundamental, radical and non-incremental. This type of change requires managers to use insight and creativity. Experience is of little use due to the radical and unfamiliar nature of the change. Managers' cognitive structures will be altered when dealing with this type of change, perhaps fundamentally. The impact of this type of change is likely to be felt right the way through the organizational structure, from the strategic apex to the operating core. The primary focus here would be on corporate strategy. The second contingent type of change – competitive – while fundamental in the medium to long term is also incremental. It is a combination of strategic and operational change which suggests elements of discontinuity in the environment but tempered by an evolutionary shift. It requires the integration of insight, creativity and experience. In essence, this type of change requires a simultaneous focus on corporate, business and production strategies. The danger is that managers may focus on either production or business strategy at the expense of monitoring and adapting to the changing long-term nature of the company with its environment – corporate strategy. Transformational change, since it involves a fundamental shift in the relationship of the firm with its environment requires a decision-making strategy of 'vigilance' and the clear demarcation between 'strategic' and 'non-strategic' issues.

2.4 Long waves and innovation in construction

Porter [1] identifies innovation as one of the key issues in sustained competitive advantage. A number of themes were highlighted in earlier chapters with respect to innovation in the construction industry. Four distinct types of innovation have been identified, as follows:

1. Technological innovation which utilizes new knowledge or techniques to provide an object or service at lower cost or higher quality.

2. Organizational innovation which does not require technological advances but involves 'social technology' – the changing relationship between behaviours, attitudes and values. In construction a number of examples were identified by Lansley – new types of business organization, new forms of contract and procurement, the opening up of new markets.
3. Product innovation which involves advances in technology resulting in superior products – services. This may have a low hardware dependency but provide better utilization of resources.
4. Process innovations which substantially increase efficiency without significant advances in technology.

In taking account of these different types of innovation, first, much of the innovation in the construction industry occurs at the workface, with individual craftsmen, on special projects, and is therefore incremental. With the increasing use of sub-contracting this type of innovation falls within the domain of sub-contractors and is lost to the possession of main contractors unless a long-standing business relationship is established. This appears to be the case in Japan and may have some impact in the United Kingdom. However, taking the UK situation, the high levels of sub-contracting mean that this type of incremental innovation is also available to competitors in the marketplace. Second, innovation in equipment or materials lies outside the industry. Construction is more involved with innovation diffusion. However, the effective utilization of equipment and materials by construction firms to maximize the benefits of innovation in other industries creates knowledge-based competitive advantages. Again, high levels of sub-contracted plant hire–leasing means that these innovations are also potentially available to competitors. Third, equipment-based innovation does occur in construction in other nations, Japan being a prime example. In its case high levels of domestic competition, skills shortages and an ageing workforce are a major impetus for the large Japanese construction firms to invest in plant and equipment development to substitute technology for labour. If successful this may well provide a competitive weapon for these firms to enter overseas markets with product innovations to service domestic industries also facing similar problems and where indigenous firms are not undertaking such development. Third, clear market pull factors in construction have, in situations of depressed demand, placed an emphasis on cost reduction and developing new services. Therefore, competitive advantage for construction firms in the United Kingdom has primarily lain with organizational innovation. Fourth, technology push has also been evident within construction with the development of intelligent buildings and robotics – an issue relevant again to Japanese construction firms. In this latter instance, we can identify that competitive advantage for Japanese construction firms lies with both organizational innovation as an immediate competitive weapon and potentially technological innovation in the future.

Lansley identified the importance of understanding the impact of long waves in the economy for the innovatory behaviour of construction firms.

Based on his empirical data in UK construction he suggests that different types of innovation may be more appropriate in periods of decline than in periods of recovery. By way of example, he indicates that in construction during the 1960s companies were involved in process innovation with a primary focus on operational change and a task-oriented style of management. In the 1970s when construction firms were faced with strategic change companies were involved in product innovation with a management style that was people and corporate oriented. Flanagan, in his analysis of the Japanese construction industry, also provides supporting evidence for Lansley's contention, in a cross-cultural context, when he indicates that during the period 1975–85 when the Japanese domestic construction industry was in deep recession – a situation of transformational (strategic) change – construction firms were strategically repositioning themselves by developing new services – product innovation – ready for the upturn in the economy. It can also be suggested that during periods of competitive change a different type of innovation is required, one that combines both product and process innovation. In this instance the company is facing change that has elements of both strategic and operational change. Process innovation – focusing on gains inefficiency – provides the company with a stable and effective resource base from which to invest in and launch new competitive initiatives – product innovations – to gain an advantage over competitors. In a construction context this would require focusing on making the production process more efficient, from which resources are generated (primarily cash, managerial and technical expertise), to launch a new service – perhaps design and build, management contracting or project management that would require investment in the upgrading or hiring in of managerial skills, a technical system or capital to fund marketing efforts.

Finally, if we compare the descriptions of the innovatory processes involved in different types of change with the strategic types identified by Miles *et al.* [2] the following picture emerges. The *defender* is characterized by a focus on improving the internal operations of the firm and a search for stability and market penetration through ruthless pursuit of cost control. This type of organization would adopt a process-based innovation approach within a business environment characterized by operational change. In a construction company the primary focus for a defender type would be on increasing production efficiency. The *prospector* has an external orientation towards the marketplace and is concerned with product development. Innovation and flexibility are high priorities. The prospector will focus on product innovation and is likely to favour a business environment characterized by transformational change where the demands for environmental scanning are high and suit this strategic type. The prospector type of construction firm would characteristically be seeking new ways to serve new or existing clients. The *analyser* combines elements of both the prospector and defender, seeking both stability and flexibility in different parts of the organization and having both an internal and external orientation. The analyser, because it is a hybrid form of organization, will effectively combine both process and product innovation. It is likely to prosper well in conditions of competitive change and, to a lesser extent, in business environments involving strategic change since the systems and procedures that are in place for achieving stability may be inappropriate in such environmental circumstances. This strategic type would characterize the construction firm that uses its strengths in production to resource new service provision.

3. 'Organization' and competitive advantage

3.1 Organizational structures and roles

Two models of an organization were presented in Chapter 1. First, a structural model that defines a company in terms of a strategic apex, middle line, operating core, technostructure and support staff. The operating core of a contracting company is based around the notion of project portfolios and is in a constant state of competitive and technological flux due to differing project life cycles. In contracting, unlike manufacturing, the requirement to maintain strategic flexibility in response to variable demand conditions in the environment is retained through the merchant producer role of the contractor. The notion of potential capacity was used to highlight the knowledge-based capacity of the contractor to gear up to increased workloads, in this instance usually located at site management level. It has been argued that due to demand variability contractors have increasingly opted for a structure that is truncated at the operating core through the use of sub-contracting. In other words they have chosen to structure themselves as administrative adhocracies to handle demand variability. Five coordinating mechanisms were identified for organizations. The diversified construction company could utilize all five within its structure depending on the degree and nature of the diversification strategy used. In addition, as Cannon and Hillebrandt report, construction companies have a structure that may be overlaid with a divisionalized and/or subsidiary configuration.

The second organizational model focused on the organizational role as a situationally defined view of an individual with a number of forces acting on it. An organization, using this model, was defined as a web or network of interlocking roles. Lansley, in Chapter 4, argues that innovative behaviour is strongly influenced by organizational position and role. For example, he suggests that the adoption of innovatory ideas is influenced by those with power, an ability to impose sanctions and with a web of communication linkages throughout the organization. In other words they use the interlocking role system to facilitate innovation diffusion. These two models of an organization were subsequently drawn together with ideas from economists' analysis of work organization to define a construction company as one that is both a business and social entity where contractual market-based and psychological exchanges takes place. The psychological contract defines the permeable boundaries of the firm and sets the parameters for defining what is internal or external to the firm. The increased use of sub-contracting means that the managerial hierarchy and psychological contract of the contracting firms, now structured as an administrative adhocracy, has become fragmented. The consequence is that the operating core is characterized by a workforce that is divided by method of payment, employment contract and company loyalty.

Using the work of Cannon and Hillebrandt, on their recent empirical studies of the national and international structuring of UK construction firms, and material from an earlier chapter, we can indicate that in UK construction for the larger construction firms, the following apply:

1. Diversification has occurred as a deliberate policy and where this has materialized internationally it has been invariably non-construction related. Where geographic diversification has occurred internationally in construction related areas it has been in housing or property development rather than contracting.
2. Construction companies are geographically mobile within the United Kingdom in terms of where they will set up a production base, both within the civil engineering and building sectors. They tend to focus their attention away from small new build and repair and maintenance projects, even at regional level, but will undertake major refurbishment work.
3. They operate as main contractors, sub-contracting supply and fix work, and increasingly use labour-only sub-contracting, although there are significant regional variations with respect to the use of the latter.
4. Labour strategy is decentralized to site level to capitalize on local knowledge of the labour market.
5. Ownership and organizational structures vary. There are a large number of family-owned companies; some management buyouts; construction firms that are subsidiaries of conglomerates; publicly owned firms but where management is still in the hands of people related to the original founders; of the remainder, approximately 30% are still in construction but with a diversified organizational configuration. The preceding indicates clearly a diversity of structures, histories, organizational cultures, strategic capabilities and directions.
6. There is an interplay between the divisional and subsidiary organizational configuration. Some firms operate on a divisionalized basis. In certain instances the divisionalized form is an overlay onto a subsidiary structure. Divisions and subsidiaries operate with their own boards of directors, as do regional subsidiaries. In the case of the latter, in certain instances where regional companies have been acquired they may continue to trade under their original names in order to maximize the benefits of being seen as a local trader.
7. The main board is usually represented with all activities. Finance is always represented and the personnel function is sometimes represented.

distinctive competencies of a contractor are to be found also in the middle line and at the strategic apex.

3.3.1 Tools, techniques and methodologies for competitive advantage

A number of tools, techniques and methodologies have been highlighted and discussed for use in a construction company. In summary, these are as follows:

1. The SWOT analysis, concerned with determining the strengths and weakness of the firm internally and the opportunities and threats in the external environment.
2. Competitor analysis, which focuses on analysing in depth the actions and moves of competitors in order to understand the context within which the company's competitive strategy has to be developed. It was argued that in contracting, competitor analysis needs to be carefully focused because of the large number of firms that may be potential competitors. It has been suggested that a firm's 'peer group' may be the best focus of attention.
3. Strategic group analysis, which is concerned with attempting to identify those firms that are pursuing similar strategies. An attempt to apply this form of analysis to construction was discussed and it has been high-lighted utilizing the knowledge that a methodology suitable for a complex industry is the best way forward.
4. The use of the strategic business area (SBA) concept in contracting. It has been argued that the SBA concept can usefully be applied in construction because it circumvents the issue of industry–market classi-fications and the product–service dichotomy, since an SBA is identified by the following:
   - a future market need, i.e. is demand-oriented;
   - a project technology, i.e. defined by the relationship and interaction of the social and technical system used by a contractor and bound together formally through a written contract, e.g. JCT 80, Design and Build, etc.
   - a customer with a need;
   - a geographical location where the customer has that need.

A construction firm's competitive strategy would be worked out in that context and would involve taking account of competitors' actions. Thus, a competitive strategy is one that positions the firm advantageously with respect to its competitors in a particular SBA. In construction this could be principally through price or through other forms of differentiation. Depending on company configuration, this could occur at three distinct levels: at bidding strategy level where the concept of contestable markets comes into play via client tendering strategy and price and pre-qualification procedures are important; at strategic business unit (SBU) level – for example a regional office or a design and build subsidiary; finally, at corporate level where the spectrum of the total firm is taken into account.

An analysis of competitive advantage should take place at SBU level. A second domain of analysis can also be included, namely, the SBA. At the heart of analysing competitive advantage is the concept of value which is created through the activities of a company in an exchange relationship. The value concept is market-based and is concerned with what the buyer is prepared to pay. The strategically important value activities are linked together in a value chain, which has both an internal and external component. Value chain analysis is concerned with understanding inbound logistics – in contracting supply inputs and the tendering process; the transformation process – organizational functioning leading to production; and finally, out-bound logistics – delivery of the facility to the client, in this case the production process and hand over. To recapitulate, the value chain is a product of a company's

- history;
- culture;
- strategic management process;
- the cost and resourcing implications of the preceding.

In construction it has been argued that a heavy reliance is placed on experience – a knowledge-based and high-order source of advantage. This requires continued upgrading through training and management development in order that the company becomes a moving target. This commitment to upgrading of knowledge-based advantages becomes crucial, especially in construction, where it has been argued that managerial entry barriers can easily be vaulted through poaching in the short term. Construction firms also compete on the basis of the relative cost of inputs compared to their competitors through their merchant producer role. This is a low-order source of advantage that can easily be copied by competitors.

An exploratory value chain analysis was conducted of the contractor's tendering–bidding process. A number of discrete value activities were identified in the pre-tender process by Male and Thorpe and McCaffer, namely the following:

- estimating;
- contracts planning–management;
- the procurement–buying function;
- the sub-contract tender process;
- tender adjudication, which was identified as both a strategic and operational activity since it involved senior managers and those from the middle line.

In the post-tender site production stage other value activities are also in evidence, namely the following:

1. The choice of labour strategy – directly employed versus LOSC
2. The site management role:
    - the organization and coordination of sub-contractors;
    - site recruitment practices;

- approaches to industrial relations in terms of employment conditions, i.e. arrangements and procedures for bonus and overtime payments;
- organization and control of boundary management between sub-contractors.

Again, since the analysis of the site management function revealed a high level of emphasis on experience this is a knowledge-based, high-order advantage requiring continued upgrading in order to meet the continued new demands of projects. However, where a proportion of the site management role falls within the sub-contractor's domain, such as the potential loss to the main contractor of the foreman, a reduction in production knowledge could ensue, and hence a source of high-order advantage.

To summarize, a number of tools, techniques and methodologies have been presented for use in the construction industry. The primary focus of their application has to be on the creation of value for the buyer (client).

3.3.2 Corporate strategy and strategic time horizons

It has already been suggested in Chapter 2 that the diversified construction firm will face different strategic time horizons. In contracting, it was suggested that a period of two years was the maximum time horizon since this tends to be the maximum length of many construction projects. Cannon and Hillebrandt suggest that with the large firms, who obtain some very large projects, this can be extended to three years. In property development the planning horizon can be four to five years and for those construction companies with a manufacturing-type subsidiary the planning horizon can extend into the long term. Thus, across different subsidiaries or divisions and at different levels within the construction firm, strategic time horizons will vary considerably. However, at main board level, where strategists develop the mission, and formulate objectives and strategy, these different time horizons have to be fused into a cognitive whole in order that a 'corporate vision' can be developed. The extent to which this corporate vision among strategists forms a 'gestalt', against which changes in the environment are judged, and which is coherent and consistent, will set the style of the company, from which all else will flow. This corporate gestalt will, in practice, be worked out over time, invariably through negotiation and compromise. However, the power of key strategists and major coalitions within the company will have a significant influence on the way strategy, within the framework of this strategic gestalt, is worked out.

Cannon and Hillebrandt have indicated the following for the larger construction firms:

1. There is often a blurred distinction between mission and objectives.
2. Ownership structure has an important influence on the type and preciseness of objectives.

3. The planning process varies between companies and to some extent depends again on ownership structure. In some construction companies it is undertaken by consensus between the main board and subsidiaries; in other construction firms it is undertaken at board level and then imposed on part of the organization, while in others it is imposed by the owning corporation.
4. The emphasis on financial policy is a distinguishing feature contracting and manufacturing. Capital is used primarily to fund housebuilding, land purchase and property development.
5. Closely related to the latter point is the importance of owning fixed assets to fund future growth through borrowing. In one sense, liquid capital has the advantage of providing strategic flexibility for the construction company. Its investment in fixed assets reduces this flexibility but creates entry barriers for other firms.
6. The capital liquidity generated by contracting makes construction firms potential targets for takeovers.
7. Acquisition is often pursued for opportunistic reasons rather than as part of a well thought out strategy. Howe [3] indicates that this could be a recipe for potential disaster and this is explored in greater detail below in the discussion of management of change.

3.4 The marketing function and its contribution to competitive advantage

Stocks has identified the fact that marketing is a management function closely bound up with the strategic management process. It is concerned with identifying, analysing and anticipating the needs of the customer and supplying those needs at a profit within the capabilities of the company. Marketing is linked to the demand side concept of the market. It also has a close affinity with the SBA concept. The three following elements comprise the marketing philosophy:

1. A customer orientation. Customers can be classified as:
   - key customers;
   - non-key customers;
   - non-customers.
2. A total company effort.
3. A profit objective.

Part of the marketing approach is to segment the market place in terms of customer needs and the way they buy and use a product or service. Market segmentation creates target markets which for industrial markets, of which construction is one, can be achieved by the following strategies:

(a) identifying market growth potential;
(b) determining the dominant competitors;
(c) determining entry barriers to markets;
(d) determining the components of value added.

Part of the marketing function involves market research, the systematic collection, recording and evaluation of data concerning the marketing of goods and services. Market research assists the firm to concentrate its resources on those parts of the market that will achieve the company's objectives. In one respect, taking the case of a diversified construction company, market research may be more applicable to its speculative house building and manufacturing subsidiaries. However, it may also be used to identify new forms of service provision for its contracting or management arms, such as design and build, management contracting and project management.

Stocks, in Chapter 3 on marketing, introduces issues associated with services and the marketing mix. The intangibility of service delivery means that performance does not result in the ownership of anything. In the context of construction this does not apply since a structure, under some form of ownership, is the result of service performance. Therefore, as Stocks points out, the delivery of a completed structure by a contractor is a mixture of both product and service. The following are required for the marketing mix in a construction context:

1. The *product* is a combination of ownership delivery – the completed structure – and service delivery – where human factors are important. The intangibility of service delivery for the contractor can only be evaluated on completion of the structure in terms of client satisfaction. The project-based nature of construction means there are problems of service substitutability by other contractors and this is tackled in two ways. First, pre-qualification makes the assumption that those contractors selected are capable of undertaking the work. In other words their service delivery is similar and price is the final arbiter. Second, differentiation, based on reputation and expertise places the contractor onto the select list in the first place. In this sense reputation embodies the fact that previous buyers are satisfied with performance. Expertise can be tackled in three ways via (a) certificated professional qualification – external validation of skills; (b) in-house training courses and on-the-job training; (c) external training courses. For example, Enderwick [4] commenting on the international construction industry, indicates that of the construction firms that he sampled, professional qualifications were seen as important by all respondents and of those companies that undertook training 50% emphasized experience and on-site training as important, and the other 50% of respondents indicated firm specific training was important for managing overseas projects. Cannon and Hillebrandt, in their empirical study of large UK contractors, also report the importance placed by companies on on-the-job training and the use of internal and external courses.
2. *Price:* in contracting, the price quoted by a contractor in advance of production represents the cost of providing the structure and the cost of service delivery. Thorpe and McCaffer indicate that in a competitive

bidding situation 90% of the tender is made up from the estimated cost of the work and the remaining 10% is the mark-up for risk, overhead and profit. In this respect the mark-up is not the most significant in determining which firm wins a contract. It was also highlighted in Chapter 2 that contractors believe that their competitive advantage comes from the pricing of preliminary items. The variability between firms in determining price is built into the tender well before it reaches the adjudication process – one of the value activities in the firm's corporate strategy.

Since it may be difficult to ascertain the true cost of service delivery until after completion, in a competitive bidding situation where the lowest price may be the deciding factor, quality may suffer during the production phase. This comment was made by skilled operatives in the NEDO study 'Faster Building for Commerce' [5]. Flanagan provides a comparative example with Japanese construction firms where quality and time are the controlled variables and cost the one that is allowed to vary.

3. *Promotion:* promotional activity provides a mechanism for differentiation and has two direct applications in contracting: first, in order to get onto select tendering lists; second, to obtain negotiated contracts. The essence of promotional activity in contracting, as any service delivery in construction, is to create the image in the recipient of performance delivery. In addition, the existence of promotional literature for a contracting company can distribute demand to a wider audience and hence create it since it provides the recipient with an insight into what the firm can potentially deliver should the recipient wish to take up the service.

4. *Place:* while it is true that there is no physical distribution system in one sense in contracting, such as a supermarket for consumer goods, it has been argued earlier that clients' consultants act as distribution channels for contractors' services. In addition, a structure is erected in a locality where the client has a need and therefore the service is consumed at the point of delivery, the construction site.

Marketing, as a competitive weapon in construction, and its influence on the strategic management process, has to be placed within the context of its location within the organizational structure of a construction firm. Earlier chapters have provided a number of clues as to how construction firms view marketing. Stocks, in Chapter 3, provided a number of stereotypes that can be used to describe a firm's orientation:

- a technology orientation;
- a production orientation;
- a sales orientation;
- a financial orientation;
- a market orientation.

We have already indicated that marketing is a customer-oriented activity. In this respect, the marketing function could be distributed throughout a contracting organization. Cannon and Hillebrandt indicate that while most construction companies are attempting to develop a marketing policy, many are finding it difficult to integrate the marketing function into corporate strategy. In addition, marketing has traditionally been seen as an operational function in construction and has not been given sufficiently high status. This is still the case in some firms, although it has increasingly been seen as a separate function. Furthermore, a financial orientation is seen to be paramount among construction firms. Thorpe and McCaffer provide additional insights into how estimating is viewed with construction firms, a value activity that can be argued to be at the front line of the relationship with customers. They discuss two types of orientation, one where estimating is seen as a technical function and forms part of the activities related to temporary works design, engineering design and work study. In this respect the estimating function is likely to report to some form of technical director. This orientation is predominant in engineering firms. A second orientation, highlighted by Thorpe and McCaffer, is where estimating is seen as part of the marketing function and reports to a marketing director. Finally, Lansley *et al.* [6] also provide corroborating evidence from their case studies of construction firms. They found empirically that the marketing function was not well developed in building and engineering firms but was in speculative house builders, where a selling orientation is imperative.

To summarize, a marketing philosophy and the associated tools and techniques can orientate the construction company towards the market place in order to fulfil the needs of the customer. The analysis above has suggested that part of the confusion over, and the reluctance to use, marketing in the industry is tied up with the issues of whether the product in construction is a service. Our analysis clearly indicates that the product in construction is both ownership- *and* service-directed, and that managers in construction are in a position to use tools and techniques aimed at both aspects. From a competitor analysis viewpoint, it is possible to work out the orientation of a firm by identifying the overriding orientation – financial, technological, marketing, etc. – by using the stereotypes as a guide. Finally, the location of the marketing function within the construction firm also gives a clue as to the orientation of the firm. However, the diversified construction company requires careful analysis in this respect since different subsidiaries may have the marketing function located at different levels in the organizational configuration. One important clue, however, can be found by analysing the functional representations at main board level.

3.5 The management of change

We have mentioned earlier in this chapter that the strategic management process involves the management of change. This is linked critically to the notion of strategy within the construction company. Male defined strategy in Chapter 2 as:

the implied or explicitly stated means that are developed by management, through cognitive and behavioural decision-making processes, to achieve the company's objectives and guide organizational behaviour

Implicit within the definition is that strategy, determining the long-term relationship of the firm with its environment, by guiding organizational behaviour, is wrapped up intimately with inducing behavioural change in people to meet the firm's objectives. In discussing change within the construction company, it is important to distinguish between the manner in which change impacts different levels of the hierarchy.

At the strategic apex senior managers are involved in more ambiguous situations where their roles are less well defined. It is at this level that changes in the environment will have its greatest impact. The problem for senior managers is whether the severity of environmental change is such that it induces dysfunctional stress and whether procedures have been put in place to ensure that their primary focus is on strategic versus non-strategic decisions. In the middle line, as roles become more formalized, change has less of an impact. However, our analysis of the operating core suggests that the project-based nature of construction, while involving the construction company in recurrent change, is of a type that ensures that site management is faced with a dynamic situation of flux.

Stocks has identified two components to the change process in organizations. The WHAT of change management can involve the following:

(a) organizational structure;
(b) technology;
(c) people.

The HOW of change management can involve the use of the following

(a) unilateral power, i.e. by decree;
(b) shared power, i.e. by consensus;
(c) delegated power, i.e. the responsibility for managing change is located at different levels in the hierarchy.

Depending on the degree of centralization or decentralization of decision-making, in a sense construction companies that are highly decentralized manage change through delegated power. Male discussed regionalization as a process of managing change. Both Male and Cannon and Hillebrandt also highlighted the fact that site management can have considerable discretion in the way that sites operate. In a situation where a construction company has to undertake transformational change, as was the case in construction firms in the United Kingdom during the 1970s and Japanese contractors during the period 1975–85, employees' natural resistance to change can be overcome through the following:

(a) education and communication;
(b) participation and involvement;
(c) assistance and support;

(d) negotiation and agreement;
(e) manipulation and cooptation;
(f) implicit and explicit coercion.

The above six methods of implementing change represents a power continuum from covert to overt and 'soft' to 'hard' uses of power. Stocks has argued that change, if it is to be managed effectively, has to be planned. This requires strategists to think through the speed of the change process, the amount of pre-planning that is required, the degree of involvement of other people and the approaches to be used. Strategists, when faced with competitive or strategic change, if they have adopted a vigilance style of decision-making, will be in a strong position to manage change and not have it forced on them.

Stocks, in the presentation of his case study of a merger highlighted a number of important points on change management in that situation. These are as follows:

1. The two companies that were to merge had planned for the process, with a pre- and post-merger timetable. Howe [7] indicates that often firms give insufficient attention to planning mergers, both in the pre-merger and post-merger phases, especially the behavioural aspects.
2. It was difficult to see every implication of the merger; the unexpected arose even though the process had been planned.
3. The merger process highlighted key problem areas. These were: employees' views of the future; modifying the culture to remove the 'them and us' issues; and the post-merger organization:

   - because of its new size the merged company would face a different set of competitors than previously, i.e. its competitive environment has changed;
   - the government could have an interest in the actions of the merged firm;
   - the organizational structure needed modification, it was over-staffed with a complex communication network;
   - a management development and training programme was insti-gated;
   - the management style was changed to produce a unified culture;
   - managers and employees had new roles to learn;
   - the corporate planning process had to be modified from that originally envisaged due to the new business environment that was faced;
   - new technology had to be introduced to compete in the new business environment.
4. The post-merger organization took a long time to settle down. Staff were still experiencing high levels of uncertainty up to 12 months after the merger; up to 18 months post-merger substantial stress was still being felt by staff due to pre-merger expectations not being met. Finally, it was expected that it would take anything up to three years after

merger for things to settle down. Thus, post-merger 'trauma' takes a long time to subside.

The construction industry has had a spate of merger activity in the recent past, not only within construction firms but also in consultancy organizations. The clear message to come from this case study is that no matter how well a strategy of acquisition or merger is planned the implications of behavioural processes in the pre- and post-merger phases may be very difficult to envisage and will require careful and sensitive handling by management. However, the transient nature of the highly sub-contracted operating core of the contracting organization suggests clearly that the main focus of change management, where transformational change is involved, rests with permanently employed staff. This does not detract from the fact that site management need operational change management skills because of the dynamic project based nature of the operating core.

3.6 Management development and operative training

Management development provides one of the key sources of competitive advantage in the construction industry since there is a heavy reliance on people at all levels of the firm. Langford and Newcombe indicate that management development is a process that upgrades a company's managerial resources to meet its present and future needs. Two aspects are involved in management development, the aspirations of the individual and those of the organization. Management development can take place in a variety of ways, as follows:

(a) through formal mechanisms;
(b) through informal mechanisms;
(c) via an individual's conscious and unconscious cognitive processes.

Integrated management development maximizes the benefits of each. Langford and Newcombe indicate that construction companies spend less than half a per cent of their annual turnover on development activities, i.e. the provision of internal or external learning opportunities for managers. Interestingly, taking the data presented in their Chapter 8 for junior, middle and senior managers who have attended development activities, in all three cases courses and training on business policy and strategy occupied third place for all three management levels.

Langford and Newcombe suggest one possible approach to management development that is advocated strongly by industrialists. This comprises the following:

1. The provision of an outward bound course to develop leadership and team skills.

2. During this time period, days are programmed in where consultants in personal development form part of the residential tutoring team and lead seminars on that subject.
3. The provision of a psychologist to undertake psychological profiling and individual counselling.

The complimentary aspect to management development is the training provision for operatives. In the study conducted by the London Research Centre [8] 70% of respondents from the construction firms interviewed believed insufficient training was being undertaken for existing needs and there was unanimous agreement that insufficient training was being undertaken for future needs. It was argued in Chapter 2 that in the building sector especially, a sizeable proportion of managerial talent was recruited from the skilled labour force. With over 50% of the UK construction labour force now self-employed, and with this section of the labour force undertaking little if any training, it suggests quite clearly that the available pool of directly employed skilled workers from which to draw potential managerial talent has diminished considerably and will continue to diminish if this form of employment continues unabated. While it could be argued that potential managerial talent could come from the self-employed sector of the workforce, it may be unlikely since their earning potential is relatively high and they will not be steeped in the systems, procedures and organizational culture of a construction company in comparison to the way in which a directly employed skilled operative will be. Finally, mention has already been made of the initiatives being taken by some of our European partners in upgrading the skill levels of their operative labour force. France, in particular, has one eye on potential management recruitment from the multiskilled workforce. Germany hopes to assist site management through the multiskilled training of operatives in order to ease boundary management problems.

4. International competitive advantage in construction

The international business environment is a special case of the general and task environment of a firm. It is characterized by increased heterogeneity, hostility and complexity in comparison to the domestic business environment. In construction the international business environment is also characterized by high fragmentation due to the diversity of buyer types, locations and needs. It also requires a high level of turnover to absorb market entry costs which sets an immediate level on the size of firm that can compete or the type of strategy employed, such as the use of joint venturing to spread risks.

4.1 Competitive advantage in international construction

Porter's national diamond and the eclectic paradigm have been discussed as analytical tools for understanding competitive advantage in international construction. Porter's national diamond is an intuitively appealing base from which to commence any analysis and, when linked with the eclectic paradigm, the two acting together provide a powerful analytical tool for strategists. It is useful to distinguish analytically between country specific (CSA) and firm specific (FSA) advantages, both forming part of ownership advantages. Country specific advantages focus attention on both home and host nation issues. Firm specific advantages focus attention on those issues that are specific to a company and distinguish it from its competitors. Firm specific advantages would also include system-based advantages, i.e. those that come from the fact that a firm is located in different nations and has the opportunity to use its international organizational structure and network of activities to assist competition. System-based advantages isolated in international construction included worldwide procurement of materials and information exchange. However, this raised the issue of whether construction firms that operated internationally could be classified as multinational enterprises with a coordinated global strategy or competed on the basis of being a multidomestic firm.

The analytical framework provided by Morris on the management of projects and the issues raised by Male and Thorpe and McCaffer in the bidding process clearly suggest that the addition of team specific advantages (TSA) as a sub-set of firm specific advantages focus attention on the importance of project management skills and the management of inter- and intraorganizational matrix structures in international construction. Depending on how an international project is set up and financed, project team skills become important where different functional specialists, experts and organizational representatives are drawn together, for example:

- at project inception level;
- at bidding strategy level;
- at design–contract team level;
- at production level, where site management may face additionally a situation of managing a multicultural operative workforce.

Faced with these potentially diverse situations, some of which may involve different cultures, Tayeb has suggested that managers have a choice of strategy to use to manage such situations. In a culturally diverse situation managers can:

- choose to ignore cultural differences and focus on the attainment of project and business objectives;
- choose to take cultural background into account and design the appropriate authority structures, control systems and methods of inducement;

- create cultural synergies by, for example, capitalizing on the group orientation of a culture, Korea and Japan being a case in point;
- create a strong 'organizational culture' where the organization's own beliefs, attitudes and accepted behaviours and norms can override or modify national cultural characteristics.

The final component of international competition in construction is the isolation of locational factors. In international construction these included advantages and disadvantages of both the home and host nation.

To summarise, competing internationally in construction involves the interplay and analysis of country specific, firm specific – including team specific and system-based advantages – and locational advantages. The pull in international construction appears to be for operating on a multidomestic footing backed up by system-based advantages.

4.2 The implications of the country chapters

Contractors are involved in a process of demand searching where, depending on the size of firm, strategists judge themselves against foreign, indigenous and home competitors. Smith, Cannon and Hillebrandt, Walker, Flanagan and Mathewson have analysed different countries and the operations of associated construction firms. A number of important issues arose from each that need to be considered by strategists:

1. Market entry is dictated by size of demand, usually by project type. Access to finance is a key competitive weapon in international construction.
2. There may be explicit and subtle barriers to entry. Subtle barriers to entry would include cultural issues. Explicit barriers to entry could include pre-qualification procedures on public projects or the need for contractors to be licensed or bonded.
3. Procurement and tendering strategies and their associated contractual arrangements will differ from country to country. There may also be a difference between bidding on publicly funded, as opposed to privately funded, projects.
4. Government policy can create a whole series of structural barriers that may make some markets more open than others. The United Kingdom and the United States are open markets. Harmonization of building codes within the EC may result in problems for non-EC nations wishing to enter this market post-1992.
5. Political stability is an important issue. In certain regions of the world, what may appear to be a stable government at one moment in time may change quickly. In such a situation it has been suggested that intuition may be the best judge of acceptable risk.
6. The climate of industrial relations in construction will vary between nations.

7. Ownership structures of construction firms will vary. Construction has a high incidence of family ownership in many nations. This may cause problems in terms of obtaining information for competitor analysis and understanding the motivating forces of companies.
8. Access to sub-contractor networks may be an important issue for foreign firms. It has been suggested as a potential problem in Japan and the United States.

The next section draws together the themes of this chapter to reach a set of conclusions about competitive advantage in construction.

5. Conclusions

This chapter has drawn together a number of major themes running throughout the book. Its primary focus has been to place construction firms in the context of theories of organization, organizational behaviour, economics and corporate strategy, with a view to developing insights into how to achieve competitive advantage in construction. One thing that has become abundantly clear is that the terminology used to describe construction firms needs to be more precise. The larger construction firms have now become so diversified that contracting forms only a part of their overall operations. Cannon and Hillebrandt alluded to this in Chapter 14 when they suggested using 'construction firm' to refer to the diversified company operating in the construction industry, and 'contracting firm' to refer to a company operating purely to erect or modify structures. A high proportion of this book has been concerned with the latter type of company. However, for the diversified construction firm, much of the discussion and concepts will be applicable in a wider context, especially in contracting subsidiaries. Where possible, reference has been made to those issues that will affect an analysis of the diversified construction company. It has also become abundantly clear that theories of 'construction companies' now need to be developed. A considerable body of literature has evolved dealing with the 'organisation' and 'economics' of manufacturing and service firms but, in the main, ignoring construction. Depending on the organizational configuration of the construction firm, these strands now need to be integrated and investigated empirically in order that a useful theory of construction firms can be developed for practical use by managers.

The analysis presented in this and earlier chapters indicates that construction firms need to be close to the market, both in terms of client and consultant contacts, and for more detailed knowledge of labour conditions and localized economic environments. This suggests that the strategic management process in construction companies should be a combination of both 'bottom–up' and 'top–down' procedures: 'bottom–up' so that strategists can incorporate localized market knowledge into their thinking in order to remain in contact with the market place, in general, and ensure that the strategic gestalt is maintained; 'top–down' to ensure that the vision and direction of the company is communicated throughout the firm to enable a common direction and purpose to be developed or maintained. This approach to strategic management should facilitate the 'loose–tight' style of management discussed in Chapter 2.

To summarize, taking an international perspective, competitive advantage in construction depends on a number of factors. These can best be posited as the interplay between the following:

(a) firm specific advantages, including team specific and system-based advantages;
(b) country specific advantages;
(c) locational advantages with respect to the domestic and host nations.

The major parameters within which competitive strategy is worked out to achieve advantages include industry and market structure; organizational behaviour and organizational structure; broadly, a nation's resources; the adequacy of management development; and operative training. In this latter instance, this is made up of two components: developing skills in general company management; and the management of projects. The foregoing involves thinking about the strategic management and competitive advantage of a construction company in terms of a hierarchy of strategies – corporate, business and operational – each level requiring a different skill base.

Finally, construction is essentially a domestic industry but with an international component. However, major international forces are now at work in the environment that will have a significant impact on domestic construction industries and those firms operating internationally. One example with far-reaching implications is the formation of the Single European Market. Another example includes the worldwide implications of a move from a centralized socialist-based economy to a market-based capitalist economy in Eastern Europe and the Soviet Union. This suggests an increasing importance being placed on the development of strategic management skills in construction as the international business environment becomes more dynamic, complex and turbulent.

References

1. Porter, M. E. (1990) *The Competitive Advantages of Nations*. Macmillan, London.
2. Miles, R. E., Snow, C. C., Meyer, A. D. and Coleman, H. J. (1978) 'Organisational strategy, structure and process', *Academy of Management Review*, July, pp. 552–574.
3. Howe, S. (1986) *Corporate Strategy*. Macmillan, London.
4. Enderwick, P. (1989) 'Multinational contracting', in Enderwick, P. (ed.), *The Multinational Service Firm*. Routledge, London.
5. National Economic Development Office (1988) *Faster Building For Commerce*. Millbank Tower, London.

6. Lansley, P., Quince, T. and Lea, E. (1979) *Flexibility and Efficiency in Construction Management*. Final Report of the Building Studies Unit. Ashridge Management College.
7. Howe, S. *op. cit.*
8. London Research Centre (1987) *Skills Shortages in the London Building Industry*. A Report by the Economic Activities Group.

Index